A CULTURAL HISTORY OF MEMORY

VOLUME 3

A Cultural History of Memory
General Editors: Stefan Berger and Jeffrey Olick

Volume 1
A Cultural History of Memory in Antiquity
Edited by Beate Dignas

Volume 2
A Cultural History of Memory in the Middle Ages
Edited by Gerald Schwedler

Volume 3
A Cultural History of Memory in the Early Modern Age
Edited by Marek Tamm and Alessandro Arcangeli

Volume 4
A Cultural History of Memory in the Eighteenth Century
Edited by Patrick Hutton

Volume 5
A Cultural History of Memory in the Nineteenth Century
Edited by Susan A. Crane

Volume 6
A Cultural History of Memory in the Long Twentieth Century
Edited by Stefan Berger and William Niven

A CULTURAL HISTORY OF MEMORY

IN THE EARLY MODERN AGE

*Edited by Marek Tamm and
Alessandro Arcangeli*

BLOOMSBURY ACADEMIC
LONDON • NEW YORK • OXFORD • NEW DELHI • SYDNEY

BLOOMSBURY ACADEMIC
Bloomsbury Publishing Plc
50 Bedford Square, London, WC1B 3DP, UK
1385 Broadway, New York, NY 10018, USA
29 Earlsfort Terrace, Dublin 2, Ireland

BLOOMSBURY, BLOOMSBURY ACADEMIC and the Diana logo are trademarks of
Bloomsbury Publishing Plc

First published in Great Britain 2022
Paperback edition first published 2024

Copyright © Bloomsbury Publishing, 2022

Marek Tamm and Alessandro Arcangeli have asserted their right under the Copyright,
Designs and Patents Act, 1988, to be identified as Editors of this work.

Cover image: © DEA / G. NIMATALLAH / Getty Images

All rights reserved. No part of this publication may be reproduced or transmitted
in any form or by any means, electronic or mechanical, including photocopying,
recording, or any information storage or retrieval system, without prior permission
in writing from the publishers.

Bloomsbury Publishing Plc does not have any control over, or responsibility for, any
third-party websites referred to or in this book. All internet addresses given in this
book were correct at the time of going to press. The author and publisher regret
any inconvenience caused if addresses have changed or sites have ceased t
o exist, but can accept no responsibility for any such changes.

A catalogue record for this book is available from the British Library.

A catalog record for this book is available from the Library of Congress.

ISBN: HB: 978-1-4742-7341-1
PB: 978-1-3504-0859-3
Set: 978-1-4742-7384-8

Series: The Cultural Histories Series

Typeset by RefineCatch Limited, Bungay, Suffolk
Printed and bound in Great Britain

To find out more about our authors and books visit www.bloomsbury.com
and sign up for our newsletters.

CONTENTS

List of Illustrations		vi
General Editors' Preface *Stefan Berger and Jeffrey Olick*		ix
	Introduction: Early Modern Memory Cultures *Alessandro Arcangeli and Marek Tamm*	1
1	Memory, Power and Politics *Jasper van der Steen*	19
2	Time and Space: Autobiographical Memory *Katharine Hodgkin*	37
3	Media and Technology: Notes, Memory and Recollection *Richard Yeo*	57
4	Knowledge: Science and Education *William E. Engel*	77
5	Ideas: Philosophy, Religion and Art *Patricia Emison*	97
6	High Culture and Popular Culture: Memory, Custom and Landscape *Nicola Whyte*	117
7	Rituals of Memory: Commemorations *Peter Burke*	135
8	Remembering and Forgetting *Peter Sherlock*	151
Notes		169
Bibliography		173
Notes on Contributors		199
Index		201

ILLUSTRATIONS

INTRODUCTION

0.1 Master of James IV of Scotland, *Procession for Corpus Christi*. Bruges, c. 1510–20.   3
0.2 Paolo Veronese (Paolo Caliari), *Costume Studies for Sophocles'* Oedipus Tyrannus (recto), c. 1584–5.   4
0.3 The epitaph of the Brotherhood of the Black Heads in Tallinn, commemorating the ten Black Heads who fell in a battle against Russians fought in 1560 near Tallinn. Tallinn, 1561.   12
0.4 The first edition of Giulio Camillo's *L'idea del theatro*, Florence (appresso Lorenzo Torrentino), 1550.   16
0.5 The first image of John. Anonymous, *Ars memorandi per figuras evangelistarum*, c. 1470.   17

CHAPTER 1

1.1 Jan Raes, Jacob Fobert, and Hans Vervoert, after Peter Paul Rubens, *The Defenders of the Eucharist*, c. 1628.   20
1.2 Column of Culemborg, Algemeen Rijksarchief, Brussels, Kaarten en plannen in handschrift.   22
1.3 Pieter Paul Rubens and Jan Wildens, *Act of Devotion by Rudolf I of Habsburg*, c. 1625.   29
1.4 Photograph of the bullet holes in the Prinsenhof Delft.   30
1.5 Dirck van Delen, *A Family beside the Tomb of Prince William I in the Nieuwe Kerk*, Delft, 1645.   34

CHAPTER 2

2.1 The Seven Ages of Man, from Johann Amos Comenius's *Visible World: or, A Nomenclature, and Picture of all The chief Things that are in the world, and of Mens Employments therein*. Translated into English by Charles Hoole, London: John Sprint, 1705.   42
2.2 Thomas Whythorne, title page of MS, *A book of songs and sonetts, with long discoorses sett with them . . .*, c. 1576.   43
2.3 Edward Barlow leaving his mother's house in the wheatfield, Journal of Edward Barlow, 1659–1703.   48
2.4 Mary Rowlandson's *Narrative*, cover image, Boston, 1773 (original publication 1682).   49
2.5 Cornelis Janssen van Ceulen, *Portrait of Lady Ann Fanshawe* (1625–80).   50
2.6 John Bunyan dreaming. Frontispiece to *The Pilgrim's Progress*, book 2, 4th edition 1680.   51

CHAPTER 3

3.1 "The outward and inward senses," with Memory located toward the back of the brain. Johann Amos Comenius, *Orbis Sensualium Pictus*, London: Printed by T.R. and N.T. Mearne, 1672. — 59
3.2 "The Study": a note-taker, possibly using a commonplace book, and apparently undisturbed by a fire outside the window! Johann Amos Comenius, *Orbis Sensualium Pictus*, London: Printed by T.R. and N.T. Mearne, 1672. — 63
3.3 Robert Southwell's commonplace book, 1660s. — 66
3.4 "A Table of ye things following," in Isaac Newton's notebook, CUL Add MS 3996, fols 87^{r-v}. — 68, 69
3.5 The Index in Locke's "New Method" of 1686 as presented in John Locke, "A New Method of a Common-Place-Book," in *Posthumous Works*, London, 1706. — 72
3.6 Hooke's "Scheme" displaying weather observations and measurements, as presented in Thomas Sprat's *History of the Royal Society of London, for the Improving of Natural Knowledge*, London: The Royal Society, 1667. — 74

CHAPTER 4

4.1 "Zodiac Man," from Jean Belot, *Oeuvres*, Lyon, 1654, fol. C8^v. — 79
4.2 "Theater of Plants," from John Parkinson, *Theatrum Botanicum*, London: Thomas Cotes, 1640, frontispiece. — 81
4.3 "Visual Contents," from Francis Bacon, *Of the Advancement and Proficience of Learning*, London: Printed by L. Lichfield, for R. Young & E. Forrest, 1640, frontispiece. — 85
4.4 "Castle of Knowledge," from Robert Recorde, *Castle of Knowledge*, London: Reginalde Wolfe, 1556, frontispiece. — 89
4.5 "Platform of the Design," from Francis Bacon, *Of the Advancement and Proficience of Learning*, London: Printed by L. Lichfield, for R. Young & E. Forrest, 1640, fol. †2^r. — 91
4.6 "Memory Grid," from Johannes Host von Romberch, *Congestorium Artificiose Memorie*, Venice: Giorgio Rusconi, 1520, fol. D5^r. — 95
4.7 "Ring Mnemonic," from Cosmas Rossellius, *Thesaurus Artificiosae Memoriae*, Venice: Antonio Padovani, 1579, fol. C4^r. — 96

CHAPTER 5

5.1 Diana Scultori, *Esther? or Aspasia with Socrates?*, B. XV, 446,32, *c.* 1570s to 1580s. — 99
5.2 Gian Lorenzo Bernini, *Costanza Bonarelli*, Bargello, Florence, *c.* 1636. — 101
5.3 Albrecht Dürer, *Nemesis*, *c.* 1502. — 104
5.4 Cornelis Cort after Michelangelo, *Tomb of Giuliano de' Medici*, New Sacristy, San Lorenzo, Florence, 1570. — 106
5.5 Hendrik Goltzius, *Circumcision*, 1594. — 107
5.6 Nanni di Baccio Bigio, *Pietà*, Santo Spirito, Florence, 1540s. — 109
5.7 Maerten van Heemskerck, *Interior of the Basilica of St. Peter's*, Staatliche Museen, Berlin, *c.* 1532–6. — 114
5.8 Anonymous, *Trinity*, Collezioni Comunali d'Arte, Bologna, *c.* 1540–60. — 114

CHAPTER 6

6.1	Map of New Buckenham (Norfolk, England) dating to 1597.	121
6.2	An example of a burial mound, in this case of Anglo-Saxon date, at Sutton Hoo, Suffolk (England).	125
6.3	Detail of the 1597 New Buckenham map showing the "the procession waie of New Buckehnam called the greene waie or hundred meare" and boundary features in question.	126

CHAPTER 7

7.1	The Solemn Mock Procession of the Pope, Cardinalls, Jesuits, Fryers &c. through the City of London, November the 17th, 1679. London, printed by G. Croom at the Blew Ball in Thames-Street over against Baynard's Castle, 1684. British Museum, 1849.	139
7.2	Luther medal 1617 (obverse).	142
7.3	A broadside commemorating the centenary of the Augsburg Confession, with a colored and partly gilded engraving on vellum by Johann Dürr. (Dresden?), 1630.	144
7.4	Medal commemorating the centenary of the 1688 Revolution, 1788. Obverse: Laureate draped cuirassed bust of William III.	146
7.5	Shakespeare Jubilee, Stratford-upon-Avon, September 6–8, 1769 organized by David Garrick (1717–79).	148

CHAPTER 8

8.1	Monument of Francis Bacon (died 1626), Church of St. Michael, St. Albans, Hertfordshire, England.	157
8.2	Woodcut, "The burnyng of the Archbishop of Caunterbury Doctor Thomas Cranmer," John Foxe, *Acts and Monuments* (London, 1563).	158
8.3	T. Cecill, frontispiece to John Weever, *Ancient Funerall Monuments* (London, 1631).	160
8.4	Monumental brass of Elizabeth Poticary (died 1590), Church of St. John the Baptist, Stockton, Wiltshire, England.	165

GENERAL EDITORS' PREFACE

STEFAN BERGER AND JEFFREY K. OLICK

Any project titled *A Cultural History of Memory* begs a number of questions from the very beginning. For instance: What does it mean that this project is a *cultural* history, rather than some other kind of history? (What other kind of history might it have been?) In turn, what makes memory a feasible and interesting topic for such a history? (It certainly isn't immediately obvious that it would be.) Finally, why a cultural history rather than *the* cultural history? (After all, with forty-eight chapters spread over six volumes, how many more cultural histories of memory could one imagine?)

CULTURAL HISTORY

A Cultural History of Memory is but one entry in a series of cultural histories already and soon to be published by Bloomsbury, including cultural histories of Animals, the Human Body, Food, Gardens, Women, the Senses, Dress and Fashion, the Theatre, Work, Law, Money, and Hair, among many others. The publisher has taken a light hand in prescribing the orientation of these projects, leaving the definition of cultural history to each project's senior editors. And this is very well, as there are many different ways to inflect the idea of cultural history, and different approaches are likely appropriate to the different subject matters. In turn, we have not imposed any particular definition on the editors of the six volumes in this current project, nor have they on the authors of the forty-eight chapters that comprise the total product. That being said, we have relied on a broadly shared understanding of the purposes and tools of cultural history in framing this particular entry in the series, and it is clear that its many authors have as well, though perhaps with occasional divergences.

Namely, contemporary cultural history, at least as it has been practiced in and on the West (and this is one of the important limitations on the project we will discuss below), has defined itself in contrast to at least three other approaches (on the historiographical developments sketched in the following pages see in greater detail Berger, Feldner, and Passmore (2020)). First, there is a broadly defined "traditional" political historiography, dominant in the nineteenth century, that wrote the story of states, their leaders, and their wars. These "high politics" approaches, of course, fully advanced the claim to "objectivity," particularly since the matters they studied—states, their leaders, and their wars—have been quite well documented. These approaches, nevertheless, not only studied the world of nation-states and their high politics but were often part of defining the claims of those states and glorifying the achievements of their leaders, so their claims to be value-free and scientific were obviously dubious ones.

Following this, though at different times in different parts of the world, and only partly under the influence of Marxist perspectives, there developed a vibrant interest in "economic" and "social" history alongside, and sometimes in contrast to, the traditional political histories: the stories not of the "great men" and the great achievements, but of economic processes and social structures. Like political history, this was often presented in national containers and sometimes served the purpose of highlighting the particular "achievements" of nations in the economic and social spheres. Only later did a nascent Marxist historiography, often relatively weak in the universities before the 1970s, come to understand this study of history to be part of a struggle not merely to interpret or understand history, but to change it, as Marx famously put it in his eleventh thesis on Feuerbach.

A stronger concern for ordinary people in social history, however, only occurred with the turn to "history from below," sometimes also referred to as history of everyday life, micro-history, or historical anthropology. This was largely a development that gathered momentum from the 1970s onwards. "History workshop" movements that often became supporters of this new, more human-agency centered understanding of social history, critiqued older forms of social history for being too focused on structures and processes and thereby for ignoring human agency. Furthermore, these approaches criticized the adherence of much of social and economic history to modernization theories and teleologies of progress that appeared to many practitioners of historical anthropology as outdated. The interest of these historians in the everyday had made them turn to anthropology and, inspired by anthropological methods and theories, they set out to change understandings of the social and cultural. As Robert Darnton has put it, "The anthropological mode of history [. . .] begins from the premise that individual expression takes place within a general idiom" (quoted in Hunt 1989: 12). In other words: history had to start from individual human agency and then locate it within a wider collective field.

More difficult to understand is the next form of "traditional" historical interest that was always a lesser strand when compared to political and economic/social history: namely, intellectual history or the history of ideas. Like "traditional" forms of history that focused on states, wars, and high politics, intellectual history has often focused on a narrow slice of life as well: the thoughts and ideas of other great men than politicians (though sometimes them too), mainly artists, scientists, philosophers, and others whose writings are seen to have captured, defined, and led the "spirit" of an age. To be sure, intellectual historians are quite interested in the contexts and structures that enabled the great thinkers to produce their great works, as well as in how those great works affected the less great thoughts of the cultures and societies that produced them. The recent influence of the so-called "Cambridge school" around Quentin Skinner and J.G.A. Pocock is a good example of such contextualization of great thinkers. Internationally even more influential has been the "history of concepts"—shaped seminally by the German historical theorist Reinhart Koselleck. Conceptual history is now a truly global undertaking and one that takes seriously the belief that we need to thoroughly historicize our key concepts in order to understand how people made sense of the world and how they consequently acted in the world.

Next to political history, economic and social history, historical anthropology, and intellectual history, cultural history now forms one of the great traditions of historical writing, reaching back to the very beginnings of professional historiography. Jacob Burckhardt and Johan Huizinga are just two examples of classical representatives of cultural history that can still be read with great pleasure and benefit by contemporary cohorts of students. However, older cultural history often had a strong emphasis on studying "high culture" and thereby distinguishing what was "true" and "worthwhile" culture from "popular culture" or simply "trash." When a "new cultural history" began to conquer history departments in the 1980s, it democratized older forms of cultural history by redefining culture in broader and more inclusive terms. Furthermore, many of its practitioners were much influenced by the "linguistic turn" and theories associated with poststructuralist approaches (Toews 1987: 879–907). Like historical anthropology the new cultural history was dissatisfied not only with an older political history interested mainly in "high politics" but an older social and economic history reducing the past to structures and processes. Unlike an older intellectual history, it was also not so much interested in "great ideas" but instead in ordinary thoughts and practices. Whilst the initial interest in language led cultural historians to study discourses, many soon realized that discourses had to be related back to practices. Furthermore, practices had much to do with things and objects, in other words, materials that needed to be considered to have an agency of their own in history. The history of material culture could thus build on the linguistic turn and practice theory, but it carved out a niche of its own in a field of cultural history that became increasingly compartmentalized as we enter the new millennium after 2000.

Marxist social historians like E.P. Thompson and Geoff Eley spearheaded new understandings of the history of society that took on board many of the insights of the new cultural history without ever abandoning an appreciation of the Marxist understanding of social developments. Thompson, for example, focused not only on the economic condition that made the English working class, but on "the way [. . .] material experiences are handled . . . in cultural ways" (Merrill 1972: 20 f). This happened, according to Thompson, through "cultural and moral mediations." In turn, however, Gareth Stedman Jones moved the discussion even farther afield from economic reduction when he declared that "We [. . .] cannot decode political language to reach a primal and material expression of interest since it is the discursive structure of political language which conceives and defines interest in the first place" (Stedman Jones 1983: 21-22). For the "new cultural historians" in this tradition, then, what they, in part following Emile Durkheim among others, called "representations" became of primary interest. And, as Roger Chartier put it, "The Representations of the social world themselves are the constituents of social reality" (Chartier 1982: 30). This is because, as Lynn Hunt writes, "All practices, whether economic or cultural, depend on the representations individuals use to make sense of their world" (Hunt 1989: 19). The goal of cultural history is thus, as again Chartier defines it, to show "how, in different times and places, a specific social reality was constructed, how people conceived of it and how they interpreted it to others" (Chartier 1998: 4). In this, Chartier followed Lucien Goldmann, who had defined worldviews—the true subject for intellectual historians who were interested in culture more broadly—as "the whole complex of ideas, aspirations and feelings which links together the members of a social group [. . .] and which opposed them to members of other social groups" (Goldmann 1967: 17). And this is indeed the approach that most of the authors in these six volumes have taken, though in an obviously wide variety of ways in and for a wide variety of contexts.

MEMORY

The turn toward memory, especially understood as a collective or cultural phenomenon, can in fact be seen as—though not only as—another inflection of the new cultural history (Berger and Niven 2014). Its interest in representations and discourses encouraged an interest in memories as constituting those representations and discourses. Whether it was written in pursuit of a nostalgic longing for a great national past, as is evident in some of the contributions to Pierre Nora's seminal seven-volume study on the realms of memory of France (Nora 1981–7), or whether it was conducted in the search for understanding and possibly overcoming the consequences of traumatic events in the past, like genocides or wars, memory history has linked contemporary memories to processes of sense-production in the present that gave rise to very different and always contested understandings of the past.

It should already be obvious, then, that the cultural history of memory undertaken in the forty-eight chapters that follow is not just about recall or other basic cognitive processes. Though the concept of memory employed across these six volumes is sometimes the lay understanding of memory as what and how people can recall in different times and places, the majority of the chapters take memory to be something broader. Memory may seem to take place within individual minds, yet for most of the last century numerous scholars both within and beyond cultural history have understood memory more broadly (Olick, Vinitzky-Seroussi, and Levy 2011). Individual memory always takes place within social contexts, with social materials, from social positions, and in response to social cues. So whatever neurological or mental processes it involves, these are obviously deeply embedded in structures and contexts that extend far beyond the individuals whose minds engage in remembering, traditionally understood. Individuals, moreover, employ many technologies of memory—for instance, chanting or writing—which exist outside of themselves and are not part of their brains, and which vary across social settings and in their impacts on individual mnemonic processes. In this way, it becomes perhaps clearer why memory is such a rich terrain for cultural (and other!) forms of history.

However, many of the chapters that constitute this cultural history of memory take yet another step beyond the mind—that is, beyond what Maurice Halbwachs, one of the key figures in contemporary thinking about memory, called the social frameworks of memory, to see memory as an inherently social activity (Halbwachs 1950). We often—even most often—remember together. Social psychologists understand that there are significant differences between remembering alone and remembering in a group, whether this is a matter of simple recall (e.g. when a group of individuals can reconstruct memorized lists more completely than the sum of individuals alone via cuing and other social processes) or in narrative process (e.g. when a family retells a story of an experience they have shared, and the complete narrative emerges from the many voices involved, which bring different pieces than everyone necessarily would have recalled). However, some scholars argue that groups themselves remember; for instance, they build libraries and fill them with materials, they curate representations of the past in museums and elsewhere in ways that transcend the resources of individuals, and they preserve knowledge that very few individuals recall (Assmann 1992). As such, scholars often refer to social, collective, or cultural memory—the forms and traces of the past that transcend the capacities or even interests of individuals—and many do not believe these forms of memories are merely metaphors (see Erll 2008). The field of memory is thus a vast one, and it is clear that understanding all the different forms of memory—from the neurological to the museological—requires, and is an appropriate subject for, all the resources of cultural history.

Having said that, the development of memory studies since the 1980s has been characterized by the gradual constitution of a new discipline that was self-consciously transdisciplinary. Of all the disciplines that constituted this new field, historians were arguably in a minority. Literary scholars and sociologists were far more numerous, and, as all six volumes in this series demonstrate, a cultural history of memory cannot do without referencing a range of literary, sociological and other disciplinary approaches to memory.

Apart from its characteristic transdisciplinarity, which had a major impact on memory history, however, the latter also remained, for quite some time, tied to the national container that, as we have already discussed, had been so strongly established in the historical sciences in the century roughly between 1850 and 1950. The move of memory history to *transnational* forms of memory has only been a relatively recent development, following a general trend in historical studies to criticize "methodological nationalism" and move to more transnational forms of historical writing, emphasizing interlinkages, adaptations, and transfers. However, as a perusal of any of the hugely successful conferences of the Memory Studies Association will show, most scholars today still focus on national memory.[1] Transnational, let alone global memory is not practiced very widely,[2] which also reflects a major difficulty for a cultural history of memory; there are simply not enough scholars who can truly synthesize vast amounts of work on a particular theme in a global perspective. Here we can only trust that our failure will be an inspiration to future generations of scholars to move to more global perspectives on memory history.

Where our six volumes have hopefully been more successful has been in moving histories of memory away from their fixation with trauma, especially national trauma. The huge body of work on the memory of genocides, in particular the Holocaust, and the equally massive amount of work on the memory of wars, especially the two world wars, but also the Vietnam war and a range of civil wars, is an indicator of to what extent memory scholars have homed in on traumatic events in the past. Undoubtedly, much of this work has been incredibly valuable and inspirational, but the six volumes that we introduce here, whilst not ignoring genocides and war, also intend to highlight a range of other areas in which memory history can be usefully applied.

If *A Cultural History of Memory* tries to escape memory history's bias toward "methodological nationalism" and toward traumatic events in the past, it also deliberately—and structurally—seeks to introduce a longer-term perspective and to show how memory history is a relevant and intriguing exercise for older periods of time. Once again, looking from a bird's eye perspective over the field of memory history, we see a massive concentration of work in the modern period, basically from the late eighteenth century to the present day. But the first four of our six volumes underline to what an extent the history of memory benefits from considering older time periods. As general editors, we particularly hope that modernists (of whom we are culpable examples) may delve into the writings on pre-modern times, as it will reveal not only substantial differences, but also, and certainly more striking to us, amazing similarities when considering the role of memory for cultural sense-production.

A CULTURAL HISTORY

Finally, what of the definite article "A" Cultural History of Memory. In the first place, across a work as extensive as this one (or these ones), it is obvious that there are many different approaches to the subject matters. Though all contributing to this cultural history, the authors come from numerous different disciplines and specialties, have different foci, bring to bear different interests and expertise even within this "one" work. We do so, moreover, from numerous different countries, languages of origin, and periods of study, though the list, however extensive, is still limited in significant ways. In the second place, however, much as the publishers did not lay a heavy hand on the forms of cultural history to be employed, they did determine that all the volumes should have the same structure. Hence, we came up with eight themes that had to be the same across all six volumes. In choosing broad themes—power and politics, media and technology, knowledge: science and education, time and space, ideas: philosophy, religion, and history, high and popular culture, the social: rituals, practices, and the everyday, and remembering and forgetting—we sought to give the volume editors the space to adapt those themes to the particular foci appropriate to different times and geographies. As any reader of the six volumes will realize, the editors made good use of that leeway, but this also leads to the phenomenon that different authors have put the emphasis of their respective chapters differently and usually in line with their own specialisms.

The publisher also dictated the epochal labels we employed, and they determined that the eight topics addressed in each chronologically constituted volume should be nominally the same as the topics in the other volumes. Much as we appreciated the reasons for this—for instance, so that a particular theme could be followed across the epochs, or that someone interested in a particular epoch could recombine the history of memory we have produced for that epoch with the history of something else addressed in other entries in the series—this constraint did raise concerns for us and our colleagues. For instance, no single chronology labeling applies uniformly for different areas of the world (e.g. not every society or culture identifies the same antiquity, or an antiquity at all). And the present chronology is a very Western one indeed. Moreover, the application of these labels can be anachronistic. After all, the people whose forms of memory we are studying in a particular age did not understand themselves as having that particular place in history (e.g. the people in the antiquity we have studied did not think of themselves as inhabiting an ancient world). Finally, had we not understood the imperative of recombination of themes and periods, the editors of each epochally-defined volume might have wanted to label the eight chapters differently from the editors of the other volumes, since the same relevances did not necessarily obtain in the same ways in different periods.

Nevertheless, much as the ground we have collectively covered here is vast indeed, we might still hope—if not for other, at least for additional work in this vibrant field on this fascinating subject. We hope that, despite the additional works that might be possible—and that we hope will be produced—what we have to offer here will be of use to as many as possible. The field of memory studies is a relatively new one. But the sophistication of the chapters (and volume introductions) we have the pleasure of presenting here shows that much as the field has a long way to go, it is well on its way.

Introduction: Early Modern Memory Cultures

ALESSANDRO ARCANGELI AND MAREK TAMM

A cultural history of memory, as pursued by this book set, is both a timely and intriguing editorial enterprise. Moreover, the period under investigation here offers particularly rewarding documentation and research questions to stimulate the appetite of writers and readers alike, especially if it be taken into account how extensively memory studies have so far been focused on modern and contemporary periods.

As defined by the chronological limits of the present volume, the early modern age is conceived as a period spanning a quarter of a millennium, from the middle of the fifteenth to the end of the seventeenth century. It was, indeed, an epoch that witnessed dramatic cultural and social developments. It was, after all, the time of major cultural encounters that produced what is currently labeled the first globalization, and intensified the worldwide circulation of a variety of cultural artifacts and material goods—as well as of people, knowledge, and ideas; of the introduction, in the West, of the printing press that contributed to re-designing systems of communication and personal access to information; of humanism and the Renaissance as artistic and literary movements and broader civilizations; of a historical rupture within Western Christianity that bore paramount consequences not confined to the religious sphere; of profound transformations in military techniques (together with other technological innovations) and in the structure and representation of political power; and, last but not least, of revolutions in the understanding of the human body and of the whole universe that surrounds and interacts with it, as well as in conceptions of knowledge in general.

Taking all these developments duly into account, it will seem inevitable that many human groups in a variety of (changing) historical circumstances should have produced and practiced, over that period, distinctive forms of memory, which it would not be easy or fruitful to amalgamate into one unifying category. Rather than attempting that, the essays that follow aim precisely to explore at least a stimulating selection of a wide range of experiences of remembering (and forgetting).

VARIETIES OF MEMORY IN EARLY MODERN EUROPE

In early modern Europe, memory was a familiar human faculty commonly understood within the framework of the predominant cultural and symbolic systems. In the learned tradition of classical philosophy, Plato had identified recollection as a means by which the human soul transcends the body, accessing eternal truths; Aristotle concentrated on the working of memory as a faculty, and described the way perceptual images (*phantasmata*) remained impressed on the mind as the shape of a seal on wax, continuing to live and operate within our cognitive experience (Chappell 2017b, 2017a; on the Aristotelian doctrine, including a sharp distinction between memory and recollection, see Chapter 3; on medical doctrines at variance with Aristotle see however Chapter 4). Thus, it could be said that Western thought tended to secularize a human activity that had previously been regarded as marking a special bond with the divine.

Perhaps closer to the experience of common people, if not by direct reading then by listening to sermons, was, however, the Christian take on the role of memory, which retained a strong connection with the sacred. As well as assigning to memory a position in his influential theology of time (where it plays the role of the "present of past things"), in the tenth book of his *Confessions*, Augustine explored memory as a godly gift that allowed the soul to recollect past experiences: a descent into oneself in order to find God (Schiffman 2011: 98–101; on the *Confessions* as model for early modern autobiographic writing see Chapter 2). After the Fourth Lateran Council of 1215, the recollection of one's sin became a crucial personal experience in Western Christianity—one that Counter-Reformation Catholicism would strengthen and develop in such directions as the Jesuit practice of spiritual exercises (O'Malley 1993).

While the predominantly oral nature of cultural transmission (which we will revisit later in this Introduction) ensured that memory skills were highly appreciated and exercised, a specific area within which they were classified, and consequently cultivated, as a constitutive part was the art of rhetoric—which traditionally listed the need to memorize a speech after finding its content, organizing it effectively and embellishing stylistically. Memory practices were employed (and underwent change) throughout early modern Europe in a variety of forms, depending on geographical, religious, social, political, and other factors. Memory was not, however, solely a dependent variable, a function of its context: memory practices could prove a significant contributing factor in determining cultural identities, customs and social behavior.

Religion, for instance, which played a major role in contemporary world views and life experiences and, as we have already mentioned, was undergoing dramatic changes, provided the ground for endless games of remembering and forgetting (see Chapters 1, 2, and 7). At the very heart of the Reformation—in the different shades of its confessional and sectarian varieties—lay a plan to remember and restore the spirit and form of early Christianity by rejecting and forgetting its medieval developments. On the other hand, the Catholic interpretation of memory consisted in keeping and strengthening ritual practice against its reformist challenges. At the same time, Catholic missionaries spanned the whole globe in their travels, and in adventuring into new spaces also faced time experiences: to some extent, their mental map was apostolic, a re-enactment of a different type of the primitive Church in its original, Mediterranean expansion (Gruzinski 2017). Distinctively Catholic rituals of commemoration, such as processions and the cult of saints and relics (see Figure 0.1), constituted the traditional form of practice that the Reformation manifestly abandoned. Nevertheless, a Protestant memory cult did not have to wait for long to emerge, as clearly attested by the celebration of the centenaries of the publication of Luther's theses (revisited in Chapter 7). All religious denominations shared a cult of their own martyrs and, in the case of displaced communities, diasporas—a feature that naturally was particularly dominant in the definition of Jewish identities.

In the realm of cultural movements and production, highly distinctive memory games were played by humanism—that renewal of the world of learning that (anticipating and to some extent indeed influencing the Reformation) posed as a recovery of ancient wisdom and knowledge. It has been noted that even an undoubtedly new medium such as the printing press—whose effects were perceived as revolutionary already by

FIGURE 0.1: Master of James IV of Scotland (Flemish, before 1465–c. 1541), *Procession for Corpus Christi*. Bruges, c. 1510–20. The J. Paul Getty Museum, *Spinola Hours*, Ms. Ludwig IX 18, fol. 48ᵛ. Digital image courtesy of the Getty's Open Content Program.

contemporaries—ended up flooding Europe with many more ancient and medieval texts than with new ones (Febvre and Martin [1958] 2010). Petrarch, a founding father of the whole tradition of humanism (who, in Chapter 5, is evoked both as a model poet and for his views on cultural imitation), was exalted within the sixteenth-century literature on memory as a master of that art: if we take properly into account the way some of his best known texts were rhetorically constructed by resorting to images as tools to remember meaningful lists, we can perhaps get closer to an understanding of how his contemporaries read (Bolzoni 2012: 85–107).

Humanism also implied and encouraged a specific historical culture and forms of history writing. The development of a new perception of anachronism, by which the widespread passion for things ancient did not impede, but actually helped to spot differences and measure distances, has long been recognized as a distinctive "Renaissance sense of the past," by which an active use of memory created symbolic myths, albeit not merely to look backwards (Burke 1969, 2001). One of the areas of experience typically displaying this was theater, where scenography aimed at recreating classical settings that so frequently formed the background of dramatic performances—to the extent that the Teatro Olimpico in Vicenza could choose to display ancient Thebes in its permanent stage set (see Veronese's costume drawings for the inaugural production in Figure 0.2). Furthermore, it may be inappropriate to attribute to our ancestors one exclusive way of negotiating the past. Even if remembering the past used to serve, in the eyes of early modern Europeans, mainly to provide lessons for the present (a tenet historians today no

FIGURE 0.2: Paolo Veronese (Paolo Caliari) (Italian, 1528–88), *Costume Studies for Sophocles'* Oedipus Tyrannus (recto), *c.* 1584–5. The J. Paul Getty Museum, 91.GG.3. Digital image courtesy of the Getty's Open Content Program.

longer hold), while looking for analogies served as a key tool in this exercise, this is not to say that they could not engage in forms of anachronism consciously and instrumentally: "rather than thinking of the history of memory as a linear process in which the rise of the new forms of engagement with the past implies the fall of all that came before, it is much more useful to conceive of it as a cumulative process" (Pollmann 2017: 72). Different manners of engaging with the past coexisted by complementing, rather than replacing, each other.

FUNCTIONS OF MEMORY IN EARLY MODERN EUROPE

Early modern memory practices performed numerous social roles, sometimes in crucial aspects of the daily life of communities and institutions, as well as of individuals. They could also be pursued within specific cultural and professional contexts, as well as more or less aimlessly, as mere forms of ludic entertainment: thus, for instance, memory was actively engaged in sixteenth-century Italian texts representing the practice of elite sociability, and specifically parlor games (Bolzoni 2001).

In the political realm, memory games were regularly played and highly visible. *Damnatio memoriae* (the condemnation of memory) was an ancient Roman practice, in use both in republican and imperial times: in memory wars played by the elite, officials could deal with their enemies (labeled as tyrants or traitors, for instance) by ordering the erasure of their names from inscriptions or of images representing them, while the disgraced could also become the target of literary attacks aimed at ruining their (also posthumous) reputation (Flower 2006). The practice did not remain confined to history books: in late medieval Italy (among other places) it was revived within the context of factional conflict. Renaissance Florence saw it implemented via the demolition of buildings, the defacement of images and symbols, and even forms of cannibalism. In its extreme manifestations, the phenomenon can be better understood when correlated with the Renaissance recovery of ancient ideas concerning fame and immortality (Robey 2013). In fact, in Jacob Burckhardt's *The Civilization of the Renaissance in Italy* ([1860] 1960: 128–34), the text that established the concept of the Renaissance both within scholarly discourse and in public opinion, fame, and the pursuit of glory were portrayed as the characteristic features of an anthropological revolution that shifted the focus on the individual human being, reversing the purported previous predominance of collective entities and supernatural principles. Although the historiography of the decades that followed has significantly revised the caricature of the medieval world picture implicit in that model, and consequently the extent of the Renaissance break with the past, it would not seem inappropriate to speak at least of a shift of emphasis, which came to put increasing weight on the public solicitousness about individuals and their families. Furthermore, rather than really new, such emphasis was itself the result of a recovery from Antiquity, one of the ways in which humanist readings of the past influenced present cultural orientations. Thus, in a way, an intellectual milieu that was looking at the past as a source of inspiration for reinventing the present and the future, recovered ancient memories of practices of social forgetting. The erasing of the memory of adversaries had clear parallels elsewhere in Europe (on acts of oblivion, see Pollmann 2017: 140–58, as well as Chapters 1 and 8).

Protestantism was partly based on deliberate forgetfulness. As Peter Sherlock (2010) has reminded us, this could take the form of widespread, bureaucratic, and authorized erasures of the names and images of saints from books and churches. In Henry VIII's

England, for instance, Thomas Becket's feast day and name were scraped out of hundreds of manuscripts, while his shrine at Canterbury was dismantled to forbid even the possibility of physical pilgrimage in his honor (Sherlock 2010: 33). Thus, a distinctively Calvinist version of *damnatio memoriae*, albeit with precedent elsewhere in the monotheistic tradition, was performed in the shape of iconoclastic outbursts, which included the defacing or beheading of statues of saints and bishops and the profanation of tombs and effigies in cathedrals and other old churches in England, Wales, and the Netherlands, sometimes deforming religious artworks that had been made and erected only a few years before their ritual desecration and ended up standing disfigured for centuries in perpetual memory of that particular spiritual orientation and policy (Schwyzer 2018).

Early modern Europeans were also haunted by the memory of violence, which left scars and was transmitted by atrocity tales. Somehow it seems that a Christian culture of negotiating pain and suffering helped them cope with the horrors of war and human ferocity (Pollmann 2017: 159–85). Traumatic memories have nevertheless remained alive for centuries, as the case of Northern Ireland clearly demonstrates. There, for instance, a divided memory of the 1641 rebellion has played central role: a rising led by Catholic landowners against Protestant settlers allegedly brought on a systematic and widespread slaughter of Protestants; however, such reconstruction is based on the subsequent testimony of thousands of Protestants, whose reliability is contested. In these conditions it has proved hard, over time, to consign such memories to history and turn the page (McAreavey 2018).

The language of custom constituted one pervasive cultural form that the memory of things past took in these times. It covered both local cultural uses and precedents to which legal value was attributed in their own rights. The general conservativeness of the customary state of mind should not be conceived of uniquely as "an elite tool to keep the poor in place" (Pollmann 2017: 91); it also provided a discursive strategy for the poor to resist unwanted change, as well as a legal ground for claims within intra-status conflict (see also Chapter 6). The way such social memory was preserved and transmitted followed some recurrent scripts. It is quite common to find documentation of old men passing on, while on deathbed, memories of local customs—for instance, gleaning rights after the harvest or rules concerning the collection of tythes in an English parish—and the narrative of that episode of oral transmission functioning as evidence, sometimes contested in its precise wording, within the framework of common law. The customs that were passed on from one generation to another—and could fuel acts of resistance when private interests and agency dared challenge them—were also ideologically nourished by, and consistent with, a discourse of communal solidarity and help to the poor that could find support and justification in significant passages of the Old Testament (Wood 2013a). Over the following centuries, one of the features of incipient modernity will be perceivable in the fading influence of this social paradigm.

Since—as already mentioned—memory was, in the classical tradition, one of the five parts of the art of rhetoric, or of the skills the good orator needed to master, its importance was transferred to a variety of different areas of human activities, partly drawing on rhetoric as their role model discipline, all of which needed to rely on the recording and recollection of knowledge, theoretical and practical alike, in order to be performed. From among plentiful examples, a significant one could be drawn from Italian fifteenth-century dance treatises: in a series of manuscripts dating from the 1440s onwards, dancing masters and other competent writers enumerated *memoria* among the elements a skillful dancer must grasp; on the list drawn by Guglielmo Ebreo of Pesaro, to confine ourselves to just one case, it appeared in the company of measure, partitioning of the ground, air, manner, and body movement. It was not just a question of memorizing the manner to perform given steps and their sequence in a specific choreography: the relevant chapter describes it as an active skill, which must be exercised in connection with a careful attention paid to the music being played, so that the implementation of the learned pattern quickly adapts to any varying circumstance that may need to be taken into account. The example may be useful, suggesting the demanding, close interaction between physical and mental skills required in such areas of social competence (Guglielmo 1993: 94–5).

The metamorphoses of the early modern self that, in their own way, were at the center of Burckhardt's myth of the Renaissance, also found expression in an increasing variety of egodocuments (that is, forms of autobiographical writing in a broad sense—not excluding unintentional self-representation) that functioned as material support for the memory of individuals and families. Notary documents, such as wills and marriage contracts as well as other personal pieces of meaningful evidence, could be preserved with care. Writing implements, such as wax tablets that allowed writing, erasing, and reusing, had a long history of popularity and were also produced in ornate and expensive presentations for a wealthy clientele. Lesser account books, usually of small format, recorded in the vernacular a variety of data and facts, from family business to external events worth noting (Castillo Gómez 2006: 59–91). Common elsewhere (it has been identified and studied in England, France, the German-speaking world, and the Iberian Peninsula, among other places), the practice was particularly rooted among the merchant classes of late medieval and Renaissance Italy, and particularly Florence, where these books were known under the name of *ricordanze* (memories), or various synonyms. The general category presented subtypes and underwent developments throughout the period. The Florentine documents peaked in the fourteenth and fifteenth century. Having first emerged toward the end of the thirteenth century, they initially evolved from the account keeping of the medieval merchant, moving "from personal account books to registers in which personal wealth was recorded. Soon the books included notations of a personal and family nature: the principal steps in the life of the author, or the evolution of his family (births, marriages, deaths)" (Ciappelli 2014: 4). Their subsequent evolution took different directions, some remaining primarily account books, enabling the author to pay special attention to the family. The fact that this material memory support also hosted and mixed with the rest, such entries as prayers, incantations, or medical and culinary recipes, further enriches our perception of what was deemed worthy of remembering, and in what company family memories traveled from one generation to the next.

The study of autobiography has been long connected to the self-portraits of great men (or, with luck, women) and men of letters, as if history from below was condemned to remain a void *petitio principii* in lack of source material. However, careful investigation has uncovered a whole world of artisanal self-writing, the story of which has been helpfully reconstructed until its nineteenth-century turning point, when individual memory becomes strongly influenced and absorbed by working class identity and trade union and socialist affiliation and militancy (Amelang 1998). Also, from the sixteenth century onwards, literate burghers discovered that they had in their hands a powerful means for safekeeping their own or their family memories. A good case in point is the German Catholic lawyer and city-councilor Hermann Weinsberg (1519–97) who spent over fifty years compiling a massive three-volume *Gedenkbuch*, or "Memory Book," jotting down everything that he thought his future family members would want to know about their forebears. He explains his enterprise as follows: "Therefore, if my book and records are preserved and continued, our descendants will also know something to say about us; otherwise, it will be as if we had never been" (quoted by Lundin 2012: 2). "Somewhat by surprise," writes Matthew Lundin in his study of Weinsberg's *Gedenkbuch*, "Hermann came to realize that he could preserve even the most mundane details of his everyday life in writing. He discovered that the practical, ephemeral record keeping of burghers—the quotidian habit of keeping track of income, expenditures, and household events—could also be used to fix forever on paper 'insignificant' (*geringen*) people and things that would otherwise be forgotten" (Lundin 2012: 202). Lundin rightly connects this particular case with the broader historical trend of the gradual penetration of literacy into ever more areas of secular life, characteristic to early modern Europe.

In writing of themselves, early modern men and women followed some socially established scripts. They did not tend to think of themselves as unique, as modern people do; rather, they lived in the shadow of examples, with an inclination to adapt their own agency and recollection of events to role models and shared value systems. It has been suggested that the reading revolution ushered in by the eighteenth-century novel may have contributed to a shift away from this attitude and practice (Pollmann 2017: 18–46; this material is the focus of Chapter 2 below, with attention paid, among other features, to the spiritual dimension of the self-writing).

In early modern memory culture, the rituals of death and commemoration played an important role. Death was ritually celebrated and memorialized in a great variety of ways, from public executions to the funerals of the ordinary people. While rituals concerning death and forms of commemoration presented unmistakable elements of long-term continuity, attitudes toward death also underwent late medieval developments, associated in scholarly consensus with the traumatic experience of the Black Death of *c*. 1350. *Memento mori*—skulls, images, or writings remembering one must die—became dominant features both in Christian devotion and pastoral literature and as desktop reminders of the inescapability and relevance of death for the learned elite. A sense of the macabre also newly developed and left a significant mark on popular imagination via images, texts, and performances (Huizinga [1919] 1996; Tenenti 1952; Gertsman 2010).

Contrary to common understanding, death rituals underwent notable changes from the middle of the fifteenth to the end of the seventeenth century, especially in Protestant societies. In a number of ways, the Reformation separated the living from the dead, both spiritually and physically, by prohibiting further urban churchyard burials in densely populated German cities for reasons of hygiene: "From extramural burial and the denial of intercession for the dead to the formation of the Lutheran funeral, the growth of the biographical funeral sermon and the rise of honorable nocturnal burial, the relationships enacted in the ritual of Christian burial were reshaped in practice" (Koslofsky 2000: 154).

If anything, the fierce theological splits that occurred over what actually happened during the celebration of the sacrament of the Eucharist can testify how seriously questions of commemoration and re-enactment were taken during the whole period, with particular intensity during the sixteenth century.

TRANSMISSION OF MEMORY IN EARLY MODERN EUROPE

The transmission of memory is a precondition for the emergence, continuity, and change of collective remembrance. At the same time, memory is deeply affected by the social organization of transmission and the different media employed. Therefore, it is relevant to pay attention to the ways in which memories were passed on and how they changed in the process. The early modern age is marked by the emergence of a great variety of new forms and media of memory transmission. Following Peter Burke (1997), we can distinguish between five main modes of transmission of memories—oral, performative, written, visual/material, and spatial—while keeping in mind their close interconnections.

Traditionally, memories have been transmitted chiefly by word of mouth. This was still the main form of conveying memory in early modern Europe. However, the rapid rise of literacy and the invention of printing brought along many changes in traditional mnemonic practices. Communicative memory, as Jan Assmann (2008) has called this form of memory shared within a social group through orality, ceded increasingly space to cultural memory, based on written and visual carriers of information. Nonetheless, oral memory remained in early modern societies the primary source to which people turned for information concerning relatively recent past—the past which was still remembered by their contemporaries. Old people especially played an essential role as preservers and purveyors of the past and were often consulted, for example in court cases to establish past practice and custom (Woolf 1991: 296).

Oral transmission of memory is not, as it is sometimes argued, a "spontaneous" mode of memory, distinct from a self-conscious written or visual form of modern memory. Oral tradition has its own stylization and genre rules. Andy Wood has pointed out, for instance, the importance of proverbs in organizing oral information about the past. "Proverbs illuminate a wider aspect of oral tradition: its potential to empower ordinary people, enabling them to make sense of their society and to communicate important aspects of local culture and memory." And Wood concludes: "Orality, then, needs to be understood not only as a mode of communicating and storing information but as a potential form of agency" (2013a: 272).

Protestantism is often considered a religion which emphasizes the importance of written communication (*sola Scriptura*). But while it is true that the Reformation embodied a massive burgeoning of writing, the Reformed church laid an equal (or even greater) emphasis upon hearing the word preached, since, as the German Reformed theologian Wilhelm Zepper put it in his *Ars Habendi et Audiendi Conciones Sacras* (1598), published in English as *The Art or Skil, Well and Fruitfullie to Heare the Holy Sermons* (1599), "the liuely voice of the teacher, is more effectual and piercing than bookes, which are but as dumbe schoolemasters or teachers" (quoted in Tribble and Keene 2011: 54, see also Hunt 2010). Many scholars emphasize today the profoundly aural nature of the Protestant Reformation: "There is growing recognition that, in the guise of preaching, catechizing, psalm singing, and godly discussions of sermons and Scripture, the Reformation actually catalyzed orality" (Walsham 2002: 180).

The oral mode of memory transmission is closely related to performative transmission of memory. Actions, rituals, and bodily practices transmit memories, but they are also attempts to impose interpretations of the past, to shape memory and thus to construct social identity (Connerton 1989). A particularly important form of memory transmission is public commemoration (see Chapter 7). Early modern societies continued to cultivate medieval religious formats of commemoration (liturgical feasts), but new forms of secular commemoration (celebration of historical events), as well as new Protestant modes of public commemoration (annual sermons, fasts, and jubilee celebrations), spread rapidly.

Early modern Europe began to punctuate the past with moments of historical significance that could be periodically commemorated through ritual performances (Sherlock 2010: 38). In early modern cities it was customary, for example, to commemorate instances of deliverance from danger, or victories won by the town, with annual processions. Thus, the city of Amsterdam instituted an annual procession to commemorate its suppression of an uprising of Anabaptist radicals in 1534 (Pollmann and Kuijpers 2013: 6). Also natural calamities, like the Black Death, which struck Italian cities in 1348 and returned every decade or so thereafter until the end of the seventeenth century, seem to have prompted intense practices of public commemoration (Cohn 1992).

In England, various historical anniversaries began to be celebrated from the late sixteenth century onwards, as Peter Burke reminds us in Chapter 7, thus establishing a new national and Protestant calendar which gradually replaced the traditional annual Catholic cycle of holy days. David Cressy (1989) has shown how in Elizabethan and Stuart times a distinct calendar of Protestant holidays was organized around national commemorations of the accession of Elizabeth I (November 17), the foiling of the Gunpowder Plot (November 5) and the Stuart accession anniversaries. In France, the sixteenth-century wars of religion offered many occasions for historical and political commemorations, but also for deliberate attempts of *oubliance* (Benedict 2013). In Germany, the very first centenary celebrated in European history occurred in 1617 when a group of German states staged a series of rituals for the one hundredth anniversary of Luther's publication of his theses in Wittenberg (see Howard 2016; Marshall 2017).

Major changes in early modern transmissions of memory took place in the realm of writing. As said above, the authority of oral information continued to be invoked, but it was increasingly important to transmit memories in written form if they were to have legal or cultural status. Contemporary thinkers often drew an analogy between memory and writing: memory becomes a kind of inner record keeping. So, for instance, according to the English clergyman and theologian Thomas Gataker (1574–1654): "As in all well-governed states there are publike registers, and records, that the memory of judgements and acts may not perish. So hath God in mans soule created a register, to wit, the facultie of remembrance, for the preservation of such occurrents, as are of weight, and may be of use for the direction of mans life" (quoted by Woolf 1991: 288).

The effect of writing on mnemonic transmission was even more amplified by the invention of printing in the mid-fifteenth century. Although the impact of printing technology made itself fully felt only from the beginning of the eighteenth century onwards, printing certainly contributed to the transformation of early modern memory. As emphasized by William E. Engel in Chapter 4, the printed book represented a new kind of visual and mnemonic aid resulting from a confluence of new technologies. Indeed, one could agree that the printing press may have impacted memory culture less in terms of its content than of media, supporting a vigorous development of oral memory culture into a written one that could then be circulated more broadly via the medium of print (Lundin et al. 2015: 112).

Literary print culture also forms a pervasive element in the Protestant Reformation. "Early modern religion is a religion of books: pre-eminently the Bible, but also a plethora of other books, devotional, doctrinal, controversial," as Brian Cummings (2002: 6) has argued. Side by side with religious texts, a particularly interesting case is that of confessional historiography which started to flourish from the sixteenth century. The moral and political authority of the past was taken for granted in the early modern age, therefore "challenges to authority had to be made through a reinvention of the past" (Pollmann and Kuijpers 2013: 10; see also Chapter 1). The past, indeed, became one of the major battlefields between Reformed and Counter-Reformed historians and theologians. Both parties rewrote history as part of a religious campaign to lead people toward their version of past events and to define their religious identity by recourse to a particular historical method (Backus 2003). Needless to say, the "history battles" transcended religious disputes since, for instance, protecting one's property could also involve making historical claims about rights and privileges.

The early modern age was a period when history writing was in transition, with new disciplinary boundaries and scholarly virtues emerging alongside new professional practitioners (Woolf 2003). Until the end of the period considered here, history was deeply connected with various memory practices: there were a great variety of contexts in which history could be listened to, heard about, and discussed. It is only from the eighteenth century onwards that the modern version of historiography that valued academic autonomy began to rise to predominance and the printed book became the main channel for conveying information about the past. "It was then that history really became a commercially successful genre, with every bookseller and publisher having to lay in a good stock of the most famous modern and ancient historians from Gibbon and Voltaire via Clarendon and Guicciardini back to Livy and Thucydides" (Woolf 2002: 119).

Written texts are one particular form of the material transmission of memory, alongside things and images. People are always engaged in the process of remembering with objects (textual, visual, material). "This is not to say," as Andrew Jones has explained, "that objects *experience*, *contain*, or *store* memory; it is simply that objects provide the ground for humans to experience memory" (2007: 22). Material images have long been used in order to assist the transmission of memories—statues, portraits, tombstones, monuments, medals, and souvenirs of various kinds. "It would be difficult to overestimate the materiality of premodern memorial culture—the ways in which memory 'stuck' to places and things" (Lundin et al. 2015: 107). In early modern Europe, material "memorials" contributed greatly to keeping public or private memory alive, but also to shaping the perception of the past, to conveying to posterity what should be known about the past. Peter Sherlock (2008) has demonstrated to what extent monuments were one of the most prominent media in the early modern period in ensuring the commemoration of people, families, communities, and events. Monuments bear witness also to changes in religious memory regimes. In post-Reformation England, funeral art changed very rapidly, "the response of the monumental tourist was no longer prayer motivated by the fear of death and Purgatory, but respect for the virtuous example and didactic power of the dead in the hope of resurrection to eternal life" (Sherlock 2010: 35).

But many other realms of everyday life also give evidence of a material transmission of memory, for instance the ways in which clothing and other domestic objects memorialize early modern traces of the body's actions, both purposeful and unintentional (Jones and Stallybrass 2000). Judith Pollmann (2017: 187–8) has recently emphasized that there was a growing commodification of secular memory-related objects in early modern Europe: people began increasingly to produce commemorative prints, medals, plates, snuffboxes, board games, and teacups. The inventories compiled by early modern craft guilds show how members established their posthumous reputations through the donation of material objects to neighboring churches and their institutional homes. Within their company halls, guildsmen were regularly reminded of the benevolence and generosity of their dead brothers: lists of their gifts were inscribed upon wooden tablets mounted upon company walls; their donations were recalled at feasts and at sermons (Kilburn-Toppin 2013: 169–73). An interesting example of the material *memoria* culture of early modern guilds is offered by the Brotherhood of the Black Heads in Tallinn (Estonia). During the Livonian War (1558–83), the Black Heads also participated in battles and helped to defend Tallinn against the Russians. After the battle, the brotherhood honored the fallen members by organizing their funerals and materializing their memories. To commemorate the ten

Black Heads who fell in a battle against the Russians fought in 1560, the brotherhood erected a limestone monument on the battlefield to honor the dead and also commissioned a painted epitaph placed in the house of the Black Heads (see Figure 0.3). The painting, which is the oldest representation of a historical event in the country, is temporally multi-layered, representing simultaneously the soldiers heading to war, the battle with Russians and the praying Black Heads, as well as listing the names of those fallen in battle.

FIGURE 0.3: The epitaph of the Brotherhood of the Black Heads in Tallinn, commemorating the ten Black Heads who fell in a battle against Russians fought in 1560 near Tallinn. Tallinn, 1561. Tallinn City Museum, Estonia. Photo: Stanislav Stepaško.

"Memory is, by nature, topophile," Joël Candau (2005: 153) argues; it is fixed to landscapes, streets, squares, houses, etc. "It is not accidental," Paul Ricoeur (2000: 49) seconds, "that we say about events that they *took place*." As a rule, people associate events with a certain location, memory is inseparable from "places of memory" that retain the remembrance of particular events. One of the main lessons of contemporary memory studies is, indeed, that collective memory is almost always located in a material context, spatially plotted, organized and understood within a reading of the landscape. Tim Ingold has written eloquently: "To perceive the landscape is to carry out an act of remembrance, and remembering is not so much a matter of calling up an internal image, stored in the mind, as of engaging perpetually with an environment that is itself pregnant with the past" (1993: 152).

Space and landscape are indeed critical to an understanding of memory transmission in the early modern period. In her innovative study *The Reformation of the Landscape*, Alexandra Walsham (2011) has explored how environment shaped the profound theological, liturgical, and cultural transformations that marked the era between *c.* 1500 and 1750 and how the senses of place and space were implicated in the series of interlinked initiatives to reform belief and behavior. An important case in point is the role of the remains of the Catholic past in the Post-Reformation landscape. In sixteenth- and seventeenth-century England, for instance, ruins became an important part of the memory landscape (Covington 2013). They proved to be especially fertile in stimulating consciousness of the past and in promoting historical activity: "The landscape held a series of signposts to the destroyed monastic era, and they led to nostalgia and poetry, as well as to antiquarianism and history. From this time on, the ruins of the monasteries entered into English consciousness of the past" (Aston 1973: 232).

There were, needless to say, many mnemonic landscapes in early modern Europe and many means of memorializing through space. Nicola Whyte points out in Chapter 6 the importance of place names and the features to which they referred in popular memory practices. She argues with good reason that the production and reproduction of customary landscapes provided temporal anchors in the organization of social memories. Likewise, Andy Wood has shown how the memory of ancient activity was preserved spatially in the present. Countless English villages, for example, were crossed by trackways named for their pre-Reformation use: "Abbey field," "pilgrim's way," "Whitefriars lane," "gospel croft," "the monkewall" (Wood 2013a: 210). Arcadian poetry, Renaissance garden design, and the beginning of the seasonal relocation of the European elites to the countryside for their vacations provide another example of entanglement between landscape and memory, albeit one in which the features of the pastoral and rural past are a product of the imagination (Schama 1995).

At the end of this brief overview of the main ways of memory transmission one has to emphasize that early modern memorial practices often gained their special dynamics and effect through the specific interfaces of their media of transmission, in which the oral transmission of memory interacted with written and/or printed memory, with symbolic rituals, with material objects and with specific urban or rural landscapes. Or, in other words, as Erika Kuijpers and Judith Pollmann have put it, "one of the most striking aspects of early modern local memory is that it was, or could be, a truly multimedia affair" (Pollmann and Kuijpers 2013: 10). A good example of how this "multimedia memory landscape" functioned is offered by Iain Fenlon's study *The Ceremonial City* (2007). Fenlon shows in great detail how in Renaissance Venice the celebration and commemoration of four major events—the victory at Lepanto, the visit of King Henri III of France, plague, and a fire in the Ducal Palace—combined various cultural media (ritual, music, art, architecture, writing, and space) and helped to transform Venetian self-consciousness and its memory landscape. It is particularly interesting to see how the changes in ceremonial practices are correlated to representations of Venetian myths and historical events in paintings, sculpture, buildings, history writing, and music.

ARTS OF MEMORY IN EARLY MODERN EUROPE

In early modern Europe, memory is something more than the transmission of collective experiences and shaping of the past perception: it is also a discipline, a form of knowledge production, which can be trained, cultivated, and developed (see also Chapter 3). The widespread attention to memory and memorization in the period attests to its status as epistemology, as does its key role in education (Clarke 2018: 86). While Mary Carruthers (2008: 9) has argued that "medieval culture was fundamentally memorial," one can claim that this "memorial culture" persisted throughout the early modern period till the early years of the Enlightenment. The Renaissance witnessed an important interest in the technologization of memory which took the form of a specific art, the *ars memorativa* or *memoriae* (see Rossi [1960] 2000; Yates [1966] 1999; Berns and Neuber 1993; Bolzoni 2001; Engel, Loughnane, and Williams 2016). The core of the *ars memorativa*, as recently explained by Stephen Clucas (2015: 143), is "a firm conviction that memory is increased and aided by order and arrangement. In the arts of memory, the themes of method (*methodus*) and order (*ordo*) are dominant." Memory training became central to humanist pedagogy, shaping the curriculum offered to students on every level of education. "The purposeful, culturally self-conscious use of the arts of memory [. . .] was designed to produce and sustain control over the self and over the material being remembered" (Chedgzoy et al. 2018: 13). William Engel's (2002) work has also shown how the tradition of the arts of memory deeply influenced early modern drama and literature. But the early modern emphasis on memorization continued to wield a potent influence not only upon education, literature, and intellectual debate, but upon the age's very understandings of epistemology and ontology, as exemplified in William Fulwood's translation of Guglielmo Gratarolo's *The Castel of Memorie* (1562): "take Memorye away: What is a man? What can he doe? / or els what can he say?" (quoted by Hiscock 2018: 72).

During the fourteenth and fifteenth centuries, the *ars memoriae* was considered first and foremost a useful rhetorical device for preachers, a learning method for teachers, or a technique that could be used by politicians, writers, and jurists to improve their public speaking. However, in the late sixteenth century, the *ars memoriae* started to acquire a rather different significance and became increasingly identified with the search for a magical "key" that would allow one to penetrate into the hidden secrets of nature (Rossi [1960] 2000: 61–2). Thus, instead of losing its importance in the age of print culture, as one would have expected, "the art of memory had actually entered upon a new and strange lease of life" (Yates [1966] 1999: 127–8). Lina Bolzoni helps us understand this unexpected turn: "The secret of this paradoxical situation lies in the fortunate encounter between the art of memory and the chief aspects of the new culture of the sixteenth century: from the flowering of arts and letters to the rebirth of hermeticism and Lullism, the interest in magic, astrology and the Cabala" (Bolzoni 2017: 66). The sixteenth- and seventeenth-century arts of memory became more and more sophisticated and claimed to present a system that was at once rhetorical, logical, and metaphysical, "capable of comprehending the infinite forms of an infinite universe" (Clucas 2015: 144).

Early modern arts of memory made maximum use of visual possibilities. From diagrams, tables and schemes to figurative images, all the means of enhancing artificial memory were explored. But on a deeper level, memorization and visualization were often considered closely linked. Thus, Giovanni Fontana writes in his fifteenth-century treatise: "There is no art or science that is more similar to painting than artificial memory. Both need places and images, and one follows the other, and for this reason it is helpful to use examples taken from painting. Indeed, we are painting when we construct images to be positioned in the places" (quoted by Bolzoni 2001: 184).

Beginning with the sixteenth century, we see the emergence of different pictorial typologies in the treatises of *ars memorativa*, but the architectural model seems to be clearly dominant. Perhaps the most famous visual-architectural interpretation of the tradition of *ars memorativa* is the "Theatre of Memory" by Giulio Camillo (*c.* 1480–1544). Camillo's ultimate purpose was "to show users how to memorize the entire encyclopedia of human knowledge by arranging its contents in a metaphysical order" (Bolzoni 2011: 16). For this, he designed a wooden building constructed like a Vitruvian amphitheater and structured according to the principles of classical rhetoric. The visitor stood on the stage and looked into the auditorium, whose semicircular construction was intended to house the memories in a clearly laid-out fashion—seven sections, each with seven arches spanning seven rising tiers. The amphitheater was divided into the seven sections according to the seven planets known at the time—they represented the divine macrocosm of alchemical astrology. The seven tiers that rose within them, coded by motifs from classical mythology, represented the seven spheres of the sublunary down to the elementary microcosm. On each of these stood emblematic images and signs, next to compartments for scrolls. Using an associative combination of the emblematically coded division of knowledge, it had to be possible to reproduce every conceivable micro- and macrocosmic relationship in one's own memory (Matussek 2001: 5). Unfortunately, Camillo's "Theatre of Memory" was never completed. The only work that presents his project in some detail, *L'idea del theatro*, appeared in print six years after his death, in 1550 (see Figure 0.4). Although some of his contemporaries called him "the divine," Camillo and his art of memory were forgotten very soon after his death. "Like any artificial system, this was doomed to be no longer understood as soon as the sets linking terrestrial phenomena to corresponding planets fell into disuse" (Couliano 1987: 35).

But the iconographic tradition of memory arts offers many more examples. Lina Bolzoni (2001: 149) observes that the use of the images of beautiful women in the arts of memory must have been a frequent practice if even an observant Minorite friar, the Calabrian Girolamo Marafioto, recommends one, in his *Ars memoriae* (1603), to walk the streets and carefully watch the most attractive women, impressing in your mind their gestures and the movements of their bodies, and using them as *imagines agentes*. Marafioto confirms that he has seen the method work and has even used it to remember some of his own sermons. Another interesting iconographic tradition goes back to late fifteenth-century Germany. In the so-called blockbooks that appeared in the Netherlands and Germany in the fifteenth and early sixteenth centuries, both pictures and text were cut into blocks of wood and printed on paper. Unlike ordinary illustrated books where pictures were used to adorn the text, blockbooks employed text merely to comment on the pictures (Carruthers and Ziolkowski 2002: 255). Around 1470, a small blockbook known today as the *Ars memorandi per figuras evangelistarum* was produced in South Germany, perhaps in a Bavarian monastery. The book with its brief text and diagrams was intended to help remember the contents of each chapter in the four Gospels in order. This

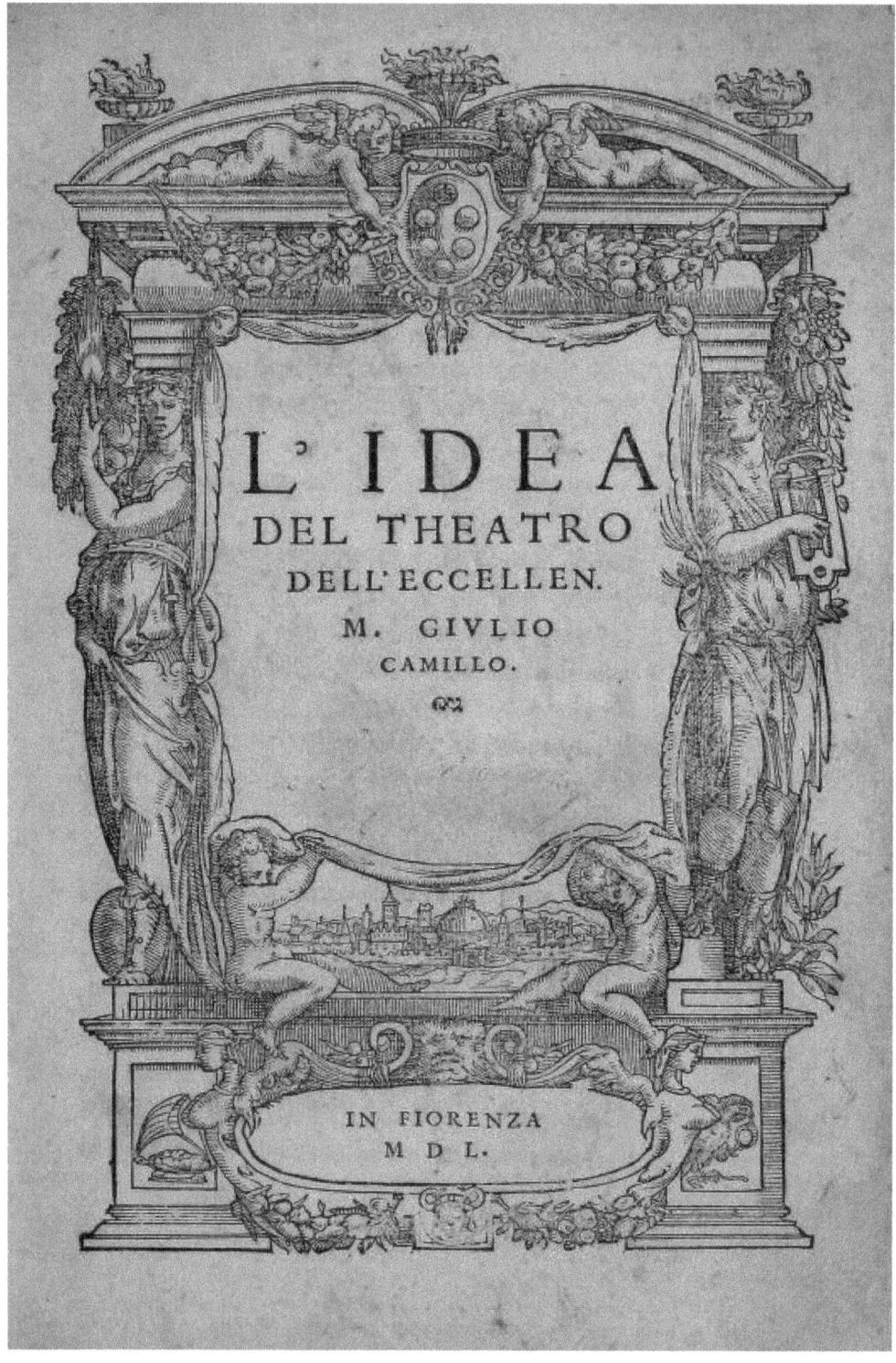

FIGURE 0.4: The first edition of Giulio Camillo's *L'idea del theatro*, Florence (appresso Lorenzo Torrentino), 1550.

blockbook enjoyed a wide popularity which led to its imitation and expansion in many later editions across Europe. The book opens with the image of St. John, accompanied by a short note: "A famous method using the images of the Evangelists worked out in what follows through visible devices for locations, which the careful reader may diligently read and try out so that he may experience them in practice" (Carruthers and Ziolkowski 2002: 258). In the image we see a large eagle, the symbol of John, complemented by a rich mnemonic iconography that captures six key episodes from the Gospel of John (see Figure 0.5).

The early modern arts of memory created also their antipode—arts of oblivion. Lina Bolzoni (2001: 142–5, but see also Cevolini 2016a) has collected a rich display of early modern tricks for forgetting things one does not need anymore. The Venetian physician and engineer Giovanni Fontana (*c*. 1395–1455), for example, explains that he commonly uses a piece of cloth to mentally cover the images he wants to forget; or else, he imagines that the place where they are positioned is crumbling, or going up in flames. The Florentine Dominican friar Cosma Rosselli suggests an iconoclastic method in his *Thesaurus artificiosae memoriae* (1579): imagine, he writes, "that a man comes home, that he throws all his images on the floor, and then he throws them out or tosses them out of the window" (quoted by Bolzoni 2001: 143). There are no fewer than eight methods of *ars oblivionalis* recommended by the Dutch educator and philologist Thomas Lambert Schenckel (1547–1625) in his treatise *De memoria* (1593). Schenckel's methods are characterized by a crescendo of destructive violence, culminating in the last method: "Eighth: let us imagine that a man in a fit of rage has taken over the fields, the houses, and the rooms with the help of a band of armed men, and he has killed some images, and wounded many

FIGURE 0.5: The first image of John. Anonymous, *Ars memorandi per figuras evangelistarum*, *c*. 1470, South Germany. Staatsbibliothek Bamberg, Inc.typ.Ic.IV.15, fol 1ᵛ–2ʳ. Photo: Gerald Raab.

others; others have fled through the doors, others have jumped out of the windows, and when you enter, you find none of them left inside" (quoted by Bolzoni 2001: 143, see also Kuwakino 2016).

Regardless of the surprising success of the arts of memory in the sixteenth century, the belief in the training of memory to the point where an individual could acquire all the accumulated human knowledge started to diminish in the early seventeenth century. Among various reasons, two seem to be crucial. First, the rapid development of the new technology of printing made it possible to record and retrieve knowledge efficiently and cheaply in books. Second, as Stephen Clucas (2015: 151) has pointed out, an important factor in the decline of *ars memoriae* was the emergence of radically new philosophical systems in the course of the seventeenth century. True enough, the philosophical critique of the arts of memory goes back to Renaissance humanism. A number of humanist scholars, most notably Erasmus, remained skeptical of the usefulness of memorization techniques. In many writings Erasmus warned against the damaging effects of artificial memory; so, for instance, in his pedagogical manual *De ratione studii* (1511), in which he severely criticized the pseudo-Ciceronian method of "places and images" which, he said, impaired and corrupted the natural memory (Rossi [1960] 2000: 2). Some twenty years later, in his *Rhetorica elementa* (1534), the Reformist Philip Melanchthon would go even further and banish recourse to mnemonic techniques for his students (Hiscock 2011: 25). But the rise of new theories of human cognitive processes in the early sixteenth century redefined the very nature and role of memory. Especially important in this regard was Francis Bacon's work on the scientific method of knowledge. "Bacon's theory of knowledge looked toward the discovery of the new and unknown, rather than the reception and fuller understanding of past truths. In this new process of interpretation, memory was displaced by reason" (Sherlock 2010: 32). Bacon, who had a very good knowledge of the arts of memory (Yates [1966] 1999: 370), considered these arts capable of providing only a superficial and useless knowledge:

> One cannot pass silently over the fact that some individuals, who are more foolish than wise, weary themselves with a method which is unworthy of this name, being in reality a method for imposture, which is only useful for swindlers. This method uses a smattering of science so that an ignoramus can make show of a non-existent erudition. [. . .] A collection of this kind is just like a junk-shop where one finds many old rags, but nothing of any value.
>
> —quoted by Rossi [1960] 2000: 104

By the end of the seventeenth century the arts of memory were considered outmoded in European intellectual circles. But the decline of the arts of memory did not mean the disappearance of memory from theoretical discussions; its importance in cognitive processes was sustained by seventeenth- and eighteenth-century thinkers, and by the end of the early modern period it was seen as key to understanding the foundation of selfhood and personal identity itself (Clucas 2015: 174).

CHAPTER ONE

Memory, Power and Politics

JASPER VAN DER STEEN

INTRODUCTION

In 1625, Infanta Isabella Clara Eugenia—daughter of Philip II of Spain and former sovereign of the Low Countries—commissioned painter Peter Paul Rubens to design a monumental series of tapestries about the triumph of the Eucharist for the Monasterio de las Descalzas Reales. This "Convent of the Royal Barefooted" was an important center of religious life in Madrid, visited by male and female members of the Habsburg dynasty, including the king. The tapestry series aimed to recreate the iconography of the Temple of the wise king Solomon and, probably based on an earlier portrait that he had painted of Isabella in 1625, Rubens included a likeness of the Infanta as the thirteenth-century saint Clare in the center-stage tapestry *The Defenders of the Eucharist* (Figure 1.1) (Libby 2015: 1–15). This kind of anachronism was a much older practice—perhaps best known in medieval Christian altar triptychs that depicted the contemporary patrons on the side panels—but continued throughout the early modern period and beyond (Burke 2001: 157–73; de Grazia 2010: 13–32). From a modern point of view, it is tempting to believe that such shameless meddling of ancient, medieval, and early modern elements betrayed a serious lack of a sense of anachronism—the ability to distinguish the past from the present. Yet anachronism was often deliberately used for political purposes, as a rhetorical technique (Pollmann 2017: 93–118). Indeed, in the case of Isabella and Rubens the "lack" of anachronism does not simply betray their inability to distinguish the past from the present. It rather demonstrates the dynamic way in which Isabella, who had been demoted from sovereignty over the Low Countries after the death of her husband Albert in 1621, availed herself of a Biblical and historical comparison. "By conflating Isabel with Saint Clare," Alexandra Libby explains, "Rubens reminded King Philip IV [of Spain] of her closeness to the Sacrament, her sacred power, and her Solomon-like, God-given authority." Isabella hoped that this message would help convince the king of Spain to give her more political freedom in his Low Countries (Libby 2015: 15).

Since the 1980s, scholars have tended to assume that only with post-1800 phenomena such as nationalism, mass media, and industrialization could memory really become an important stake in political debates (Gillis 1994: 6–7; Smith 2000: 52–77; Bayly 2004: 202). The focus on the period after 1800 of two important anthologies of memory studies testifies to this modern bias (Erll and Nünning 2008; Olick, Vinitzky-Seroussi, and Levy 2011). Eric Hobsbawm, who is included in the latter anthology, has suggested in the pathbreaking *The Invention of Tradition*, first published in 1983, that the convergence of state, nation, and society can explain the growing attention to and political exploitation of national history in the second half of the nineteenth century (Hobsbawm 2000a: 1–8,

FIGURE 1.1: Jan Raes, Jacob Fobert, and Hans Vervoert, after Peter Paul Rubens, *The Defenders of the Eucharist*, part of the tapestry series *The Triumph of the Eucharist*, c. 1628, wool and silk, Convent of the Descalzas Reales, Madrid. © Patrimonio nacional.

2000b: 263–5). Especially in those circumstances, authorities and interest groups had the political motivation and an increasing number of mass media at their disposal to spread a national outlook on their past. Aleida Assmann, one of the most astute memory scholars in the present day and included in both anthologies mentioned above, has convincingly argued that "forgetting is the normality of personal and cultural life." Not entirely satisfying for early modernists is her subsequent remark that precautions against forgetting are a costly government business normally requiring mass media, monuments, school curricula, etc. (A. Assmann 2008: 101). Since these phenomena are typical for the nation-state, she too highlights the importance of modern developments in the politicization of memory.

Yet the strategic rhetorical usage of anachronism exemplified in Isabella's tapestry series has suggested that early modern people, too, were aware of the political potential of the past. And this was just one example. As Judith Pollmann and Erika Kuijpers pointed out, a central consensus in medieval and early modern approaches to the relationship between past and present was that things were "true or legitimate only if they could also be proven to be old" (2013: 6). This chapter will demonstrate that precisely for this reason people at all levels of society used references to the past to defend their claims in the present. Due to the importance of the past in establishing (political) legitimacy, historical references were also often objects of fierce contestation, especially in Reformation and Counter-Reformation Europe, where religious wars and revolts challenged the existing order. In trying to explain the crises in Europe, the exemplary function of history as *magistra vitae* (teacher of life) lost some of its usefulness. Daniel R. Woolf argues convincingly that it was complemented by an emerging "sense of the past as continuous process and the establishment of the primacy of causal relationships between diachronically or proximate events" (Woolf 2005: 38). The French Wars of Religion, the Revolt of the Netherlands, the Thirty Years' War in Germany and beyond and the Civil Wars on the British Isles intensified the politicization of the (recent) past and stimulated interest in historical development.

This chapter will show that modern phenomena such as the emergence of the nation-state and nationalism were no prerequisites for memory to play an important role in political life and that at all levels of early modern European society, memories of the past were politically potent and objects of fierce political discussions. The main theme of the chapter is power and politics, defining *power* as the "control or authority over others" and *politics* as the "actions concerned with the acquisition or exercise of power, status, or authority" (OED 2006). Rulers, contenders for power, opinion-makers, and other political stakeholders in a great variety of social contexts drew on references to the past in support of their political arguments in the "present." I will give an overview of political memory practices in early modern Europe, discussing the importance of cultural memory for fighting out political conflicts and exploring the continuities and discontinuities in the early modern political usage of memory. In doing so, I will demonstrate that while memory was an important source of legitimacy for political groups, it could for the same reason be used to delegitimize political opponents. And even though memory seemingly offered an endless supply of politically useful supporting material, existing storylines also limited the way memory could be deployed successfully in political discussions.

Since the author's research expertise primarily concerns the Dutch Republic and the Habsburg Netherlands, the material will be skewed a little toward this region, yet attention will also be paid to other parts of Europe. The chapter begins with a Netherlandish case study about the destruction of the Palace of Culemborg, which beautifully illustrates how and why memories of the past carried such political potency and identifies the diversity of stakeholders involved in the management of memory. The subsequent sections will zoom in on each of these stakeholders: dynasties, religious groups, government authorities, and opposition movements.

THE DEMOLITION OF THE PALACE OF CULEMBORG

On March 29, 1568, the duke of Alba, Philip II of Spain's representative in the Low Countries, gave orders to demolish the Culemborg palace on the Sablon in Brussels. In 1566, this palace of Count Floris I of Culemborg had been the location of an important assembly of nobles, dissatisfied with the Habsburg policies in the Low Countries. What began as loyal opposition soon turned into a revolt against the regime and prompted a bloody civil war known both as the Revolt of the Netherlands and the Eighty Years' War. Alba wanted to destroy this physical reminder of the place where, in his eyes, the first rebels had prepared their insurgence (Schuermans 1870). In the sixteenth century, the practice of demolition as a punishment already had a long history from antiquity (Roller 2010), which early modern people in this instance seem to have been familiar with. A contemporary observer later wrote that "the entire palace was leveled to the ground and the place was sprinkled with salt and awful curses in accordance with the duke of Alba's command" (Junius 1595: 72). The inspiration to use salt, probably to make the soil infertile, in all likelihood had its origin in stories about the destruction of Carthage in 146 BCE, where Roman soldiers had supposedly sown the ruins of the city with salt (Ridley 1986: 140–6).

The demolition took place on May 28, 1568 and, a few days afterwards, Antoine II de Lalaing, count of Hoogstraten wrote that "a column will be erected in the middle of the spot with a notorious dictum beneath" ([1568] 1836: 242). The column was built and in Latin, French, Dutch, and Spanish an inscription declared that it had been placed there "in memory of the execrable conspiracy made here against the religion of the Catholic

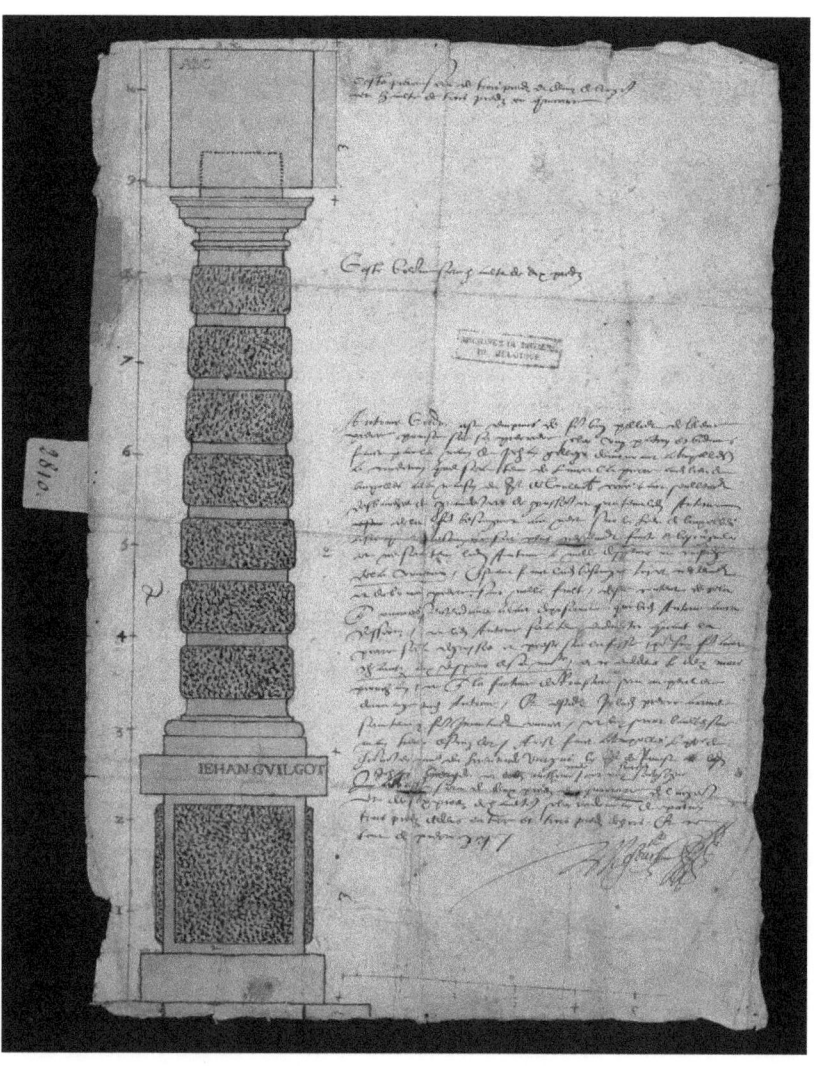

FIGURE 1.2: Column of Culemborg, image reproduced with the kind permission of the Algemeen Rijksarchief, Brussels, Kaarten en plannen in handschrift. Nr. 2.810.

and Roman church, against the king and against his lands" (Figure 1.2) ("Suite du rapport" [1568] 1961: 528). While the demolition of the palace removed a physical memory of what was in the Habsburg regime's view the first cause of the rebellion, the subsequent placement of a column did the exact opposite by drawing attention to the "execrable" past. Here, too, ancient examples probably were inspirational, at least indirectly. In the Roman Empire, the senate could, for instance, issue a "damnatio memoriae," or a "memoria damnata," to damn the public memory of persons who were charged with crimes against the state (Vittinghoff 1936: 64–74). Clearly, such management of memory was a central concern of Alba and his regime. But they were not the only stakeholders. As political circumstances changed, so did the politics of memory.

The column did not serve its original purpose as an eternal *damnatio memoriae* for long. In 1576, the Revolt flared up again when soldiers in Habsburg service mutinied, killing thousands of citizens notably in the city of Antwerp. As a reaction to these mutinies, Netherlandish political elites agreed in the Pacification of Ghent (1576) to drive away the Spanish troops. Article 13 of the Pacification ordered that all "the pillars, trophies, inscriptions and effigies erected by the duke of Alba to the shame and disgrace of the afore-said and all others, shall be destroyed and demolished" (Kossmann and Mellink 1974: 130). The Brussels column was probably demolished soon afterwards. According to the Reformed clergyman Johannes Gysius the column "was knocked to pieces by the citizens, yes in such a manner that each sought a piece thereof to show that they had helped to destroy such a work" (Gysius 1616: 272).

In 1585 and under military pressure, Brussels reconciled with the Habsburg regime. The Culemborg site remained underdeveloped for decades, during which the Revolt separated the Low Countries into a Northern part, continuing its rebellion, and a Southern part, returning under Habsburg authority. The former palace grounds in Brussels only received a new purpose when the daughter of Philip II, Isabella, and her husband Albert of Austria began their joint reign over the Low Countries in 1598. Re-appropriating the location, the archducal couple invited the Discalced Carmelite Friars to settle on the location of the demolished palace (Juste 1855: 504). The new Discalced Carmelites were a mendicant order from Spain, founded in 1593 to contribute to the Counter-Reformation struggle against heresy. On September 8, 1611, the archdukes laid the first stone of the new church and convent (van Gestel 1725: 38; Sanderus 1629: 273; Eusebius 1737: 43–4). Significantly, they required that the exact place where the nobles had assembled be left vacant (Schuermans 1870: 101). Albert and Isabella apparently wanted to keep alive the memory of how things had gone very wrong in the sixteenth century but also to show by antithesis what the outcome had been: a successful religious restoration. Initially known for heresy and insurgence, the Culemborg site thus became a symbol for the Habsburg Counter-Reformation (Jacobs 2006: 150). Curiously, the location of the nobility's gathering in 1566 remained recognizable as such for a long period of time. When the Catholic Northerner Gerard van Loon visited the convent more than a century later in 1720, he wrote that "in the courtyard of this convent has been shown to me by the priest a square place dug out with care, where the room is supposed to have been in which the confederated nobles formerly held their assemblies" (1723: 115). The priest's awareness of the place's significance and his act of sharing the information with visiting strangers suggests that in the eighteenth century the Discalced Carmelite Friars in Brussels still cherished the symbolism of their convent's location and their triumphant struggle against heresy.

The Culemborg family, too, had a stake in keeping alive memories of the past. Floris I of Culemborg died in 1598. He had never been able to reclaim the confiscated family property in Brussels. In 1619, the United Provinces and the Habsburg Netherlands were exploring the possibilities for extending the Twelve Years' Truce (1609–21). In this context and after earlier attempts, Floris II requested compensation for the confiscation and destruction of his family's palace in Brussels where, after all, "the first fundaments were laid for our victory and triumph."[1] He outlined the history of the house in order to convince his audience that his father had played an important role in the liberation of the land and that they should therefore help him in his efforts:

> In the year 1566 the principal nobles of the Netherlands assembled in the house of the lord the count of Culemborg's lord father of honourable memory in order to consider as good and loyal vassals—seeing the great troubles of the common land's unrest, bloodshed and other calamity [...]—how these troubles and calamities could be soothed, which is why they presented a request to the duchess of Parma, governor of the Netherlands.[2]

It is unclear whether the States General offered further assistance to Count Floris. What is clear is that it took until 1674 for the Culemborg lobby to succeed. In that year, the great-great-grandson of Floris I, Count Henry Wolrad of Waldeck, obtained from the States of Brabant an annuity of 5,000 guilders.[3] In 1732, 164 years after the demolition in 1568, the debt was redeemed for a lump sum of 100,000 guilders (Voet van Oudheusden 1753: 380).

The Culemborg case indicates that government authorities and other stakeholders in the early modern Low Countries were keen managers of memory: the duke of Alba, the burghers of Brussels, the archdukes Albert and Isabella, the order of the Discalced Carmelites, and the Culemborg family, each for their own reasons kept alive their interpretation of this particular episode. Hence, memories of the past survived for a long period, but only when people had a stake in keeping them alive and acted accordingly. And at different times memories could serve different functions. Alba wanted to show force by damning the memory of the rebels. The drafters of the Pacification of Ghent desired to forget the episode altogether in order to restore peace and stability. Local inhabitants kept pieces of the stone column as souvenirs. The archdukes, together with the Discalced Friars, framed the place's history as a triumph of both the true faith and the house of Habsburg over heretics and rebels. The following sections will discuss the political usage of cultural memory by these different groups, beginning with early modern church authorities and religious stakeholders.

CHURCH AND RELIGION

Religion and politics were closely entangled in pre-modern Europe. When Albert and Isabella gave the grounds of the Culemborg palace to the Discalced Carmelites they were contributing to the Catholic Revival in the Netherlands. Seeing the restoration of Habsburg authority and Catholicism as two sides of the same coin, they were also making a political statement. It would, for this reason, make little sense to exclude church authorities and religious stakeholders in a chapter on memory, power, and politics. Until recently, however, religion did not feature prominently in memory studies, partly because of the close connection between memory and modern nationalism research, which has neglected the importance of religion. It also has to do with the way in which religion has long been considered as the domain of church history rather than cultural history. This has been changing recently as numerous studies have begun to emphasize the connection between religion and memory (e.g., Louthan 2009; Walsham 2011; Pollmann 2011; Janssen 2014).

The striking Habsburg recatholicization of Bohemia, an important cradle of Protestantism, after 1620 relied not only on force but also persuasion. Memory played a big role in this process. Bohemian antiquarians, notably the Jesuit Bohuslav Balbín, placed the Protestant past between brackets and sought to connect the pre-Hussite, Catholic past to the Counter-Reformation "present" and frame the period in between as an undesirable disruption of normality. Religious authorities also reintroduced and widely disseminated triumphalist Catholic imagery in the Bohemian landscape (Louthan 2009: 115–44). Defining both the natural and the manmade landscape as "a porous surface upon which each generation inscribes its own values and preoccupations," Alexandra Walsham has argued that it should not simply be seen as the static backdrop of historical developments such as the Reformation and Counter-Reformation. It both reflected and shaped religious history (Walsham 2011: 6). This interplay between religion, landscape, and memory was of course not linked to a particular confession. Iconoclastic violence in Britain eliminated Catholic "idolatry," but stories and legends of saints, martyrs, and miracles survived nonetheless, and Catholics continued to harbor nostalgic feelings for the time before the Reformation. For Protestant iconoclasts, too, total oblivion was not desirable. Ruins, empty spaces of dissolved abbeys, stumps of "holy" trees, and pieces of stained glass reminded English Puritans of the ongoing struggle against Catholic "dilutions" of the word of God. Keeping memories of destruction alive allowed also the symbolism of iconoclasm to survive (Walsham 2011: 147–8).

Inherent to the power struggles between Catholics and Protestants during the Reformation and Counter-Reformation were disagreements about memory. Catholics viewed Christian doctrine as "true and orthodox because it was conserved by a continuous succession of bishops" (Cameron 2012: 31). Since continuity in church traditions was such an important doctrinal justification, the Catholic accusation of innovation was enough to frame Protestants as evil "heretics." In doing so, Catholics had the advantage of being able to fall back on existing strategies to legitimate their faith. We see this, for instance, after the Revolt of the Netherlands had split the Low Countries into a Northern and Southern polity—the Dutch Republic and the Habsburg Netherlands, respectively. The North had a Reformed public church while authorities in the South organized a very effective Counter-Reformation. Around 1600, church authorities on both sides of the political and religious divide sought to point out the "mistakes" of the other side. In 1595, Franciscus Costerus, a Jesuit living in Brussels observed in his *Proof of the Old Catholic Teachings* that "it is in the manner of all heretics, to introduce some novelty in the world, never heard of or known by their parents" (1595: f. 3r). Clerics, like Costerus, were quite resourceful not only in demonstrating the longevity of Catholicism but also in incorporating recent developments in the long-term history of the Roman church. Take for example the first centenary in 1640 of Pope Paul III's confirmation of the Society of Jesus in 1540, which Jesuits celebrated with splendid festivities all over the world. A group of Netherlandish Jesuits wrote the *Imago primi saeculi Societatis Iesu* and also brought an abridged Dutch edition on the market, in which they explained how their centenary was in line with tradition. Emperor Constantine (*c.* 272–337 CE) had transformed the "heathen" *ludi saeculares*, which at least in 47 CE were celebrated as a commemoration of the foundation of Rome, into a jubilee of the birth of Christ. In the year 1300, Pope Boniface VIII confirmed this practice in his bull "Antiquorum habet fide relatio." During these jubilees, the church offered penitent pilgrims absolution of their sins. Later successors of Boniface VIII, Paul II, and Sixtus IV, even decided to hold the jubilee every twenty-five years, so as to enable more people to participate in the festivities—which, significantly, were highly lucrative for the Catholic church (Bollandus et al. 1640: 3). In 1640, the Jesuits were appropriating the jubilee tradition to celebrate both the ancient history of the true faith as well as their hundred-year-old struggle against the Reformation, which had helped transform the Southern Netherlands from a cradle of heresy in the 1540s to a bulwark of the Counter-Reformation in the 1640s (van der Steen 2015: 262–3).

Remembering intercessions of the Holy Virgin and other miracles also served to demonstrate the verity of Catholicism. Benedictine monk Jacobus Lummenaeus à Marca recalled in 1626 that during Archduke Albert of Austria's lifetime, the archduke asked him to write a chronological history of the Revolt, to support the political objectives of the regime. Lummenaeus told Albert that the subject was very delicate and that he would much rather devote his time to studies of the Virgin Mary, which indeed he did with his *Corona Virginae*, published in Ghent in 1618. Writing in the second half of the seventeenth century, the Catholic author of a manuscript chronicle explained the political interest in miracles: "the heresy of our time cannot be vanquished but by miracles because one does not dispute with words but with actions and only with actions can the impudent lies of heresy be repudiated."[4]

Condemning Catholic church traditions as a dilution of the word of God, Protestants claimed to return to the doctrinal purity of the early Christians (Cameron 2012: 27–32). Yet, despite attempting to do so in doctrinal treatises, they found the political rhetoric of seniority irresistible as well. They, for instance, took over the Catholic practice of celebrating jubilees and, as Peter Burke shows in this volume, in turn inspired the 1640 Jesuit jubilee. In 1617, Elector Frederick V of the Palatinate led an assembly of the Protestant Union—an important alliance of Protestant imperial princes against Catholic rulers in the Empire. The elector organized a day of thanksgiving in commemoration of the Reformation, to strengthen bonds in the divided Protestant world. This centenary resulted in a true commemoration competition. As a reaction Pope Paul IV organized a Catholic jubilee on June 12, 1617, even though the next jubilee was only planned for 1625. The organization of Protestant centenaries also served an internally divisive function. Lutheran preachers in Saxony held a jubilee to emphasize their status as protectors of Lutheran orthodoxy (Schönstadt 1978: 13–19).

Internal disagreements between different Protestant confessions in the Dutch Republic in the 1610s further demonstrate the irresistibility of using the recent past in support of one's own agenda. A religious quarrel broke out between the supporters of Franciscus Gomarus and Jacobus Arminius, two theologians at Leiden University. The disagreement between them was about the Reformed concepts of predestination and human free will. Whereas Arminius argued that the doctrine of predestination allowed for the human initiative to reject God's offer of salvation, Gomarus contended this would impinge intolerably on the Lord's absolute sovereignty. As a minority group in the public church, many Arminian clergymen were threatened with suspension. In 1610, prominent Arminian clergymen therefore presented a remonstrance to the States of Holland, asking for political protection. Hence, they became known as Remonstrants. Initially a matter for academics only, the conflict brought the young state on the brink of civil war.

Just as Catholics argued that Protestants wanted to undermine church teachings, Gomarists (or Counter-Remonstrants) accused their Arminian opponents of introducing novelties in the public church. The most serious charge was that Arminians wanted to alter the doctrinal foundation of the Reformed church in the Netherlands, which ever since the Synod of Emden in 1571 consisted of the Heidelberg Catechism (1563) and the Belgic Confession (1561). Gomarists considered altering these as tantamount to casting off the hard-fought achievements of the Dutch Revolt against the Catholic Habsburgs (Trigland 1650: ff. *3r–4v, pp. 18–9). Arminians scoffed at this accusation and claimed that they acted more in the spirit of the Reformation. One of their clergymen, Johannes Uytenbogaert, sneered: "the history of forty years on which the Counter-Remonstrants pride themselves is real novelty compared to the history of Holy Scripture and the first Christendom" (1617: f. a3r).

But even a learned clergyman such as Uytenbogaert seems to have felt the lure of seniority. Even though he fundamentally argued that Arminian ideas about predestination were more in the spirit of the Bible and the early Christians than those of the Counter-Remonstrants, he also wrote that "there are in these lands many preachers now dead, and some still alive, old men: who have declared and still declare never to have had a different sentiment than the current Remonstrants do now" (Uytenbogaert 1617: f. a4v). He subsequently named the Rotterdam preacher Jan Ysbrantsz who had allegedly always disapproved of Calvin's ideas about predestination and one of the oldest retired clergymen in Holland, Clement Maertensz, who "frequently declared that [. . .] he had had and had learned no other feeling regarding the predestination than that of Melanchton" (Uytenbogaert 1617: f. b1r). Another Remonstrant preacher, Jacob Taurinus from Utrecht, in 1617 even appropriated Prince William of Orange, the leader of the Dutch Revolt, who had died in 1584, as the retrospective protector of the Arminian cause (Taurinus 1617).

DYNASTY

Princely dynasties have long understood the political usefulness of history. New dynasties that replaced old ones, by conquest, inheritance, or other means, often covered up any discontinuities by creating an image of permanence, of "having always been there." Capetian kings of France, once their throne had been secured, from the second half of the eleventh century presented themselves as the heirs of the Carolingians (Gabriele 2011: 22). This tradition of camouflaging dynastic change continued after the agnatic extinction of the house of Capet in 1328. Its successor dynasty, the house of Valois, conveniently "rediscovered" the old long-neglected Salic Law to bar female succession and, thereby, oppose the claims of rival pretenders to the throne, notably Edward III of England whose mother was a Capetian princess (Taylor 2006: 543–4). Furthermore, thirteenth- and fourteenth-century members and successors of the French Capetian dynasty established a tradition of commemorating the holy crusader-king Louis IX, who had died in Tunis during the Eighth Crusade. He was canonized in 1297. The last Capetian women, not qualifying for succession themselves, nonetheless played a central role as guardians of Louis IX's legacy to bolster their status as the last of the line (Allirot 2013: 243–60). At the beginning of the Hundred Years' War, both Edward III of England and the Valois king of France Philip VI presented themselves as the true heirs of Saint Louis. In the fifteenth century, the political usage of memories of Louis IX waned, which shows, just like the unused Culemborg site at the end of the sixteenth century, that commemoration of the past is not a self-evident phenomenon. Memories of Saint Louis were only revived at the beginning of the seventeenth century, when they began to serve new political functions for Bourbon kings of France, who had succeeded the Valois in 1589. Successive monarchs, for instance, commissioned images of Louis IX with their own facial characteristics. Such references to the sainthood of Louis IX served to support their (controversial) claims about the divine right of kings (Gaposchkin 2008: 238–41).

Naming practices in the Bourbon dynasty also evoked memories of Louis IX and reflected the renewed interest in the holy king's legacy. The later Louis XIII (1601–43)—when still a child—was deeply unhappy about being named not after his father Henri IV or his favorite ancestor Gaston de Foix but after his distant forefather Saint Louis. Almost a year before he was actually baptized, on October 25, 1605 he had already told his court physician Jean Héroard, who kept a meticulous diary, that he wanted to be named Henri. To Héroard's question why this was so, the royal infant responded: "Papa is called that; I do not want the name Louis" ([1605] 1868: 158). In 1607, when the duke of Verneuil, an illegitimate son of Henri IV, was named after his father, Louis was displeased. "I don't want [that]; I will not call him Henri, it's the name of my papa," he told Héroard ([1607] 1868: 297). In reaction to the child's dismissal of the name the court physician "took the opportunity to tell him that his name was much prettier and spoke to him about the king Saint Louis, his piety, his fairness, and how he had gone to war against the Turks" (Héroard [1607] 1868: 297). It seems the young Dauphin had listened attentively to his physician and developed a certain admiration for his distant ancestor. In August 1618, Louis XIII formally re-established the cult of Saint Louis and, from then on, all Bourbon monarchs grew up with the myth of religion and justice embodied by Louis IX (Mormiche 2009: 232, 252).

Although dynastic exploitation of the past spans the medieval/early modern-divide, dynastic awareness of the political potential of cultural memory grew in the early modern period. One reason for the change is the increasing reliance on male primogeniture for the succession of lands and titles. According to an influential grand narrative in studies of European kinship, the medieval devolution of property was relatively egalitarian but changed in the early modern period, when "patrilineality, primogeniture, and other single-heir principles" were on the rise (Sabean and Teuscher 2007: 1–16). A ruler's political emphasis on vertical family relations to legitimate his, or sometimes her, exercise of power thus required commemoration of ancestors. Apart from slowly changing conceptions of kinship and succession, the turmoil of the Reformation and Counter-Reformation also changed the outlook of dynasties on their past. These conflicts undermined continuity and negatively affected the credibility of dynastic pretensions of longevity. Kevin Sharpe argued that in this period the creation of a public "image" of rulers and their family became more than before "inextricably connected to cultural memory" (2009: 12).

This certainly holds true for the Habsburg dynasty. An important element of the Habsburg public image was the piety of its members: the *Pietas Austriaca* (Coreth 1982). This image of piety was an old tradition that can be traced back to the medieval period, but it was also a reaction to the "heresies" that jeopardized Habsburg rule throughout Europe. In his *Reason of State* (1589), the Italian political thinker and cleric Giovanni Botero argued that princes should be pious and serve God, "because from Him proceed the power of a ruler and the obedience of his subjects. The higher he is raised above his fellows, the lower he should abase himself in the face of God" ([1589] 1956: 63). The Habsburgs were definitely not the only rulers emphasizing their piety and interweaving their political and religious aspirations, but they did develop a particularly strong tradition of piety. Botero himself attributed the rise of the dynasty to its devoutness and traced this practice back to a legendary encounter of Count Rudolf I of Habsburg (1218–91). Hunting in the woods on a rainy day, Rudolf met a priest carrying the viaticum—the last Eucharist—to a dying person. According to Botero:

Rudolf dismounted at once, and humbly making obeisance to Jesus Christ in the species and form of bread, he laid his cloak over the priest's shoulders to give him more protection against the rain and so that the Host should be carried with more dignity. The good priest, wondering at the courtesy and piety of the count, gave him eternal thanks and prayed that the divine majesty would reward him from the abundance of His grace. A miracle followed: soon afterwards Rudolf became emperor, and his descendants were archdukes of Austria, rulers of the Low Countries, kings of Spain and sovereigns of the New World, lords over innumerable states and immense territories.

—Botero [1589] 1956: 63

From 1600, this narrative gained new relevance when the Habsburgs began to use it to demonstrate that religion was the firmest base of their authority. Instructing his son Philip III, Philip II told him about the legend and added that Rudolf had actually given his horse to the priest as a magnanimous gesture and demonstration of his devotion. Philip IV had his apartments in the Madrid Alcazar decorated with a painting depicting the actual scene of Rudolf's generous act of devotion, painted by Pieter Paul Rubens and Jan Wildens (Figure 1.3) (del Rio Barredo 2010: 57–64).

The Bourbon and Habsburg commemoration of distant ancestors, Louis IX and Rudolf respectively, partly served to camouflage dynastic and political uncertainty. The "new" Bourbon dynasty presented itself as the rightful successor of Saint Louis while Habsburg references to Rudolf justified the dynasty's bloody struggles against "heretics" and "infidels." Both dynasties used the pious credentials of their distant forefather to bolster

FIGURE 1.3: Pieter Paul Rubens and Jan Wildens, *Act of Devotion by Rudolf I of Habsburg*, c. 1625. © Museo Nacional del Prado, inv. P01645.

their claims of divine right. But sometimes political turmoil actually provided a dynasty with its best claim to power. In such cases, historical depth was less necessary in dynastic self-representation. The German house of Nassau is a prime example. Like the Bourbons and Habsburgs, the Nassaus prided themselves on a distant kinsman: Adolf, who had been elected king of the Romans in 1292. As ruler of the principality of Orange, an enclave in the kingdom of France, the senior agnate of the family later also came to enjoy the status of sovereign prince. Yet, despite claims of ancient descent or sovereignty, dynastic representations of the house of Nassau in the Dutch Republic did not so much rely on the dynasty's real or imaginary ancient lineage but rather on the military participation of Prince William of Orange-Nassau, and his sons Maurice and Frederick Henry, in the Revolt of the Netherlands.

In the seventeenth century, many inhabitants of the Republic considered Prince William as a popular prince and as their *pater patriae*. The historian Louis Aubery, born in 1609, observed in the 1680s that tourists visited the Prinsenhof where William had been murdered: "in the city of Delft in Holland, strangers are still shown the marks of the bullets that entered the stone of the doorway after having pierced the body of the prince: and it was shown to me in my youth" (1687: 151) (Figure 1.4). However, the heroic reputation of William of Orange in the seventeenth century does not reflect the prince's public image at the time of his death in 1584, when there had been little reason for celebrating his life. The Revolt was not going well at all and had almost bankrupted the Nassau family. In 1584, the second son of the late prince William, Maurice, was in a

FIGURE 1.4: The bullet holes can still be seen. Image courtesy of Museum Prinsenhof Delft.

difficult position. His impoverished family depended financially on the States of Holland, and only in 1609 were the fierce conflicts about his father's inheritance resolved. The high gubernatorial office to which Holland and Zeeland appointed the young count Maurice in 1585 (the provincial "stadholderate") remained non-hereditary. Due to Prince William's lack of popularity, neither the provincial States nor the States General made much effort to commemorate and celebrate his life. As Olaf Mörke has rightly observed, the fact that the Orange-Nassau family became a powerful European dynasty in the seventeenth century was, at least in the 1580s, an unforeseen development (2010: 259–263).

The position of the Orange-Nassaus changed around 1600. Once Maurice had gained a reputation on the battlefield, his father's reputation, too, improved, which is reflected by the fact that most of the existing plays about William of Orange were published and performed around 1600 (Bloemendal 2007: 99). Several reasons may account for the sudden interest in the life and death of the prince, but the most important one was that in the 1590s Maurice and his uncle William Louis of Nassau-Dillenburg—facilitated by the statecraft of the Holland "Land's Advocate" Johan van Oldenbarnevelt—recaptured important cities in the east of the Union. William of Orange's unimpressive grave may further illustrate the fact that his later reputation was far from self-evident. After a visit to Delft in 1593, traveler and author of the *Itinerary* Fynes Moryson noted in his diary: "In the New Church is a monument of the prince of Orange, the poorest that ever I saw for such a person, being onely of rough stones and mortar, with posts of wood, coloured over with black, and very little erected from the ground" (Moryson [after 1609] 1918: 229). Financial difficulties are insufficient explanation for what was in Moryson's eyes a gross neglect. After all, while William of Orange was still lying in his nondescript grave, in 1607 the States General commissioned an ornamental tomb in Amsterdam's Old Church designed by Hendrick de Keyser for Vice-admiral Jacob van Heemskerck, who had died at the Battle of Gibraltar in 1607 (Scholten 2003: 73). Gibraltar was an important victory for the Republic against the Habsburg overlord. It is telling that the States General commemorated Jacob van Heemskerck as a national hero immediately after his death while no such honor had yet been extended to Prince William of Orange.

Only during the Twelve Years' Truce (1609–21) did the States General commission a worthier grave for the late prince of Orange. The deferral of hostilities removed the immediate threat of the enemy and diminished the military importance of Prince Maurice as army commander. In 1613, the States General began to discuss draft designs by several artists. In 1615, William's widow, the dowager princess of Orange, Louise de Coligny, urged the States to speed up their efforts for "an honourable sepulchre" for her late husband. The dowager princess understood that the actions of the house of Nassau in the war against Spain were the dynasty's main claim to fame. In a non-monarchical polity such as the Dutch Republic, there was no guarantee that future princes of Orange would come to occupy high offices of state. Stories about the dynasty's role in the foundation of the Republic, however, would remind people of the gratitude that they owed to the dynasty, and this was an idea successive princes of Orange grew up with (van der Steen 2015: 133–4). The tutor of William II (1626–50), the Huguenot theologian André Rivet, for instance, taught his pupil that he should learn about his family's history because "memory is the chest that guards the acquired treasure" (Rivet 1642: 246). As we will see in the next section, the funerary monument of William of Orange, which was ultimately finished in 1623, demonstrates that there was some truth in Rivet's lesson.

GOVERNMENT AUTHORITIES AND OPPOSITION GROUPS

The pursuit of modern nationalist governments to have their own interpretation of the past be accepted as authoritative has long been well-evidenced. Research on the early modern period has begun to reveal that governments before 1800 also engaged in top-down manipulations of the past. An early example of this phenomenon is the state in Tudor and Stuart England, which took an active role in the management of memory, as David Cressy has shown. Whereas before the Reformation, English history had no part in the liturgical calendar, this situation changed under the reign of Elizabeth I. Her government created its own Protestant calendar: it reduced the number of holy days and introduced new secular commemorations, such as "the queen's holiday" on November 17, a commemoration day of Elizabeth I's accession in 1558, followed at a later stage by anniversaries of the defeat of the Spanish Armada. The Stuarts continued this new practice by adding anniversaries to the calendar such as a day of thanksgiving commemorating the Gunpowder Plot in 1605. Government authorities developed "a mythic and patriotic sense of national identity," focusing less than before on traditional Catholic frames of reference such as religious doctrine and more than ever on the recent past. The intention was to create a "rhythm of the year" that supported the political aspirations of the government (Cressy 1989: xi–xiv).

In politicizing the national calendar top down, however, the English state also turned the past into a rhetorical battleground on which later opposition groups settled their disputes. Elizabeth I became in the seventeenth century a heroic figure in the minds of English Protestants. After her death in 1603, the pamphleteer and poet Anthony Nixon presented her successor James VI and I as "a Phoenix from Elizaes ashes bred / Though she possesse a place among the dead" (1603: f. d3r). Supporters of Elizabeth's legacy, like Nixon, developed a selective account of her reign that ignored most of its shortcomings. The popularity of these narratives rendered them politically useful, especially from 1625 onwards when Charles I became king of England, Scotland, and Ireland and started a quarrel with the English Parliament, resulting in the Personal Rule of 1629–40 and the English Civil War (1642–51). David Cressy has shown that in this political context opposition groups began to use commemorations of Elizabeth I as "a safe and discreet way to criticize the current regime." When tensions between Spain and England grew during the Anglo-Spanish War of 1625–30, in 1626 clergyman Thomas Gataker commemorated the successful victory of Elizabeth I, whom he presented as an instrument in the hands of God, against the Spanish Armada of 1588. In 1639, at the end of Charles I's Personal Rule, an anonymous pamphleteer eulogized Elizabeth I and evoked the memory of her cooperation with Parliament: "her Commons all were joyn'd to her in love" (anonymous 1639: f. b6v). And at the height of the crisis, in the 1640s, Elizabeth's last speech to Parliament in 1601—in which she had emphasized the good relationship with the Commons that she enjoyed in her reign—was reprinted twice (Cressy 1989: 134–8). In some ways, the reputation that Elizabeth had built during her life was a millstone around the neck of her Stuart successors.

Although the English case above is a good example of state-driven national memory politics, opposition to Charles I demonstrates that the state was not the only stakeholder in the political exploitation of the past. The following case about disagreements between supporters of the Orange dynasty and the grand pensionary of Holland, John De Witt, shows that in the federal Dutch Republic, the state was even a relatively powerless actor. Furthermore, it demonstrates that public memories about the past did not simply constitute an endless supply of examples, supporting just any political argument. Existing memories could also limit the possibilities of rulers to use historical arguments in support of their own political agenda.

Citing the termination of the Eighty Years' War in 1648, the States of Holland decided in 1650 to discontinue paying its share of the state's military budget. William II of Nassau, prince of Orange, deeply resented this decision. As the highest army officer and stadholder of several Dutch provinces, including the influential province of Holland, he had a vested interest in maintaining military expenditure, which for him was an important source of power, income, and prestige. He therefore tried to intimidate Amsterdam—Holland's most powerful city—into paying its fair share. He was unsuccessful and a few months later he died unexpectedly. William II's only child, William III, was born a few days after his father's death. The States of Holland were afraid that the young William would ultimately follow the footsteps of his father and they agreed in a secret addition to the Treaty of Westminster (1654), which ended the First Anglo-Dutch War (1652–4), to bar the new prince of Orange from political office. English republicans feared that the young prince—a nephew of Charles II—would ultimately turn the Dutch Republic against the English government to help the Stuarts re-establish monarchical authority. In the Act of Seclusion, as the secret agreement between Holland and England was known, John De Witt promised England's lord protector Oliver Cromwell never to appoint the young William III to the stadholderate. When news about the secret agreement broke in Holland and the other provinces, a political conflict broke out between supporters and opponents of the house of Orange, in which memories of the Revolt of the Netherlands became politically relevant once more.

To understand why memories of the sixteenth-century Revolt suddenly became politically potent halfway through the seventeenth century it is important to know that the Revolt had become an important foundation narrative for the Dutch Republic. This foundation narrative had its origin in the anti-Spanish propaganda that Dutch opinion-makers had spread during the late sixteenth and early seventeenth centuries (Pollmann 2008: 6–13). Leaders of the Revolt, William of Orange and his successors Maurice and Frederick Henry (and their supporters) had linked the Orange dynasty to the success and survival of the Republic. According to the influential contemporary political commentator Lieuwe van Aitzema, this Orangist interpretation of the conflict was told everywhere: "on the chair, in barges, and on carts [. . .] yes for children to learn at their mother's knee [. . .] It would well-nigh be idolatry, should one not believe it" (van Aitzema 1669: 1234). And, indeed, when news about the Act of Seclusion leaked, the States of Friesland protested in the States General against this ungrateful action against the descendant of "the lord prince William the Elder [. . .] whose bones are in Delft beneath a tomb erected in his honor and in his eternal memory by the State itself" (van Aitzema 1663: 110) (Figure 1.5). With this reference to a physical reminder of the house of Orange's active role in the Revolt, the States of Friesland sought to convince the States General that they owed gratitude to the Orange dynasty.

A memory war was in the making. John De Witt reacted personally to the accusations of ingratitude by writing and presenting on August 6, 1654 in the States General his *Deduction*. A contemporary observer estimated that the text was "as big as half the Bible." This was an exaggeration, but it did take De Witt no fewer than five hours to deliver his argument. His fundamental point was that gratitude toward William of Orange was not incompatible with denying high political office to his great-grandson William III. However fundamental this principle may have been in 1654, he spent much of his *Deduction* painstakingly trying

FIGURE 1.5: Dirck van Delen, *A Family beside the Tomb of Prince William I in the Nieuwe Kerk*, Delft, 1645, Rijksmuseum Amsterdam, SK-A-2352.

to disentangle the history of the Republic from the role the princes of Orange played in the sixteenth-century struggle against the Habsburg overlord. In doing so, he did not shun radical statements. He even wrote that the murder of William of Orange had not necessarily been a bad thing. At the time, the States of Holland—who had abjured their overlord Philip II in 1581—were namely in the process of making Prince William count of Holland. De Witt explained that after the Catholic zealot Balthasar Gérard assassinated the prince, "God Almighty has nonetheless created light from such deep darkness and not only kept the state standing, but also preserved its inhabitants, and guarded them from the new subjection they were already being rushed into" (De Witt 1654: 50). With this "what if"-perspective, De Witt suggested that William of Orange would have become a tyrant had he not been murdered. On top of that, the grand pensionary downplayed the role of the house of Orange in the Revolt by emphasizing the influence of divine intervention. Further on, he gave the States of Friesland a taste of their own medicine. Reacting to their accusation of ingratitude toward the house of Orange, De Witt evoked a memory of 1584, when Friesland had refused to let William of Orange's son, Maurice, succeed as stadholder. Instead they employed Prince William's nephew William Louis of Nassau-Dillenburg. Pointing out the hypocrisy of the Frisian States, De Witt jeered: "where, at that time, were those who now dwell on due gratitude?" (De Witt 1654: 74).

To modern readers, the argument in De Witt's *Deduction* appears sensible, but to the majority of early modern people—for whom the heredity of status was a fact of life—it probably did not. This is why De Witt and other opponents of Orange princes having a say in Dutch politics time and again needed to position themselves—however grudgingly—against the dominant Orangist narratives about the Dutch Revolt and debunk the historical interpretations of their adversaries.

CONCLUSION

Already in the medieval period, church authorities, dynasties, and governments but also non-elite stakeholders in a very multi-medial and dynamic way cloaked their political arguments with the authority of precedent and, in doing so, attempted to manipulate the past to their advantage. The commemoration of distant ancestors to legitimate one's position in the "present" and to camouflage discontinuity was a practice predating the early modern period. This chapter has shown, however, that great upheavals—the Reformation, the Counter-Reformation, as well as revolts and religious wars—stimulated the competitive usage of conflicting interpretations of historical development in the period 1500–1800. After their succession to the French throne, Bourbon kings of France used Louis IX, through worship and naming practices to give but two examples, in order to make the family connection to the Capetians seem a bit less remote and to lend weight to their claims of divine right monarchy. The Habsburgs, plagued by the Revolt of the Netherlands, commemorated their ancestor Rudolf's act of piety in the thirteenth century to demonstrate that unlike some other dynasties (including the Bourbons) they had always prioritized religion over reason of state. In Counter-Reformation Bohemia, Catholic antiquarians emphasized the bonds between the world before early reformer Jan Hus and the present day to demonstrate the antiquity, and therefore verity, of Catholicism. And on the British Isles, but also elsewhere in the Protestant world, memories of the Reformation could both vindicate hardline Protestants in their struggles against Catholic "superstitions" and nourish Catholic feelings of melancholy as well as nostalgia about a lost world.

The past was malleable but in politicizing memory, memory makers also set a standard that could turn itself against them. Like their post-1800 successors, early modern communities could not simply use the past as an inexhaustible supply of historical examples. They were constrained by the existing dominant storylines in the community. On a national level, government authorities played a role in setting these standards. Elizabeth I politicized the national calendar by adding secular commemorations of political events to the previously predominantly religious feasts. A figure of great popularity after her death, Elizabeth set a kind of benchmark for her Stuart successors, who generally did not compare favorably to the last Tudor monarch. But the early modern state was not necessarily the most important actor in establishing dominant interpretations of the past. National government authorities in the federal Dutch Republic did very little to spread their vision on the Revolt of the Netherlands. This allowed the Orange-Nassau dynasty and its supporters to step in and create a pro-Orange narrative of the conflict. They used this highly popular narrative to argue that state authorities in the Republic should express more gratitude to the dynasty for its military leadership during the rebellion.

The most important conclusion of this chapter is that overreliance on modern state formation, nationalism, and mass media in explaining the political potency of memory neglects the dynamic usage of the past in the early modern period. We have seen that due to the public authority of history, the political usage of memory was rarely uncontested, which explains why—so often—political disagreements in the contemporary "present" turned into conflicts about the right interpretation of the past. Despite the importance that scholars of memory politics have long attached to post-1800 developments, early modern people, too, purposefully and resourcefully used memory to serve their political needs through commemoration, rediscovery, and deliberate oblivion.

CHAPTER TWO

Time and Space: Autobiographical Memory

KATHARINE HODGKIN

Autobiography, as retrospective first-person narrative, occupies a distinctive place in the exploration of memory. Recent scholarship has opened up the field of early modern life-writing in rich and exciting ways, locating autobiography and memoir in relation to a range of other texts and genres, including family memory books, almanacs and account books, diaries and letters, spiritual meditations and recipe books (Dragstra, Ottway and Wilcox 2000; Bedford, Davis, and Kelly 2007; Smyth 2010). Many of these genres are memory texts of one sort or another. Diaries and letters recall thoughts and events; family books perpetuate memories collectively within the family group across generations, animating a sense of contact with ancestors and descendants. But it is in autobiography that writers engage actively with their own memories across an extended period of time. The memories recorded are selective and subject to forgetfulness; they are constrained by generic conventions, propriety, the narrative's purpose and its intended audience, among other things. But if, as Paul Ricoeur (2004: 84) suggests, "it is through the narrative function that memory is incorporated into the formation of identity," then in retrospective narrative especially, we see the work of memory in action.

Ricoeur's assertion that the key term uniting memory and identity is narrative—the sequential story of a life—may be juxtaposed with Georges Gusdorf's ([1956] 1980: 30) point, from a very different moment in the history of autobiography and the self: "The man who takes the trouble to tell of himself knows that the present differs from the past and that it will not be repeated in the future." Gusdorf's paradigmatic autobiographical self—masculine, western, individualist—is very much at odds with the variety of autobiographical voices uncovered in recent years, but it is worth recalling for his emphasis on time as change, and how this is embedded in the act of telling. Research on self-writing has, as the term suggests, focused on the concept of the self (and often put it into question). But self-writing emerges in relation not only to a changing sense of self but to a changing sense of the past; time itself is historical, lived in and understood differently at different moments, and the early modern is a period of developing awareness of historical difference (Woolf 2003; Baggerman, Dekker, and Mascuch 2011). Early modern memory narratives inhabit different temporalities to ours—cyclical and providential as well as linear and chronological; internal as well as external—and structure the remembered life in unfamiliar ways. Nonetheless, the remembered self of retrospective narrative is located in time, and to some degree understood in relation to temporal and historical change.

Memory is anchored not only in time, but space; and space, like time, is imagined and experienced historically and socially. Michel Foucault, in a characteristically suggestive aside, describes medieval space as the space of "emplacement", stable, hierarchically organized, and divided into opposing pairs (sacred/profane, protected/open, urban/rural), and identifies the seventeenth century as a moment of transformation in which (following Galileo) space becomes unbounded and "infinitely open": "a thing's place was no longer anything but a point in its movement, just as the stability of a thing was only its movement indefinitely slowed down" (Foucault 1984: 1–2). This contrast is perhaps less convincing as a historical transition than as a way of imagining different inhabitations of space. Early modern autobiographies offer many variations on these themes: places of security or enclosure, sacred places, places of mobility. The relation between the site of memory as at once an actual and an imagined place is shifting and unstable, and complicated in early modern narratives by the symbolic meanings attributed to places of spiritual significance. But the attribution of specific qualities of memorability to defined locations also recalls the most well-known Renaissance configuration of memory, the memory palace or theater, whose symbolic locations underline the importance of spatial remembering. Early modern culture, indeed, could be seen as bracketed between two modes of memory that are significant cruxes for memory studies today: the Renaissance *ars memoriae*, and the concept of nostalgia, emerging at the end of the seventeenth century. Both these modes construct memory in relation to spatiality as well as temporality, focusing remembrance on an inner space that is materially absent; and for both also memory is sustained by affect, with the dramatic or emotional charge of images and places constituting their memorability.

MEMORY TEXTS

The last few decades have revealed a great range and quantity of retrospective narrative autobiography in early modern Europe, and have generated a correspondingly great volume of critical commentary. A genre once studied through a small canon of famous and exceptional exemplars, almost all male, is now seen as offering access to the mental worlds of marginal people who left few other historical traces. Narratives written by prominent public figures are joined by those written by the obscure and unknown; not only aristocrats and gentry, but merchants and artisans, preachers and travelers, women and men, left accounts of their lives (Graham, Hinds, and Hobby 1989; Amelang 1998). Those caught up in political and religious conflict recorded their experiences, and people from all confessional groups wrote spiritual autobiographies, focusing on inward experience and the relationship with God. In England, the upheavals of the mid-seventeenth-century revolutionary period generated a particularly substantial outpouring of religious narrative, sustained by small sectarian churches, much of which found its way into print; while among Catholics spiritual autobiographies were required by confessors as devotional exercise. This proliferation of material—print and manuscript, spiritual and secular, appearing unevenly and intermittently across Europe—is impossible to capture in a brief discussion. In this exploration of retrospective narratives as memory texts I focus on spiritual autobiography, especially the wealth of English puritan and sectarian writings of the seventeenth century, though I include comparative material from other times and places and more secular perspectives. But important differences within the genre are inevitably flattened out, along with regional and national variations, and changes over the two centuries or so covered. These texts are written for diverse audiences and purposes, in different times and places, and much more could be said about their differences than can be addressed here.

Spiritual narrative poses particular challenges to memory. Characteristically inward-looking, it is a record that depends on the memory of the writer; the remembered movements of the soul cannot be verified with reference to external events. Moreover, narratives published under the auspices of a church or written at the behest of spiritual authorities are often required to conform to a rigorously defined framework of spiritual growth, and subject to editing and censorship, widening the gap between remembering subject and recorded text. Indeed, spiritual autobiographies have often been regarded as too constrained by the imperatives of the form to offer any insight into the remembering self behind the text; the presumed authority of God compromises any other claim to authorship (Mascuch 1997). But while attention to the historicity of early modern selfhood is a necessary corrective to the universalizing assumptions of writers such as Gusdorf, we should also be attentive to the many different modes of self. Definitions of genre and selfhood that exclude groups which have been traditionally refused autonomy and self-authorship are a problematic starting point for a debate on the nature of the self inscribed in these texts. The fundamental precondition for such writing is the remembering self: without a subject presumed to remember, there can be no autobiography.

Memory is perhaps especially significant in spiritual autobiography, too, because it is closely tied to devotional and spiritual practice. The idea of memory as a spiritual duty is repeatedly invoked in early modern culture. Forgetfulness is construed as not merely personal weakness but moral failing, connoting neglect and ingratitude; disobedience, to God, a parent, or anyone in between, is characterized as forgetting one's duty. Remembrance is placed at the heart of the story of the spiritual self—"a manual, a bosom book" as John Donne describes it (1967: 188)—from St Augustine onwards. The seventeenth-century autobiographer Elizabeth Isham, modeling her "book of remembrance" on Augustine's *Confessions*, marvels at memory as an "everlasting library," and addresses God directly to wish "that I may neither ungratefully remember thy benefits nor ungraciously forget thy severe judgements" (Isham *c*. 1639: ff. 32r, 2v). Memory was central not only to educational practice in general, with schools teaching through rote learning and repetition, but specifically to spiritual and devotional training. Memorizing and repeating biblical passages was part of the routine of the godly Protestant household, as was training children to remember sermons—an activity recalled in the autobiographies of a number of writers—and the catechism; Catholic children learned the prayers and practices associated with the church rites and sacraments. Learning by heart was deployed to embed religious principles and knowledge from an early age.

Memory is thus central in autobiographical narrative, both as purpose and as problem. As writers note, it is often fallible, needing to be sustained by divine aid, or by written materials. It is structured by loss, whether it appears as pleasure, connecting the writer to a happier past, or as a reminder of still painful sorrows. Additionally, memory is engaged with and located in time and place. Writers place themselves within wider temporalities—historical, divine, and personal; and they organize their narratives around the memories recorded and recalled. They orient their lives through remembered journeys, placing themselves and their stories in relational space; and they identify key memories by anchoring them in place. The discussion that follows explores these various deployments of time, space and memory.

PROVIDENTIAL TIME AND THE NUMBERING OF DAYS

Personal memory is at the heart of self-narrative; but personal memory is embedded in the longer structures of historical time, and individual lives intersect with extended pasts and futures. "It is to memory that the sense of orientation in the passage of time is linked," writes Ricoeur, ". . . from the past to the future [. . .] following the arrow of the time of change, but also from the future toward the past [. . .] across the living present" (2004: 97). But memory is not only an arrow; alongside this forward drive sit other temporalities. The memories recorded by early autobiographers engage with different time frames: providential, historical, episodic, calendrical, cyclical. The sense that lives are situated in the great temporality of God's providential time, and the working out of divine intention, is characteristic of spiritual autobiography, but writers may also situate themselves in relation to historical events, or in the arrow of family time (as Natalie Zemon Davis (1977) describes it), or in its repetitive cycles; they may structure their lives around the ages and phases of life, or around turning points and moments of transformation. Memories are situated in juxtaposed and overlapping temporalities, inner and outer.

The temporal structure of spiritual narrative is often radically unfamiliar. Its drama is largely internal: what is worth remembering is the story of the relation to God, not the "outward Calling" (Thurgood [c. 1636] 2005). Conversion, often assumed to be the transforming moment of spiritual narrative, is less clear in practice than we might expect. The conversion narrative in its pure form, oriented around the transformation of self from unregenerate to reborn, is complicated by the many accounts which describe younger selves as living in a state of anxious uncertainty rather than sin, and conversion itself as a process rather than a moment, drawn out sometimes over many years and characterized by movements backwards as well as forwards, and continuing self-interrogation. Dates are few—writers are largely indifferent to chronology—and information about everyday life scanty; a few weeks of spiritual struggle may occupy a quarter of the narrative, while years of marriage and childrearing are passed over in a few lines. The temporal structure is governed not by chronology but by providential and mystical time, in which past, present, and future are present simultaneously in the frame of divine intention.

Providential time also reinforces the process of retrospective interpretation characteristic of autobiography: the backward gaze takes in the life as a whole and frames its meaning, reading the future in the past. It is a time of hindsight, in which the meaning of life's accidents, always already present, becomes clear only in retrospect. The task of spiritual awakening is to uncover that unknown meaning; conversion is a revelation of what has always been there as much as a radical transformation. So the Quaker Dorothea Gotherson recalls her first encounter with a Quaker preacher as an event that transforms her understanding of her own past: "the Lord's time was then to direct me by the mouth of his Prophets," and the words of the preachers "did show me all that ever I had done" (Gotherson 1661: 91–2). Her life is governed by the Lord's time, and he chooses the moment in which its true meaning becomes clear. This structure—the time of the Freudian *nachträglichkeit*, in effect—is reiterated in the instances of providence and foreshadowing that are so characteristic of spiritual autobiography, as well as in the mystical dreams recorded by many (Hodgkin 2008). However important the moment of grace, it has always been anticipated by divine foreknowledge; spiritual autobiography remembers the past in the light of "an eternity which is always in the present," as Augustine called it (1991: 230).

This structure also governs the rare memories of childhood recounted in spiritual narratives: its primary significance is in its capacity to prefigure divine intent, both through providential escapes from disaster, and through character. Writers remember themselves as serious children, worrying about sin and salvation, rather than going out to play. John Crook describes his anxiety at seeing other children "merry and cheerful, and not at all as I was" (1706: 6); Richard Norwood frets over whether his recollections of early childhood piety are true "fruits of regeneration" ([*c.* 1639] 1945: 8). Teresa of Avila recalls planning with her brother to become martyrs or hermits, and "to go to the country of the Moors [. . .] that we might be there beheaded" ("our greatest difficulty seemed to be our father and mother," she adds [1561–5] 1962: 4). Continuity across time is guaranteed not only by the act of memory that holds together past and present selves, but by the divine reassurance that finds the signs of the adult to come in the child.

Providential time faces not only backward but forward, toward the millennium, locating the soul in the frame of eternity. Thus when Lucy Hutchinson notes the date and time of her birth (four in the morning on January 29, 1620) it is in order to locate this precise moment both in an extended chronology of British history (from ancient Britons and Romans through Saxons and Normans to the present), and also at a high point of Christianity, "not in the midnight of popery [. . .] but when the Sun of truth was exalted in his progress and hastening towards a meridian glory" ([*c.* 1671] 2000: 7). Norwood similarly counts his birth in 1590 as a mark of God's favor, having been "born in those days of the glorious sunshine of the Gospel in the reign of that blessed Queen Elizabeth of famous memory, the second year after the great overthrow of the Spanish Armada [. . .] in the most prosperous and happy age that ever England enjoyed" ([1639] 1945: 4). The repeated image of the sun evokes both cosmic and diurnal cycles, tying the time of memory to the long sweep of Christian history and the time of divine intention: individual lives and national history are set against a backdrop of immutable eternity, and also implicitly against the drive toward apocalypse. Both calendar time and the time of an individual life represent moments in a cosmological time which is always simultaneously past, present, and future—"A state but of one Day," as Donne described it in 1626, ". . . yesterday doth not usher it in, nor to morrow shall not drive it out" (1967: 271).

As Bedford, Davis, and Kelly suggest, "time [. . .] functions as a God-organized enabler of the process of individual sin, repentance and salvation" (2007: 42). Mystical temporalities govern the placing and shaping of the course of life, and the time of God's great plan lends significance to trivial details. The counting of numbered days draws attention to the cosmological frame, and to the shortness of human moments measured against eternity. Calendrical time in individual life memories is marked chiefly through significant dates; birth dates in particular are read for providential and auspicious meanings. Thomas Platter's birth "on the Shrove-Tuesday of the year 1499, just as they were coming together for mass" led his family to believe that he would become a priest ([*c.* 1573] 1839: 1). Thomas Shepard was born "In the year of Christ 1604 upon the fifth day of November, called the powder treason day, and that very day wherein the Parliament should have been blown up by Popish priests" ([1646] 1972: 37). Disconcertingly he mistakes the year; November 5 is evidently the date of real (providential) significance, rather than the specific year.

Astrology adds a further cosmic frame, as well as another model of time in which the future is to some extent predetermined. The British Library copy of Thomas Tryon's 1705 *Memoirs* includes a (damaged) copy of his astrological chart as frontispiece; while for the Calvinist pewterer Augustin Guntzer, the details of his birth define his humoral complexion (and thus future character) in relation to star sign and weather:

> I was brought into the world in the year 1596, on Tuesday the 4th of May, according to the old calendar, between one and two o'clock in the morning [. . .] the moon was in the Ram [. . .] I was melancholic by nature, the earth was cold and dry.
> —Guntzer 2010: 55

The "old calendar" is the Julian calendar, a reminder that calendar time itself was subject to change. It was also a subject of religious contestation. Quakers refused to use the pagan names of days of the weeks and months; other writers refer in passing to days and dates as "Monday (so called)" (Rogers 1653: 421), or as September 6, 1634, "according to our common computation" (Tryon 1705: 7). Placing the self in time thus has a religiopolitical dimension even in its minor form, in the choice of terminology and of significant dates. November 5 is a birth date of another kind for Rose Thurgood, whose spiritual rebirth is magnified by association with the date of Protestant triumph: lying sick in bed on "the day before the Gunpowder treason day" she felt "a sweet Flash coming over my heart" and is told, "Thy name is written in the book of Life: Thou hast [. . .] a new name" ([c. 1636] 2005: 14). And underlying the attention to days and dates is the knowledge that they are

FIGURE 2.1: The Seven Ages of Man, from Johann Amos Comenius's *Visible World: or, A Nomenclature, and Picture of all The chief Things that are in the world, and of Mens Employments therein. Translated into English by Charles Hoole*, London: John Sprint, 1705, plate 37 at p. 44.

countable and limited by God. "Oh reader," wrote the Augsburg merchant Matheus Miller, "think of me that I must die and that my days are numbered. And that I must live those days as the Lord did, must die as the Lord did" (Safley 2000: 15). The days of human life repeat the days of Christ; and memory of the past presses against the limits of the future.

MEMORY IN TIME: FROM YOUTH TO AGE

Providential and mystical time are powerful structuring models for memory, but other organizing temporalities also appear. The idea of life as a sequence of determinate stages, the ages of man, is widespread. Thus the sixteenth-century musician Thomas Whythorne (Figure 2.2) locates himself in a structure of defined temporal change ("as I have been changed from time to time, by time, so altered mine affections and delights"

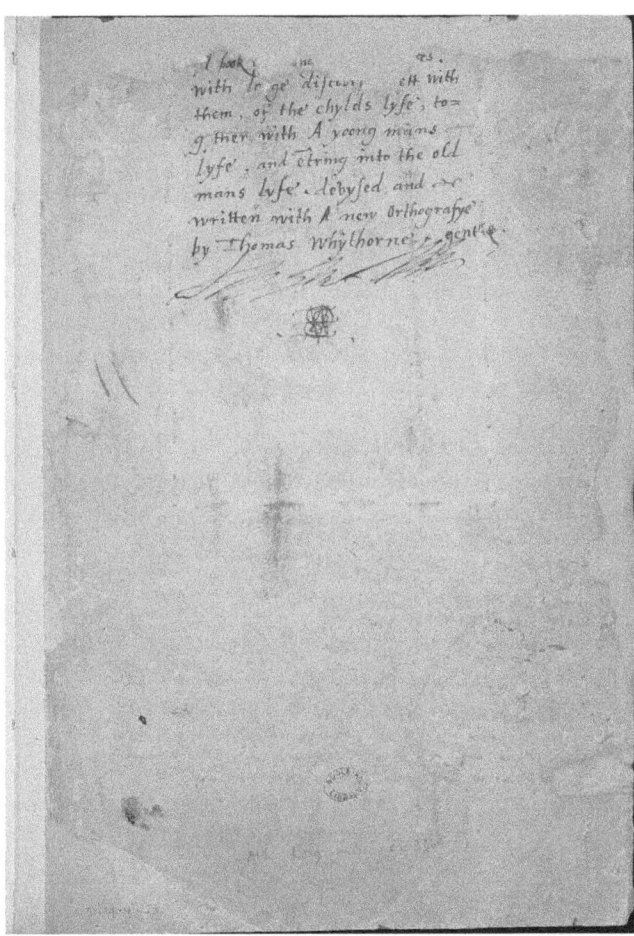

FIGURE 2.2: Thomas Whythorne, title page of MS, *A book of songs and sonetts, with long discoorses sett with them* . . ., c. 1576. Bodleian Library, MS. Eng. misc. c.330, fol. 1r. Courtesy of the Bodleian Libraries, The University of Oxford.

[*c*. 1576] 1962: 1). His description of his narrative—"the child's life, together with a young man's life, and entering into the old man's life"—underlines the generic character of his life story: temperament, horoscope, and age determine his character, as he considers the "ages of mankind, what humours have most dominion in every age" (so "the blood reigneth chiefly in the juventute [. . .] from the twenty-fifth until forty years of age," [*c*. 1576] 1962: 66). Understanding himself in time, he is subject to preordained and determinate changes shared with a horizontal group of those of his age.

Other narratives too suggest the influence of this model. John Dunton, writing at the beginning of the eighteenth century, suggests that his *Life and Errors* (as he calls it) will be "digested into Seven Stages," though in fact his narrative offers only four (birth to fifteen; seven years apprenticeship; from freedom to marriage; and the years of his marriage), and those are eccentrically juxtaposed with his "Idea of a New Life," which describes everything he would do differently if he were to live those years over again (1705: title page). The Jewish autobiographer Glückel of Hameln in the late seventeenth century divides her life into seven books, one for every decade of the scriptural lifespan (though the narrative is not divided into decades). Others begin with a similar structure and divert from it or reduce the number of stages. Guntzer outlines his life in three phases: "my bitter youth and apprentice years [. . .] my travels and wandering over water and land [. . .] my marriage and housekeeping, my happiness and unhappiness up to my final end" (Guntzer 2010: 27).

The limitations of the fixed chronological temporality implicit in the idea of the ages of man are apparent in the narrative structure, which generally gives variable attention to different life phases, rather than aiming for a balance. Youth, between about fifteen and thirty, is a particular focus for memory. The often vividly recollected conflicts and choices of these years—struggles over apprenticeships and education, marriage, work or religion, leaving home and traveling, encounters with faith and doubt—highlight their centrality as a moment when choices are made and pathways laid down for the future. Attention to subsequent decades is often comparatively cursory. Miller, for example, gives a chronological account of his early life which more or less stops at his marriage, followed by a three-sectioned house book recording family matters, public offices, and social connections. John Dane's brief account of his life takes him through childhood, youth, and migration to New England in ten pages or so, with a few paragraphs covering the remaining thirty years.

For women, the story of youth is often concerned with courtship and marriage, rather than apprenticeship and travel. Narratives by elite women in particular often feature versions of the marriage plot: romantic encounters, heightened emotions, difficult choices, parental reservations, and the eventual triumph of love. But marriage is seldom the end of the story. For some the love story is the background to a married life conditioned by war, politics, and childbearing. Spiritual autobiographies, meanwhile, may vary this plot by describing struggles to stay single or to become a nun, against the wishes of parents who are set on advantageous marriages, though both men and women frequently fail to mention when they marry or have children at all.

Memories of youth in spiritual accounts, indeed, often focus on sorrow and loss, or sin. "Dancing, Singing, telling idle stories" (Hayes 1723: 14), "vain company [. . .] wearing long Hair [. . .] spending my Money in vain" (Crook 1706: 9–10), reading romances, playing cards, and temptations to sexual misbehavior (generally heavily coded, and almost always invisible in the writings of women) belong to the phase of life before spiritual awakening. When writers regret their youth, it is more usually as a period of wasted or misspent time and foolish decisions than as a time of lost happiness. Few of these narratives dwell on a sense of loss, or display nostalgia for the past more generally. The upward trajectory of spiritual autobiography, leading from spiritual darkness into the light of divine grace, is at odds with a nostalgic perspective at least on a personal level, though the condition of the world may be lamented.

In contrast to the prominence of youth, it is unusual to find writers reflecting on their own ageing process, or defining their lives in relation to the other ages of man. Whythorne identifies the moment when he "began in my diet and government of the order of my body to do as the youngest sort of old men do" ([c. 1576] 1962: 117), but does not say what factors led him to do this. Norwood on his forty-ninth birthday reflected on the effects of age on memory: "some things began to grow out of memory, which I thought I should scarce ever have forgotten [. . .] considering that as age came on, forgetfulness would increase upon me," he decided to write them down ([1639] 1945: 3). Thomas Platter also identifies memory as a weakening faculty, recollecting how he used to tell stories of his wandering youth to his teacher, "which I could much better remember then than now" ([c. 1573] 1839: 47). But descriptions of bodily ageing are rare; the passage of time is marked, if at all, by inward rather than outward change. Time as the devouring enemy of youth and the body, so prominent a theme in the poetry of the age, is almost absent from autobiographical writing.

FAMILY MEMORY: TIME PAST AND FUTURE

Past and future are both invoked in the idea of lineage, which links ancestors and descendants through the hinge of the present moment. Many autobiographical accounts situate themselves in relation to family history, sometimes reaching back many centuries; Hutchinson, embedding her own life story in English Protestant history, traces her paternal descent to the Normans and her maternal to the Anglo-Saxons. The record of lineage was a basic component of gentry identity, often formally remembered in the written account in a more or less explicit claim to status, especially where it seemed to be in question. Hutchinson's insistence on her husband's ancient and honorable family counterbalances his death and the loss of his estate following the Restoration; Huguenot exiles wrote memoirs intended to establish lineage, replacing lost family documentation and "re-establishing social identity for the writer and the writer's family" (Hodgkin 2013; Chappell Lougee 2002: 96). Less elevated writers too locate themselves in genealogy. Thomas Platter, as if to offset the poverty and suffering of his early years, emphasizes the importance and "greatness" of both paternal and maternal families, and the Welsh prophet Arise Evans gives his genealogy in the Welsh memorial tradition, to ten generations: "*Arise* the Son of *Evan* the Son of *Arise* the Son of *Owen* the Son of *Arise* the Son of *Evan* the Son of *David* the Son of *Arise* the Sonne of *Griffith* the Son of the *Red Lion* the Son of the *Ren*" (Evans 1653: 1).

For others, however, the lineage narrative might be neither available nor desirable. The proclamation of a poor and simple birth was often a rhetorical means to establish God's providence in raising up the humble (Bunyan describes his family as "low and inconsiderable" and his father's rank "the meanest and most despised," [1666] 1998: 6), or to demonstrate the writer's initiative and energy in moving beyond this birth (Thomas Tryon was the son of "a Tiler and Plasterer, an honest sober Man of good Reputation," whose efforts brought him prosperity, 1705: 7). But in most spiritual autobiographies descent is stripped back to a minimum or omitted. The only significant information relates to the level of piety in the family; what counts is what is inherited from God. As Gotherson declares, "When I came first from my mother's womb, I was as all are in that state, an heir of heaven" (1661: 82); the fleshly womb is secondary to the divine. The soul exists in its own moment of time, without precursor.

Family memory also reaches toward the future; family and personal recollections are frequently directed toward children, as the bearers of their parents' memories and of their more distant lineage. "My dear children," writes Glückel of Hameln, "I write [. . .] lest today or tomorrow your children or grandchildren may not know about their family [. . .] that they should know from whom they are descended" (Glückel [c. 1690–1719] 1962: 37). Ann Fanshawe's narrative is directed to her one surviving son (and not to his two sisters), as the heir of his father's lineage, to acquaint him with "the most remarkable actions and accidents of your family" ([c. 1676] 1979: 102). And if lineage memories acquaint children with their useful allies and sponsors, spiritual autobiographers transmit memories of spiritual experience not only to their descendants but to the future community of the faithful. "Now my Children," writes Elizabeth Stirredge, at the end of her long narrative, "the End and Aim of my leaving this to you, and all upon Record, is, that future Ages may know [. . .] the great God of Heaven and Earth" (1711: 161). And her children, as believers, must repeat her own experiences: "keep faithful to the Lord, and his blessed Truth, that you have been trained up in, and your Eyes shall see for your selves, as mine eyes hath for my self" (1711: 165). This is an inheritance for the future in which blood links take second place. Bunyan, whose four children are mentioned in his narrative as objects of tender concern ("the parting with my wife and poor children, hath often been to me in this place, as the pulling of flesh from the bones," he writes of his imprisonment) nevertheless addresses his memoirs to his children in the spirit, who will carry forward his message; when those he had converted fell back, he writes, "their loss hath been more to me, than if one of my own children, begotten of my own body, had been going to its grave" ([1666] 1998: 89, 80).

Repetition, then, is part of an engagement with the future: children (spiritual and fleshly) reaffirm the memories of their parents and ancestors by repeating them. Family history ties children to the lineage, enjoining them to repeat the virtues of their ancestors, maintain traditions and honor the past. This sense of heritage and continuity, in both spiritual and secular contexts, provides an alternative temporal structure to the millennial time that hurtles toward the final apocalypse: a cyclical and repetitive time follows established patterns of experience and affirms the enduring truth of repeated variations on a theme.

Such cyclical and repetitive temporalities, it is worth noting, have often been linked with femininity, tied to the rhythms of the female body. But the "monumental time" identified by Julia Kristeva in relation to femininity has a wider purchase in the context of spiritual temporalities; Ricoeur's concept of cosmic time evokes something similar (Kristeva 1986; Ricoeur 2004). If women are often the guardians and transmitters of family memories, their relation to temporality is nonetheless complex and variable. In spiritual narrative, in so far as the body is represented at all, the gendered body of sexuality and childbearing is often replaced by the suffering body that imitates Christ: the story of the body is told through imprisonment, whippings, fasting, and sickness, rather than through gender-specific temporalities, as both women and men position themselves variously in relation to different conceptions of time.

REMEMBERING PLACES: MOBILITY AND SETTLEMENT

Geographical spaces, Doreen Massey suggests, should be conceptualized "as temporal as well as spatial"; place is intrinsically historical, an "envelope of space-time" (1995: 186, 188). Place in memory is similarly both temporal and spatial, and much recent work has focused on the ways that early modern collective memory is embedded in place; Alexandra Walsham describes post-Reformation Britain as a society "in which historical consciousness was intimately connected with topography [. . .] space rather than time often provided the most significant fillip to remembering" (2011: 7; see also Wood 2013a; Stock 2015). But if the deep historical memory of communities was held collectively in a fixed location, individuals, with the possibility of geographical mobility, had a different relation to the memory of place. Place in personal memory narrative is remembered and represented in complex ways. The meaning of place is inscribed temporally; the particular house, town, hill, river, may have been long left behind, but the memory of the place summons up the past. The symbolic resonances of places in the memory identify turning points and powerful emotions, lost homes and the liberation of travel. Spiritual and affective experiences are mapped onto the physical and spatial world, working differently for men and women, for spiritual and secular travelers, for those who choose to travel and those who are forced; the memory of place in personal narrative is legible in the dynamic of imagined relations between movement and stillness, home and abroad, security and danger.

Early modern attitudes to mobility were deeply ambivalent. The expectation that everyone should have a fixed place of origin and residence was embedded in frameworks for employment and poor relief as well as in cultural unease over vagrancy and displacement; gadding and wandering were potentially transgressive activities. But the principle that people should stay put was under pressure. Geographical as well as social mobility seemed to be continually on the rise. Young people left their homes as apprentices or servants; journeymen traveled to develop their skills; increasing numbers traveled for pleasure or curiosity. Explorations and colonial settlements brought young men into military and naval expeditions, and both men and women traveled willingly or unwillingly to the New World, as missionaries, settlers, traders, bonded servants. War and persecution displaced many: Catholics or Protestants fleeing hostile authorities, peasants and townspeople fleeing the line of danger, left their place of birth, often never to return. In this sense, early modern spatiality was perhaps experienced as increasingly unbounded, even if authorities continued to display a strong preference for emplacement. The link between place of origin and identity remained strong, but the place of origin for many was to become a place of memory rather than settlement.

Departure from home thus appears repeatedly in autobiographical narratives, as young men leave their families and go traveling. Their journeys may be haphazard, driven by poverty, chance encounters, or employment, or they may be directed and purposeful; often there are elements of both, at least with hindsight. But leaving is a memorable act, recorded with a sense of momentous detail. Edward Barlow, son of a poor laboring family in the north of England, illustrated his departure with a picture of himself as he leaves; his mother beckons to him at one edge of the picture as he heads out of the image on the other (Figure 2.3). The young John Dane, having been "basted" by his father for attending a dance, rises early in the morning, taking "two shirts on my back and the best suit I had," and a Bible, "and went to my father's chamber door and said, Goodbye father, Goodbye mother. Why, whither are you going? To seek my fortune, I answered" ([c. 1670] 1854:

FIGURE 2.3: Edward Barlow leaving his mother's house in the wheatfield. Journal of Edward Barlow, 1659–1703. National Maritime Museum, JOD/4. © National Maritime Museum, Greenwich, London.

150). This abrupt departure eventually becomes a determination to leave for New England, validated by the familiar technique of opening the bible to find guidance (here 2 Cor. 6: 17, "Come out from among them"). Providence governs place as well as time.

To travel is to enter into danger, leaving the predictable and known for a world of chance and risk; journeys are commonly remembered as encounters with hazard. Shipwrecks, robbers, hunger, illness, loneliness, are juxtaposed with friendship, sustenance, and the offer of help. Platter recalls the journeys of his early youth as a repetitive cycle of suffering, in which he was bullied, made to steal, and always hungry; the education he seeks is always somewhere else, and the kindness he occasionally encounters only highlights the general lack of care. Contentment comes only with settlement, and late in life his success is ratified by his enumeration of the properties he owns—a secure identification with place that affirms the distance in time and space from his unhappy wandering youth and recaptures the stability of his village childhood, with a family name derived from "a broad plat [. . .] on a very high mountain" nearby ([c. 1573] 1839: 1).

As the colonizing impetus of the period suggests, travel often aims at mastery, both as the journeyman's goal—to become a master of his craft—and as the effort to master strange worlds. The traveler must take possession of the spaces traversed, negotiating the dangers, and naming and disciplining new peoples and places. This urge takes different forms. Journeymen like Guntzer, who includes itineraries of his journeys over years and many countries, with lists of all the places he went to and the distances between them; settlers like Dane, recording his encounters with Indians and the places he lived in and farmed; or colonial administrators like Norwood, who ends his life as the surveyor of Bermuda, mapping a new world and identified with the colonial project, all assert some kind of ownership and knowledge of the unknown. Travels in strange places are remembered as hazards successfully overcome.

But loss as well as peril accompanied such displacements. In her late seventeenth-century captivity narrative (Figure 2.4), Mary Rowlandson describes herself carried away into the unknown depths of North America in a structure that does away with the

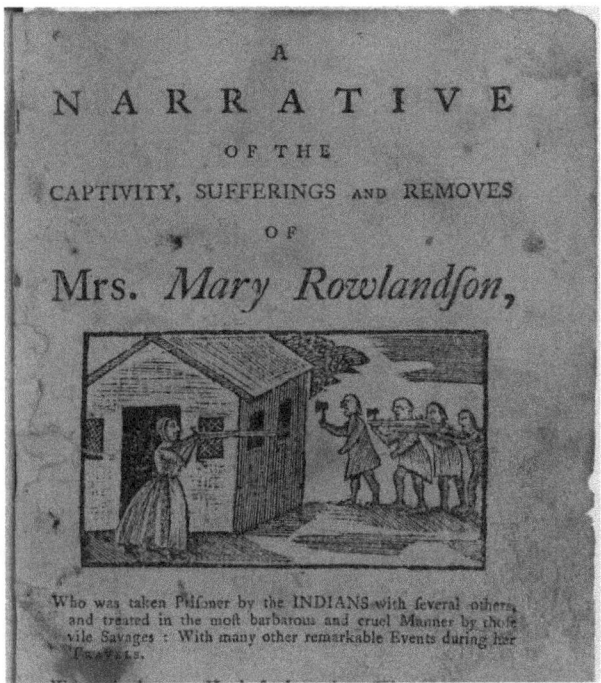

FIGURE 2.4: Mary Rowlandson's *Narrative*, cover image, Boston, 1773 (original publication 1682). Brown University, John Carter Brown Archive of Early American Images.

distinction between time and space altogether: her account is divided into a series of "Removes" as her captors journeyed on, each section a reluctant displacement which also measures the passage of time. Through the frame of involuntarily changing place, she remembers the events and emotions that accompanied each new location; and the nomadic life she is forced into by her captors also reinforces the colonizer's division between settled civility and unsettled savagery, named repeatedly as "wilderness". Constant removal dislocates the order of life, both temporally and spatially. Her six-year-old daughter, wounded during the raid, dies in the course of the third remove; Rowlandson records the exact date of death but cannot identify the burial place, writing, "I left that child in the wilderness, and must commit it, and myself also in this wilderness condition, to Him who is above all" (Rowlandson [1682]: 1977: 6; and see Chedgzoy 2007: 173–86). The lost wilderness grave stands in for her many other losses.

Ann Fanshawe (Figure 2.5), whose memoirs recall repeated displacement and separation as she and her husband travel with the exiled Stuart court, also leaves her dead children scattered across the space of travel. She enumerates with careful attention the burial places of the nine children who died during the years of exile: "the parish church of Tankersley in Yorkshire," "the chapel of the French Hospital at Madrid," "the parish of Fotts Cray in Kent," "in the Esperance in Lisbon in Portugal," and so on ([1676] 1979: 106–7; Hodgkin 2013). Fanshawe's wandering life has dispersed these remains, and again her careful recollection of the bodies of her children, with their repeated names (two Anns, three Elizabeths, two Henrys, three Richards), represents a recurrent scene of loss, of both homes and children.

FIGURE 2.5: Cornelis Janssen van Ceulen, *Portrait of Lady Ann Fanshawe* (1625–80). Valence House Museum, London.

Robert Burton in his *Anatomy of Melancholy* regards the pain attached to the loss of home with some disdain. "Banishment is no grievance at all [. . .] 'Tis a childish humour to hone after home," he declares ([1621–38] 1927: 201, II.iii.iv). But the experience of exile for the displaced is often one of yearning. The diasporic communities of early modern Europe also took with them remembered places, to be transmitted to the next generation. In reconstituting memory cultures for the new environment, they recollected places and property at the same time as remembering fears and violence. Huguenot memorialists, writes Chappell Lougee, felt themselves exiled from a local rather than a national place; they "might evoke Poitou or Rouen or Saintonge, but not France" (2002: 93). And even if home was not remembered as a specific place, displacement generated a wish for settlement, and a yearning for imagined homes (Wilcox 2006).

For many travelers even temporary departures bring a heightened awareness of nationality and difference, sharpening the memory of—and desire for—home. Barlow's youthful longing to travel, once he actually gets to sea, is transmuted into a bitter sense of the hardships suffered by seamen, and a longing to escape from bad food, bad masters and dangerous seas; England becomes "more dear than all the other lands I had ever been in in all my travels" ([*c.* 1703] 1934: 244). Love of country is associated with a sense of the danger of foreign parts, especially (for many English) the spiritual dangers of Catholicism. Richard Carpenter, a youthful convert to Catholicism, traveled around the Continent with increasing disillusionment; returning, "I came out of the noise, and tumults of other Countries, into England, as into a silent harbor, and haven of rest [. . .] I kneeled down, and kissed the very sands, and gravel on the shore" (1642: 173). Norwood is not only drawn to Catholicism during his European travels, but also suffers from "that nightly disease which we call the mare," along with "nocturnal pollution [. . .] horrible dreams and visions." In an increasingly allegorized journey, he is literally led astray: "every step I went, as it was further from my native country so it led me and alienated my heart farther from God, from reason, and from a desire to return." Eventually, "the Lord [. . .] set limits to my wanderings," bringing him away from "the places of confusion and destruction," and his return home frees him from both nightly afflictions and heretical temptations ([1639] 1945: 22, 28). In such retrospects, the remembered errors of youth are symbolized through foreign places and foreign religions, and the return to England is also a return to the true self and the true faith. Wandering as metaphor for spiritual confusion in Norwood's narrative becomes also its reality, and the return to England inaugurates his spiritual journey away from internal and external pollutions.

Danger to the soul is also implicit in the wanderings of Dionys Fitzherbert, whose departure from home followed a disagreement with her father about marriage plans. Moving from one aristocratic household to another, against the wishes of her family, she eventually suffers a collapse into a mental and spiritual crisis which she attributes in part to her "gadding humour," and the word's connotations of misbehaving and undisciplined femininity underline the gendered aspect of her error: a daughter who leaves home against her father's wishes wanders off into trouble ([*c*. 1608] 2010: 179). Fitzherbert's

FIGURE 2.6: John Bunyan dreaming. Frontispiece to *The Pilgrim's Progress*, book 2, 4th edition 1680.

journeys from one household to another enact her unsettled and restless condition, and her increasing departure from godliness; her eventual recovery is figured in the narrative both as a retracing of her steps (from London to Oxford, to her father's house, and from there to Wales, to her mother), and as a retracing of memory, involving meditation on "all this which I have written," with "many tears and sometimes trembling of my body" ([*c.* 1608] 2010: 221). Again, her journeys are both internal and external. The father's house is a resonant image in early modern writing, echoing the biblical house of many mansions as a place of homecoming; Donne's sermon on this text, quoted earlier, identifies the mansion with God's time, explaining that the word "signifies a Remaining, and denotes the perpetuity, the everlastingness of that state" (1967: 271). Fitzherbert's wish to return to her father's house evokes a location of dream and memory (like Bachelard's oneiric house) in which her life will be resolved.

PLACES OF MEMORY, SPIRITUAL JOURNEYS

In the preface to *Grace Abounding*, John Bunyan (Figure 2.6) urges his congregation to remember the word of God, and the moment they first heard it. He also urges them to remember the place it happened:

> Remember, I say, the word that first laid hold upon you: remember your terrors of conscience [...] remember also [...] how you sighed under every hedge for mercy. Have you never a hill Mizar to remember? Have you forgot the close, the milk-house, the stable, the barn, and the like, where God did visit your souls?
>
> —Bunyan [1666] 1998: 5

As Bunyan's own memory narrative returns to the doorstep in Bedford where he saw a group of women sitting in the sun and speaking "as if joy did make them speak" ([1666] 1998: 14), so he summons up for his listeners a concrete world of common places, imbuing the mundane environment of milk-houses and barns with spiritual resonance and memorial significance, and reminding his congregation that God is in all these places and does not need churches or rich houses to speak to his children: the image of a barn, resonating in the soul, will reignite fervor. Agnes Beaumont, locked out of the house by her father after going to hear Bunyan preach, recalls a night of unforgettable spiritual illumination in the barn where she took shelter: "it was a blessed night to me; a Night to be remembered with comfort to my life's end." But "the heart ravishing visits" are not the only things she will remember. "It froze vehemently that night," she writes, "but I felt no Cold; the dirt was frozen on shoes in the morning. My heart was wonderfully drawn out in prayer" ([*c.* 1675] 1998: 200). Beaumont's memory holds in place the barn, Satan's assaults, God's protection, and the frost sharp enough to freeze the mud on her shoes.

Few writers summon up their own hill of Mizar with such vividly concrete detail; in the inwardly directed spirituality of the seventeenth century the significant journey is internal, and outer places of memory exist primarily as prompts. But the recollection of place to depict moments of spiritual awakening is widespread. For Arise Evans, the "hill Mizar" is a more literal hill: his place of memory is the mountainous landscape of Wales, where God first spoke to him. Thus he remembers "a high place called *Bwlch Ryw Credire*" where "the dark Clouds about me by the wind were driven swiftly," and the power of prayer lifts him over the pass; "a place called Gole Ronnw," where he saw "the Sun at its rising Skip, Play, Dance, and turn about like a wheel." Evans summons up a landscape drenched with visionary meaning, already present in the Welsh place-names, to be opened to him subsequently in dream. His translations of place-names ("*Bwlch ryw credire* in *English is,* Believe ascend the gap") display the entire landscape as a symbolic commentary on the struggles of seventeenth-century England (1653: 5–6). The Welsh mountains, collapsing time and space into a single system of mystical meaning, have been waiting for both the events and the prophet who will disclose them.

For Catholic mystics too the place of awakening is often imbued with symbolic resonance. Claudine Moine, embarking on an extended period of spiritual austerity while alone in Paris, similarly collapses spiritual and physical location to identify her room as the place of divine service:

> It is time, my God, that I enter that bedroom which your divine and loving Providence prepared for me. When they brought me the key, you, O my sweet Jesus, put into my head the idea that I should go off in front of the most Holy Sacrament and present it to you [. . .] I should enter that room as your poor, little servant [. . .]
> —Moine [c. 1645] 1989: 60

The physical world here is indistinguishable from its spiritual place-mate. The chamber is both the place where she pays rent and sleeps, and the home of her spirit, in which material needs are irrelevant; her master God will find the money to pay the rent.

Place is an anchor for memory, then, in complex ways. The symbolic value assigned to place may or may not correspond to a place in the real world, and real-world places are also inscribed with spiritual significance, constructing the landscape as simultaneously material and mystical. This doubling effect also shapes the meaning of the landscape traversed by spiritual travelers, imprinting it with a changing devotional and memorial significance. The post-Reformation world remapped sacred space; late medieval Catholicism's landscape of pilgrimage, shrines, wayside crosses, churches, and monasteries came under pressure in what has been described as "a rearrangement of space according to a new conception of the sacred" (Coster and Spicer 2005: 6). But it was a contested rearrangement in which laws against vagrancy and sedition were mobilized against radical preachers, policing the boundaries of acceptable spirituality as well as acceptable travel.

Radical preachers interpret their journeys and their conflicts with the authorities in relation to spiritual histories and geographies. George Fox's travels around England trace a map of sacred paths which is both new—marked by the places in which he preaches and finds Friends—and ancient, as he inscribes the landscape of the apostles onto the towns and hills of England. In Mansfield, he writes, "the Lord's power was so great that the house was shaken," and people said "it was now as in the days of the apostles, when the house was shaken where they were" ([c. 1675] 1997: 22–3). He walks in his stockings through channels of blood, crying "Woe to the bloody city of Lichfield," realizing afterwards that he was called to "raise the blood" of "Christian Britons" martyred there by Diocletian ([c. 1675] 1997: 72). And the founding places of Quaker gathering—Pendle Hill, Nottingham, Derby—were imbued with spiritual resonance, as new places of memory for the new religion.

The common metaphor of spiritual awakening as journey intensifies the meanings of the actual journeys undertaken. "I speak my Experience of the Dealings of the Lord with me, in my Travels and passings through my Spiritual Journey, for the benefit of those that Travel rightly after," writes the Quaker Barbara Blaugdone; and her spiritual is also her physical journey, as it alternates between the open road and the enclosed prison (1691: 8). Her relation to the social and physical places she inhabited in the past has been transformed. Former friends she tries to visit have her driven away: "when I would go to their Houses to reprove them," she writes, ". . . their Servants would come [. . .] and hale me out and shut the Doors" (1691: 28). The meaning of place in her narrative is shaped by exclusions and transformations; safety is found not in places of settlement, but in the power of God that accompanies her. A similar dynamic shapes the journey of many preachers, perhaps particularly Quakers, who practiced a traveling ministry and for whom imprisonment under vagrancy laws was a repeated threat (Hinds 2011: 100ff.). Fox's narrative juxtaposes the open spaces of field and orchard, barn and haystack—places of communion and communication—with the deathly confinement symbolized by steeple-houses and prisons.

Women preachers and missionaries such as Blaugdone claimed with varying success an exception to the general rule that good women stay at home (Flather 2007). Anna Trapnel records an exchange with a hostile Cornish magistrate who interrogates her over her reasons for traveling alone to a place where she had no family or connections—"having no hindrance, why may I not go where I please, if the Lord so will?" she asks, asserting her independence both as unmarried and as in the Lord's service (Trapnel 1654: 26). And the Lord's will took some women great distances. Katherine Evans and Sarah Cheevers, Quaker missionaries attempting to reach Turkey, spent two years imprisoned in Malta, and in their account again the enclosed space of the prison defines both the open but perilous world traversed, and the inner spaciousness of divine grace that allows them an internal escape from imprisonment, to be remembered with joy (Evans and Cheevers 1663). When the French missionary nun Marie de l'Incarnation set off for Canada, after a lengthy struggle for permission, she recalled, "When I put my foot on the boat, it seemed to me I was entering Paradise"—the boat, Paradise, and Canada remembered as merging into one place, reached with a single step (quoted Davis 1995: 83). In women's narratives, the pleasures of travel seem accessible more readily through spiritual rather than secular journeys.

TIME, PLACE, AND MEMORY

Time and space are experienced and understood differently in these accounts. The structure of life and the relation between past and present are unfamiliar; likewise, the ways that place is shaped and occupied, reinvented and traversed. The expected details of time and place that for us orient and anchor memory are often bypassed in favor of other priorities, both spiritual and secular. The memories recalled and recorded in early modern autobiographical narratives are radically other, and the work memory is doing seems to be different.

At the same time, the mere possibility of reading these accounts as memory texts, of reflecting on and engaging with their different senses of the past, raises the question of how fundamental the differences are. Debates about formations of cultural memory which are seen as distinctively modern have been questioned by historians in recent years (Pollmann 2013; Sherlock 2010). In relation to the specific question of autobiography the issue is sharpened by parallel arguments about the history of the self and subjectivity: how far is it justifiable to read these documents as if they were modern memory texts, founded on linear and secular time and space, and autonomous subjects? One answer to this would be that modern subjects are not necessarily as autonomous, nor as firmly rooted in a linear chronology and secular landscape, as they might suppose, and neither are their self-narratives. The boundaries of subjectivity, like other boundaries, are not fully secure in any epoch; and to say that memory operates differently, as time and space are different, does not mean that memory is not at work in these narratives.

The relation of time, space, and history once again suggests the resonance of nostalgia, a concept which despite its early modern origins is often tied to modernity, among historians as well as cultural theorists. Rudolf Dekker and Ariane Baggerman, among others, have persuasively argued that nostalgic sentiments about the past, especially childhood, do not emerge until the early nineteenth century, when they register a significant change in the ways that people understood the processes of historical change and their own place in relation to those changes (Baggerman, Dekker, and Mascuch 2011). However, Kristine Johanson has recently questioned this, suggesting that nostalgia may exist in different forms at different historical moments, and that the ways in which a culture conceives of time may generate other forms of nostalgia: "the longing for an idealised, unobtainable past may possess different cultural or rhetorical weight if that past is imagined or understood as able to return, an idea encouraged by cyclical and momentary notions of time" (Johanson 2016: 7). The same might be said of the desire for lost place. A lost real place, rather than a lost illusory time, is at the heart of the concept as originally formulated by Johannes Hofer in 1688; and in devising the term he is building on existing words and ideas (*Heimweh*, banishment) (Starobinski 1966). Nostalgia, suggestively described by Atia and Davies as correlating "place, time and desire" (2010: 184), might thus take other forms and other names in early modern Europe, but still retain recognizable elements of a shared emotional structure.

Time, space, and affect are also brought together in the model of remembering symbolized by the memory palace. One of the principles of the memory arts was that the objects chosen to evoke specific memories should themselves be memorable, and one way of ensuring this was to choose symbols that were resonant, that evoked emotion: "merry, cruel, injurious, marvellous, excellently fair, or exceedingly foul things, do change and move the sense and better stir up the Memory," according to Guglielmo Gratarolo (Engel, Loughnane, and Williams 2016: 64). Place memories in autobiographical narratives often seem to work similarly, summoning up a memory of emotional significance alongside a lost moment, something irretrievable in time. The displacement of *ars memoriae* by other discourses of memory (such as nostalgia) might thus be understood as a reconfiguration of elements, rather than a radical transformation.

If we place ourselves differently in time and space, then, we might also consider the elements that go to shape that placing; and if we remember differently, and think about memory differently, we do also use it in some similar ways. Memory is what enables the writer to hold together the idea of the self in time. But memory also needs anchorage. In these narratives of fracture, loss and change, to remember and record in writing a place and a time may secure the continuity of self in a world of change.

CHAPTER THREE

Media and Technology: Notes, Memory and Recollection

RICHARD YEO

There has long been agreement in Western culture that memory is an indispensable faculty. Writing in the first century of the common era (CE), Pliny the Elder called it "the boon most necessary for life" (Pliny 1938–63: vol. 2, 563; Small 1995: 159). Stories about the memory feats of certain individuals are perennial. In the early modern period, the English preacher, Thomas Fuller, was renowned for his ability to recite, backwards and forwards, the names of the shop signs between Ludgate and Charing Cross in London, thus emulating the famous performances of the ancient Greeks and Romans, such as Simonides and Seneca the Elder (Aubrey 2016: vol. 1, 555; Yates 1966: 17–18, 31). Yet the very celebration of these people underscores the more usual weaknesses of memory, both in terms of loss of content over time and slowness in retrieval of what is stored. Clearly, memory needs help.

In his *Micrographia* (1665), the natural philosopher and inventor, Robert Hooke, identified the task of "rectifying the operations of the *Sense*, the *Memory*, and *Reason*." He imagined extensions to natural capacities that anticipated cyborg forms: "The next care to be taken, in respect of the Senses, is a supplying of their infirmities with *Instruments*, and, as it were, the adding of *artificial Organs* to the *natural*" (Hooke 1665: "Preface," sig. a1r; a2r; emphasis in original). In the case of the senses—vision, hearing, touch, smell, and taste—some progress had already been made: spectacles, telescopes, and microscopes enhanced vision, ear trumpets improved hearing. It was not impossible to imagine augmentations of the other three senses. However, Hooke recognized that memory posed special challenges: its role was to retain and supply information from *all* the senses. Although he contemplated the action of chemicals on the brain, his preferred response was the design of an external framework of support. As he put it:

> The next remedies in this universal cure of the Mind are to be applied to the *Memory*, and they are to consist of such Directions as may inform us, what things are best to be *stor'd up* for our purpose, and which is the best way of so *disposing* them, that they may not only be *kept in safety*, but ready and convenient, to be at any time *produc'd* for use, as occasion shall require.
>
> —Hooke 1665: "The preface," sig.b1v

In this passage these "remedies" are not specified, but in his "General Scheme" (*c.* 1668), Hooke announced that they included diagrams, filing systems, and methods of note-taking and indexing (Hooke 1705: 1–70). I will focus on note-taking, especially as it was promoted by Renaissance humanists and adopted as a scholarly practice throughout Europe. I also consider how this practice was applied to empirical scientific inquiry by English *virtuosi* (Yeo 2014). But first we need to return to the weaknesses of memory, and then to consider some distinctions between different kinds of remembering.

FORGETTING

The prevailing view in the early modern period was that the process of forgetting could not be controlled: important and trivial ideas, experiences, and information were all candidates for oblivion. Forgetting was endemic because the faculty of memory was an inner corporeal sense (Harvey 1975). Two major writers on the limits and capacities of human understanding, Thomas Hobbes and John Locke, made the consequences clear. In his *Elements of Law* (1640), Hobbes said that memory "may be accounted a sixth sense, but internal, not external as the rest," and he regarded forgetting as the natural, gradual decay of a conception originating in sensory perception. This, he said, often happens "by little and little," with memories growing more obscure as the original impressions in the brain fade away (Hobbes [1640] 1969: 11; see Figure 3.1). Yet loss could also be sudden. Soon after he arrived at Trinity College, Cambridge in 1661 the young Isaac Newton began a notebook which, by 1664, hosted his thoughts and questions on natural philosophy, including speculations about the workings of the mind. In an entry under the heading "Of Memory" he recorded some accounts about dramatic memory loss after physical trauma:

> Messala Corvinus forgot his own name. One, by a blow with a stone, forgot all his learning. Another, by a fall from a horse, forgot his mother's name & kinsfolk. A young student of Montpelier, by a wound, lost his memory, so that he was fain to be taught the letters of the alphabet again.[1]

As both a physician and a philosopher, Locke was well aware of the dependence of memory on bodily health. It was probable, he thought, that "the Constitution of the Body does sometimes influence the Memory; since we oftentimes find a Disease quite strip the Mind of all its *Ideas*" (Locke [1690] 1975: II.x.5).

It was commonly believed that the likely physical causes of impaired memory could be partially counteracted by physical means. In his *A Helpe to Memory and Discourse* (1630), the poet, William Basse, listed "things hurtfull for the Memory to be avoyded," such as noisome vapors, unripe fruits, strong drinks, and "all cold in the hindermost part of the Head." On the positive side, things that strengthened memory included nourishing meats such as the brain of partridge, the ingestion of herbs such as rosemary, and other practical measures that assisted sleep and general good health (Basse 1630: 10–12). All these examples seem mild when compared with one remedy recorded in Hooke's diary on September 11, 1677:

> Mr. Melancholy told me that a freind of his had been recoverd of a bad memory and severall other distempers by carrying a small box full of very fine filings of the best refined silver and now and then licking of it with his finger and swallowing it.
>
> —Hooke 1968: 311–12

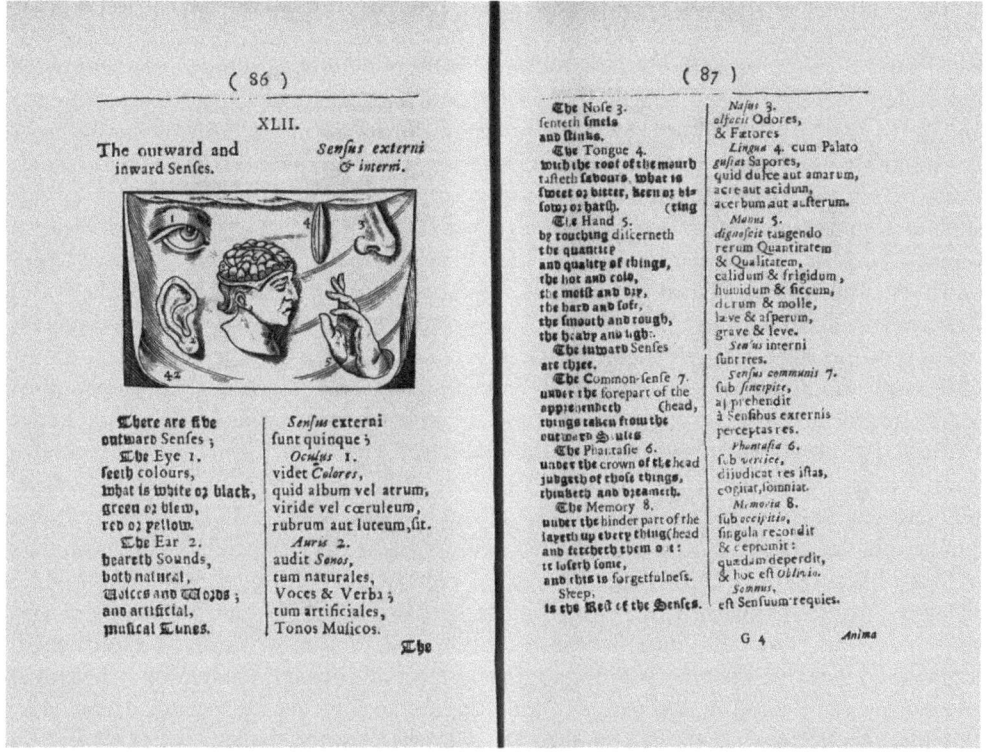

FIGURE 3.1: "The outward and inward senses," with Memory located toward the back of the brain. Johann Amos Comenius, *Orbis Sensualium Pictus*, London: Printed by T.R. and N.T. Mearne, 1672, plate at pp. 86–7. Kindly supplied with permission by Rare Books and Special Collections, The University of Sydney Library.

Even without bodily disease, however, decay of memories over time was to be expected because the brain could not retain the material impressions of all the sensations it received from the senses. Locke admitted that the memory of some individuals was "tenacious, even to a Miracle: But yet there seems to be a constant decay of all our *Ideas*, even of those which are struck the deepest, and in Minds the most retentive." Without special precautions our ideas fade rapidly, "leaving no more footsteps or remaining Characters of themselves, than Shadows do flying over Fields of Corn; and the Mind is as void of them, as if they never had been there" (Locke [1690] 1975: II.x.5 and II.x.4). He mentioned two such means by which Memory, the "Store-house" of our *Ideas*," might be "renewed": by "repeated Exercise of the Senses, or Reflection on those kind of Objects, which at first occasioned them" (Locke [1690] 1975: II.x.2 and II.x.4). In specifying these two ways of helping memory, Locke indicated two different kinds of performance: rote memory and recollection. The first was often referred to as memory "without book," a form of automatic recall; the second, recollection, was the recovery of forgotten memories by a process of reflection or meditation; it was thought to be improved by external aids, such as diagrams, note-taking, other forms of writing, and the arrangement of material.

ROTE MEMORY

Expectations about memorizing, either with or without initial consultation of a text, were embedded in religious and educational practices. There was widespread respect for the ability to perform "without book"—to recite information or knowledge without consultation of a text or a notebook that summarized it. It was demonstrated by individuals in the pulpit, the lecture hall and the law courts, and by groups of individuals in situations such as the classroom and church congregation (Halbwachs [1952] 1992; Tribble and Keene 2011). In 1612, the schoolmaster, John Brinsley, declared that students must "have daily some special exercise of the memory, by repeating somewhat without booke; [. . .] The reason is, because the daily practice hereof, is the only means to make excellent memoryes" ([1612] 1968: 51). Here was a version of Locke's "repeated Exercise." At university, undergraduates were required to argue the "pros" and "cons" of propositions set in formal disputations. A study manual, composed by the Cambridge don, James Duport, and circulated from the 1660s, advised that "When you dispute be sure you have your arguments by heart," so as to perform convincingly "without book."[2] Richard Holdsworth, Master of Emmanuel College, Cambridge between 1637 and 1643, wrote a similar manual that influenced generations of tutors. He stressed the need to get grammars by heart because the acquisition of a language necessitated "this getting without book." He urged students to write down Greek words "as you doubt you cannot remember," and cautioned that "Gramers must not be forgotten." Significantly, however, Holdsworth maintained that rote memory was not appropriate for all subjects, contending "that [this] plodding way of conning doth tire and lode the memory rather then beget a readiness" (Holdsworth 1956–61: vol. 2, 639–41). Later in the century, the call for exactness, in both textual study and the new sciences, reduced the prestige of rote memory. In *Some Thoughts Concerning Education* (1693), Locke castigated the notion of "exercising and improving the Memory by toilsom Repetitions without Book" (Locke [1693] 1989: 233, section 176); and elsewhere imputed a lack of care and precision to those who relied on memory in matters of detail. Thus in replying in 1697 to Edward Stillingfleet, the Bishop of Worcester, he said, with some menace, that "To show the reader that I do not talk without book in the case, I shall set down your lordship's own words" (Locke [1697] 1823: 212; also Yeo 2014: 55–6).

These caveats about the function of rote memory point to another contemporary ideal—a learned memory that was capacious, but more flexible. Hobbes claimed that over-reliance on rote memory delivered parrot-like talk, comparing it with that of "beggars, when they say their *paternoster*, . . . having no images or conceptions in their minds answering to the words they speak" (Hobbes [1640] 1969: 23). His criticism resonated with the adage that quick memory and acute reason rarely coexisted. In 1575 this opinion had been influentially embedded in a psychological and medical framework by the Spanish physician, Juan Huarte, in a work translated into English as *The Examination of Men's Wits* (1594). Drawing on Hippocrates and Galen of Pergamon, Huarte asserted that good understanding required a certain dryness of the brain, whereas good memory needed moisture, which allowed impressions to be made more easily. "By this doctrine," he inferred, "the understanding and memorie, are powers opposite and contrary, in short, that the man who hath a great memorie, shall find a defect in his understanding" (Huarte [1575] 1594: 60–3). In 1673, Obadiah Walker, Master of University College, Oxford (from 1676 to 1688) reported this as a prevailing view: "They that excel in it [memory] are accounted many times *greater Clerks* than *wise men*" (Walker 1673: 126).

RECOLLECTION

This sharp contrast between memory and reason (or understanding) was complicated by Aristotle's distinction between *memoria* (memory) and *reminiscentia* (recollection). He argued that memory was a corporeal faculty displayed by some animals, whereas recollection involved a deliberate search for something stored in memory and was therefore akin to reasoning. Recollection was a rational activity involving a process of searching, reviewing, and comparing ideas stored in memory; as such, it was "a sort of reasoning" (Aristotle 1972: 52–60). In line with this view, Walker cautioned that many remarks about individuals who displayed amazing memory required qualification. He mentioned the Spanish philosopher, Francisco Suarez (1548–1617), who knew Augustine's works "by heart," but added that this was "not *memory*, but *reminiscence*; for it was indeed as much *judgment* as memory" (Walker 1673: 128). This distinction between memory and recollection was often obscured (as it is today) by the tendency to use memory, or remembering, as general terms. In his *Leviathan* (1651), Hobbes wrote that recollection is a "Calling to mind: the Latines call it *Reminiscentia*, as it were a *Reconning* of our former actions" (Hobbes [1651] 2012: vol. 2, 42).[3] Elsewhere he said that *reminiscentia* is the attempt to "recover something lost, proceeding from the present backward," and that it involved the "Sagacity" displayed in "hunting or tracing" (Hobbes [1640] 1969: 14). The trick was knowing how to restrict the space to be searched, as when "one would sweep a room, to find a jewell; or as a Spaniel ranges the field, till he find a scent" (Hobbes [1651] 2012: vol. 2, 42). In his *De augmentis* (1623), Francis Bacon, who for a time employed Hobbes as his secretary, warned against casting about "hither and thither as if in infinite space," likening the preferred effect to "the hunting of a deer within an enclosure" (Bacon 1963: vol. 4, 436; and vol. 5, 648 for the original Latin).[4] As these metaphors suggest, recollection involved deliberate searching, something that contrasted with what Hobbes and Locke understood to be the default mental state, namely, that of "wandering" (Hobbes [1651] 2012: vol. 2, 38–42. Compare Locke [1690] 1975: II.xix.1 on "Recollection" as involving "pain and endeavour").

The ancient Greek art of memory, referred to by Roman authors as *ars memoriae*, used internalized cues to trigger recollection of names, texts, and arguments. Its proponents claimed that it enhanced the natural ability to recollect. Cicero referred to the Greek mnemonic technique as *artificiosa memoria* (artificial memory), a term found in the earliest extant exposition, an anonymous Latin text (*c.* 88 BCE) titled *Ad Herennium* (that is, addressed to Gaius Herennius). The author referred to earlier Greek practices involving two principal components—backgrounds or places (*loci*) and images (*imagines*). Hence the method came to be known as "local" or "place" memory. The practitioner of this art imagined a structure of some kind, such as a palace with several rooms, and took care to furnish it with clearly marked places, such as "an intercolumnar space, a recess, an arch, or the like" (*Ad Herennium* 1954: 209; for examples, see the images in Yates 1966: between 224 and 225). These places were memorized as an ordered series, thus forming a familiar, permanent mental background. In the next stage, specially chosen vivid images (*imagines agentes*) were deposited in these places as reminders of the things, quotations, or arguments. When one walked mentally through this imagined space, the images in each of the places gave up their associated content—but only if approached in the sequence originally set down; one could move forwards and backwards, provided that this was done without skipping any places (Yates 1966: 22; Small 1995: 159–60). Crucially, the choice of images was an individual affair: as the text explained, an image "that is well-defined to us appears relatively inconspicuous to others. Everybody, therefore, should in equipping himself with images suit his own convenience" (*Ad Herennium* 1954: 223). If strictly followed, this art would support both *memoria verborum* (memory of words) and *memoria rerum* (memory of things).[5]

During the early modern period, the classical art of memory continued to be discussed, and sometimes promoted (Beecher and Williams 2009). By this time, it was well recognized that the technique presupposed a reliable natural memory. Thus when the Italian Jesuit, Matteo Ricci (1552–1610), explained this Western art to the Chinese elite, the son of the governor of Macao offered a comment: "though the precepts are the true rules of memory, one has to have a remarkably fine memory to make any use of them" (Spence 1984: 4). Indeed, the art of memory involved the double task of remembering the stable background and a personal set of mental associations between images and content. The payoff was that this background could be internalized as mental scaffolding that stimulated recollection (see Carruthers 1990 for the medieval period). However, critics contended that there was a danger that the task of choosing and retaining idiosyncratic visual images (as the cues) would debilitate natural memory. In *De incertitudine et vanitate scientiarum et artium* (1531), the German physician, Heinrich Cornelius Agrippa von Nettesheim (1486–1535), made this point: "It [artificial memory] cannot stande without natural Memorie, whiche oftentimes is dulled with monstrouse Images [. . .]" (Agrippa [1531] 1569: 24–5). In what might seem to be the last word, the Oxford don, Robert Burton, recommended the art of memory as a cure for melancholy—on the grounds that, like the practice of "Brachygraphy" [shorthand], it "will aske a great deale of attention" (Burton [1621] 1989: vol. 2, 92).[6]

Nevertheless, an emphasis on ordered storage of information and ideas as the key to retrieval from memory was widely accepted in the seventeenth century—as it had been in the middle ages and the Renaissance—and no plausible aid could be ignored. In his word portraits of famous contemporaries, now known as "Brief Lives," the antiquarian and naturalist, John Aubrey, often commented on his subjects' memory. In a few cases he surmised that they practiced artificial techniques. In alluding to Bacon's house in which the glass windows of a gallery were painted with images of beasts, birds, and flowers, he remarked that "perhaps his Lordship might use them as Topiques for locall memor[ie]" (Aubrey 2016: vol. 1, 217). And of John Birkenhead (1617–79) he reported that he "had the Art of locall memory, and his Topiques were, the Chambers etc in All Soules Colledge. about 100. so that for 100 errands etc: he would easily remember."[7] The allusion to a decidedly unscholarly application—to help remember shopping lists—might reveal skepticism in Aubrey's assessment. Indeed, he was keen to notice that many individuals with powerful memories did not rely on such a specific technique. The scholar and lawyer, John Selden, "never used any artificiall help to strengthen his memorie: 'twas purely naturall." Aubrey believed that methodical ordering of thoughts was just as helpful, suggesting that the poet, John Milton, "had a very good memory: but I beleeve that his excellent Method of thinking, and disposing did much helpe his memorie" (Aubrey 2016: vol. 1, 405; and 664).[8]

MEMORY AND NOTES

Aubrey's reference to thinking and "disposing" nicely captures the early modern concept of note-taking as an aid to recollection. This was a legacy from Renaissance humanist ideas on methods of reading and study. In his *De ratione studii* (1512), the Dutch scholar,

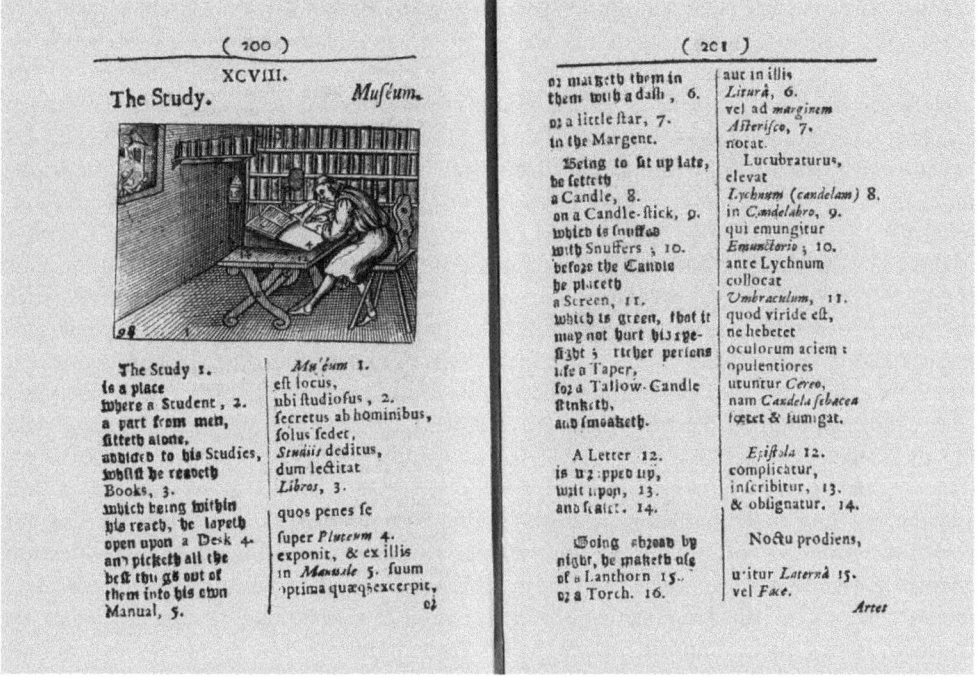

FIGURE 3.2: "The Study": a note-taker, possibly using a commonplace book, and apparently undisturbed by a fire outside the window! Johann Amos Comenius, *Orbis Sensualium Pictus*, London: Printed by T.R. and N.T. Mearne, 1672, plate at pp. 200–1. Kindly supplied with permission by Rare Books and Special Collections, The University of Sydney Library.

Desiderius Erasmus of Rotterdam, urged that every student "have at the ready some commonplace book of systems and topics, so that wherever something noteworthy occurs he may write it down in the appropriate column" (Erasmus [1512] 1978: 672). Erasmus described the method of establishing *loci communes* (common places) under which cognate material was collected in designated pages of a notebook. By the late sixteenth century this practice of commonplacing became established in grammar schools, universities, and private scholarship (Bolgar 1963; Moss 1996; Havens 2001; Décultot 2003; see Figure 3.2). Works on moral and political philosophy by Roman authors such as Ovid, Virgil, Horace, Cicero, and Seneca the Younger were among the favorite texts. Accordingly, topics such as honor, friendship, truth, constancy, happiness, together with the virtues and vices of Christian doctrine, or concepts from natural philosophy such as matter and motion, became the "Heads" (headings) expected in the commonplace book of any educated person. The maker of such a notebook selected textual passages and entered them under appropriate Heads, thereby signifying a common place (*locus communis*). This process of selection and allocation was said to strengthen both memory of the quotations and understanding of their relationships with similar themes. It encouraged the ability to retain and recollect *copia* (abundant material) for the purposes of conversation, oratory, and literary composition.

Significantly, however, note-taking had to be defended against the charge that it weakened memory. In his *De augmentis* (1623), Bacon acknowledged that "transferring things we read and learn into commonplace-place books" was denounced by some as inviting "the memory to take holiday" (Bacon 1963: vol. 4, 435). Promoters of scholarly notebooks responded by clarifying the kind of intellectual processes at work in commonplacing and other kinds of note-taking encompassed by the concept of *ars excerpendi* (the art, or skill, of excerpting). Two influential Jesuit authors, Francesco Sacchini (1570–1625) and Jeremias Drexel (1581–1638) published, respectively, *De ratione libros cum profectu legendi libellus* (a little book on how to read books with profit) in 1614, and *Aurifodina artium et scientiarum omnium* (the goldmine of all arts and sciences) in 1638 (Sacchini [1614] 1615; Drexel 1638; on these works, see Cevolini 2006; Blair 2010: 77–80, 84–6). Later, the German scholar and jurist, Vincent Placcius (1642–99), reviewed and extended these and other manuals on note-taking in his *De arte excerpendi* of 1689. Those who affirmed the power of notes did not deny that rote memorization fostered the ability to perform "without book." Rather, they argued that it failed to evince the full possibilities of recollection. Methodical note-taking involved choice and judgment at the time when extracts were selected and assigned to appropriate Heads (Sacchini [1614] 1615: 75–6, 81). Consequently, when one returned to an excerpt, this original mental effort stimulated recollection via a pathway of categories and associations that delivered more than the actual content of the note. The aim was not verbatim recall of a specific passage, but scholarly improvisation on a topic. Recollection enabled recombination of ideas, thus aiding thinking as well as memory. In contrast, rote memorizing or, in the language of the day, conning, parroting, learning by heart, or "without book" elicited nothing more than fixed content.

The time and labor involved in careful note-taking created a potential disincentive. Indeed, Holdsworth conceded that for lazy students, the proper keeping of large commonplace books was a bridge too far, due to the effort "to rise evry foot to a great Folio book, & toss it and turn it for evry little pasage that is to be writt downe" (Holdsworth 1956–61: vol. 2, 651). He suggested that the full range of notebooks (called "paperbooks"), including waste books, diaries and journals be used as temporary receptacles. However, even those with good intentions sometimes reported failure. The diarist and antiquary, Sir Simonds D'Ewes, first baronet (1602–50), confessed in 1620 that:

> I spent a great part of this month (July, 1620) amongst other private studies in framing several scholastic heads, as physics, ethics, politics, economics, and the like, and inserting them into two great commonplace books I had newly caused to be bound up in folio; but this cost and labour, by my sudden departure from the University, was in a manner lost, those paper books remaining still by me with little or nothing inserted into them.
>
> —quoted in Costello 1958: 32

Yet for those who persisted in the habit of making (and reviewing) notes, the benefits were believed to be considerable. Holdsworth promised that from "frequent reading them [notes] over on evenings [. . .] they will offer themselves to your memory on any occasion" (1956–61: vol. 2, 651). The French philosopher and mathematician, Pierre Gassendi, believed that such practices supported the "happy memory" and copious conversation of the great antiquarian and collector, Nicolas Fabri de Peiresc:

> Now he wrote things down in his Memorials, because he then judged they were out of danger of being forgotten, seeing he could not trust his memory as Socrates or Pythagoras were wont to do; and had found by experience, that the very labour of writing did fix things more deeply in his mind.
>
> —Gassendi [1641] 1657: 188, 191

Careful note-taking was thus understood both to preserve material that required memorization, and also to prompt recollection of more than the note itself. Notebooks aided memory; they did not render it superfluous (Yeo 2008).

Systematic arrangement of a commonplace book was recommended as the best support for memory and recollection. Such organization became especially necessary when Renaissance authors began to see these notebooks as a means of summarizing *all* knowledge. In her pioneering work on this genre, Joan Marie Lechner observed that a "desire for copiousness of material became almost an obsession" (Lechner 1962: 168). This wider compass of material entailed thoughtful ordering. In *De locis communibus ratio* (1531), the Protestant theologian, Philip Melanchthon (1497–1560), issued a warning: "Do not think commonplaces are to be invented casually or arbitrarily: they are derived from the deep structures of nature, they are the sets and patterns to which all things correspond" (quoted in Moss 1996: 121). An insistence on topical organization, albeit less severe than this one, became entrenched in subsequent advice on note-taking. Indeed, before any entries were made, Heads were usually *pre-assigned* to pages of the notebook—on the assumption that reading and study would inevitably generate appropriate excerpts. By the mid-1600s, alphabetical rather than thematic arrangement was more usual, but in some subjects there remained an expectation that a pre-selected group of Heads would be sufficient. We can see this outlook on a grand scale in the commonplace book of Robert Southwell, English diplomat and fellow of the Royal Society of London (he served as President from 1690 to 1695). In this notebook, used in the 1660s (and possibly started earlier), he pre-allocated Heads across 572 pages.[9] These Heads (usually one per page) registered topics and themes in moral and political philosophy. Southwell's reading included ancient, humanist, and contemporary authors from Ovid, Tacitus, Pliny, and Seneca to Erasmus, Machiavelli, and Bacon. His excerpts and comments are entered under Heads from "Abstinentia" (abstinence) to "Uxor" (wife)! Ironically, the page headed "Meditatio" is blank (along with many others), even though meditation and reflection were regarded as crucial partners of "Memoria," the Head on the facing page (see Figure 3.3).

The note-taking of the young Isaac Newton also reveals the choices that needed to be made about organization. The front flyleaf of his quarto-sized paperbook (mentioned above), one of his early Trinity College notebooks, bears his name and is dated 1661. Newton used this notebook to make reading notes on the Aristotelian texts of the Cambridge curriculum. About three years later, he turned the notebook upside down and began a very different set of notes, starting from the back. He titled this section "Questiones quædam Philosophicæ ("Certain Philosophical Questions") and numbered its pages 1–95.[10] The first page, begun no earlier than March 1664, opens with a motto: "Amicus Plato amicus Aristoteles magis amica veritas" (Plato and Aristotle are my friends, but the greatest friend is truth). Yet the entries show Newton reading the moderns—such as René Descartes, Henry More, Walter Charleton, and Robert Boyle—and using his notes on them as the basis for thinking for himself and, in many cases, proposing experimental tests of his ideas (Westfall 1993: 25–30). Although his notes were unusual in being a series of queries rather than strictly excerpts, Newton started out with a traditional format, pre-allocating topics to pages like Southwell did at about the same time. Initially, he chose thirty-seven Heads relating to some standard concepts in natural philosophy.[11] But unlike Southwell, he decided on a systematic (not alphabetical) order, beginning with fundamental matter, then its qualities as exhibited in celestial, terrestrial, and human bodies. The opening topic is "Of ye first mater" [matter], followed by topics including density,

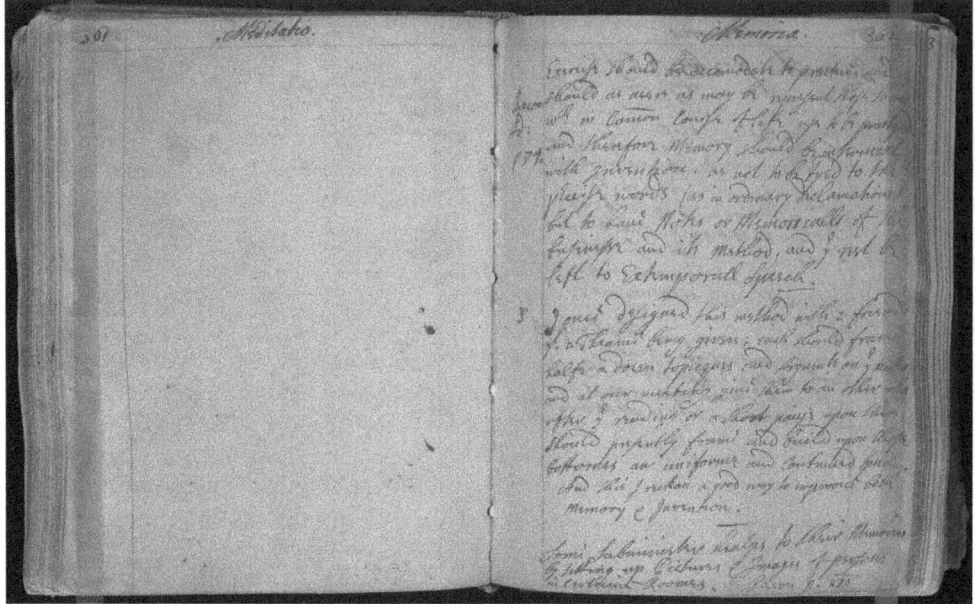

FIGURE 3.3: Robert Southwell's commonplace book, 1660s. MS Osborn b112, 361–2. Kindly supplied with permission by the James Marshall and Marie-Louise Osborn Collection, Beinecke Rare Book and Manuscript Library, Yale University.

condensation, fluidity, heat, and cold; the traditional elements of fire, air, water, and earth; the nature of light; and finally a sequence on the sensations available to the human brain and the faculties of vision, hearing, touch, taste, and smell; and memory. After setting out the original topics he needed to add others, so that eventually there were seventy-one (the final entries were made in late 1665). Newton's experience showed the risk of pre-assigning Heads to pages when one's reading and thinking extended beyond a canonical set of texts. At some stage he must have found it difficult to locate previous entries, because he inserted an index on two unused leaves before the start of the "Questiones"; this listed all entries alphabetically, giving their page numbers (see Figure 3.4).

Deviations from traditional methods were being discussed before Southwell and Newton began their commonplace books. Sacchini, Drexel, Holdsworth, and Placcius allowed some flexibility, especially for mature scholars. In 1638, Drexel advised that individuals make notes as they were reading, perhaps using a waste book and journal, and only later transferring material to entries under Heads in a separate commonplace book (Blair 2010: 79–80). Similar departures from earlier precepts were evident throughout the seventeenth century, but they were not always endorsed. We can sense this reservation in the remarks of Roger North, the lawyer and musical scholar, about the note-taking of his elder brother, John North, Master of Trinity College, Cambridge from 1677 to 1683. Presenting John's habits as atypical, Roger explained that "He noted as he went along, but not in the common way by commonplace, but every book severally, setting down whatever he found worthily to be observed in that book" (North 1984: 107). In other words, John North simply jotted down points of interest (as we tend to do today) without bothering to place them under a common Head and, *a fortiori*, without any reference to a larger set of key topics.

The most radical scenario was one in which notes were treated as autonomous bits of information unrelated to a specific topic. In *Of Education* (1673), Obadiah Walker moved in this direction when discussing commonplace books. He made this seemingly paradoxical suggestion: "The best way I know of ordering them, is; To *write down confusedly* what in reading you think observable"; then to write a number in the margin next to each note, and later to transfer these numbers (and the relevant page numbers) from "these Note-books" to an "Index" listing Heads to which they belong. Walker did not abandon the idea of placing material under Heads: indeed, he continued to assume that the index could be pre-stocked with these, "yet not too much multiplied, least they cause confusion" (Walker 1673: 130–1). However, his mention of numbers assigned to entries opened the possibility that these alone, not topics or categories, could be effective markers. This implication is present in the collaborative note-taking advocated by the Oxford graduate, Thomas Harrison (1595–1649), in his *Arca Studiorum* (Ark of Studies), described in a manuscript of 1640 later printed in Placcius' *De arte excerpendi* (1689). Harrison invented a cabinet that stored loose slips of paper on hooks pinned to rods labelled with thin metal plates arranged in alphabetical order (for images of this, see Malcolm 2004: 211–4; Blair 2010: 95; Yeo 2014: 115, 117–8). In the examples he gave, the labels on these plates were quite conventional Heads, such as Amor, Deus, Fides, Virtus; but he also mentioned the option of numbers as a way of identifying single slips (Placcius 1689: 124–59; Cevolini 2016b: 28).[12] Jan Comenius, the Czech pansophist and educational reformer, admired this invention and believed that with this giant index it would "be possible readily to ascertain the opinions of divers authors on any specific point of interest" (cited in Young 1932: 66).[13] Yet Comenius continued to link the data entered on slips to authors, whereas Harrison seemed to think (albeit opaquely) of his basic units as non-repeated propositions detached from books, and available for recombination (Malcolm 2004: 208–9; Yeo 2014: 113–23).

Despite the acknowledged need for collaborative note-taking—within the Royal Society, for example—personal notebooks remained the starting point. Those who favored flexibility of note-taking practice advised that individuals choose their own methods. Nevertheless, there were two main alternatives: setting out a notebook with pre-allocated Heads, or making notes in chronological order, with entries later assigned to a Head, or not at all. The advantage of the former (and older) method was that everything was entered in a commonplace book which, if set out with Heads in alphabetical order, did not require an index. The new approach involved at least two notebooks: a waste book or journal for notes taken on the run, and a commonplace book to which some of them were transferred. This practice coped better with novel and unexpected information that did not fit under the usual categories: a note could be made immediately, perhaps assigned to a temporary Head, or simply left for later attention.

BACONIAN NOTE-TAKERS

Bacon's natural histories demanded massive collections of empirical data that required detailed description and analysis. He published such histories of the winds and of life and death, and planned others on qualities and processes including dense and rare, heavy and light, sympathy and antipathy (Bacon 1963: vol. 2, 11). He admitted that this effort would produce a multitude of "particulars" beyond the capacity of memory (Yeo 2007: 3, 7–12; Yeo 2014: 53–5, 83–7). As he explained in the *Novum organum* (1620):

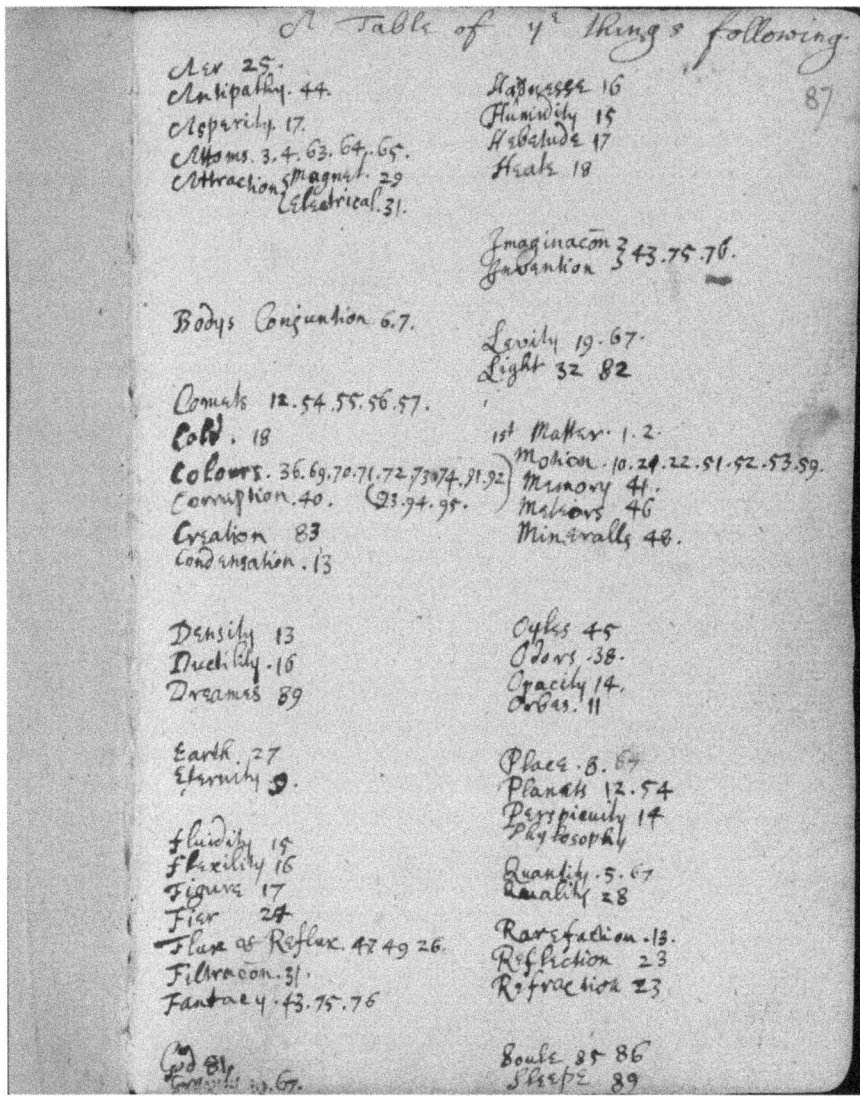

FIGURE 3.4: "A Table of ye things following," in Isaac Newton's notebook, CUL Add MS 3996, fols 87^{r-v}. Reproduced by kind permission of the Syndics of Cambridge University Library.

But even after the abundance and matter of natural history and experience that we need for the work of the intellect or philosophy is all present and correct, the intellect is still quite incapable of working on that matter unprompted and by memory: you might just as well expect to be able to calculate and get through an ephemeris by force of memory. (Bacon [1620] 2004: Book I, aphorism no. 101, 159; also Bacon 1963: Book I, aphorism 101, vol. 4, 96; and vol. 4, 435 for a similar remark in *De augmentis*)

In this connection, Bacon regarded notes as encompassed by what he called "writing in discontinuous sections"—notes were "tags" that jogged the memory (Bacon [1620] 2004:

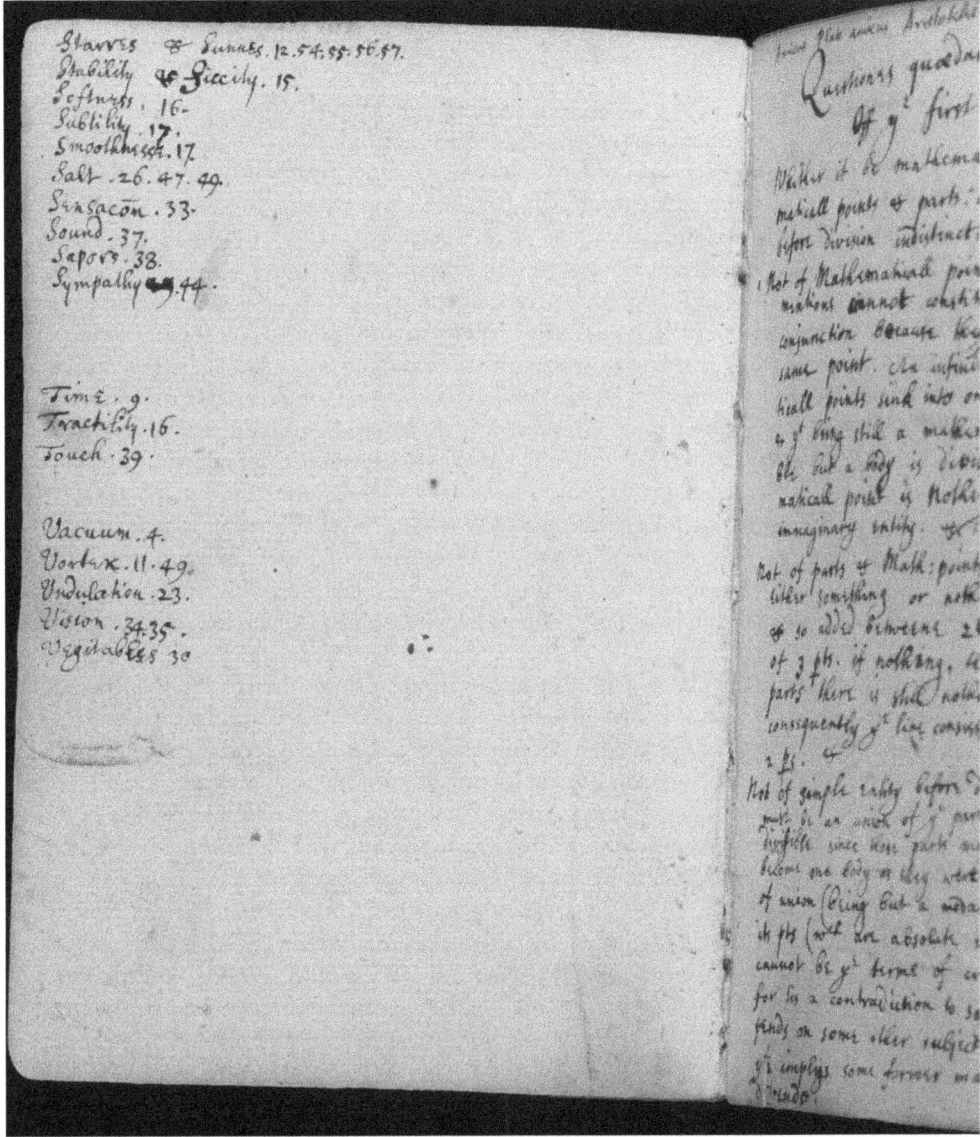

FIGURE 3.4 (continued)

Book II, aphorism 26, 287). We know that he kept paperbooks of various kinds because one of his extant notebooks (most have not survived) contains an audit of these that he conducted in July 1608.[14] As part of this audit, Bacon sought to reduce his material, transferring a redacted version into a smaller number of notebooks. Moreover, in the case of commonplace books, he reflected on whether to reduce the number of Heads (or "Titles," as he called them), making these "fewer and lesse curious and more sorted to use than to Art." He believed this process would render the notes more suitable for the "better help of memory and judgment" (Bacon 1963: vol. 11, 61–2; Vine 2011). This preoccupation with condensing and abbreviating personal notes is also apparent in

Bacon's ideas about the collective management of information. In *New Atlantis* (1627) he imagined a utopian scientific academy, Salomon's House, which orchestrated the collection and gradual refinement of data, potentially leading to knowledge of fundamental laws of nature. In both individual and institutional quests for knowledge, Bacon stressed the need for aids to memory and understanding. In the *Novum organum*, he declared that the "army of particulars is so vast and so scattered" that it "confounds the intellect." This plethora of data had to be brought into order, such as that afforded by "appropriate tables of discovery, well drawn up and ready, so to speak, for action"; only then might the intellect begin to distil patterns (Bacon [1620] 2004: Book I, aphorism 102, 159–61).

Bacon's admirers in the Royal Society welcomed his call for methodical gathering and recording of information. John Evelyn, Robert Boyle, and John Locke, for example, were interested in compiling natural histories as a basis for inductive generalizations in chemistry, botany, physiology, medicine, and meteorology. However, they contended that Bacon's insistence on tables and other ways of refining data could lead to premature abstraction, and even loss of the original notes that captured preliminary information. Although these men were dedicated note-takers, by the 1660s they had moved away from traditional commonplace books, making a shift from pre-selected topics to notes (called *adversaria*) taken in the course of reading, observing, and experimenting (Yeo 2014). They did not doubt the power of personal notes to trigger recollection and to assist thinking; but for this to happen, notes had to be found easily. When excerpts were made from well-known texts, such as those recommended by humanists or set for reading in universities, the standard Heads served as guides to the location of particular entries. This was not so when material was collected from a wider range of sources and from observation and experiment as well as reading, the combination encouraged by the new sciences. In this case, individual entries needed to be identified by a memorable tag, or by a set of letters or numbers. An index containing these labels thus became the key to one or more notebooks. Evelyn was the only one of these three figures who began with more or less traditional commonplace books. In about 1649, he instructed his amanuensis, Richard Hoare, to pre-format three folio-sized notebooks (approximately 22 cms × 48 cms) with subject Heads for theology (including ethics), the mathematical and physical sciences, liberal arts, and politics (one of these notebooks, BL Add. MS 78330, is titled "Loci Communes Theologici"). However, about a decade later in a letter to his brother he implied that he had adopted the habit of entering notes as they occurred to him, as summed up in the title of one notebook used from the 1680s: "Adversaria Historical, Physical, Mathematical . . . promiscuously set downe as they Occur in Reading, or Casual Discourse" (Evelyn to George Evelyn, October 15, 1658, BL Add. MS 78298, fol. 88^{r-v}; and BL Add. MS 78333, fol. 1^r). Evelyn marked such notes with marginal Heads and collated these in indexes.

As a young aristocrat, Robert Boyle was privately tutored; he was not indoctrinated at university in the early and regular use of commonplace books (Hunter 2009: 45–56). Of course, he knew about them, but he preferred what he called "loose notes," referring to "a Chaos of Promiscuous Notes confusedly thrown together."[15] But this depiction gives a false impression: Boyle usually wrote Heads or numbers in the margins next to entries, thus allowing these to be indexed. His extant papers include forty sets of folio sheets stitched together and folded to make small, pocket-sized booklets; these are now known as his "workdiaries," although Boyle called them "Memorials," or simply "loose notes." They contain chronological sequences of short entries, often numbered in "centuries," that is, from 1–100, emulating Bacon's *Sylva sylvarum* (1627) with its ten centuries, or

1,000 observations and experiments. Boyle described this method as being "by way partly of a *Diary,* and partly of *Adversaria,* register'd and set down one Century after another" (Boyle 1999–2000: vol. 11, 169). This combination of diary-like entries and Heads matched the definition of *adversaria,* a contemporary term for commonplace book, though crucially, one no longer set out with pre-selected Heads.[16] Yet Boyle's preference for making notes first and assigning Heads later, or not at all, did not affect his conviction that notes and Heads stimulated recollection. Thus in a manuscript draft, he explained that he had lost the original version "but yet, since I retaine some memory of the chief heads it consisted of, I shall here present you with a summary of them."[17] Indeed, it appears that Boyle's confidence in his memory, and also recollection prompted by notes, is one reason why he neglected the proper indexing and cataloguing of his papers (see Yeo 2010; Yeo 2014: ch. 6). His friend and sometime collaborator, John Locke, tried to ensure that his own notes could always be found.

In an anonymous article published in the *Bibliothèque universelle* of July 1686, Locke shared his "New Method" for making commonplace books or, more strictly, *adversaria* ([Locke] 1686). The novel component was his way of *indexing* notes, one that radically disaggregated topics that would be grouped together in a traditional commonplace book. Entries were indexed as they were made, rather than when the notebook was full or had been used for some time (as in Newton's case). A two-page index (see Figure 3.5), placed at the beginning or end of the notebook, governed both entering and retrieval of material. This index consisted of 100 ruled cells, each containing a two-letter combination.

This is how Locke described his method.[18] In an unused paperbook, he went to the first double opening and made his note (whether an excerpt, an observation, or a thought) on the left-hand page. He wrote the Title of his note (like Bacon, he did not use the term Head) in the generous left-hand margin ruled on each page. Locke mainly used Latin for these Titles. The next step was to register this Title in the Index. Locke's novel approach was to reduce the first word of his Title to just two letters—the first letter and the next vowel. He then recorded the page number of the note in the cell that contained this code (which Locke called a "class").[19] In the sample index which Locke provided, the page number for his note on *Adversariorum Methodus* (way of making *adversaria*) was written in the *Ae* cell of the Index, and the page number for his note on *Confessio fidei* (confession of faith) was written in the *Co* cell. In his notebook, all entries sharing the same class were made on the same double opening, even though their subject matter, inevitably, could be quite disparate—for example, *adversaria, aer,* and *abscessus* all belong to the *Ae* class and could be found on the same double opening. When making a new note, Locke found the appropriate page number of the notebook from the Index and wrote under the previous note until the page was full. He then continued the note on the next available double opening. If the very next page was available, he would write "v" (for *verte,* that is, turn over) at the bottom of the page; or he would add the relevant page number if the next available page was further on. As Locke explained: "By these figures at the bottom of one of these pages & the top of the other referring to one another reciprocally things that are sometimes written at 100 pages distance are as easily continued as if they were the very next page, all that is between them being turned over as it were one single leafe" (BL Add. MS 28728, fol. 59ᵛ).

What were the consequences of Locke's "New Method"? First, because pages were not reserved for topics, this method avoided the prospect of unused pages when topics did not attract entries and, conversely, the problem of overflowing notes when certain topics produced full pages. Second, this procedure came at a cost: it made entries harder to find

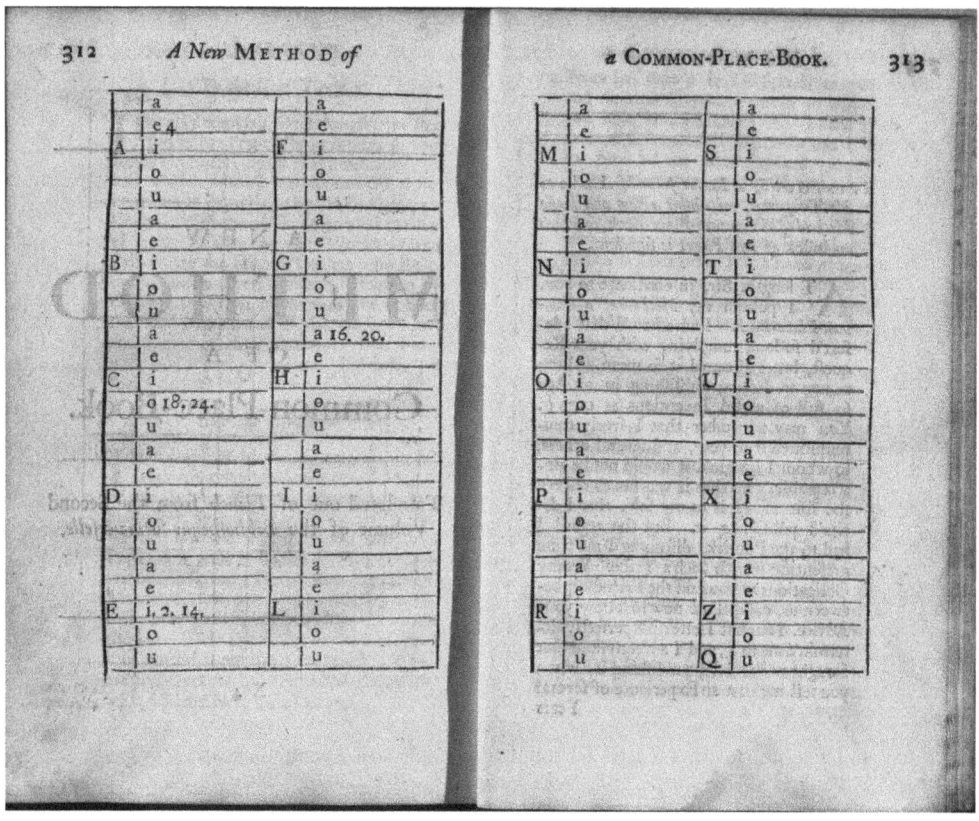

FIGURE 3.5: The Index in Locke's "New Method" of 1686 as presented in John Locke, "A New Method of a Common-Place-Book," in *Posthumous Works*, London, 1706, 312–3. Kindly supplied with permission by Rare Books and Special Collections, The University of Sydney Library.

than those in either a thematically arranged commonplace book, or one like Southwell's that used a strict alphabetical order of pre-allocated Heads. By treating the first letter/next vowel of Title words as the determining factor, Locke allowed disparate topics (for example, *Veterinaria* and *Vertigo*, or *Respiratio* and *Reumatismus*) to appear on the same page and cognate ones to be scattered throughout a notebook. The special type of index was therefore essential. As seen above, such an index worked well to find entries of a particular class, even though in a much-used notebook several pages might need to be checked. We can say that Locke was more interested in locating material than in any thematic arrangement of it; however, he did use different notebooks for moral and philosophical subjects as opposed to medical and physical sciences, and this made it easier to start a search. The third point is that the "New Method" was a very personal information system; it required the owner of the notebook to remember the Title assigned to an entry. The two-page index displayed only letter/vowel classes, not the full word of the Head or Title as would be the case in a more conventional index (see Figure 3.4 for Newton's); it was thus imperative to choose a memorable word. As Locke said, "When any thing occurs that I thinke convenient to write in my Adversaria I first consider under what title I thinke I shall be apt to looke for it" (BL Add. MS 28728, fol. 58ʳ).

There is a discernible shift in the practice of these English note-takers from thematic or systematic arrangement of notebooks to an emphasis on making and finding notes easily. This is in keeping with the advice and practice of continental European scholars. However, abandonment of some earlier precepts did not weaken the conviction that notes stimulated recollection. The people I have discussed relied on their notes as external triggers—by way of intellectual links or associations—of material built up in personal memory over a lifetime. They realized that this process worked fully only for the person who made the note. Bacon emphasized this in a letter of *c.* 1589 in response to a question about the delegation of note-taking for a large project:

> Therefore to speake plainelie of the gathering of heades or Common places; I thinke firste that one mans generall notes will litle profitt another, because one mans conceipt doth so much differ from anothers, and also because the bare note it self is nothing so much worth as the suggestions it geves the reader.
>
> —Bacon 2012: 211

Obviously, this had implications for the function of notes in collaborative inquiry. Steps were needed to ensure that notes acted as stable records able to be shared and analyzed by groups. Hence the insistence on order—a legacy of the commonplace method—continued to have application, although in collaborative projects it provided strategies for observation and recording rather than aiding personal memory. Boyle's assistant, Robert Hooke, considered this issue when thinking about how the Royal Society should manage the data it collected (Yeo 2007: 23–30; Yeo 2014: 238–51). After acknowledging the frailties of memory, he concluded that there had to be an external storehouse of material which could be analyzed and re-arranged. He described a method of keeping a "large Book" into which slips of "very fine Paper" could be inserted; this would help the process of sifting and resorting, which could not be accomplished so well by natural memory (Hooke 1705: 64). These paperbooks would assist

> the Memory by writing and entering all things, ranged in the best and most Natural Order; so as not only to make them material and sensible, but impossible to be lost, forgot, or omitted, [and thereby] the Ratiocination is helped first, by being left alone and undisturbed to it self, having all the Intention of the Mind bent wholly to its Work, without being any other ways at the same time imployed in the Drudgery and Slavery of the Memory.
>
> —Hooke 1705: 34

Hooke did not imply that individual memory ceased to play a role in science; his point was that external records could remove an unnecessary load on the mind and also facilitate communication of ideas. Personal mastery of empirical data and ideas, developed over a lifetime, continued to depend on memory and recollection, the latter being supported by institutional protocols, diagrams, tables, indexes, and catalogues (see Yeo 2016 for comparisons with the recent concept of "external memory"). For example, he suggested "A Scheme" arranged in columns displaying weather observations, including wind direction, temperature, humidity, and barometric pressure (see Figure 3.6). The beauty of this, as Hooke said, was that observations and measurements of "a whole Moneth, may at one view be presented to the Ey," thus offering a "Scheme" that could be used by many people in different places, encouraging comparative observations likely to generate "*Axioms*, whereby the Cause or Laws of Weather may be found out" (Hooke 1667: 175).

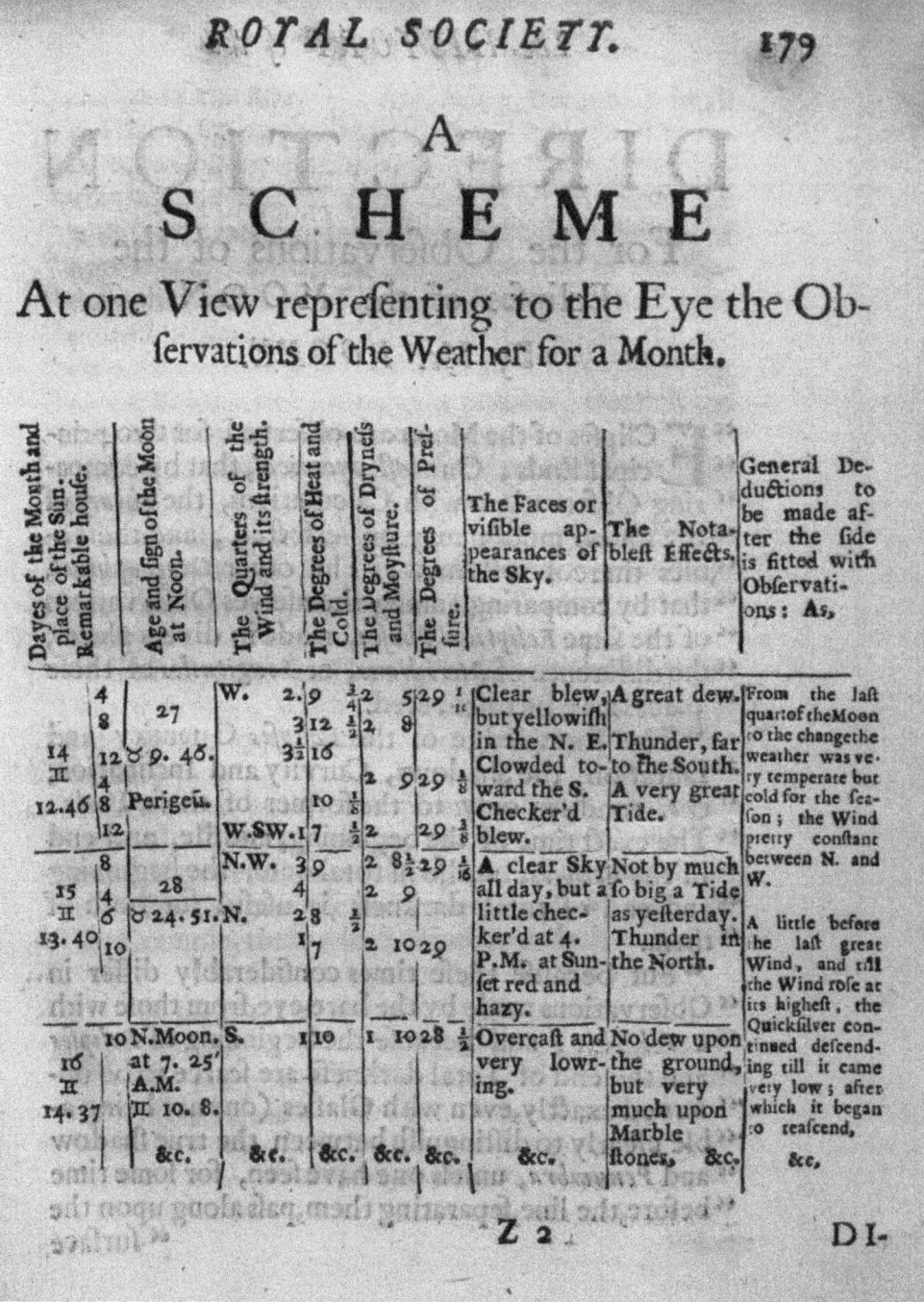

FIGURE 3.6: Hooke's "Scheme" displaying weather observations and measurements, as presented in Thomas Sprat's *History of the Royal Society of London, for the Improving of Natural Knowledge*, London: The Royal Society, 1667, plate at p. 179. Kindly supplied with permission by Rare Books and Special Collections, The University of Sydney Library.

CONCLUSION

In the early modern period, memory was regarded as a crucial faculty, but one that needed support of various kinds. At a physical level, its nature as an inner corporeal sense meant that impairments due to disease or accident could sometimes be ameliorated by medicine and diet. At a cognitive level, different kinds of remembering called for different aids: automatic recall from memory might be facilitated by repetition, perhaps especially in group situations such as the classroom and church. Recollection could be triggered by internalized cues, such as the images recommended by the ancient art of memory, but more usually by written notes in various kinds of notebook. There was a shift away from the practice of pre-allocating Heads to pages of a notebook to a more flexible one in which notes were made in chronological sequence and later labeled with Heads chosen by the individual. This method required indexing so that notes could be found. In addition, we can conclude with three points. First, there was recognition that memory functioned in different ways for various purposes. Rote memory was useful, and necessary, for some tasks such as learning arithmetic, grammar, new languages, and factual information. However, there was a growing belief that reliance on memory, on performance "without book," could no longer be paraded as an achievement. In the case of empirical inquiry, this conviction was reinforced by the plenitude of particulars demanded by Baconian natural histories; consequently, the institutional archives imagined by Hooke secured information that could never be memorized. Second, the concept of recollection as an intellectual process implied that notes both relieved memory and prompted it. Well-taken personal notes stimulated memory of more than the note itself. In this way, individuals were able to assimilate and recover both general and specialist knowledge; but this process could not work in the same way for notes and records made in collaborative data gathering. The latter kind of inquiry required protocols for the collection of information, and well-organized and retrievable records able to be consulted by many people, including those of future generations. Third, the emergence of better external repositories did not entail an unqualified eclipse of memory. Rather, the use of various "technologies," which included intellectual strategies as well as material supports, indicated a more complex scenario in which note-taking was a component in the interaction of mind, memory, recollection, and the external world.

ACKNOWLEDGMENTS

Thanks to the editors for their invitation to contribute, and for their helpful comments; and to Mary Louise Yeo for reading early drafts.

CHAPTER FOUR

Knowledge: Science and Education

WILLIAM E. ENGEL

RECKONING WITH NEW KNOWLEDGE

An unprecedented reformation of science and education took place during the early modern age coincident with an explosion of knowledge in all areas of inquiry. Ongoing discoveries in the heavens, around the globe, within the human body, and in smaller worlds still were made available to a wide range of new readers by virtue of advances in print technology and the mechanical reproduction of images. The present study seeks to highlight and examine critically some representative moments associated with these seismic shifts in the history of Western thought by paying special attention to the place of memory in this time of rapid epistemological change. A recurring motif will be that the old and the new overlapped in telling ways, each impinging upon and to some extent and in varying degrees interpenetrating the other.

For example, Robert Recorde's *Castle of Knowledge* (1556), an astronomical treatise written as a dialogue between a master and his student, although concerning and grounded in traditional Ptolemaic cosmology also contains a sympathetic reference to Copernicus and the heliocentric theory. The student dutifully recites from rote memory principles of the old learning, vehemently rejecting that "the earth should move out of his place" (1556: O5^r).[1] He is rebuked by his teacher—Recorde's subtle wink to the reader:

> You are too young to be a good judge in so great a matter, it passeth far your learning and theirs also that are much better learned than you, to improve his suppositions by good arguments; and therefore you were best to condemn no thing that you do not well understand. But, another time, as I said, I will so declare his supposition that you shall not only wonder to hear it, but also peradventure be as earnest then to credit it as you are now to condemn it.
>
> —Recorde 1556: O5^r

Shakespeare likewise sports at times with this idea of the new learning casting all in doubt. Hamlet's love letter addressed to Ophelia includes the following verse: "Doubt thou the stars are fire, / Doubt that the sun doth move, / Doubt truth to be a liar, / But never doubt I love."[2] This poem succinctly reflects early modern anxieties about the predicaments posed by advances in science, the accuracy or inaccuracy of memory, and the quest for certain knowledge.[3] The same can be said of Hamlet's chiding Horatio for so readily deferring to easily remembered scholastic methods when confronted with a new problem: "There are more things in heaven and earth, Horatio, / than are dreamt of in our philosophy" (1.5.168–9). The term philosophy in the Renaissance, it should be noted, implied simply human learning, especially as regards the theme or activity of education (Gish 2013: 198).

The old ways and the new also overlap with respect to how Hamlet signs his letter to Ophelia: "Thine evermore, most dear lady, whilst this / machine is to him, / Hamlet" (2.2.123–5). By the mid-sixteenth century, the human body was thought of as a mechanism; the word machine referred to a "complicated structure composed of many parts" (Jenkins 1982: 234). The word machine, furthermore, took on an additional resonance at this time with respect to the book. Specifically, Peter Ramus (1515–72), a French logician and Protestant reformer, conceptualized the book as a "memory machine" (Ong 1991: 134). Although manuscripts preserved and conveyed in uniquely crafted artifacts the words and deeds of the ancients (along with a backlog of accreted authorial commentaries), the printed book both represented—and itself was—a new kind of visual and mnemonic aid resulting from a confluence of new technologies in the West (Eisenstein 2012: 54–7). Printing, with the capacity to reproduce hundreds of more or less exact copies of a text, revolutionized Western memory, but it did so slowly (Le Goff 1992: 81). André Leroi-Gourhan describes this revolution in memory as follows: "With the advent of printing [. . .] not only was the reader faced with an enormous collective memory whose subject matter he could no longer assimilate *in toto*, but he was frequently put in a position to exploit new works. We then witness a progressive exteriorization of individual memory; the work of orientation in a written text is accomplished from the outside" (quoted in Le Goff 1992: 81).

In ways that exceeded even the voyages of discovery during this period of accelerated global exploration, printed accounts of which making possible a new kind of "collective memory" (Neuber 2009: 71), the mechanism of book production brought forth a new world, "a paperworld" (Rhodes and Sawday 2000: 1–6). The book "rendered the older education obsolete" and "was literally a teaching machine where the manuscript was a crude teaching tool only" (McLuhan 1969: 176). Essentially the book, as a new kind of machine, relied on old learning and looked forward to new domains for collective memory resulting in a daunting influx of information (Blair 2010). And so while humanist educators were eager to publish translations of newly rediscovered works of classical learning, they also recognized something unsettling about accumulating and putting into circulation these often outmoded preserves of ancient knowledge, "skeptical about a system while still functioning wholly within it" (Eggert 2015: 30).

The Italian physician Guglielmo Gratarolo (1516–68) is a good case in point. His innovative works on medicine and natural philosophy were widely read and translated, as were his backward-looking treatises on alchemy, plague epidemics, and health regimens. Renaissance medicine, after all, was tied into astrology (see Figure 4.1), and charts of the human body were drawn to create a memorial landscape that revealed "which parts were under the influence of which stars and planets" (Whitfield 2015: 14). Among the innovations of Gratarolo's wide-ranging *De memoria reparanda* (*Memory Restored*) (1553) was the easy commerce between modern cures for head ailments and classical place-system mnemonics. He differentiates natural memory and its medicinal aids from mnemotechnics, saying "we will briefly entreat of Artificial Memory" ([1553] 1562: B4ᵛ).[4] Alongside ancient learning (especially Aristotle), he discusses the latest medical advances (Vesalius). He describes memory as the means by which the mind repeats things that are past; it is

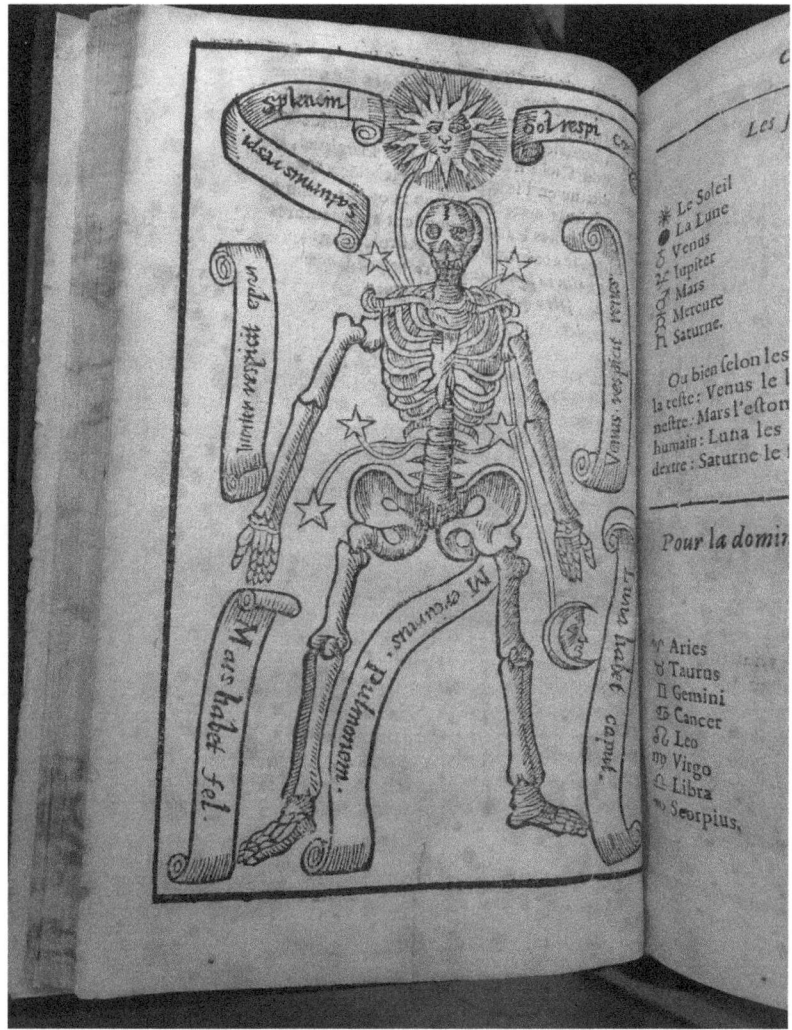

FIGURE 4.1: "Zodiac Man," from Jean Belot, *Oeuvres*, Lyon, 1654, fol. C8ᵛ. The Huntington Library (600149).

a steadfast perceiving in the mind of the disposition of things and words. Or, as Aristotle supposeth, it is an imagination that remaineth of such things as the sense had conceived [. . .] Yet have ancient writers, not without a cause, said that divers parts of the head and brain be occupied of these functions of the soul. Memory, therefore, hath his seat in the hinder part of the head in the third ventricle, which is also called *Puppis*. It would be long and altogether superfluous here—where I study brevity—to describe the anatomy of the whole brain, the which is to be seen in the books of many, especially of the learned, yea, and diligent Andreas Vesalius.

—Gratarolo [1553] 1562: B1ʳ–B2r

In this passage Gratarolo refers specifically to Aristotle (2004: 450a22–3) and to the preeminent experimental anatomist of the age, Andreas Vesalius (1514–64). Originally from Brussels, Vesalius was a professor at the University of Padua's celebrated medical school when he published *On the Fabric of the Human Body* (Vesalius 1543). It was so popular that he brought out an epitome of the same with large woodcuts of the dissected human body, including two sheets that could be cut up and glued together to make layered paper manikins, male and female (Saunders and O'Malley 1973: 204–5). This empirical approach to science (verifiable by observation or experience rather than theory or pure logic) engendered new learning techniques.

KNOWLEDGE AS POWER AND THE "NEW SCIENCE"

The word science during the early modern age meant "knowledge." Francis Bacon (1561–1626), like his Florentine counterpart in statecraft, Niccolò Machiavelli (1469–1527), maintained *"ipsa scientia potestas est"* ["knowledge itself is power"] (Bacon [1597] 1826: 308; Bacon [1597] 1892: 253). This same aphorism appears as a commonplace in Hobbes's *Leviathan*, which he may well have recalled from the time when he was a secretary to Bacon, assisting in the translation of his *Essays* (Collins 2005: 53). Hobbes, moreover, establishes early in *Leviathan* some preliminary understandings prerequisite for any sustained inquiry into human nature, reminiscent of Bacon's treatment of "Idols of the Mind" (Bacon 1620: F2^v–F4^r). Hobbes looks at imagination, memory, dreams, apparitions, and visions to demonstrate the extent to which what and how we think is conditioned by our training and natural predispositions—and, as such, subject to error.

Building also on *The Law of War and Peace* (1625) by the Dutch legal scholar Hugo Grotius (1584–1645), Hobbes begins with a purely mechanistic view of the world and goes on to consider what human life would be without legitimate government, "the state of nature"; his conclusion is the now famous tag-line: "solitary, poor, nasty, brutish and short" (Hobbes 1651: I2^v). By using the very methods he would discredit, Hobbes sets up within the reader's mind's eye a resonant image concerning memory's fallibility. He remarks on the after-image resulting from staring at something for a long time—whether the sun or mathematical figures—and gives a physical and material explanation for what, in an earlier age, had been taken as a truth by analogy or metaphor (Nicolson 1960: 2–9). Hobbes, who corresponded with one of the foremost authorities on optics of the day, René Descartes (1596–1650), understood the modern scientific explanation of how impressions form in the mind (Hobbes 1651: B2^v). Still he was very much aware of how the persuasive power of classical rhetoric, coupled with the memory arts, could enable an adept practitioner, such as Thucydides, to make "his auditor a spectator; for he setteth his reader in the assemblies of the people, and in the senates, at their debating; in the streets, at their seditions; and in the field, at their battles" (Hobbes 1629: A3^v). From the earliest times knowledge and memory danced hand in hand, but, by the sixteenth century, the tune was beginning to change.

Desiderius Erasmus (1466–1526), like Michel de Montaigne (1533–92), openly and repeatedly questioned "the Renaissance pedagogical assumption that memory and knowledge were coidentical" (Rossi 2000: 3). Whereas *scientia* previously referred to the knowledge gained from books (and especially their glosses and commentaries), from the time of Vesalius to Hobbes "science" was beginning to mean knowledge that could be learned from experience and observation. The latter is signaled explicitly in the title of Bacon's *Novum Organum Scientiarum* (literally, a new system of the sciences or branches of knowledge), which sought to renovate human learning through a method surpassing the syllogisms associated with Aristotle's body of work, the old instrument as it were

(Anderson 1948: 130–1). This impulse toward renovation and reform, especially when cultural memory was concerned, gave rise to the "New Science" (Nicolson 1960: 45).

Among those actively participating in this approach to handling what was remembered from the past and renegotiating how it counted as knowledge, were Nicholas Copernicus (1473–1543), armed with new observational methods to chart the movements of heavenly bodies; Vesalius moved medicine away from Aristotelian strictures and long-entrenched views of a humoral-based theory of the body originally championed by Galen (130–216 CE); and Galileo Galilei (1564–1642), about whom more will be said later, advanced mathematics, music theory, optics, and astronomy. Consider also John Parkinson (1567–1650) who, although steeped in an herbalist tradition stretching back to Dioscorides (d. 90 CE), was among the first botanists to concern himself with the soil science underlying

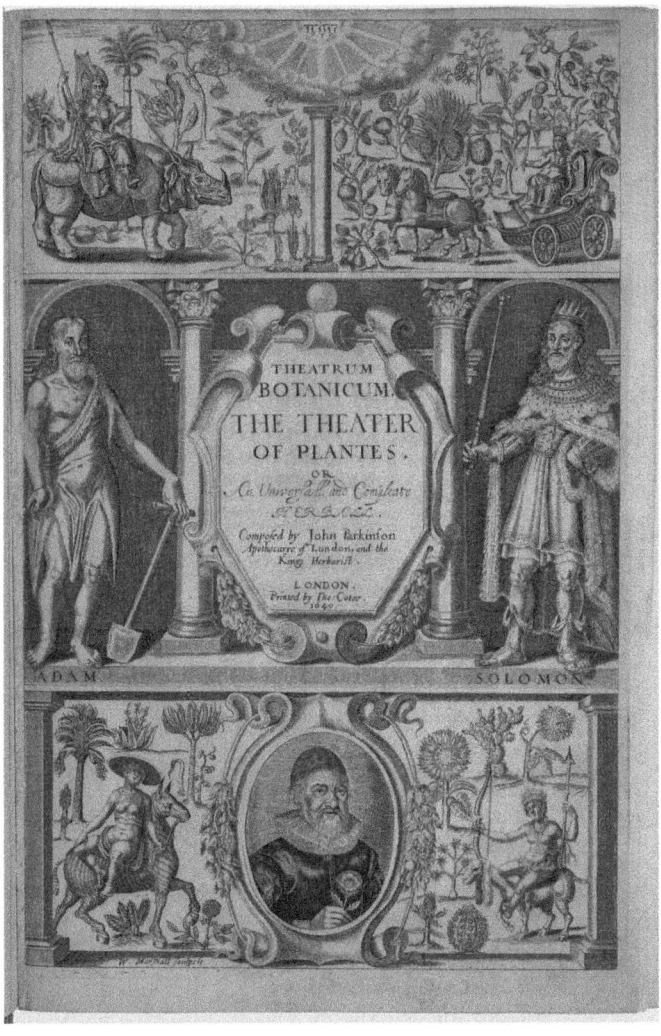

FIGURE 4.2: "Theater of Plants," from John Parkinson, *Theatrum Botanicum*, London: Thomas Cotes, 1640, frontispiece. Used by permission of the Folger Shakespeare Library (Luna 43953).

plant cultivation (see Figure 4.2). Parkinson, typical of this new stamp of seekers of the truths to be found in nature, says he published his observations to correct earlier accounts "whose slips and errors I unfold likewise," and asks his readers not to "tear this book in pieces" because he did not follow the familiar method of long-cherished authority (in particular John Gerard) but instead standardized "the English names"—all of which he undertook, not "to teach Doctors [. . .] but to help their memories" (1640: "To the Reader"). The philosophical underpinning of this self-conscious looking backward to move forward is expressed succinctly in Heidegger's suggestive premise: "Whatever and however we may try to think, we think within the sphere of the tradition" (Heidegger [1957] 2002: 41).

Aristotelian faculty psychology (with its taxonomic topography of the mind having discrete modules, or faculties, each with different tasks) held sway well into the sixteenth century (Bloch 2007: 140). And yet even Galenist physicians, like Helkiah Crooke (1576–1648), were beginning to maintain, contrarily, "that all the principal mental operations were diffused throughout the brain's substance" (Engel, Loughnane, and Williams 2016: 145). Crooke further contended that the presentation and labeling of the body's parts by previous authors "distract the mind and defraud the storehouse of memory," thus hampering the work of doctors and surgeons (1616: A3^v). Likewise, the Dutch experimental physician Levinus Lemnius (1505–68), who studied under Vesalius, wrote on "preservatives of memory" and rationalized their efficacy in terms of Galen's humoralism (the balancing of the body's four humors, or governing fluids).

> For even as too much dryness of the brain [. . .] is very hurtful to memory, because that quality is nothing apt to take any impressions, or forms of things (for dryness and hardness taketh no prints nor images), so also too much moisture (proceeding of idleness, sloth, immoderate sleep and moist meats) quite destroy and drown memory. Moisture, indeed, is more capable, and will sooner take the print and forms of things, but, by reason of softness, the same tarryeth not, but passeth away again, even as stamps or seals, being affixed and imprinted into substance or matter that is too moist, liquid and fluible, maketh therein no stamp, form, or print, but such as presently fleeteth and immediately vanisheth away again.
> —Lemnius 1576: P8^r

The appropriation and repurposing of Aristotelian and Galenic faculty psychology was part of a larger movement coincident with methodological developments in observational and inductively driven practices that led to advances not only in medicine but also in astronomy and agriculture (Wear 2000: 224). At the heart of this approach was the reconceptualization and invention of new instruments (precision honed scalpels, telescopes, microscopes, and mathematical notational symbols—to name a few) as well as concomitant new methods of interpreting nature and the place of the individual within an increasingly accessible cosmos. Of this approach, the English explorer and courtier Walter Raleigh (1554–1618) quipped: "I shall never be persuaded that God hath shut up all the light of learning within the lantern of Aristotle's brains" (1614: B6^r). During the Latin Middle Ages, Aristotle's thought had been rigorously scrutinized, codified, and systematically arranged by such authorities as Thomas Aquinas (1225–74), which in turn formed many of the positions about human learning sanctioned by the Roman Catholic Church (Martin 2014: 16–26). Aquinas himself was particularly qualified to deal with memory insofar as he is reputed to have had "a phenomenal natural memory, and his artificial memory had been exercised by Albert the Great's teaching at Cologne" (Le Goff 1992: 78).

Foremost among the new instruments that recast how objects of human knowledge—and this includes notions of human subjectivity and memory—were to be assessed, judged, and applied was Pico della Mirandola's *Oration on the Dignity of Man* (1486). Pico's syncretism (his bringing together the common truths shared by opposing schools of thought) was, in and of itself, a carefully reasoned justification "of this Humanist procedure" that for the first time "gave to it something like a positive method" (Kristeller 1948: 222). He published in Rome the introductory outline of his much longer public discourse, thus making Pico among the first to recognize and take full advantage of the book as a memory machine, seeing as he did, quite early on, the intellectual purchase made possible through the process of printing. To return to a theme already mentioned but seen now in a more nuanced context, printing gave rise to a special kind of artificial memory in the brave new "paperworld" (Rhodes and Sawday 2000: 14). Pico fundamentally remapped the domains of knowledge by giving primacy to the individual and centering on human capacity, thus lending dignity to the human perspective. His program had far-reaching implications for the dictum of Protagoras that "man is the measure of all things."[5]

During the Renaissance, this concept was imagined in terms of Vitruvian principles of order and arrangement, consonant with the architectural schemes used in the memory arts (Yates 1969: 20–59), drawn from the methods and designs of Marcus Vitruvius Pollio (81 BCE–15 CE). His richly illustrated *On Architecture* was rediscovered in 1414 by the Florentine humanist and manuscript-hunter Poggio Bracciolini (1380–1449) and popularized in the writings of Leon Battista Alberti (1404–72). Many people today are familiar with the drawing by Leonardo da Vinci (1452–1519), sometimes called "Vitruvian Man," of a person inscribed within a "squared circle," arms and legs out-stretched showing the harmonious mathematical proportions of the human form. "Man" was taken to represent the universal *metron*, or measuring stick, by which all things were to be divined and assessed. This concept was true as well for the traditional memory arts familiar to those trained in rhetoric and oratory, insofar as one imagined oneself walking through a house with rooms convenient for the disposing of things later to be recollected and used. Vitruvian artificial memory schemes thus were scaled to the human body's size so that one imagined entering and moving commodiously around within a mnemotechnic construct.

THE MEMORY ARTS AND THE RENOVATION OF KNOWLEDGE

Cicero invented a certain familiar house, severed or parted into many places, and he thought it good that we should devise after every fifth place either a golden hand or some other distinction whereby the one might be discerned from the other, and also in them to observe a steadfast and unmovable order, that we might always enter in and go out at the right side.

—Gratarolo [1553] 1562: G7^r

Order was the primary concern, not only in the building of material edifices but also imaginary ones. Classical rhetoricians advocated strolling through an imaginary dwelling as a way of composing, recalling, and delivering a speech: "The first thought is placed, as it were in the forecourt; the second, let us say, in the living-room; the remainder are placed in due order all round the impluvium [atrium cistern] [. . .] all these places are visited in turn and the various deposits are demanded from their custodians, as the sight of each recalls the respective details" (Quintilian 1961: 11.2.20). Consistent with this aspect of the rhetorical tradition already part of the humanist curriculum, Hugh Plat (1552–1608) instructs his readers:

> you must make choice of some large edifice or building, whose chambers or galleries be of some reasonable receipt, and so familiar unto you, as that every part of each of them may present itself readily unto your mind when you call for them. In every of these rooms you must place ten several subjects at a reasonable distance one from the other, least the nearness of their placing should happen to confound your memory.
> —Plat 1594: N1^r

What can be done with the most common sort of memory plan, "a spacious house divided into a number of rooms," Quintilian relates, "can equally well be done in connexion with public buildings, a long journey, the ramparts of a city, or even pictures" (1961: 11.2.21).

Classical formulations of the memory arts were fundamental to juridical oratory; the Latin Middle Ages revived these arts for the study of rhetoric and grammar; Dominicans used them to order and recall the Bible and its commentaries; and Jesuits, to organize and teach the truths of religion harmonized with natural science. All of these uses were recognized in Peter of Ravenna's *The Phoenix*, which advertises the art of memory as "profitable to all Professors of Sciences," including teachers of the liberal arts, "Grammarians, Rhetoricians, Dialecticians," as well as people in the professions, "Legates, Philosophers, and Theologians" ([1491] 1548: title-page). Peter of Ravenna's influence on the promulgation of mnemotechnical methods throughout Europe was notable, to the extent that he was considered an authority together with Cicero, Quintilian, and Thomas Aquinas (Yates 1978: 119–21). To use place system mnemonics one invented backgrounds (*loci* or places) and then fixed and arranged a series of striking and lively images. He likened the places to "cards or scrolls or other things for to write in. The images [are] the similitudes of the things that we will retain in mind" ([1491] 1548: A2^v–A3^r). These similitudes were part of a visual shorthand expressed variously as emblems and other symbolic images whose meanings were assigned to them, often idiosyncratically. As John Willis, the popular writer on stenography (or shorthand), says:

> The first kind of compound ideas is of them which consist partly of a direct idea [image or visual conceit], partly of a scriptile [written in words]. Of this sort are, an history painted in a fair table with verses underneath explaining it; a libel or epigram made upon something done, supposed to be written in a paper and pasted upon the opposite wall, and the thing done expressed in action upon the stage: an armored knight bearing a scutcheon and imprese written therein, and the like.[6] The second kind of compound idea is of them which consist partly of a relative idea and partly a scriptile. Of this sort are innumerable examples in emblems written by Beza, Alciato, Peacham, and others. For in all emblems, the picture occupying the upper part of the table is a relative idea, and that which is written underneath, a scriptile.
> —Willis 1621: C5^v

As for the place of emblems in the advancement of knowledge, Bacon advocated only the most judicious uses:

> This art of memory is but built upon two intentions; the one prenotion, the other emblem. Prenotion dischargeth the indefinite seeking of that we would remember, and directeth us to seek in a narrow compass, that is, somewhat that hath congruity with our place of memory. Emblem reduceth conceits intellectual to images sensible, which strike the memory more; out of which axioms may be drawn much better practice than

SCIENCE AND EDUCATION 85

that in use; and besides which axioms, there are divers more touching help of memory not inferior to them.

—Bacon 1605: Pp2ᵛ

Bacon—along with Erasmus, Descartes, and Cornelius Agrippa (1486–1535), the German polymath and legal scholar who wrote *The Uncertainty and Vanity of the Sciences* (1527)—was skeptical about the long-term utility of involved mnemotechnic systems; and yet still he acknowledged their place in the progressive renovation and widening of fields of human knowledge (Engel, Loughnane, and Williams 2016: 197–201). He was attuned to the intellectual pressures of the day, for his *Novum Organum Scientiarum* was among the most consequential new instruments to aid in the recalibration of knowledge with respect to human memory, seen now as more than a place to store and stockpile information whether in one's mind or in books. Bacon's plan for a "Great Instauration," or all-inclusive restoration and renewal for "the advancement and proficience" of human learning, is expressed visually on the frontispiece of his ambitious work (Figure 4.3).[7] The

FIGURE 4.3: "Visual Contents," from Francis Bacon, *Of the Advancement and Proficience of Learning*, London: Printed by L. Lichfield, for R. Young & E. Forrest, 1640, frontispiece. Used by permission of the Folger Shakespeare Library (Luna 77261).

mission that he launched (figured by a trade-ship sailing through the Pillars of Hercules, or Strait of Gibraltar, symbolic of the limits of the known world, labeled with England's two main centers of learning, Oxford and Cambridge), would in time be taken up and put into practice by the Royal Society. Christopher Wren (1632–1723), renowned for his modernizations of Vitruvian principles in his architectural designs, was a professor of astronomy at Gresham College, London, in 1660 when he proposed to a group of like-minded friends (including Robert Hooke, inventor of the microscope) to establish "a College for the promoting of Physico-Mathematical Experimental Learning," which, in 1663, received the king's approval and thereafter was known as "The Royal Society of London for Improving Natural Knowledge" (Bryson 2011: 3; Purver 2013: 136–7).

And so memory, as a subject of inquiry in the history of thought was Janus-like in the early modern period, at once looking back to earlier models and looking forward toward new methods and approaches in the interest of taking care of the truths of the natural world. Reference is made here to the history of thought rather than the history of ideas, following Foucault's helpful, if subtle, distinction.

> The history of ideas involves the analysis of a notion from its birth, through its development, and in the setting of other ideas, which constitute its context. The history of thought is the analysis of the way an unproblematic field of experience, or set of practices, which were accepted without question [. . .] becomes a problem, raises discussions and debate, incites new reactions, and induces a crisis in the previously silent behavior, habits, practices, and institutions. The history of thought, understood in this way, is the history of the way people begin to take care of something.
> —Foucault 2001: 74

There is an additional advantage in looking at the history of thought as proposed here, in that many of the existing histories of memory seem to be much better at "describing what they [their authors] consider to be new features of engagement with the past than in specifying what cultures of memory these replaced" (Pollmann and Kuijpers 2013: 3). Pierre Nora, for example, sees the historian's task as decoding the hybrid aspects of what amounts to the mnemonic schemes that often unwittingly are employed by those who previously have given a nation or culture its sense of history and identity (Nora 1989: 19).

However, as Pollmann and Kuijpers contend, it is all too easy—and erroneous—"to conflate pre-modern mnemonic theory with actual memory practices in early modern European societies" (2013: 3). With this caveat in mind, let us turn once again to examine more particularly the Baconian inductive method, which basically is the deductive method turned on its head, and nowadays is called the "scientific method" (Betz 2011: 21–2).

Whereas the Aristotelian syllogistic deductive method started with a few true statements (axioms) with the goal of proving many true statements (theorems) that logically followed from them, the inductive method, used by experimental scientists such as Galileo in Italy and Tycho Brahe (1546–1601) in Denmark, started with many observations of natural phenomena with the goal of finding a few powerful statements about how nature worked so as to derive thereby laws and theories that held up to repeated testing. Although Bacon was adept at systematizing categories of thought each with its own special discursive concerns, as is evident from his *Sylva Sylvarum* (1627) which presents a thousand experiments concerning "natural history," he should not be seen as "the inventor of modern science on the grounds that he discovered the inductive method," since he proposed and categorized but did not actually carry out quantitative and mechanical analyses to form mathematical theories as did Galileo (Rossi 1968: 138). All the same, knowledge for Galileo as for Bacon is not described in terms of recovery, storage, and retrieval, but instead, with respect to a model of performativity involving images in motion. A shift can be observed "in the prevalent model of human memory: from a repository to a theatrical stage. The objects of our recollection no longer seem to us to constitute a passive inventory for deposit and withdrawal; rather, they seem far more like actors in a succession of changing *mise-en-scène*," or placements on stage (Matussek 1999).

This insight into dynamism and performance points the way to the next steps in giving an account of knowledge in the early modern age with respect to the place of memory in the history of thought. Memory Theaters required imagining one's body reduced to scale and moving about inside that construct built to fit the dimensions of one's body. Once inside, one needed to keep all components sufficiently realistic so as not to restrict movement or disrupt the flow of retrieval. The successful mnemonist therefore (both the subject of and, as it were, an object within such a system) had to make certain the entire construct conformed to the rules of mnemonic decorum. The stakes of such ludic configurations at times were nothing less than the acquisition and transmission of the extent of human knowledge, as was the case for Renaissance magi and polymaths such as Giulio Camillo (1480–1544) and Giordano Bruno (1548–1600), who emphasized both the generative and mystically divine aspects of such schemes (Ong 2012: 107).

CONTESTED KNOWLEDGE AND INNOVATIVE PEDAGOGY

Esoteric luminaries like those just mentioned, as well as Paracelsian physicians like Robert Fludd (1574–1637) who valued occult or divinely hidden understandings of the macrocosm (Debus 1970: 81–105), were celebrities in their own day. As such, they remind us that it is deceiving to imagine a narrative of steady progression stretching "from Vesalius to Harvey to Newton," presented largely in terms of "the mathematicalized physical science," as there is ample evidence of a "Neoplatonic revival and the prevalence of interest in natural magic, Hermeticism, and alchemy" (Debus and Walton 1998: vii–viii). It would be wrong, therefore, to assume that "the scientific revolution" eliminated the memory arts (Yates 1964: 148), notwithstanding that this period is marked by monumental efforts to bring about "a great forgetting, a clearing away of the textual and humanist accretions built up around natural philosophy" (Engel, Loughnane, and Williams 2016: 146). Aristotelian natural philosophy, which understood experience quite differently from the Baconian view of empirical observation and experimentation, equated experience with sensory impressions and presupposed that memory always mediated between perception and experience (Dear 2009: 5).

To combat and supplant this Aristotelian view of the natural sciences, Thomas Sprat wrote an account of the Royal Society, an organization that embraced Bacon's reorientation of the relationship between traditional and innovative knowledge and which promoted the advancement of science. Neither a natural philosopher nor an experimental scientist, Sprat wrote what amounts to a defense of the society's activities and objectives rather than a celebration of its members' achievements (Wood 1980: 1–3).

> Nay, what if I should say that this honor for the dead, which such men pretend to, is rather a worshipping of themselves than of the ancients? It may be well proved that they are more in love with their own commentaries than with the texts of those whom they seem to make their oracles; and that they chiefly dote on those theories, which

they themselves have drawn from them, which, it is likely, are almost as far distant from the original meaning of their authors as the positions of the new philosophers themselves.

—Sprat 1667: F4^v

Sprat is a representative spokesman for this new attitude toward traditional textual authorities that early modern empiricism and experiment fostered. And so, while the memory arts in the sciences underwent revisions according to the emerging materialist assumptions (Rossi 1968), they continued to preoccupy the humanities—especially when education was concerned.

The political dimension of formal schooling, as a means of promoting a preferred strand of cultural remembrance and inculcating prevailing values and habits of thought, has long been recognized as an essential feature of education. Diogenes of Sinope (404–323 BCE), popularly portrayed holding a lantern in daylight searching for an honest person, helped his students "get by heart many passages" from poets and historians, teaching them "every short cut to a good memory" (Diogenes Laertius 1925: 6.2.31). He is also credited with the adage: "The foundation of every state is the education of its youth." Humanist educators were especially attuned to this aspect of disseminating and defining what counted as knowledge in this age of especially rapid mercantile development and concomitant social mobility. Thomas Elyot (1490–1546), advisor to Henry VIII, used examples he recalled from Latin and Greek authorities, coupled with his own experience in "daily affairs of the public weal," to describe the education of those "hereafter deemed worthy to be governors of the public weal under your highness" (Elyot 1531: A2^v). The basis of such a program of learning was consonant with the ideas of Diogenes, a founder of Cynic philosophy that promoted aligning human will with knowledge of the ways of nature.

The revival and repurposing of this cognitive orientation of the individual's place in the world was vigorously embraced, both in its more refined form of Roman Stoicism following Cicero and Seneca, as well as the Pyrrhonist skeptical tradition so evident in Montaigne's *Essays* (Schiffman 1984: 499), Sanchez's *Quod Nihil Scitur or That Nothing Is Known* (Popkin 2003: 38–40), and Descartes's *Meditations* (Judovitz 1988: 139–52). At the same time, with the rediscovery of Cicero's and Quintilian's core texts on rhetoric and oratory by Renaissance humanists hungry for learning about classical literature and culture, rhetoric underwent a pedagogical revival. The educational ideals and study of practical arts throughout Europe during this age, although steeped in traditional liberal learning of the past, questioned the custodial approach to understanding the world. This much, along with rudimentary distinctions about memory in the educative process, is made clear by Obadiah Walker (1616–99) in his pedagogical reflections written prior to his being appointed master of University College, Oxford:

Memory is the calling to mind or recollecting of what hath been before known and apprehended. They that excel in it are accounted many times greater clerks than wise men, are able to cite many books and authors and their editions, can tell their opinions and interlace their discourse with ends of gold and silver. Yet, if not managed by judgement, their opinion or learning is of little force or esteem amongst knowing men, who yet can gather many useful things out of their confusion. This faculty is necessary for lawyers, whose learning lies in quotations and records, and who number, rather then weigh, their authorities. 'Tis also proper for learning languages, criticisms, philology, antiquities, for putting out, commenting upon and making indexes to, authors.

—Walker 1673: 128

SCIENCE AND EDUCATION

The word education derives from the Latin *educare* meaning to rear or bring up, closely aligned with *educere* connoting to lead out or away from (Raylor 2008: 219), in this case from ignorance to knowledge—a commonplace theme emblematized and glossed on the frontispiece of Robert Recorde's *Castle of Knowledge* (1556) (see Figure 4.4). Ignorance is personified using features associated with unstable Fortune, blindfolded and dancing unsteadily upon a turning ball, her wheel bearing the motto *Qui modo scandit corruet stadium* ("Whoever rises, will soon fall") (Sawday 2007: 155). Opposite this figure is

FIGURE 4.4: "Castle of Knowledge," from Robert Recorde, *Castle of Knowledge*, London: Reginalde Wolfe, 1556, frontispiece. Used by permission of the Folger Shakespeare Library (Luna 42055).

Destiny, firmly placed atop a stable cube, symbolizing a solid foundation upon which to build, pointing toward the Sphere of Fate "whose governor is knowledge." Along the same lines Plato's doctrine of *anamnesis*, pithily expressed by Bacon in the adage "all knowledge is but remembrance" (1605: A2^v), found practical application in a new kind of approach to learning that relied heavily on images.

Consistent with Bacon's view of the emblem as compressing much information in a compact expressive form (Bacon 1640: Ii3^v–Ii4^r), which paralleled his advocacy of the axiom as a succinct statement conducing to the discovery of universal truths (1605: Pp2^v), the Czech reformer Iohannes Amos Comenius (Jan Amos Komenský, 1592–1670) pioneered the first school primer based on pictures. He used images to stimulate and aid the student's memory in *Orbis Sensualium Pictus* [*The Visible World in Pictures*] (1658), which covered the rudiments of reading and disputation as well as supplied digressions on moral philosophy and natural science.

Still some regional educators such as Edmund Coote (head of the Free Grammar School in Suffolk, whose *English Schoolmaster* went through sixty-four printings between 1596 and 1737), set out to teach people of all ages to read using associative schemes of memorization, thereby addressing the need for vernacular literacy in a society where this skill was becoming increasingly more important. Richard Mulcaster, first headmaster of the guild-funded Merchant Taylors' School in London, advocated using memory techniques to help students think beyond mere retention and recitation so as to be able spontaneously to compose original dialogues: "If the nine muses and Apollo (their president) were painted upon the wall, he might talk to them without either laughing or lowering, they would serve him for places of memory, or for hieroglyphical partitions" (Mulcaster 1581: Aa2^v). Elsewhere, when explaining his teaching methods, Mulcaster declares that he selects "some certain figures proper to architecture, picture, embroidery, engraving, statuary" as "seem most fit to teach a child to draw, and withal I will show how they [are] to be dealt with even from their first point, to their last perfection" (Mulcaster 1582: H1^v). His culling of images, like his alphabetical list of 8,000 "hard-words" at the end of *Elementary* (which paved the way for future English dictionaries), indicates Mulcaster appreciated the pedagogical and mnemonic value of an orderly disposition of the matter to be managed, as does his innovative staging of plays, improvisational debates, and orations for his students.

This technique of having students learn how to dispute propositions, as well as engage in dialogues drawn from classical texts, was becoming the norm in grammar schools throughout Europe—especially with the aid of standardized texts, perhaps the most popular being *Cordier's Colloquies*, which contained hundreds of approved Latin conversations (Green 2016: 176–81). Typical of this approach, John Brinsley (1581–1633), also a promoter of the memory arts, used a "mode of daily disputing and opposing," first peer to peer and then pupil to teacher to make sure knowledge was being advanced rather than puerile simplicities merely circulating among the students unchecked (Brinsley 1612: Hh1^r–Hh2^r). Another educator, William Kempe (1560–1601), clearly familiar with the writings of Ramus (whose work he had encountered while a student at Cambridge), was interested in the more practical ways in which memory is connected to pedagogy and behavior. As part of a step-based system conducing ultimately to original compositions, Kempe developed a lively way to help students memorize precepts and grammar (1588: E3^r–E4^v).

In light of these widespread dialogical practices, Mulcaster's reference to an imagined mural of the muses can be understood in terms of a new attitude toward pedagogy designed to incite students to develop their own viable memory places, seen now as both instrumental to the development of expository conversation as well as a pathway to critical judgment. Such examples reflect the extent to which value was still ascribed to collecting and engaging actively with one's own mnemonic treasury. The Spanish humanist Juan Luis Vives (1493–1540), considered the forerunner of modern psychology because of his insights into the interplay of emotions, memory, and learning, advised his students

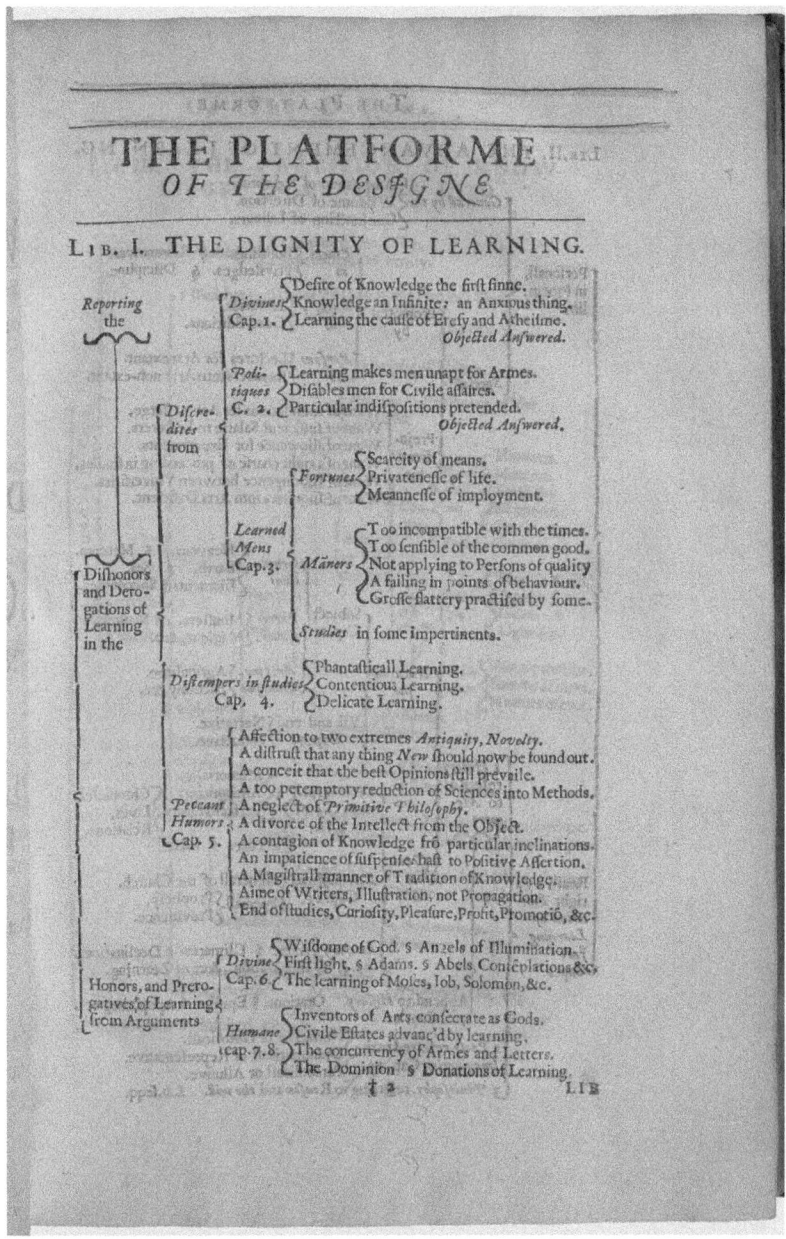

FIGURE 4.5: "Platform of the Design," from Francis Bacon, *Of the Advancement and Proficience of Learning*, London: Printed by L. Lichfield, for R. Young & E. Forrest, 1640, fol. †2ʳ. Used by permission of the Folger Shakespeare Library (Luna 62766).

to "have always at hand a paper book, wherein thou shalt write such notable things as thou read thyself, or hear of other men worthy to be noted [. . .] that thou may have in a readiness when time requireth [. . .]. The more often thou commit things to her [memory's] custody, the more better and faithfully will she keep them" (1563: E4ᵛ–E5ʳ). Consonant with this precept, all manner of techniques were devised to gain access to "notable things" gleaned from classical texts, including collections of adages, anthologies and epitomes with topical headings, compendia and encyclopedias with indexes arranged alphabetically or topically (and sometimes according to both systems), as well as elaborately ramified charts outlining a book's contents. A representative example of the latter is "The Platform to the Design" in Bacon's magnum opus (Figure 4.5).

These various approaches toward augmentation and organization were designed to help readers find their way around a book, or simply determine which parts were most useful to their present purposes. With characteristic wit Montaigne reported that his book, bristling with quotations drawn from his reading, in an effort to record and reflect on his own experience as things occurred to him, inadvertently crafted an artificial memory: "For lack of a natural memory, I make one of paper" (Montaigne 1958: 837). While the theme of an unreliable memory is a central and animating feature of Montaigne's mode of composition (Engel 1995: 108), the real issue at stake here "is not whether or what someone does or does not remember, but rather how a good or a bad memory impinges upon one's relations with others" (Frisch 2006: 23).[8]

Ethics, as discussed by Montaigne among others, infuses new implications into the memory arts that originally emerged from classical rhetoric's preoccupation with helping public orators recall suitable matter for the composition and delivery of their arguments, which were aimed at persuading, if not instructing, others. It is not surprising, then, that larger claims have been made for the art of memory itself as being hidden within the rhetoric of modern forms of discourse (Hutton 1993: 29).

THE ART OF MEMORY AND THE REFORMATION OF KNOWLEDGE

Traditionally, thanks to the humanist program of learning that scholars knew so well (people like Vives, Ramus, Erasmus, Bacon, and Montaigne), classical oratory was organized around five canons, or rules: invention, arrangement, style, memory, and delivery. The fourth canon, the art of memory, specifically gave strategies for recalling a speech's primary points, usually involving an architectural mnemonic design or some other decorous method of creating a series of linked images.

Philip Sidney, for example, adapts to poetry the commonplace view that "writing resembles an art of memory, where stanzas function as *loci* and rhythmical and rhymed words as the securely placed images" (Engel, Loughnane, and Williams 2016: 124). As Sidney said:

> Now that verse far exceedeth prose, in the knitting up of the memory, the reason is manifest, the words (besides their delight, which hath a great affinity to memory) being so set as one cannot be lost, but the whole work fail: which accusing itself, calleth the remembrance back to itself, and so most strongly confirmeth it. Besides one word, so as it were begetting an other, as be it in rhyme or measured verse, by the former a man shall have a near guess to the follower. Lastly even they that have taught the art of memory, have showed nothing so apt for it, as a certain room divided into many

places, well and thoroughly known. Now that hath the verse in effect perfectly, every word having his natural seat, which seat must needs make the word remembered.

—Sidney 1595: F3^v

The art of memory thus associates things worth remembering with images and then mentally locates those images in an appropriately hospitable setting. And yet, beyond its being merely an expedient way of managing information, it also shaped and informed many intellectual domains of the age. These included Renaissance aesthetics, ranging from iconographic programs of tapestries, to triumphal entry arches, and to the encoded signifying elements in portrait paintings; also in architecture, for example Shakespeare's Globe, both for its exterior design and what happened inside the playhouse (Yates 1978: 330–54); and epistemology, especially systems for disclosing the extent of human learning. Examples of the last include the diagrammatic method of Peter Ramus, schematically outlining ever more precise branches and sub-branches of a topic; Giulio Camillo's celebrated Memory Theater, as both a storehouse and generator of all knowledge; and Giordano Bruno's Hermetic principles used to discover and reveal occult truths of the universe. Many such systems were indebted to the Spanish logician Ramón Lull (1232–1316), especially those reproduced in books by the French occultist, Jean Belot (*Oeuvres* 1654), and the English almanac writer and promulgator of palmistry and other arcane forms of divination, Richard Saunders (*Physiognomy* 1671). Lull's astrolabe-inspired diagrams of combinatory wheels within a wheel, known as the *ars notaria*, was a prefiguration of later memory machines. The practitioner of Lull's system reverentially gazed upon and engaged with figures and cryptic diagrams (*notae*), a different *nota* provided for each discipline, so as to gain knowledge—and thus memory—of all the arts and sciences (Yates 1978: 175–96).

Notwithstanding its many variations and forms, the memory arts all promised pragmatic applications—whether devising a rhymed song to fix in mind one's market list en route to a trade fair, or constructing a Memory Theater for arranging and delivering legal cases, or any of many methods suited for oratorical performances ranging from sacred sermons to secular plays. In all such cases, images—whether virtually in the mind or represented in the world—remain the rudimentary and initiating component. Leon Battista Alberti, for example, maintained that the starting point for any painting should be a memorable story, and that painting itself was an art of memory (Hulse 1990: 65–8; Nadav-Manes 2006: 9).

Although applications of the memory arts proliferated during the early modern period, the rules of classical mnemotechnics remained unchanged. Place system mnemonics required the arrangement of lively images in pre-designated places (usually in sets of five or ten), the more grotesque or ludicrous the image the better because the more easily recalled (Gratarolo [1553] 1562: H6^r). A convenient backdrop was selected—whether wall, room, theater, house, castle, or city; flower, tree, garden, or grove; body, hand, or finger—onto which these telling images were placed in sequence. Obadiah Walker of University College, Oxford, speaks to this directly:

> Yet there is also an artificial help to memory, which is variously and obscurely delivered by many authors. The shortest and easiest is this: make use of a sufficient number of places best known to you: as of towns [on] the way to London, the streets of London, or the signs in one street, such in fine as are well known to you. Keep their order perfectly in mind, which first, which second, etc., and when any word is given you to remember, place it in the first town, street or sign, joining them together with some

fancy, though never so extravagant, the calling to mind your known place will draw along with it the fancy, and that the word joined to it. And these you may repeat afterwards either in the same order as they were delivered, or backwards, or as you please.

—Walker 1673: 131–2

Students and other beginners in the art tended to favor the simplicity of a single room of manageable size like the one illustrated, for example, by Johannes Romberch, his own version of a Vitruvian image, showing a person standing with arms held at 90 degrees to indicate the proper dimensions of a room to be used on its own and perhaps as one of many within a more involved Memory palace (1520: C5ʳ). More elaborate designs lent themselves to accommodate more places still, such as any of the mnemonic itineraries presented and discussed in Romberch's handbook. He proclaims it was compiled specifically for the benefit of theologians, statesmen, university professors, jurists, lawyers, notaries and civic officials, doctors, philosophers, teachers of the liberal arts, as well as traders and merchants (1520: title-page).

Among his many illustrated schemes is what amounts to a City of Memory, depicting a winding street with labeled destinations corresponding to the letters of the alphabet. One moves from the "A" part of town through a distinctive starting gate to five places beginning with the letter "B" (the second letter of each term being a vowel proceeding in alphabetical order from "a" to "u" thus assuring a systematic means for retrieving the *loci*), thereby indicating how one might construct similar sets of images for one's own mnemotechnic needs (Engel, Loughnane, and Williams 2016: 20–21). This sequence, along with further successive alphabetically organized blocks of five items, is spelled out explicitly a few pages later to give readers more sets of ready-made models for constructing their own arts of memory (Romberch 1520: D4ʳ).

Romberch's compilation gives another useful scheme (Figure 4.6), presenting visually three decades (or sets of ten, in keeping with Cicero's advice) of neatly arranged items, divided and numbered for placing in each slot what one wants to retrieve (Romberch 1520: D5ʳ). The fifth place is marked with a hand (again, following Cicero), and the tenth by a form of a cross with different numbers of strokes as one progresses decade to decade thereafter. The top rank concerns domestic items ("**A**vla," *aula* is Latin for house-courtyard); the second, things at a bookstore ("**B**iblioteca"); and finally, the bottom, things found in a chapel ("**C**apella") [emphasis added].

As a through-thread in the history of thought with regard to the topic of knowledge in the early modern age, the art of memory offered a way to organize one's experience within the world itself, as well as with respect to one's reading and learning; and also, along with it, the symbolic world one has constructed to contain it. The heuristic pedagogical value of applying the memory arts to organize and make sense of one's reading experience reveals that the inverse obtains as well—namely seeing in one's reading a viable mechanism for creating an art of memory to house the extent of what one learns experientially in the world.

Such a plan was recognized and commented on by the Florentine Dominican friar Cosmas Rossellius (d. 1578), in his discussion of Dante's *Divine Comedy* with respect to a series of rings forming a linked and coherent background mnemonic against which various allegorical tableaux are situated and visited in turn (see Figure 4.7). The variety of punishments in the *Inferno*, together with the locations where sinners suffer, Rossellius explains, will become clear and distinct memory places that, in turn, facilitate the

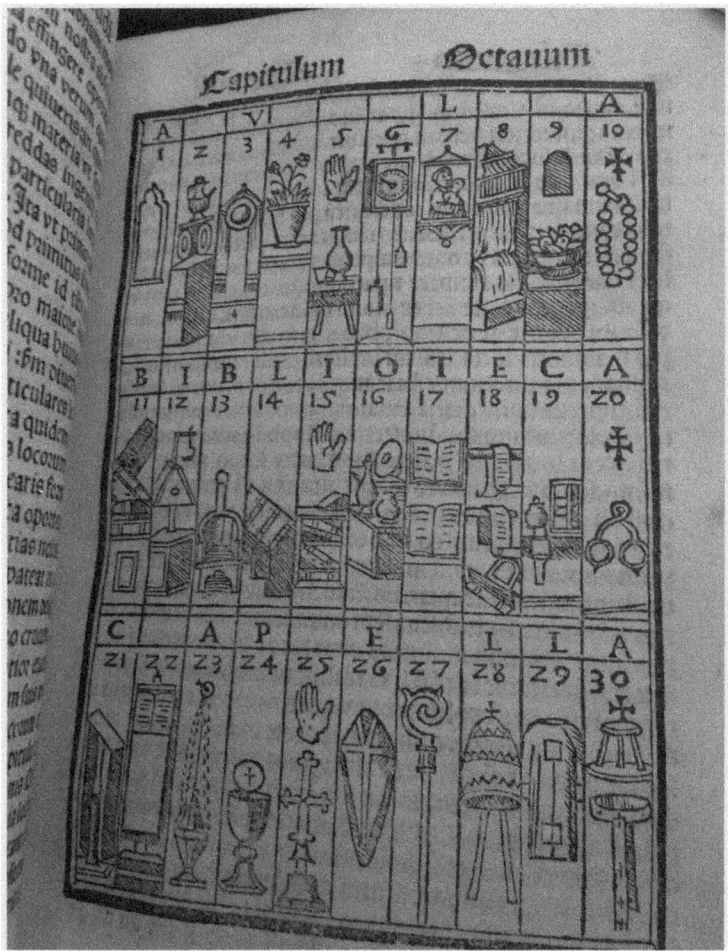

FIGURE 4.6: "Memory Grid," from Johannes Host von Romberch, *Congestorium Artificiose Memorie*, Venice: Giorgio Rusconi, 1520, fol. D5ʳ. Huntington Library.

improvement of one's memory by providing apt places for future uses when relieved of their original Dantean content (Rossellius 1579: K2ᵛ). Such memory schemes, understood as machines for generating knowledge, offer modern readers a credible way to retrace key steps in the intellectual movement of an earlier age, not only the dynamic movement within such imaginary constructs, but also in the history of thought with respect to the productive tension existing then between science and education.

The various and representative examples presented here, any one of which will reward further study along the lines outlined, all showcase the importance of memory in a range of intellectual and pragmatic endeavors. During the early modern period renewed attention to memory made possible an immense broadening and a general reconfiguring of human knowledge, which included the beginnings of modern science and systematic educational reform. Samuel Hartlib sums up well this impulse of the age to put memory to new and far-reaching uses when, following Comenius, he declared: "that which we desire is to have a living tree with living roots and living fruit of all arts and sciences, I

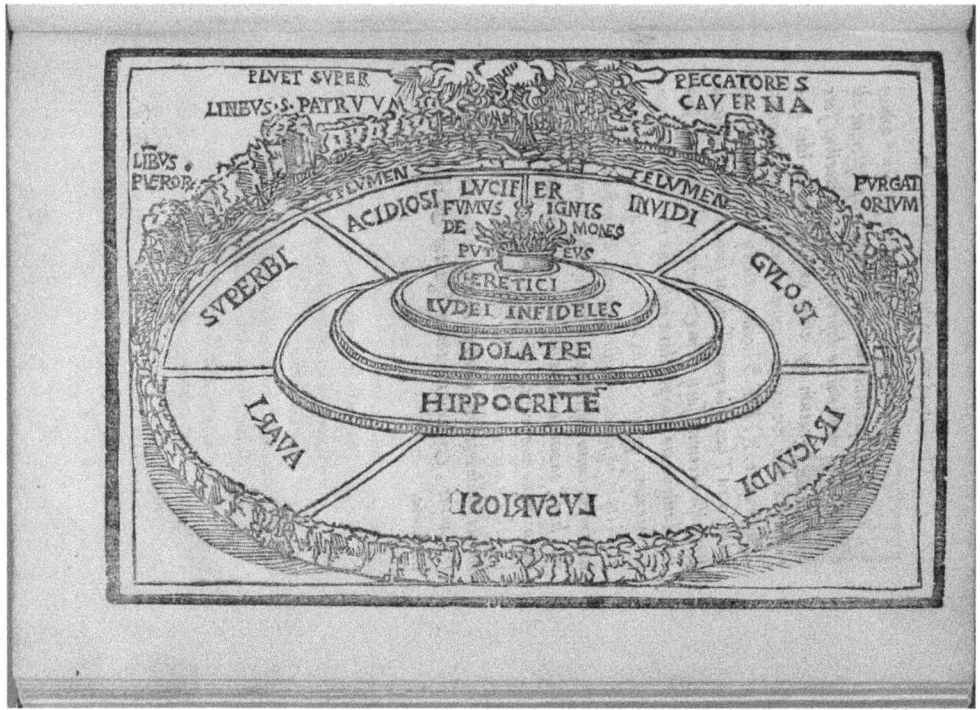

FIGURE 4.7: "Ring Mnemonic," from Cosmas Rossellius, *Thesaurus Artificiosae Memoriae*, Venice: Antonio Padovani, 1579, fol. C4^r. Huntington Library.

mean pansophy, which is a lively image of the universe, every way closing and agreeing with itself, everywhere quickening itself and covering itself with fruit (1642: D1^v). Knowledge during the early modern age, figured as a mirror of the universe's true operating principles, was conceptualized as a kind of organic mechanism set in place—and set to work—by men and women. Indeed Comenius, among others, insisted "that youth of both sexes should be put to school" (1672: M4^v).

Knowledge in every age, of course, is made and regulated in the context of assumptions, presuppositions, available vocabularies, and methodologies of the day. What is extraordinary about the renovation of knowledge during the early modern era, however, are the powerful ways that memory was mobilized systematically to recover, accommodate, reconfigure, and transform nearly 2,000 years of reigning scientific assumptions and pedagogical methodologies, thereby refashioning the epistemological terrain which, to a large extent, we still occupy today.

CHAPTER FIVE

Ideas: Philosophy, Religion and Art

PATRICIA EMISON

A chamber must have more than four corners which is to contain the gods of memory.
—(Albrecht Dürer to Willibald Pirckheimer, from Venice, September 8, 1506 Conway 1889: 55)

Visual memory is but a subset of cultural memory, and works of art but a subset of visual memory. That given, this chapter proposes to examine a few instances in which the history of art helps us to address the issue of how cultural memories and present exigencies interacted during the period we call early modern. Just as, traditionally, artists have been understood as imitators of nature and it has been the task of art historians to explicate the complexities inherent in that theory of art, so artists were supposed to create *istorie*, narratives or allegories about the past, and it is increasingly the task of art historians to interpret this function within the larger context of cultural memory as it impacts politics, intellectual life, and devotion.

A MORE VISUAL AND A MORE CONTINGENT WORLD

Forgetting and remembering were dialectically interlocked with particular acuteness in the early modern period. How else could a Christian culture hope to succeed in deliberately imitating a pagan one? What a strange project it was, and accordingly no wonder that there were many wrinkles along the way. Church and state, artists and writers, each had something to gain and something to lose in the complicated process of assimilating that beguiling and ever-shifting amalgam of writings, objects, and ideas called the antique. It might appear to be a process by which early modern Europe overcame its newfound shame vis-à-vis the ancient world, its regretful apprehension that much had been lost during the wars and deprivations in the aftermath of the Roman Empire, and gradually emerged as a continent of proud nation states that relegated antiquity to the role of mere ornament to modern glory, while keeping the Papacy neatly in check as a vestige of the long Middle Ages. However, not only was the vanquishing of ancient pre-eminence more often announced than completely accepted, but it was also true that the modern was a complex concept in a world that had previously habituated to simpler (if sometimes mystical) dogmas. In the early modern period rhetoric and dialectic offered new challenges and intellectual strategies; concurrently, a new love of literature, especially lyric poetry, validated introspection and emotions quite beyond the range even of those aroused by the more emotional Franciscan religious devotion. The forgetting and remembering both happened in relation to an incipient modernity which was alternately more nuanced, more materialistic, at least as violent, and more wide-rangingly imaginative than what had gone before. Part of what the shapers of modernity imagined was the past, and in particular, how that past might be made useful. Aristotle's exposition of the concept of magnificence in the *Nicomachean Ethics* (the book held by Aristotle in Raphael's *School of Athens*) is but one instance of a fragment of ancient culture whose retrieval and assimilation had enormous consequence for the making of modernity.

The vectors of the triangle constituted by antiquity, the modern, and nature were ever shifting in dynamical relationship to the cultural development of early modern Europe, which was a tangle of unresolved religious and political affiliations, as well as of morphing social relations, not only those of class but also gender. Nevertheless, whereas the medieval period might be characterized as—overall—a period of much forgetting, of concentrating attention on relatively few and new foci, and in some cases of cocooning from a hostile environment, the early modern period was distinguished by its eagerness to remember.[1] Its great project was to construct a collective memory that spanned both Christian and pagan history and that brought religion and philosophy into alignment with each other and ideally also with the study of ancient literature. Erasmus was a leading exponent of this project. Terence, he wrote in a letter of 1489, "no one but a barbarian has ever failed to love" (Erasmus 1974: 60) and Terence it was who famously declared: "I am human. Nothing seems strange to me which is human." Erasmus echoed the sentiment in 1522, writing to the radical reformer Huldrych Zwingli: "My own wish is to be a citizen of the world, to be a fellow citizen to all men—a pilgrim better still" (Erasmus 1988: 185). Montaigne had Terence's declaration inscribed on a ceiling beam in his study, amid other epigraphs. Humanists of various national origins so believed in the value of a common cultural heritage from antiquity that their project survived (not without damage) the Reformation; conversely, we may wonder how much more grievous the impact of the Reformation might have been had there not been this shared and fairly neutral intellectual ground.

The humanists' project entailed a huge expansion in reading, both the construction of a public that read and a vast broadening of the texts available for reading; an epoch-making integration of visual imagery into the stuff of communal ponderation, such imagery to be found now variously on majolica, rock crystal engravings, jewelry, prints, tapestries, frescoes, cabinet paintings, colophons, and personal emblems; and a newly keen pursuit of the art of conversation, interactions sometimes captured for us in the revived literary genre of the dialogue and occasionally in visual imagery. An engraving such as Diana Scultori's figures seated at a table in lively discussion (Figure 5.1) (Bartsch [1805] 1970: XV, 446.32) encapsulates these various cultural strands: the scene is set in antiquity; the figural design derives from Michelangelo, the most radical of early modern artists (specifically from the background of the *Crucifixion of Hamon* in a Sistine lunette, *c.* 1512); and whether its subject was thought to be a religious or a philosophical discussion, the active role taken by a woman provides a rare visual correlate for early modern literary dialogues, which were markedly more inclusive than their ancient precedents.

Much can be learned from the conversational snippets and fragments recorded from artists, not only about the history of art but about how the reception of art fit into the greater whole of religious, philosophical, and historical thought. Artists of the period were remembered in newly bantering anecdotes, storytelling in which a versatile wittiness (the sort of quality we might now designate as street-smartness) comes to the fore as much as specifically artistic intelligence. Might this kind of banter, which transformed the stiff

FIGURE 5.1: Diana Scultori, *Esther? or Aspasia with Socrates?*, B. XV, 446,32, c. 1570s to 1580s, engraving. Diana portrays an articulate woman, variously supposed to belong either to Greek antiquity or to the Old Testament, who seems a surrogate for the women who participate so actively in Renaissance literary and philosophical dialogues.

norms of hagiography into a kind of proto-documentary biographical style, have helped to shift the norms of analytical thought from the rigidities of scholastic discourse toward the more speculative, sometimes strikingly inventive philosophical ruminations of Montaigne or even Descartes? The stern Dominican reformer Girolamo Savonarola imagined a painter remonstrating with an engraver who had not followed the pattern properly when he wanted to explain the necessity of following God's plan precisely (Emison 2004: 101–2; cf. Berger 2017: 184–6, on Descartes' using visual art as a metaphor for the brain's processing of nature), a striking instance of the imagery of artists (specifically the new art of printmaking) infiltrating unexpected realms of thought.

Montaigne and Descartes see themselves as the subject of their meditations, literally as well as figuratively. They identified their physical instantiation as the frame of their window onto the world, and their philosophy is founded in that selfhood. It is not so very far from Brunelleschi's practical joke played on Grasso the woodcarver, convincing him that he had awoken to a different identity to the one he had supposed to be his own (Martines 1994: 171–212, written in the 1480s), to Descartes' quandary about the relationship between the ratiocinative and the subjective. He sits at his desk, wondering, analogous to Grasso's waking up thoroughly befuddled by the practical joke being played on him; Brunelleschi is Grasso's personal evil genius, set out to trap him in true-seeming falsehoods. The two were writing at vastly different times and places, yet we might ask, is there not in both cases a more improvisatory, investigatory attitude toward where words and images might lead, and a taste for the games one might play with one's own and others' sense of reality? Cosimo de' Medici's sponsorship of Marsilio Ficino's translations of Plato into Latin must surely be accounted a factor in the validation of these new habits of questioning the foundations of knowledge.[2] At the other end of our period, paintings such as Velázquez's *Las Meninas* (Prado, 1656) and Vermeer's *Woman Holding a Balance* (National Gallery, Washington, *c.* 1663)—the former which shows from the back a canvas as large as that of *Las Meninas* itself and the latter which shows a painting of the *Last Judgment* on the back wall (an occasion for weighing souls even if, in this painting from a Protestant country, no St. Michael appears)—demonstrate how art and nature had come to be seen as parallel realities rather than as copy and original. For all their differences, they are both paintings in which reality is found to be what landscape painters would later call picturesque, i.e., suitable for art. Analogously, the past came to be seen as that which might be explored or even exploited, rather than only as that from which came inviolable precedent. The relationship between past and present, like that between nature and art, was full of possibilities.

The whole project of systematic linear perspective construction had been an attempt to erase the line between reality and the appearance of reality. Yet there was nothing improvised about Brunelleschi's system; its appeal was lodged in the geometric certainty with which it promised perfection (that same certainty to which Descartes turned), every proportion exact, as in his new architecture, the very epitome of rule-boundedness. Nevertheless, both the history of art and even more so the history of preserving the memory of artists depended, beginning in the fifteenth century, on a new tolerance for the anecdotal, the relatively random, sometimes amusing, actions. Character and the cast of a person's intelligence might be revealed by accidental encounters. Instead of merely sin and virtue, the whole of human subjectivity was now open to scruple. "What's he to Hecuba or Hecuba to him, that he should weep for her?" Hamlet asks himself of the First Player (II, ii), in a moment that crystallizes centuries of meditation on the value of ancient history and literature, as well as signaling a newly modern sense of interior selfhood, one's own and that of others.

THE ARTIST AS KEEPER OF PUBLIC MEMORY

When Michelangelo struck out the teeth of his head of an old faun carved in marble, simply because Lorenzo il Magnifico (whom, Vasari tells, the young artist both loved and feared; Vasari 1991: 419) had criticized it as unrealistic, he was young and inexperienced; when he brushed off the marble dust from the nose of the David and convinced Piero Soderini that he had made the recommended changes, he was momentarily in control of those ostensibly in political power. When in the wake of the assassination of Duke Alessandro, first Duke of Florence, he made a bust of Brutus, he was helping the Florentine exiles in Rome to see themselves as heirs to an ancient republican tradition. Each of these sculptures, though, belonged to the overarching project by which he helped his contemporaries to see themselves as like the ancients, as mirroring the greatness of ancient times. In concert with humanists, he helped to construct a novel pride in the present as a time that combined the accomplishments of the ancients with Christianity, or in other words, a time whose project was the discriminating resuscitation of various layers of cultural memories. Incipient nation states would nurture this evolving pride in the present, though with diminishing emphasis on the cultural memory that had helped to instigate it. Bernini's bust of Louis XIV (Versailles, 1665), for example, shows the subject in armor, wig, and lace collar, very much a figure of his own time, not only in his dress but in the obtrusive stylistic markers left by the sculptor—in particular, the flamboyant drapery that becomes a human wing surrogate, used to activate the bust rather than to stabilize it and to assert a sort of signature for the artist that establishes a counterpoint to the attention directed at the King's visage. Even in the visage itself the sculptor took a certain liberty (for which he was criticized) in exposing the forehead, leaving one obtrusive curl at the center. Bernini may well have meant to recall the hairstyle of Alexander the Great (his leonine *anastole*), as sculpted by Lysippos. The sculptor is reported by Paul Fréart de Chantelou, Bernini's guide around court, to have said that "His Majesty had something of Alexander about him, particularly in the forehead" (Chantelou 1985: 121).

The viewer cannot understand Michelangelo's bust without thinking of its antique prototypes (for both form and content); the bust of the King of France by Bernini is predicated on but a faint memory of the tradition, an optional memory we might deem it. The startlingly informal bust of his lover *Costanza Bonarelli* (Figure 5.2) (Bargello, 1635), her blouse rumpled and askew, her lips relaxed and slightly open, essentially reinvents the art form. The *Costanza* is for the history of art what Descartes' *Meditations* is for philosophy: a declaration of a modernity that consciously suppresses its debt to the past and establishes a new, and distinctively modern, intimacy of discourse—a correlate to the close bond between reader and printed book, especially the neat quarto-sized editions inaugurated by

FIGURE 5.2: Gian Lorenzo Bernini, *Costanza Bonarelli*, Bargello, Florence, c. 1636, marble. Bernini, who elsewhere reinvented the Roman portrait bust with startlingly vivid details, explores here an intimate rapport with the sitter that seems to have correlated with the frank self-examinations recorded by Descartes and Montaigne.

Aldus at the end of the fifteenth century. There is room in this newly intimate discourse for empathy, whereas the ancient world had tended to prioritize rationality as the means by which human communities that were not totalitarian established themselves.

The weight of cultural memory could be oppressive: no early modern author managed to write an epic that could compare with Homer's or Virgil's, despite much effort, and it was partly in compensation for that dearth that Michelangelo's acclaimed superiority to the ancients was so vaunted. In the arts, the nude, colossal, and equestrian statue types had been reinvented, whereas in literature, instead of writing epic, Shakespeare, Cervantes, and Rabelais worked outside the confines of ancient genres, much expanding the role of comedy in the process. Accordingly, Terence and Lucian gained in prestige. Aristotle had had relatively little to say about comedy, whereas Baldassare Castiglione recognized it as the key to a convincing imitation of life: "writers of comedy [. . .] more than the others, reflect the nature of human life" (1967: 107). In that claim we recognize an early modern voice, far from any medieval one—not meaning that people in medieval times had no capacity to laugh, but only that they tended not to take their laughter seriously. The dialogue Castiglione penned was meant to preserve the memories of his dead friends, yet it is full of wittiness and laughter, and includes a lengthy discussion of humor, as being a device by which the courtier can ingratiate himself with his prince. Laughter was being legitimized.

Tragedy and epic featured rulers; Castiglione was writing about the next step down in the hierarchy, and the period in general was one in which the mercantile class was rising in power, so comedy—especially comedy refitted so that the old master/slave tensions suited the contemporary world—had an enlarged role to play, a role that exceeded the bounds of literature. It was becoming a tool by which to shape society, rather than primarily a release and recreation. When Willibald Pirckheimer, Dürer's close friend, wrote to Erasmus in 1523 about the deeply troubling religious strife in Nuremberg, he reported of the papal legate, "No one—I repeat, absolutely no one—pays him the slightest respect, and he is the laughing stock and butt of the whole population" (Erasmus 1988: 404).

The modernity crafted by intellectuals and artists was complex: it fostered a new sense of empathy but also—not entirely compatibly—amusement. This latter can be found both in the biographical writing about artists, in which they astound their contemporaries with their wit as well as their extraordinary talent, but also in the art itself, which now and then engages the viewer's sense of humor in place of religious or patriotic devotion. Often it is the present situation that is mocked, and sometimes with the help of history. Sir Thomas More's *Utopia* (1516), for instance, criticizes the shambles of present-day society that drive men to criminality due to poverty, by wittily holding up as preferable a place that so disdains gold that it uses it for bedpans. That model society is not a historical one, but like its name (a new Greek word) it could claim to be both ancient and invented. The idea of Utopia owes at least a little to ancient lore about uncorrupt and exotic societies like Arcady, the rural version of antiquity.

In Molière's *Tartuffe* (1664), the disordered world of the comedy is set to rights by the King's Officer in the final scene by a *deus ex machina*, laughter was ultimately aligned with authority—although for most of the play the head of the household was the chief fool on stage, his ridiculous religious advisor a figure of unalloyed vice. The potential threat to order presented in such a satirical comedy was acknowledged when the play was censored (presumably at the instigation of the Church). State and Church demanded stability; contingency and comedy were bedfellows.

Artists, unlike the other typical objects of biographical writing such as hereditary rulers and saints, were expected to confound those around them, so whether it was Donatello smashing a portrait bust rather than delivering it to a patron who wouldn't readily pay for it what the artist had decreed to be the price (Vasari 1991: 153–4) or Dürer pulling an ordinary paintbrush out of his pocket when Bellini asked to see the tool with which he made his amazingly precise marks, the amusing or surprising anecdote was a staple of their biographies from the time of Vasari onwards. Sometimes the episode is pure theater, as when Bernini presents his bust to Cardinal Scipione Borghese, the marble of the forehead scarred by a flaw in the marble, only to astound the disappointed Cardinal, after a prolonged interval, with a second bust, sans flaw. The Cardinal displayed then a notable *allegrezza*, all the greater, Filippo Baldinucci tells us, because he had suffered so in receiving the flawed bust without wanting to betray his disappointment to the artist (Baldinucci 1847: 590). Benvenuto Cellini describes how he presented his silver statue of *Jupiter* by candlelight in the gallery at Fontainebleau, sliding it forward to enhance the lifelikeness of the figure. He assures us on the one hand that it left the casts of antiquities in the dust ("alquanto . . . indietro"; Cellini 1985: 498), and on the other, that the act of dramatically removing the scarf from the statue's genitals gave offense to the King's mistress, Madame d'Étampes. He presents it as a joke on an envious, conniving woman whose plans to shame him in the end shamed her. Women and antiquity figure in his account both as opponents for whom he has no respect, as entities he wishes to humiliate. It is as though he wants to declare his independence from the past, but lacks the concept of originality and so remains bound to the norm of ancient art, as personally, it appears, that because of the lack of the concept of legitimate homosexuality he was bound to the appearance of heterosexuality, all the while despising (at least unconsciously) that which constrained him.

Cellini admires Michelangelo, a generation older than he, more than he does the ancients, and yet his work is not much like Michelangelo's (typically bronze instead of marble, delicate figural types and intricate ornamentation), so there could be no praise that would satisfy him, only riches, and his patrons continually disappoint him in this regard. A case in point is the account he gives of using his now-famed saltcellar himself with his confrères before delivering it to King Francis I—using it privately would be cheeky enough, but writing about doing so long after he had fallen out with Francis elevates the stakes to revenge (or possibly revenge fantasy) (Cellini 1998: 292). Still, the episode is presented as merely an amusing incident.

It is not only the stories told about art that entertained, but the art itself. From Botticelli's *Mars and Venus* (National Gallery, London, *c.* 1485) to Caravaggio's *Fortune Teller* (Louvre and Capitoline Museum, 1590s) (in both of which the woman has the upper hand) to Quentin Matsys's so-called *Ugly Duchess* (National Gallery, London, *c.* 1513), painting was now used to divert its private patrons, whether via mythological situations, genre scenes, or caricature. Like the courtier who sets out to amuse his prince and thereby gain influence, so the artist entertains his patron. Even more than in painting, prints, a low-cost art form, allowed for jocularity.

Dürer's engraving of *Nemesis* (Figure 5.3) (*c.* 1502, B.VII, 91.77, so named by Dürer in his journal of his trip to the Netherlands in the early 1520s) translates an ancient concept into a contemporary hallucination we might say, rather than a vision, and changes the tenor of his public's approach to the idea of Fate from frightening into an entity at least slightly ludicrous.[3] If Nemesis is the antithesis of free will, we may well wonder what Christians at this critical moment in the history of religion made of this personification of Fate in the guise of a middle-aged nude woman, an image at once antique and contemporary but with a good deal of friction between the two. Precursor to Dürer's *Melencolia*,

FIGURE 5.3: Albrecht Dürer, *Nemesis*, *c.* 1502, engraving. Dürer portrays the antithesis of free will, in the decade before the Reformation begins, as a dubious goddess. © The British Library Board.

likewise a middle-aged woman seen as a personification of human defeat (broadly speaking) and also with an unstable sphere as attribute, both engravings were widely imitated and adapted within the artistic community and, we may assume, ruminated over by a wide range of collectors. Melencolia's chief ancestor is the medieval sin of Sloth; Nemesis descends, ultimately, from the ancient goddess of Fortuna.

Dürer's *Nemesis* may be taken to be distinctly irreverent in tone: the woman has not one, but two, trailing reins between her legs threatening to trip her up; her forelock has blown back so as to be ungraspable; her balance seems to rely on the particular positioning of her big toe, working separately from the other toes; the goblet she proffers is seriously askew and off balance; and she is much less winsome and youthful a creature than his own *Small Fortune* (B.VII 92.78), engraved just a few years earlier. There, Fortuna seemed the personification of the vagaries of love;[4] the later, bigger version has shifted the implied topic from Love to Fear: she has wings like Nike, she soars over the landscape, but she is not akin to Machiavelli's Fortuna, who he says deserves to be mastered by the tyrant-type exalted by *The Prince* (Machiavelli 1950: 94).[5] The drapery in the later, larger engraving is used to desexualize the profile presentation of the body, breasts and buttocks. She is such a bizarre creation that when Aldegrever went back to the imagery more than fifty years later (B. VIII 407.143), he made the woman nubile, turned her to face the viewer, and gave her a snake to hold.[6] Dürer's middle-aged *Nemesis* is a hapax legomenon whose isolation from other pre-existing imagery leaves open the possibility that it may have been intended as humorous[7]—not lightheartedly so, but rather anticipating the vein of Erasmus' *Praise of Folly* (written 1509), in which that female personification is ironically praised as a vehicle by which to satirize a range of human foibles. Perhaps Dürer expresses—discreetly, impishly—his disrespect for Nemesis. If the consensus that the landscape is identifiable is even approximately correct, it is worth noting that she sails over a place very remote from Dürer's native land, which enhances the likelihood that she is to be viewed without real angst.[8] If we scoff at Nemesis, do we not assert free will (and thereby affirm our discretion in appropriating from the past)? Just as the early modern period is marked by a shift from the uniformly respectful attitude toward images that had earlier been the rule, so too do we find artists and thinkers behaving cheekily toward the past, appropriating at will and ignoring equally at will. The unruliness of images, like that of artists, acted as cultural catalyst.

Although Michelangelo is not known for his sense of humor, he did write poems that display some sense of irony or parody, even burlesque ones, and made many grotesque drawings; he famously included a prominent papal official in the Hell of his Sistine *Last Judgment*, an act Vasari called capricious, which was as close as he could come to criticizing the artist whose life encapsulated for him the culmination of the Florentine accomplishment. What Vasari would never acknowledge and we may always be left wondering about, is whether Michelangelo (consciously or not) mocked the Medici in that string of grinning grotesque heads along the wall of the New Sacristy (Figure 5.4). They complement the grotesque heads ornamenting the figures of the two Dukes (one of them on the back of Duke Lorenzo), as well as the leering mask of *Night*. There are more such amusing heads, quite small, in the capitals of the Laurentian Library vestibule. In the context of the Sacristy, they might be explained as a kind of reinvention of the death's head; there is at least a faint trace of the traditional exhortation Michelangelo knew well, e.g., from Masaccio's *Trinity* in Florence: "I was once as you now are; you shall be as I now am;" and possibly the taunt is intended here, subtly, for the pretentious and increasingly autocratic ruling Medici. Possibly they signal the irascible Michelangelo's rebelliousness, not against death but against the Medici, dead as well as alive. The grotesque heads in the wall play the part of an egg in the egg-and-dart pattern as used in antiquity, but they also initiate a new tradition of the amusing mascaron, a distortion of the appearances of nature for the sake of humor, but also for the sake of signaling the limitations of the ideal. Michelangelo, so dedicated to the ideal in art, allowed himself also to be slightly fascinated by the grotesque—as was also true of Leonardo.

The antique had long oppressed Michelangelo. An early work of his was presented in Rome as an antique and when it was discovered to be modern it was rejected. As a young artist, he made drawings which he faked to look old (Vasari 1991: 418, 423). Hendrik Goltzius after him, at least as described by Karel van Mander in his biography of 1604 (Van Mander 1936: 365–6), seems also to have been annoyed by those who were so bound up with the past that they could not recognize what was new and good. He circulated a fake "newly discovered" Dürer (as Alberti had presented a new dialogue by

FIGURE 5.4: Cornelis Cort after Michelangelo, *Tomb of Giuliano de' Medici*, New Sacristy, San Lorenzo, Florence, 1570, engraving. Cheekily or not, Michelangelo included numerous grotesque masks into the ornamentation of the funeral chapel for the Medici, most insistently in the frieze along the wall behind the statues. © The British Library Board.

Lucian, to prove his worth as a writer). Van Mander called it "a funny trick," and it did make others look foolish when they declared it Dürer's best print (Figure 5.5). He then issued a series of engravings in the manner of esteemed predecessors such as Lucas van Leyden or the more recent though geographically more distant Federico Barocci. Goltzius made sure he would be remembered not for his originality but for his having assimilated the recent past; he complicated cultural memory not only by intruding there, but also by preferring the recent past to the antique past. Goltzius and Michelangelo each in their own way wanted to make the present invisible, to validate the present by rendering it continuous to the point of indistinguishable from the honored past. Modern art would in that case be an extension rather than a descendent of ancient art (in Michelangelo's case) and sixteenth-century art (in Goltzius' case). It was comparably said of Parmigianino that

FIGURE 5.5: Hendrik Goltzius, *Circumcision*, 1594, engraving. Goltzius proudly asserts his ability to mimic the styles of modern artists, namely the northerner Albrecht Dürer, rather than turning only to ancient and classical models. © The British Library Board.

he wanted to be the new Raphael, and Pope Paul V pronounced of Bernini, "We hope that this youth will become the Michelangelo of his century" (Baldinucci 1966: 10); i.e., that he would relieve the Pope of any anxiety about how the present measured up against the recent past by making the present absorb that past. Artists were expected to perform cultural memory rather than to generate it. And yet, modernity was in itself a value, modernity understood sometimes as this capacity for recapture and other times as competitive with precedent. Early modernity was transitional in this important sense: it respected the past and wanted to displace it, both. In their eyes it made sense to dismantle mighty ruins for the sake of scavenging building elements for new projects.

BELIEF IN THE IDEAL AND ITS CONSEQUENCES FOR CULTURAL MEMORY

Michelangelo is reported to have said of his portraits in the New Sacristy of San Lorenzo (which ostensibly portrayed the two Medici dukes, Lorenzo, Duke of Urbino and Giuliano, Duke of Nemours, who died at a young age) that no one would remember what they looked like in 1,000 years, i.e., when his present would itself have become an antiquity.[9]

From the remoteness of Roman antiquity he had learned the opposite lesson from that Christians typically absorbed from sacred history, i.e., he had recognized the unimportance of the distant particular. Michelangelo's idealizing style neither looked particularly like works from antiquity (what could be less like a Roman portrait than either of Michelangelo's dukes, smooth-skinned and finger-obstructed visages as they are?), nor did they claim closeness to nature. Instead, he perfected a self-conscious abstractness, a freedom from any model combined with a devotion to ideal beauty, which was recognized by his contemporaries as proclaiming a modern style—albeit a modern style imbued with antique forms. Michelangelo's work allowed for antiquity to be vaguely remembered rather than revived. As Parmigianino performed Raphael and Goltzius did the same for a handful of near predecessors, and as Poussin would in the seventeenth-century perform Raphael, and Bernini would enact Michelangelo, so Michelangelo had performed antiquity, i.e., each of them presented a version of that cultural past translated for the present, a past whose cultural force was weakened by that translation. Michelangelo's style provided a visual correlate for remoteness and so freed itself from needing to imitate antiquity faithfully.

Castiglione in his *Courtier* acknowledged that he presented the court at Urbino not as it actually had been but as it might have been. Artifice in making the historical record was sanctioned, as was artifice in life, on the presumption that such artifice served an abstract sense of truth or virtue. Castiglione defended his ideal courtier by saying that it was by having an ideal in mind that one could do as well as possible in actuality. What he explained shares a certain commonality with Michelangelo's description of his sculptural practice: that he aimed to release what was already in the block, by removing all that was not part of the perfection buried within. Implicitly, any shortcoming in the final sculpture had to do with his carving rather than with the idea for the work, an idea inherent in the marble itself—and likewise, presumably the ideal he never perfectly achieved was still possible in any work left unfinished. Whereas according to traditional theological thought, history was heading toward post-Apocalyptic perfection, for Castiglione as for Michelangelo the ideal was already fully accessible, mentally. One did not study antiquity because it had been more ideal than the present, but because the ancients too had understood that the ideal was to be found in the present.

Throughout the *Courtier*, Castiglione reiterates the theme that use (referring in particular to language and dialect) is a measure of excellence that competes with any idea of authenticity located in the past, and that one ought not sentimentalize past glories like an old man nostalgic about his youth.[10] He likewise presents the argument that use does not necessarily translate well across time or place, and that the project of his interlocutors is to find an ideal that is, one might say, like the ideal of linear perspective: it is a fiction that mirrors reality (historical as well as contemporary) sufficiently well that, being seen and admired, it can affect reality. Castiglione presents an ideal that is a rarefied and distilled form of both present and past realities. He does not expect his ideal ever to be more present than it is to the interlocutors in the palace at Urbino, just as for Michelangelo, the marble contains the ideal whether or not it has yet been revealed, whether fully or partially.

The great cultural revelation inherent in this way of thinking was that one need no longer think of the past as the locus of authenticity, the past with its relics and with Jerusalem and the Holy Sepulchre as its center, as well as their being no push toward a more perfect future. The sense of contemporary flourishing of which Lorenzo Valla in the fifteenth century was as aware as Vasari in the sixteenth was not so much a revival (Renaissance was Michelet's term in the nineteenth century, it is worth reminding ourselves) as an ability to rethink the local present as incorporating within it, by art and by study, whatever was worthwhile from the past. One might say they had discovered cultural thickness and that cultural thickness was understood as a kind of perfection to which authenticity was irrelevant. When Michelangelo carved his *Pietà* of 1500, it transformed but did not renounce the medieval versions that accentuated the pain and sorrow of the occasion; it freely imitated the style of the *Apollo Belvedere*, with as much emphasis on the freedom as on the imitation; and there was no offense in the close copy made for Santa Maria dell'Anima in Rome in 1532 or for the second one made for Santo Spirito in Florence in the 1540s, both by Nanni di Baccio Bigio (Figure 5.6). The early modern period initiated the age of reproduction because the value of the ideal challenged that of authenticity. When even Giulio Romano could not tell Andrea del Sarto's copy from Raphael's own portrait of Leo X (as reported by Vasari), Raphael had become performable (i.e., as imitable as the antique) in paint, as he had been already in engraving. The issue was not authenticity but the ideal, and that exists in the mind of the person with judgment, be it Michelangelo with his block of marble, Brunelleschi with his linear perspective, or Castiglione who is

FIGURE 5.6: Nanni di Baccio Bigio, *Pietà*, Santo Spirito, Florence, 1540s, marble. Michelangelo's *Pietà* of 1500 is here essentially reproduced, demonstrating the early modern era as inaugurating the age of reproduction, a consequence of valuing the ideal more highly than the authentic.

able to imagine the perfect courtier by close study of real ones. It is judgment that Castiglione's dialogue extolls, much more than grace or *sprezzatura*. And it is because so many early modern intellectuals believed in the ideal that humanists and artists, theologians and philosophers, were able to think and share so readily across disciplines.

Dürer comparably and during the same years was seeking for ideal beauty, which he had originally thought he would find by studying antique precedent and by consulting with Italians who could teach him the laws of perspective and proportion. He ended up believing no simple codification was possible, that beauty was a complex mystery known only to God (Parshall 2013: 403). Michelangelo, who is reported to have criticized Dürer for trying to rely on actual compasses rather than incorporating his compasses in his eyes, might have been more sympathetic to Dürer's ultimate position, though it meant that Dürer fell back on following nature closely rather than seeking the ideal.

Michelangelo's work was predicated on a culture that had already well launched the vast and epochal project of taking the antique as exemplary. But whereas the humanists had no real debate about which ancient authors displayed exemplary style, Michelangelo had his own ideas about which antiques were most to be admired. The *Laocoön*, like the *Belvedere Torso* before it, allowed the mature Michelangelo to forget the *Apollo Belvedere* and its sleek, debonair ideal in favor of something that was ideal without being either effete or predictable. Like Masaccio before him, Michelangelo moved bodily proportions away from elegance and, in his case, toward something capable of expressing world-weariness. His *David* of 1504, made without knowledge of the *Laocoön*, is a figure with furrowed brow, but in a posture of relaxed confidence, a posture that has much to do with the athlete type from antiquity; the *Slaves* or *Prisoners* for the Tomb of Julius II, like the *Dukes* and the *Times of Day* for the New Sacristy, instead express anguish through their twisting postures. Even the figure symbolizing the "pensive" Lorenzo (as Vasari called him), features a rotated forearm. Michelangelo's figures do not convey the traditional idea of stable power but suggest instead disquiet. The *Dying Slave* (Louvre) is not so much an imitation of the left-hand son of *Laocoön* as a bravura challenge to that revered monument. It is a study of a similar formal problem, the waning of life in a youthful body, made in self-conscious rivalry not just with that one statuary group but the whole package of the apparently unassailable prestige of the past. That there existed a public ready to rethink the attitude toward the past is attested to in Castiglione's *Courtier*, in which recent experience is repeatedly held to be more credible than things said about the distant past, things which might or might not be true. The prestige of the ancients was already showing some signs of tarnish before Ptolemy or Galen was challenged. Michelangelo, like a good relay runner, transformed the cultural momentum of *rinascita* into modernity. He broke with the past in the very act of doing homage to it, and he utilized the humanists' definition of imitation as a creative act in order to accomplish this. The modernity he created was characterized by the selfsame troubled and restless subjectivity that we recognize in Luther, Montaigne, and Descartes.

Whether or not Michelangelo had heard enough about Platonic philosophy as a young man at the Medici table to think of his approach to the block of marble as analogous to a person's attempt to remember ideal Forms within a distracting world of sensory experience, his attitude toward the mimetic challenge was distinctive. His turn away from detailed naturalism was not akin to Raphael's foundations of classicism but an alternative to it. In some versions of the history of art Michelangelo's abnormalities have been seen as the gateway to the mistake called Mannerism, corrected in time by a Baroque return to naturalism. According to this view Michelangelo insinuated the stylistic decadence Vasari worried about even as he, too, spent less time studying nature. Instead we might consider Michelangelo's achievement to lie in having created the type of an ascetic and austere artist nevertheless capable of exploring a visual vocabulary that might readily be castigated as excessive or mannered. His relationship to his complex cultural past—the antique with its cult of power, Platonism and Petrarchism with their yearning, Christianity's guilt—was encoded in that achievement. His fellow artists tended to understand their cultural heritage more simply and to design more naturalistically.

When Hamlet arranges for a play within what we as audience know to be a play, the title—the Murder of Gonzago—sets the action in Italy, and plausibly in the ambient of the Gonzaga family of Mantua, Castiglione's native city. Francesco Maria I della Rovere, Duke of Urbino after Guidobaldo (and the man who plagued Michelangelo about the unfinished tomb of his uncle, Pope Julius II) died under circumstances deemed suspicious, and in some accounts his death is described as having been effected by his barber's poisoning him through the ear (Bullough 1935: 433–44; Thompson and Taylor 2016: 62). Art mirrors life in the play, disturbingly so, and also outside the play, since its fiction is built on what was taken to be historical fact. Shakespeare, the great borrower of plots, seems often to have started from historical legend; he was as little bound to the facts of these stories as Michelangelo was to ancient precedent or to Vitruvian theory, but he often started from stories purported to be true. Italy was for him something like what antiquity was for the Italians, that remote but real place that was distinctive, and which reveled in the passions, in eloquence, and in bold gestures. The sonnet, that poetic form which with great discipline presented the world of subjectivity, originated in Italy with Petrarch. Shakespeare's sonnets achieve a tone not of peevish discontent but of genuine regret, or foreboding, or threat, a kind of psychological darkness Petrarch never knew and which finds no resolution in a hymn to the Virgin, as Petrarch does. Unlike the bloody and conventionally heroic Fortinbras, Hamlet is a figure with a vivid and distracting interior life. Shakespeare benefitted from emulating that which was distant and believed only as myth is believed, rather than as dogma.

TREATING THE PAST LIKE A COLONIAL TERRITORY

Castiglione's dialogue balances its memorial function, preserving the memory of the court of Urbino under Duchess Elisabetta, with its polemic against obeying the rules of the past. There is a brief discussion of how an older courtier would comport himself, but the dialogue portrays all its principal participants in an ideal state of youth. Castiglione was twenty-eight at the time the dialogue is set.

His dialogue recalls Plato's *Symposium*, its fellow dialogue on love, as well as a variety of treatises on the education of a prince—one might go so far as to include Machiavelli's *Prince*, which although it was not published until four years after the *Courtier*, was being written during the same years and circulated to some extent in manuscript, as was the *Courtier*. The original dedicatee of the *Prince* was Giuliano de' Medici, who describes the perfect female counterpart to the ideal courtier in Castiglione's Book III and who is memorialized by Michelangelo opposite his cousin Lorenzo, the Duke of Urbino after Francesco Maria's death.[11] Machiavelli's text is like the verso to Castiglione's recto: instead of a description of a courtier admittedly too ideal ever to exist, Machiavelli takes as his prime example of rulership a master of perfidy and violence, Cesare Borgia, who did not succeed due to the power of Fortune over the lives of men, rather than for any hesitation about making others defer to him out of fear. A ruler may be loved, Machiavelli allows, and perhaps he implicitly alludes to Federico da Montefeltro of Urbino as he does so, but just as Castiglione's interlocutors dismiss discussing a perfect courtier not of noble birth because they want to deal with the simplest possible instance, so Machiavelli soon moves from the premise that a ruler may succeed either by exciting love or fear to a thorough examination of the latter case. The ill health of Duke Guidobaldo, like the sudden sickness of Cesare Borgia (Montaigne's lead example in his essay "Fortune is often found in Reason's train"; Montaigne 1991: 247), proves for both Castiglione and Machiavelli the power of Fortune—envious Fortune, Castiglione calls her—which can undo the good effects of precept, whether the goal is virtue or *virtù* (power).[12]

Castiglione himself in the prologue to the first book of the dialogue casually turns on its head the normal assumption that the courtier is secondary to the prince, by asserting that no matter how small the domain, if exemplary courtiers flock to a prince, that alone suffices to win him honor. The facts of Urbino under the invalid Duke Guidobaldo may have stimulated such a comment; nevertheless, the claim implies precedence for learned discourse over feats of war. Emilia Pia, lady-in-waiting to Elisabetta, cites with equal respect examples of slight topics seriously treated by Lucian and by Erasmus (Castiglione 1967: 125). Neither is named, but Castiglione's readers would have understood the implicit equivalence of past and present authors. In such respects the book asserts its fundamental modernity, its reluctance to hold the past in higher prestige than the present and its willingness to disagree with what had previously been taken for granted. Castiglione's interlocutors allow that antiquity itself provides examples of how rules can lead us astray, as in the case of Torquatus' execution of his son (Castiglione 1967: 132), so direly punished for breaking a rule, despite good intentions and good effect. When a Renaissance author cites an antique example as an anti-example, this is a clear sign that cultural memory is unsettled.[13]

Not only may the past not be as ideal as we remember, but memory itself is inadequate to the task of preserving the past, the dialogue implies. For Castiglione purports to record the conversations held over four evenings when he was not present, as told to him by an unspecified person who had been there. Yet he describes how on the second day, when the prefect (the seventeen-year-old Francesco Maria), lately arrived, asks to be told what had been discussed the previous evening, no one was able accurately to recall. Thereby Castiglione cagily acknowledges that his reconstruction of these evenings at the court of Urbino is a fabrication.

When Pietro Bembo weighs in on the question of friendship, he demonstrates that he has the standard citations of ancient friendship at his fingertips, but then says that for his own part, he would never trust a friend as another self (Castiglione 1967: 137–8). It is a staggeringly unexpected move, this rejection of precedent and of trust in favor of suspicion. Malice or envy or inconstancy will eventually mar any friendship however dear, "for there are so many concealed places and recesses in our minds that it is humanly impossible to discover and judge the pretenses hidden there." He thereby implicitly rejects Cicero's valuing of his friend Atticus as his alter ego; more than that, he rejects belief in an ideal world, though not necessarily the resolution to act as though one believed in it.

Courtiers are like caged birds, Castiglione's interlocutor declares at one point, unable to leave their lord (Castiglione 1967: 130). Their *grazia*, like the license Vasari accords artists of his third period, must be understood in the context of all that confines them (Emison 2012, see also Mac Carthy 2020: 50–75). Part of that is precedent, which establishes decorum, a sense of what is right that can be as culturally specific as dialect. In a typically witty convolution, Castiglione invokes the past to license forgetting the past, by invoking the example of Themistocles, who prized "the secret of forgetfulness," i.e., being able to forget selectively (Castiglione 1967: 108). But license is also the quality for which Erasmus excoriated the followers of Luther: "Those who are naturally prone to license easily snatch an excuse out of Luther's books; more modest folk are left between the devil and the deep sea" (Erasmus 1988: 47, writing in 1522 to Pirckheimer).

License was a quality much identified with Michelangelo and his evident freedom from the rules of the ancients.[14] In architecture in particular, he created a modern idiom that declared both dependence on the ancients and independence. He modified the ancient architectural forms and composed with them as though he had been able to recoup the lost momentum of ancient architects; he created walls and spaces unlike any seen before and yet inextricable from cultural memory.

He made it plain to see that the cultural accomplishments of the Greco-Roman tradition could be fully assimilated, so that instead of Petrarch's model whereby cultural imitation mimicked the resemblance between one generation and another, the moderns might think of themselves as the new imperialists, exploiting the past at will—and because the past was pagan, without compunction.

Michelangelo was willing to break any rule and any convention; he admired the *Belvedere Torso* when no one else did and he instantiated the oval in the design of the Campidoglio pavement and pedestal. His friend and biographer Ascanio Condivi tells us that he could ever hear the warning words of the radical preacher Savonarola echoing in his head (Condivi 1999: 105). Not without reason does Vasari sound genuinely worried about Michelangelo's artistic license, as the Inquisition would be later about the relatively mild-mannered Veronese's. Horace's much-developed idea that poetry and painting had creative license was potentially disruptive, and that mixed with lingering affiliation to Savonarola even more so. The *Last Judgment* as painted by Michelangelo is still censored. License might be either admired or feared; it was, after all, the ruler's license that made him either loved or feared.

Michelangelo, whose oeuvre had made remembering antiquity less imperative, was himself being selectively committed to oblivion even before he died, his nudes covered up on the Sistine altar wall. Soon his tomb, adorned with Vasari's bombastic creation rather than his own *Deposition* (now in the Museo dell'Opera del Duomo, Florence), appropriated his memory for the glorification of Cosimo's ducal and declining Florence. Meanwhile, the work to which he had dedicated his old age, completing the rebuilding of St. Peter's, was drastically rethought and his plans for a centralized basilica, the proper base for his dome, abandoned.

When Luther visited Rome in 1510–11 and called it Babylon, he would have seen the old basilica in ruins with Bramante's new one just starting to rise around it, a visible embodiment of the rivalry between authenticity and a new grandeur. For the next hundred years, anyone visiting Rome would have witnessed the spectacle of the gradual obliteration of European Christianity's holiest building (Figure 5.7). Drawings show the Tiburio, the small building designed by Bramante to protect the altar area during the construction works, built in 1513 and dismantled in 1592 (Bosman 2004: 105–18), looking to our eyes rather like what a fallout shelter might look after a catastrophic bomb. It sits there as a little bastion of modern classicism amidst the early Christian ruins. Eventually it too was replaced by the Baroque basilica and its giant piazza, an obelisk—like an ancient battlefield trophy—at the center. The new basilica treated the past (and not only the pagan past) like a colonial territory, now subdued. The inscription of 1612 across the entablature of the façade, at its center section, jutting forward, proclaimed "PAULUS V BORGHESIUS ROMANUS"—the very man who had decided that Bernini would be his Michelangelo.

FIGURE 5.7: Maerten van Heemskerck, *Interior of the Basilica of St. Peter's*, Staatliche Museen, Berlin, c. 1532–6, pen and ink and wash. The destruction of the early Christian basilica of St. Peter's, a process here recorded by an artist from Haarlem, was an astonishingly bold assertion of the right to appropriate cultural memory.

FIGURE 5.8: Anonymous, *Trinity*, Collezioni Comunali d'Arte, Bologna, c. 1540–60, oil painting. Early modern artists tried to visualize what was important to their contemporaries, and it was not only the famous artists who produced images that demanded attention, in this case an image that was at once familiar and new, theologically motivated and provocative.

Early modern Europe was better read, more musical, and had a significantly more developed visual culture than its predecessors. A painting in Bologna of the *Trinity* has precedents in the most traditional icons as well as in a few other tricepahlic images, but it offers the viewer an experience of great interest both artistically and theologically (Figure 5.8).[15] Early modern culture had made a new place for works of art and for artists as the companions of intellectuals rather than only as the servants of rulers. It could see itself in many objects, not only the increasingly available mirrors. Its artists were students of nature, starting down the path that scientists would soon co-opt: they thought about underlying structures, about the vision of infinite space, about how light helps us to understand what we see. Artists challenged the paradigms of ancient knowledge before anyone else, crossing the threshold between admiration and appropriation with nonchalance, in part because so much of their place in society was anchored in the religious role of visual art. Raphael, for example, used the pose of the *Apollo Belvedere* for the Christ Child (*Madonna of the Goldfinch*, Uffizi, 1506) and felt presumably that he had honored both.

The importance that the concept of free will had for humanists may have owed a great deal to the evolving sense of historical dynamics, of not feeling oppressed by the past and of feeling able to reach out to posterity. Modernity had become an important concept, and the moderns were themselves intent upon being remembered. At the end of the fifteenth century a plaque was put up to mark the house in Ferrara at which Cardinal Bessarion had stayed during the Council between the Eastern Orthodox and the Roman churches, a plaque with an inscription in Roman lettering and his profile portrait. One lesson learned from antiquity was how to create cultural memory.

Yet even as philosophers, theorists, and artists were growing more open to Galileo's idea of the "book of nature" which one read and interpreted in combination with revered and carefully revised texts, they were also growing increasingly mystified by the depths of their own individual minds and motivations. They were realizing that, even as knowledge increased, so did the shortfalls of reason, shortfalls as likely to be demarcated by laughter as by reverence for things mystical. Theologians and rulers found themselves less and less able to curb multiple impulses toward mockery, satire, and general irreverence. The past—that traditional source of authority—had been to some extent neutered by the advance of pride in a modern sensibility, on an individual and civic, and sometimes now also on a national level.

If, as Stephen Clucas (2015) has argued, the early modern period produced a blurring of the distinctions among perception, imagination, and cognition, this was partly due to the epochal change in the cultural role of the visual arts, which had morphed from an ancillary function in religion and politics to becoming a pillar in the public understanding of cultural hegemony, as well as playing a vital role in the thought of philosophers, historians, and theologians: witness even Savonarola readily turning to the visual arts when he wanted a metaphor. By the close of our period, the past could no longer be remembered apart from the visions of modern artists.

CHAPTER SIX

High Culture and Popular Culture: Memory, Custom and Landscape

NICOLA WHYTE

Writing in the 1970s, Peter Burke ([1978] 1994: xiii) defined culture as "a system of shared meanings, attitudes and values, and the symbolic forms (performances, artifacts) in which they are expressed or embodied." At the time of writing, Burke was particularly interested in elucidating the processes of cultural change in Europe between the sixteenth and eighteenth centuries. He argued that at the beginning of the period, popular culture was everyone's culture, however increasing polarization between the "high" culture of the learned elite and the popular culture of ordinary people occurred over the course of the period. Historians have since found elements of this cultural division in a number of themes and processes including the rise of literacy and demise of oral culture; the separation of the pious from the ungodly; the growth of agrarian capitalism and dissolution of customary culture; and shift from highly localized and heterogeneous cultural practices toward a national historical consciousness and cultural identity. In more recent years, however, there has been a growing concern to dismantle unhelpful binary classifications in order to better understand the complex web of values, beliefs, and community ties that drew people together across rank and status. In revealing the inadequacies of elite/popular categorizations, not least the problems of reaching adequate definitions of such broad social classifications, this body of work invites readers to think about the ways social values and interests overlapped and intersected, suggesting greater complexity in the ways social identities were formed, articulated, and responded to by others. As Tim Harris argues, rather than viewing culture as a static structure, we should consider it a process in order to allow for the possibility of adaptation and reinvention in the face of change (Harris 1995: 23). In understanding culture as a mutable process, historians have since opened up debate to consider appropriations, transformations, and above all diversity in the ways various cultures and subcultures came into being (Burke 1989; Scribner 1989; Harris 1995).

In foregrounding cultural interactions and interconnections, we are also prompted to consider the drivers of change over time, and whether historical change was imposed upon local societies through external "elite" forces, the campaigns for the reformation of manners for example, or the enclosure of the commons by a wealthy minority of landowners; or whether the momentum for change occurred from within local societies and through the dynamic interplay of social allegiances and cultural expectations that cut across rank and status. These are big questions with significant ramifications for thinking about causation and agency in history. Overarching models of historical change tend to overlook the complexity and contingency of social and cultural relations as they were played out at the micro-level; while the reverse focus can lead to a burden of multiplicity and plurality, with historians dealing with a myriad of cultural perspectives and social aspirations. As no one group (nor locality) can be reduced to a single set of determinants, it is important to consider how cultural meanings and values were reproduced through constant rearrangement, adaptation, and fusion of their constituent elements. To understand cultural change, therefore, is to move beyond straightforward binary oppositions which in turn requires careful consideration of the spatial scale of analysis we are to work with. The region has offered historians one scale, whether at the level of the early modern "pays" or "country," or emergent nation state (Woolf 2003). However, the sheer complexity of local differences cautions against drawing boundaries around regional "types" that often results in making links which artificially tie social, economic, and cultural conditions and relationships together. Rather than necessarily striving for the neatness of closure, our interest here is to investigate memories and experiences situated in places and landscapes that are by their nature fragmentary. This requires a micro-scale approach, and though the archival materials employed in the following discussion are from England and Wales, it is hoped that readers will find comparisons with other European localities.

Historians have long been interested in the findings of anthropological research in providing theories and methodologies for approaching early modern experiences and cultural practices from a micro-historical perspective (Darnton 1984). In Sigurður Magnússon's (2016: 190) words, it is by revealing "the endless contradictions, incongruities, oddities and unmotivated events that characterize people's daily lives" that complicates overarching explanations of historical change. Magnússon is interested in developing a micro-historical approach and what he terms the "singularization of history," by aiming to address the past in all its diversity and multivocality, "without becoming bogged down in predetermined categories of the grand narratives" (Magnússon 2003: 701–35; and 2016: 190). His decontextualizing approach may prompt criticism from some, and yet there is a great deal to be taken from this and other work interested in exposing traditional historiographical approaches and assumptions. In starting with the evidence itself, and exploring instances that do not necessarily fit comfortably within the contextual frameworks provided by conventional historical questions, we find a useful way of approaching our topic of focus here. Investigations of memory are necessarily about multiplicity and plurality, contradictions and peculiarities that are revealing of contemporary knowledge, experiences, and motivations. It is by exploring the work of memory and the uses of the past among elite and non-elite alike that we can piece together points of connection and interaction, which can serve to modify and nuance expectations of historical change that are often shaped by the anticipation of modernity. In this regard, Judith Pollmann's and Erika Kuijpers' discussion of memory and historiography offers a useful critique of modernization theory. They expose the assumptions contained in the literature on memory and modernity as being categorically different to the pre-modern past by showing how in attempting to make sense of the present, contemporaries purposefully drew upon past experiences and historical analogies (Pollmann and Kuijpers 2013; Pollman 2017). Episodes of apparent rupture and transformation identified by historians may have been rather more muted for contemporaries, for whom change was a constant in their day-to-day lives.

From the perspective of the everyday we can begin to understand the ways ordinary people were active creators of their own social and cultural identities. In Bob Scribner's (1989: 185) words: "to understand processes of cultural differentiation, modification, domination or subordination, we need to explore more carefully certain key areas of life which served as loci of cultural formation." In this he includes the acquisition of practical life-skills, the production of food, formal and informal education, experience, the role of the household and institutions such as the church and arenas of local governance. There is yet another social dynamic to be folded into the mix, and that is the activity of sharing knowledge and memories and the processes whereby evidence of the past was actively sought to inform cultural practices and social relationships in the present. Just as historians drawing on the research of cultural anthropologists like Clifford Geertz (1973), have shown how the past entered festivals and ceremonies through ritual performances, we can turn to more recent anthropological and archaeological works to think through the evidence for everyday routine practices which might also be described as ritualized (Hendon 2010). Rituals performed on special occasions and routinized, customary practices performed in everyday life produced communities of learning through shared practices, and a common sense of the past. Small-scale everyday resistances, whether through the appropriation or adaptation of what was believed to have come before, had the potential to produce subtle but no less important changes to the ways people lived their day-to-day lives. By moving away from considering top-down renderings of the past, and turning instead to an embedded understanding of memory as situated in ordinary everyday practices we can explore the complex entanglement of elite and non-elite attitudes toward the past in the making of local memory cultures.

To understand culture as practice, rather than as a thing, necessitates consideration of the ways in which social interactions and cultural beliefs were situated in ordinary landscapes and places. Physical contexts and social settings have long been recognized, particularly for the ways in which physical space structures events, whether in church, the alehouse, or the piazza (Burke [1978] 1994: 111–2). With this in mind, we can turn to the role of memory and the uses of the past as an important dimension in the formation of social and cultural identities. The following discussion seeks to do this by bringing into focus the concept of landscape in order to reach an understanding of memory as not only communicated through language and discourse, but as embedded in everyday material and temporal practices (Hendon 2010: 27).

LANDSCAPE AND MEMORY

While the concept of landscape is hugely significant across a number of disciplines—archaeology, anthropology, cultural geography—few social historians have taken seriously the possibility of pursuing landscape as a methodological and theoretical framework for further research (see Whyte 2009; Walsham 2011; Wood 2013a). More typically, they have turned to theories of space for inspiration. This work has resulted in finely grained and compelling accounts of the social production of space in defining class and gender relations, the worlds of work and domesticity, religious cultures, local political structures, and the spatial mediations and limitations of power in everyday life (Coster and Spicer 2005; Stock 2015). It is my contention that these spatial considerations might be usefully developed by drawing on current research on the themes of temporality, materiality, and memory in landscape studies. In Tim Ingold's (2000: 192) words, "with space, meanings are attached to the world, with the landscape they are gathered from it." Questions of landscape and temporality complement recent theorizations of space, by bringing into focus contemporary engagements with the landscape and how the physical evidence of the activities of past generations was incorporated in the production and reproduction of social and cultural relationships in the present (Whyte 2015, 2018). Yet more might be done to align both areas of research on memory and spatiality as a way to further explore the interactions and interconnections of the collections of people living in rural societies.

Though we might take issue with binary accounts of elite/non-elite culture, landscape history has often developed along similar lines with the material landscapes of wealthy elites providing evidence of the withdrawal—culturally and spatially—of landowners and affluent tenants from village life. Modern appreciations of landscape emerged in the eighteenth century, as an aesthetic and ideological understanding of property, ownership and improvement (Williamson 1995; Tarlow 2007). From this perspective, landscapes were re-written by enclosure, privatization, and capitalism, which erased the traces of former customary regimes, and symbolized the rational, civilized, improved culture of "polite" society. Yet the extent to which the past was entirely severed from the present, with landowners re-designing the land without recourse to what had gone before, is not as clear as it might at first appear. Of the estate maps surviving in English county record offices, at least, the imagery suggests landowners remained interested in the past histories of their estates, as indicated in the recording of minor names, places, landscape features, old boundary marks, and structures surviving from the pre-Reformation and even earlier pasts. More than a matter of antiquarian interest, the physical evidence of the past provided an important and necessary connection linking estate owners to their forebears (Figure 6.1). It was not simply a matter of wiping the slate clean in the name of progress. The re-modeled "improved" landscapes depicted by professional surveyors depicted old, apparently redundant landmarks and standing structures, for they gave structure and authenticity to the organization of landscapes in the present.

Archaeologists and anthropologists have long been concerned to break down, often implicit, assumptions that landscapes provide neutral backdrops to cultural values and social action. There has been a particular concern to look beyond the idea that landscapes can be read as objects of study by experts who have acquired the skills to decipher the chronology of landscape change (Bender 1999). Landscapes are the accumulated traces of human activities surviving from multiple pasts. Just as archaeologists have shown for earlier epochs, the relics of the past continued to be appropriated and re-used in the early modern period for a number of reasons far removed from their original purpose (Bender 1998; Bradley 2002). In Ingold's words: "To perceive the landscape is therefore to carry out an act of remembrance, and remembering is not so much a matter of calling up an internal image, stored in the mind, as of engaging perceptually with an environment that is itself pregnant with the past" (2000: 189). The tangible presence of old, crumbling, and weathered features often originating in a time beyond the lifespan of anyone living, connected the lives and actions of former generations of inhabitants to the present. Over the course of our period of focus, the material traces of the past in the landscape mattered to tenants, commoners, and wealthy landlords alike.

Court deposition evidence offers invaluable insights into the ways people remembered and experienced the landscapes around them, and the ways in which old monuments and landmarks were incorporated into memory practices. For example, during litigation proceedings concerning the Manor of Lledwigan (Anglesey, Wales) at the turn of the seventeenth century, local people were called to give account of the history of the landscape in question based on their knowledge and experience. The cause of contention

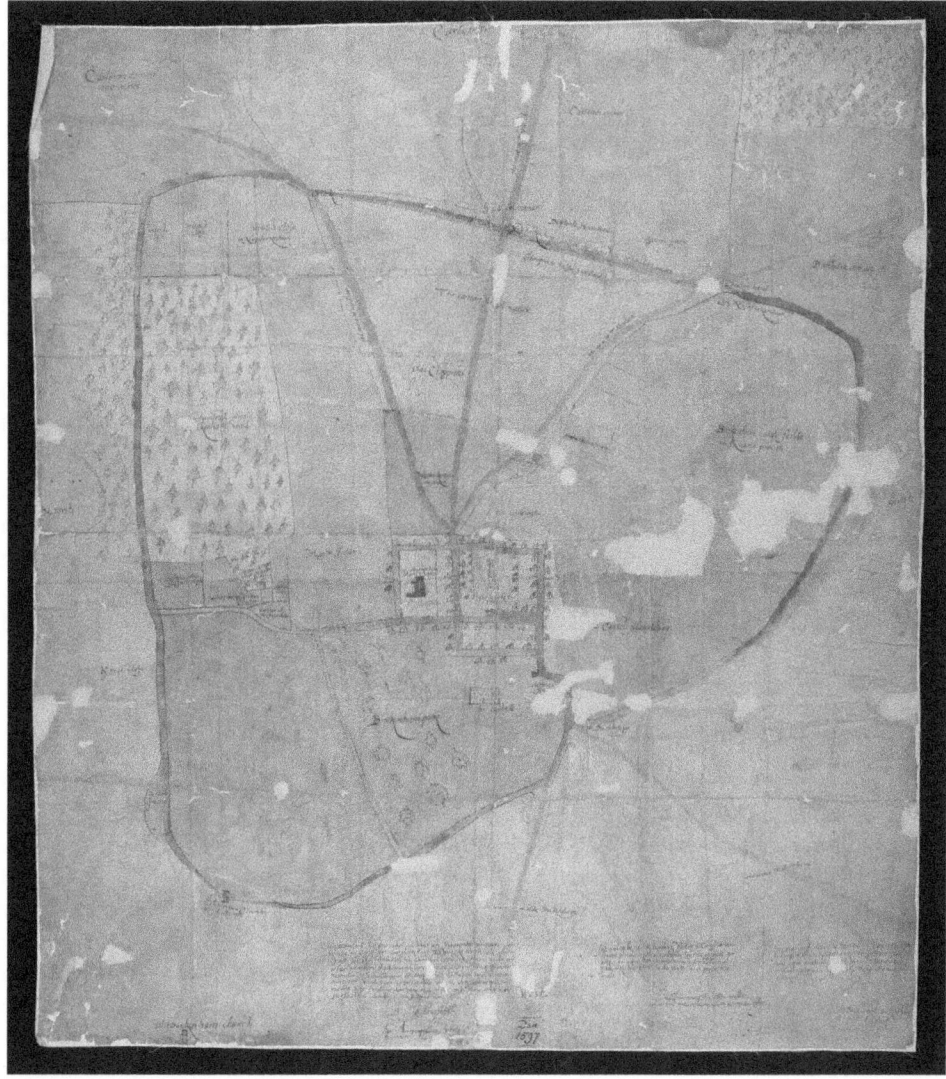

FIGURE 6.1: Map of New Buckenham (Norfolk, England) dating to 1597, offering an insight into elite responses to the material remains of the past in the landscape. New Buckenham castle and deer park are shown, the village, market cross, and church, with special attention evidently being given to depicting the old perambulation route and boundary marks especially those demarcating "the common in variance" (top). The map can be interpreted as celebrating manorial longevity and proprietorship over land, resources, and local society. Yet, it also reveals the interactions of elite culture and popular culture in the formations of landscape and memory. Courtesy of the Norfolk Record Office, NRO, MC22/11.

concerned the demarcation of common land between the neighboring townships of "Skeiviog" and "Berow," and access rights to graze livestock, gather hay for overwintering animals, and digging turves for fuel. The history of the landscape was encapsulated in the oral testimonies of deponents, who described how long-term physical changes to the common had been caused since the flow of the River Keveny was redirected, affecting them, their household economies, and local social relations. Deponents reported that during the time of Henry VIII, the commoners agreed to cut a mere or boundary ditch across the common to soothe tensions arising between the neighboring townships. Some ten years later, the landscape was altered again when the plaintiff's father instructed the diversion of the river from its ancient, meandering course and into the boundary ditch. Deponents spoke about "the marks and precinct" of the old river "as yet is to be seen about 30 roods from the arable lands of Lledwigan." Sixty-year-old laborer Thomas Geffrey, remembered being with the village elders when the story of the old river was explained to him: when "in the company of diverse old men long ago they passed over some water and over some lower ground where the precinct of a river seemed to be [he] did enquire the cause thereof by way of talk. And the same old men told him in these words: you do marvel at it for the River of Keveny heretofore had his course this way until it was diverted."[1] Thomas Geffrey's testimony reveals both the social and material contexts of memory practices. The political economy of memory worked to contest local histories of landscape, which drew upon everyday experiences, talking, and remembering with others, and interpreting the physical traces of the past on the ground. Each generation lived in a landscape shaped and modified by the activities of previous generations, which demanded interpretation, even neglect can be viewed as a deliberate act of misremembering and forgetting. An understanding of the relationship between landscape and society in the early modern period, requires detailed consideration of the material contexts and meanings of custom.

CUSTOM AND PRACTICE

Early modernists have explored the multiple, often ambiguous ways in which power was claimed and negotiated within local societies. Among these studies, the functions of oral memory and the uses of the past in plebeian political culture have been highlighted, with particularly illuminating studies focusing on the contemporary concepts of custom and right (Wood 1997, 1999; Pollmann 2017: 73–92). It is well attested that oral memory was highly valued both in local customary culture, and the official arena of the early modern law courts (Wood 1999; Fox 2000; Houston 2016). Across Europe, customs and rights structured local use rights to land and resources, and to ensure continuity between past and present, from one generation to the next. In the sixteenth century, a Flemish jurist defined custom as "unwritten law, that originates in usage and continuous acts of successors and practitioners, used publicly without being challenged by the greatest majority of people, for such a long time that it can be considered a custom" (cited in Pollmann 2017: 76). Although varying from place to place, some common themes emerge: customs were to be reasonable and equitable, and in continuous usage since before anyone could remember. Customs were not always codified in written form, but were reliant on oral memory and practice. This created a necessarily flexible and adaptable system whereby customs could be adjusted to suit changing needs and circumstances, caused by inclement weather for example, but it also meant customs came under sustained scrutiny and were open to question and manipulation, resulting in litigation in some places.

A well-established literature exists on the politics of custom and the value contemporaries placed on the spoken word as credible evidence before the law courts in the sixteenth and seventeenth centuries. Historians have shown the importance of understanding collective memory in solidifying a common sense of identity among plebeian groups. Strongly held beliefs in the validity of custom brought people together in defense of rights and privileges they claimed to be held in common (Thompson 1991; Wood 1997, 2013a). In this threading together of memories, a collective sense of the past was summoned against the deleterious actions of wealthy elites accused of dismantling customary rights in the pursuit of status and profit. Court deposition evidence reveals how the past was purposefully narrated to portray a lost golden age defined by a harmonious hierarchical order, in which everyone knew their place according to the principles of rights and duties, and patronage and deference (Wood 2013b). Prescription, practice, and memory were called upon in defense of local, time-honored systems of production in order for a collective stand to be made against "improving" landowners and affluent tenants. For our purposes, two significant insights emerge from the research on customary law. Firstly, the past provided a powerful mobilizing resource in strategies of resistance among the lower orders, and secondly, local societies took particular care in maintaining shared practices of remembering.

One way of interpreting the documentary record is to consider how knowledge and memories made through customs, rituals, and everyday practices led to meanings being attached to the landscape. It follows that the constituent marks of the landscape were transformed into a text that could be read as a repository of memory and series of reference points. However, taking seriously the notion that landscape and materiality matter in memory work, we might reconsider this analytical order by foregrounding the ways in which people drew meaning from the physical evidence of the actions of past generations. The landscape was not simply a store of memories. Memories were made and remade through embodied practices, daily movements through the landscape, and through deliberate observance of material markers. It is the ongoing recognition and incorporation of features such as trees, wells, pits, stones, posts, old wayside crosses, and earthworks, that gave context and coherence to customary practices (Whyte 2007, 2009, 2013). Paul Connerton's concept of "incorporated practices" is particularly useful for opening up the possibility for substitutions and transformations in the ways people remembered and drew meaning from the landscapes they inhabited (Connerton 1989; Ingold 2000: 193). This conceptualization moves us away from the idea of landscape as a static representation of social and cultural values, toward a realization of the multiple and diverse ways in which people drew meanings gathered from the worlds in which they lived. Following Ingold, to assume that meanings are inherited and worlds are made before they are lived in, is an oversimplification of the ways people dwell in the landscape, how they create meaning and give context to everyday practices in the present (Ingold 2000: 199).

Returning to the court proceedings from Anglesey, recourse to the physical evidence of the past gave material context to local memories, indeed for Thomas Geffrey the earthwork imprint of the old river was a wonder to behold. Meanings were not self-evident, they were remembered through the experience of being in and walking through the landscape often in company with others, when the important things to remember were told to those gathered to listen. The evidence shows nothing was to be taken for granted, mnemonics were not simply fixed but needed constant recognition and renewal. In Emma Blake's cautionary words, "memory and tradition alone do not preserve an object's identity, it is the ongoing incorporation of that object into routinized practices that generates meaning" (2007). The disparate character of local disputes reveals the complex and contingent processes of landscape and social change and difficulty of compartmentalizing social and economic activities as either elite (enclosure and improvement) or plebeian (custom). In the Manor of Lledwigan, neighbors agreed to make a boundary ditch across the common, and the ensuing complaints were not about enclosure but the flooding caused by the diversion of the river and diminishment of customary ways of life caused by subsequent changes to the local ecology and landscape. People were well aware that landscapes constantly changed whether due to natural or human processes, and in turn weight was given to the constancy of memory, sustained by handing on knowledge from old to young. For the inhabitants of the Manor of Lledwigan, it was important to remember the course of the old river, for its imprint on the ground provided tangible evidence of an earlier configuration of landscape and social relations.

The significance of landmarks and monuments in the work of memory is of course an established topic of discussion and debate across disciplines. From this literature, a number of themes emerge including a recognition of the dynamic interplay of official and unofficial meanings and practices, and inadequacy of assuming that monuments simply fix meaning in the landscape (Savage 2009; Bender 1998). Monuments and memorials are usually erected in order to remember a particular event or individual, and yet their meanings and associations are unstable, influenced over time by shifting cultural practices, political agendas, and societal expectations. Understanding the "afterlives" or biographies of monuments and landmarks invites consideration not only of the purposefully constructed memorial, monument, or building intended by its makers to prompt engagement with a particular past as a lesson for the future, but also the ways in which existing features were incorporated within memory practices over time (for example, Bradley 2002). Such investigations raise important questions on the themes of change and continuity, and processes of destruction and preservation in the landscape. This was not merely the product of an oral customary culture held onto by lower sorts of people, but rather old landmarks were points of connection in the landscape where various meanings and interests intersected.

These issues are illustrated in another collection of depositions dating to the 1590s, concerning a tract of intercommon claimed by the inhabitants of New Buckenham and Carlton (Norfolk, England). Shared by neighboring parishes and manors the common was exploited for grazing livestock, gathering fuel, digging for clay and stone, which was apparently used to build the parish church. These patterns of interconnectivity between different sites and places are important for understanding the temporal meanings of landscape expressed through material practices and imagined associations, such as the customary place where stone was quarried for local building for example. In attempting to prove the boundary across the tract of open common grazing land, local inhabitants and manorial lords sought to claim the antiquity of various features, as having existed since time out of mind.[2] One feature, an earthwork mound, was reported to be particularly contentious with both sides insisting upon very different origins for the feature. The villagers from Carlton claimed it was known as Windmill Hill, and therefore not of particular note, but their neighbors from New Buckenham claimed it was known as Haugh Head and had served as the open-air meeting place of the hundred court, which served to administer the law and keep the peace in the medieval period. Described as a "grassy knoll," the etymology of Haugh Head, suggests a burial mound of prehistoric or Saxon origin (Figure 6.2) (Lawson, Martin, and Priddy 1981).

Recognized as ancient and in that sense permanent landmarks, evidence shows that it was not unusual for barrows and other prehistoric features to be incorporated in the organization of customary landscapes in the early modern period (Whyte 2009). For the inhabitants of New Buckenham, the authenticity of Haugh Head as an ancient boundary

FIGURE 6.2: An example of a burial mound, in this case of Anglo-Saxon date, at Sutton Hoo, Suffolk (England).

mark of the common, was given further credibility through the memory of its functions as a meeting place of the Hundred court. John Sharping, a glover of sixty-seven years, remembered his grandfather seeing the Hundred court meet at Haugh Head, on the boundary of Shropham Half Hundred.[3] Others laid claim to its local significance, remembering the route of the perambulation of the bounds. Thomas Neave, a seventy-six-year-old yeoman, recalled as a boy walking to "Buckenham Haugh" on the third day of Rogation week. Peter Cullyer, a shoemaker aged sixty-six, and Peter Underwood, a sixty-nine-year-old mason, both living in New Buckenham, recalled the Rogationtide procession of the bounds stopping to drink beer at Haugh Head, which as they remembered marked the boundary of the common (Figure 6.3).[4]

Place names and the features to which they referred, might typically be overlooked as seemingly prosaic and insignificant in charting historical processes of change. Yet, in the production and reproduction of customary landscapes, the physical identifiers of the past provided temporal anchors in the organization of social memories. Place names did not merely fix or encode meanings in the landscape. Practices of naming, and the continuity of certain names, evolved from socially embedded memories made over time during routine activities and also official rituals. In another example from Cambridgeshire (England), the inhabitants of Swaffham Prior knew the boundary bank and ditch across their common as the Reach Ditch, while their neighbors from Burwell claimed it was known as Burwell Ditch.[5] There are numerous other examples of boundary features being referred to by different names (Whyte 2009, 2013). With names being a deliberate matter of contention, a politics of "place naming" existed within and between village communities. In New Buckenham, an earthwork mound would have certainly provided a convenient location for erecting a windmill, making it possible that both sides of the dispute offered

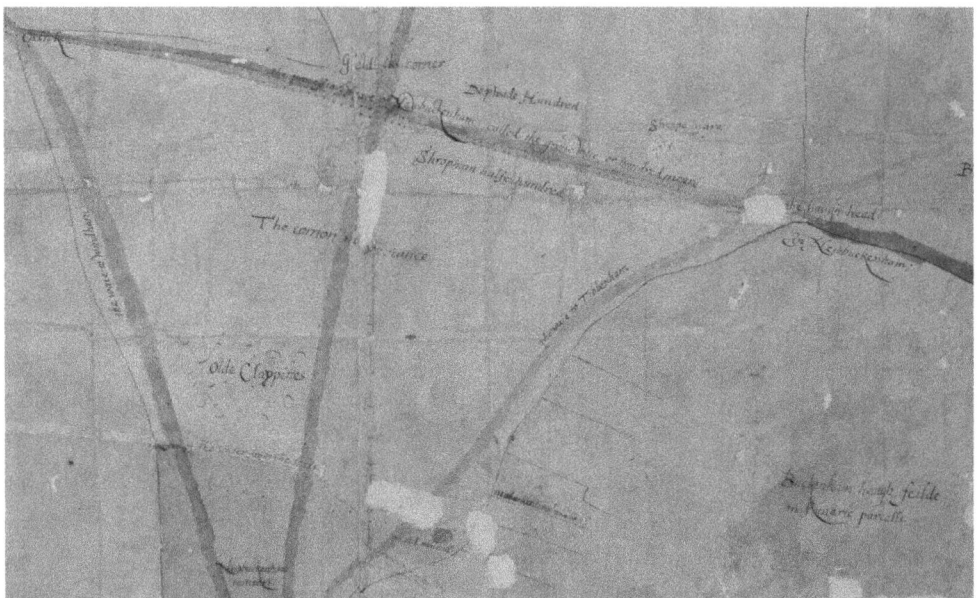

FIGURE 6.3: Detail of the 1597 New Buckenham map showing the "the procession waie of New Buckehnam called the greene waie or hundred meare" and boundary features in question. The feature at Haugh Head (top right) has unfortunately been erased, but its name is still discernible as the boundary mark claimed by New Buckenham. Conversely, the inhabitants of Carlton claimed the "Old Mill Hill" (bottom, right) as the boundary mark of their common. Courtesy of the Norfolk Record Office, NRO, MC 22/11.

up plausible place names. However, each name carried different connotations and were weighted differently before the courts. As an ancient meeting place and administrative boundary mark, Haugh Head suggested longevity and permanence in the landscape. In attempting to claim the authority of the past, place names were vital in either authenticating or bringing discredit to the claims to customs and rights being made in the present.

HOUSEHOLD MEMORIES

Experts in the field of cognition and memory have discussed, how "we have learned (both culturally and individually) to integrate our relatively vulnerable and permeable biological memory with more stable external scaffolding" (Sutton, Harriss, and Barnier 2010). Of particular interest here is how the foundations of this scaffolding were formed within the social arena of the household. Building on Burke's concept of multiple memory communities, Julia Hendon has explored the functions of the household as a memory community, in which individual experiences and memories were shared through everyday practices (Burke 1989; Hendon 2010: 60). This is not to assume households were bounded and atomized groupings, rather they formed part of a community of practice, with each household aware of their mutual responsibility to nourish and sustain the conditions of local life. These ideas connect with contemporary ideals of neighborliness, and awareness among rural communities that they were held together through collaborative, albeit frequently strained, social and cultural relationships (Wrightson

1996, 2005; Rodgers et al. 2011; De Moor 2008). The failure to maintain good practice and order was all too evident in the material traces of abandoned fields, denuded commons and deserted settlements (Dyer and Jones 2010). By examining the ways everyday practices and patterns of remembrance were situated in the physical landscapes in which people lived and learned, we can also explore the material and temporal contexts of households as communities of practice. Though, as others have pointed out, there are similarities and overlap in the ways people narrated the past through the construction of social memory (Wood 1997, 2013a), the depositions are often highly revealing of individual and personal experience in the construction of household identities.

Social historians have shown how the elderly, especially men, were purposefully sought during litigation proceedings for their knowledge of local customary law (Wood 1997). As the custodians of memory, their authority could override socio-economic standing, thus laborer Thomas Geffrey was called to give evidence in the Lledwigan case. The evidence suggests that it was as children that boys and girls were considered the future curators of local knowledge. Children learned about time and place through memory-sharing practices within the social arena of the household and through their own applied knowledge of working in the landscape. Knowledge was handed on from parents to children, and from grandparents to grandchildren. In the case concerning "Reach Ditch" in Swaffham Prior, sixty-year-old Elisabeth Edwards of Burwell referred to the feature as "Burwell Ditch," confirming that she knew the correct course of the boundary as she tended to her father's sheep flock on the common when she was eight or ten years old. He instructed her not to allow the sheep to graze the ditch and bank.[6] Among the deponents called to give evidence in New Buckenham, eighty-four-year-old widow Cicely Hunford of neighboring Carlton Rode, described to the court how she heard her grandfather confirm that the wife of one Overton, an inhabitant of New Buckenham and bailiff to the lord of the manor, confessed that her husband attempted to defraud Carlton of their common by forging "a writing" describing the boundary. The story handed on from grandfather to granddaughter was made all the more memorable with details of how Overton made the forged document look old by hanging it in the smoke above the fire place.[7] As Pollmann notes, memories are molded by the memories of the people around us, and the cultural settings in which they are remembered (Fentress and Wickham 1992; Pollmann 2017: 3).

Eviatar Zerubavel (1997) describes this as mnemonic socialization that is "a subtle process that usually happens rather tacitly; listening to a family member recount a shared experience, for example, implicitly teaches one what is considered memorable and what one can actually forget" (cited in Misztal 2003: 15). Children and new members to the group were thus introduced to and familiarized with what was important to remember. But importantly, such knowledge was situated in local and familiar landscapes. The Reach Ditch and the boundary features separating New Buckenham from Carlton were encountered on a daily basis, especially by children and young women who were often given the task of tending to livestock on the commons (Capp 2003; Whyte 2011). It was their responsibility to know where they could graze stock and gather fuel, and where they might not, in predominately open landscapes with few landmark features. Boundaries were interpreted by sight, and by the distance walked from one boundary mark to the next. In other words, boundaries were made and remembered through embodied practices. Even when a person had moved away from their place of birth they might still be called upon as witnesses in disputes, for it was expected that as children they would have been well taught to know and to remember the names and places that mattered to their families and households. Among the deponents called as witnesses during the New Buckenham dispute, sixty-six-year-old yeoman Thomas Rutland, from Wymondham (some eight miles away) knew the boundary of the common, for he accompanied "his father in the perambulation when he was very young his father told him that the green way was the true & ancient perambulation of New Buckenham. And his [. . .] father told him also that his father being this deponents grandfather told him the like concerning the said perambulation."[8] It was through the process of mnemonic socialization that instilled household knowledge of landscape and place. Thus communities of practice could extend beyond the boundaries of the locality in question, encompassing family and kin living in neighboring villages or even further afield.

RITUAL PRACTICES

Rituals were an important part of the process of organizing memories through social practices whether at the level of the household or wider community of neighbors. While outward displays of solidarity were publicly maintained, rituals were polysemous and occasions of multiple, overlapping experiences, perspectives, and interests (Burke [1978] 1994: 191; Muir 1997; Feuchtwang 2010). Research has shown the contradictory responses to rituals and ceremonies associated with late medieval religious culture. Campaigns for the reformation of manners, and emergence of private property together with the withdrawal of elite participation and support, led to the demise of local festival culture. While some rituals were actively suppressed or went out of fashion, others were purposefully adapted and renewed. Rogationtide processions were one such ritual, with their post-Reformation survival often being attributed to the "community spirit" they elicited (Muir 1997: 67). In England, in some villages, the occasion was presided over by parish (male) elites in demonstration of their political authority over the administrative terrain of local life (Hindle 2000; Hindle and Kümin 2009). Rogations performed on the three days before the Ascension were to be found across Europe. The priest would lead his congregation about the fields carrying banners, crosses, relics and statues, chanting psalms and singing gospels, stopping to bless the crops with holy water. There is evidence of great variety in the customary culture of villages across Europe (Burke [1978] 1994; Hutton 1996; Muir 1997; Wilson 2000). In some villages livestock was blessed and crosses planted in the fields. Stephen Wilson gives an example from Franche-Comté (eastern France), where the priest gathered up stones as he went around the village, made wax crosses on them and threw them into the fields that had been sown, to protect against bad weather. The blessed stones were known as the cure's manure (Wilson 2000: 38). That the practice was retained in Catholic and Protestant regions, suggests its importance as a time for prayer and thanksgiving to God for the fruits of the earth and to beseech the lord for seasonable weather (Wilson 2000: 39).

In customary landscapes, boundaries did not simply exist since time immemorial without close attention being paid to their ongoing maintenance and preservation. In many parishes, the social production of parish space drew upon re-imagining the late medieval past, a past that could be corroborated in the activity of identifying physical structures and place names surviving in the landscape. In this process, the disparaged rituals and ceremonies of the late medieval church were not simply erased from local memory, as throwbacks to an outmoded and redundant past, rather they were re-packaged as a valuable resource in establishing the course of boundaries in the present. In the case from New Buckenham, for example, Thomas Neave, seventy-six-year-old yeoman of

New Buckenham, told the court that he was a "singing boy" and used to help "sing the procession," while sixty-five-year-old husbandman John Roberts, remembered "a firkin of bere" for the procession of New Buckenham to drink, and Thomas Rutland, sixty-eight-year-old yeoman from Wymondham, remembered drinking from a hand bell.[9] The best hospitality and the ritualized consumption of food and drink was important for reinforcing memories, and the social and cultural obligations expected of local landowners in making such provision. Old monuments, such as wayside and boundary crosses provided stations for eating and drinking and saying prayers. Among the deponents called to give evidence in Swaffham Prior and Burwell (Cambridgeshire), many remembered Rogationtide when they carried banners, often struggling to hold them up against the prevailing winds, and pausing to sing gospels at the boundary crosses.[10] Reliant on memory and practice, the unity of the parish as an autonomous bounded territory was not clearly defined. Indeed, the weight given to recording the remembrances, perhaps also misremembrances, of local people during court proceedings, reveals the production of parish space as an active, ongoing process through which various, and not always compatible memories intersected. Perambulations continued to be important for they provided a time for people to assemble together to share their experiences and knowledge, to reach agreement on changes that may have taken place, to acknowledge old boundary marks and with common consent create new ones. On occasion, disagreement over the correct alignment of the boundary could result in heated confrontation, with residents protesting against unwarranted changes to customs and rights (Burke [1978] 1994: 199–204; Thompson 1991: 98–100, 117–20; Wood 2002: 102–3; Walter 2006: 22–3).

Close examination of the deposition evidence also highlights the importance of household memories in the articulation of community boundaries. In the evidence for English villages at least, old perambulation routes and rituals were remembered as an extension of household space. As the authenticity and power of memory rested on proof of long-term settlement and knowledge of a place and landscape, memories of old rituals served more than one function. They were used to promote a shared sense of the past, against the transgressors of time-honored customs, they also demonstrated within an official arena the longevity of household attachments to place. Among the deponents who recalled taking part in Rogationtide perambulations, many talked about their parents and grandparents taking them aside and instructing them to remember the bounds. Ritual occasions such as this were opportunities for families to reinforce their knowledge of specific boundary features that were vital to the ongoing economic subsistence and social identity of their households, especially where they demarcated grazing and fuel rights across open commons. Economic subsistence was a central matter for concern, as was social place and standing endorsed through long-term settlement. Deponents gave up their experiences of Rogationtide, and it was by showing subtle differences and nuances in their experiences based on family knowledge handed on from one generation to the next that rights to dwell in a place were substantiated.

The physical traces of the past were incorporated into ritual and customary practices for they gave substance and meaning to claims of authenticity and permanence, against the reality of constant change whether through natural processes or human intervention. The concept of ancient time was frequently used by deponents to denote a time beyond generational time. Given the internal logic of custom, which rested upon flexibility, mutability, and adaptability, decisions were always made as to what aspects of the past were remembered and what was to be forgotten. Contemporaries understood customs and rights, everyday routines and practices to be susceptible to change, and the documentary evidence reveals heightened levels of concern within local societies for the destabilizing consequences of momentary ruptures and discontinuities of practice. As a counterpoint, the evidence shows how from one generation to the next memories were threaded together to produce an apparently seamless connection to the past. To bring a degree of stability to the otherwise fluctuating and unstable circumstances of the everyday, the material evidence of the past was actively sought on the ground. The landscape and its constituent features provided evidence of a longer history of land use that had existed before anyone could remember, beyond the span of generational memory. Furthermore, the physical appearance of decay—veteran trees, weathered stone crosses, denuded earthworks for example—was interpreted as an indicator of deep time, extending the experience of lived memory into the deep past. The visible signs of aging in the material world not only corroborated ancestral memory, it gave credibility to the notion that customs and rights had existed since time immemorial, and that an ancient order of landscape and custom had once existed before being eroded by the activities of those who would deny the past. Therein lay the power of the past, made visible in the landscape as a physical process of erosion and disintegration, and rather than bringing an end to memory, it was through encountering these dynamic material and visible processes of decay and decomposition that memories were made and remade. Contemporaries narrated landscape histories of place, which gave temporal depth to the meaning of customs and practices and in turn shaped their household identities.

Laying claim to the physical relics of the past surviving in the landscape was not simply the preserve of a non-elite, oral, ritual culture hanging on to the vestiges of the past. In England, parishes governed by middling male householders reinvented Rogationtide perambulations and sought to establish the course of boundaries by examining the material relics of the past on the ground, especially across open commons (Whyte 2007). Elsewhere, wealthy landowners were also keen to determine the longevity and credibility of customs and rights pertaining to their manorial jurisdictions, which set the grounds for later encroachment. Maps of estates were commissioned with particular attention paid to boundary features and old landmark features, essential to the ongoing assertion of manorial jurisdictions and rights originating in the medieval past. Just as the inhabitants and commoners of New Buckenham sought to clarify and confirm the extent of their rights to access land and resources, the boundary demarcated the extent of manorial rights too. Surviving map evidence includes details of the boundary, relating to the oral testimonies presented to the court, alongside fine drawings of Buckenham Castle, the park, and village. Not only were common rights at stake, so were the grazing rights of the manor. Unsurprisingly, the decisions made as to what to include and what not to include were weighted in the favor of its maker, the owner of the manor, indicating the complexity of boundaries and difficulties of disentangling them in a social context defined by competing interests, and alternative memories. Investigating cartographic material and the deposition evidence together, reveals how different perspectives and agendas were held in tension with one another in the landscape.

Some historians have argued that from the mid-sixteenth century, the increasing interest in record keeping together with surveying and map-making, signaled a shift toward modernity: from oral to literate culture, and from customary to capitalist modes of production. Rather than necessarily being the cause of rupture and discontinuity, methods of documentation and map-making were closely bound up with attempts to lay claim to customary rights, which stood for good order in the organizational structures of everyday life. The interpretation is a subtle one, but one worth making not least because it shows the memory work of landowners and commoners combined in making and remaking landscapes through differing, sometimes aligning interpretations of the past. Map evidence further reveals the appropriation of features surviving from the deep past including holy wells and crosses, prehistoric earthworks, and standing structures, in giving material substance to claims being made in the present. They gave tangible context to manorial jurisdictions, and processes of marking and claiming manorial rights. The physical relics of the deep past gave material context to the actions of the present, by clarifying and preserving the connectivity between past and present. As late as the eighteenth century, when elite culture becomes associated with taste, civility, and improvement, maps still depicted old monuments and structures as marking out and giving context to the economic and cultural organization of landscapes.

CONCLUSION

Finally, to return to the case from the Manor of Lledwigan, the social and environmental consequences of redirecting the River Keveny into a relatively small boundary ditch, had become a grave matter of contention by 1605. Agnus Gruff, widow of sixty-five-years, reported that she had known the place in question for forty years for "she hath long dwelled near to the same." She described the extent of local flooding when the dam made to divert the river was broken and "quite overthrown by the course of the water" and "thereby the water recovered his own ancient course again." She described how forty years previously the boundary ditch or mere was a little channel "over which a man might step" to gather sedge and thatch from the adjoining grounds. But in recent times the ditch had become so great and broad that a horse could not cross without difficulty, and thus movement and access to the meadows was impeded. She went on to give "her opinion" that the diverting of the river and subsequent flooding of the meadow grounds that "she seeth and she heareth" that many others complain that they find themselves "damnified by the said diverting."[11] Ninety-two-year-old husbandman Llewellyn ap David of Skeiviog, who could recall the river and meadow grounds when he was a boy, before the boundary ditch was dug, reckoned that "if the River of Keveny were suffered to Run in branches as he hath seen it to his ancient course and not hindered by stops it would be very beneficial to the inhabitants on both sides."[12] Seventy-six-year-old Owen ap Robert, husbandman, told the court how he saw the river break the dam and to flow once more to its ancient precinct, but the dam was repaired and once more the old river was kept from its prescribed course. Further alterations were made in 1585 and again in 1605, the year of the court proceedings, when the damming caused the river to flood the "hay and turves," of the neighboring inhabitants "to their great loss." Hay was essential for overwintering livestock and dried blocks of "turf" provided a necessary source of fuel.[13] This network of rights which entitled local inhabitants to access the land to gather natural resources, served to connect individual households to the communing community though the memories and meanings drawn from their lived experiences of being in the landscape.

The evidence highlights the complex, entangled, and contradictory motivations leading to landscape change and the lasting, perhaps unintended, social and environmental consequences of those actions. Earlier attempts at reconciling differences between commoners, by digging a boundary ditch, had been undone by the actions of the lord of the manor. The re-routing of the river increased the flow and volume of water in to the boundary ditch, causing the meadows to flood and in some years the river to return to its "ancient" course. But its construction had long-term, perhaps unforeseen consequences, in altering the ecology of the land. The oral testimonies here and in many other cases offer fragmentary moments which nevertheless show memory to have been a social and material process. We gain insight into different versions of reality in the historical record—the changing physical and ecological qualities of the meadows brought benefits to some but not all. Sixty-year-old yeoman Hugh Howell, told the court that when he was a boy the meadows were "but boggs and used as comon" and since the ditch was made "without doubt doth better and must nedes make drier the lands round about." Better drainage dried out the land and evidently for some the potential for grazing was greatly improved. The complaints made against the "improvements" were directed at those who would dissent from the prescribed natural order, not only concerning social ideas of equitable customs and practices, but also the physical environment and the attempts to force the river from its ancient course.

Perceived by contemporaries to originate in the deep and ancient past, old monuments and standing structures surviving from the late medieval and earlier periods were purposefully claimed to give clarity and substance to the organization of social and economic landscapes in the present. Explorations of the life histories of landmark features, thus, offer useful insights into the work of memory in early modern society that cannot easily be categorized into elite/non-elite, oral/literate culture. The material traces of the past were purposefully sought by tenants, commoners, and manorial lords to substantiate their claims to customs and jurisdictional rights. Archival material, including court records and maps, reveals two themes worth emphasizing here. Firstly, at a time when proof of the past was paramount in disputes over rights and boundaries, earthworks, and standing structures surviving from the deep past, including features of prehistoric origin, were incorporated into the practices of the present as authentic monuments to customs and rights. Secondly, the evidence reveals the interconnected meanings of landscape and the significance of apparently commonplace, and not obviously connected features, in structuring knowledge and everyday practice.

Memories of Rogationtide and other perambulations offered up to the court commissioners, defined and reinforced knowledge that came with long-term residency in a locality, with deponents re-imagining the footsteps and pathways created by their forebears. Household memories embedded a sense of identity and belonging, of being settled in a place, created through sedimented and routine practices that extended the spatial parameters of the household into the wider landscape. Through the practices of remembering, the landscape became an active background, with old earthworks, standing structures, trees, and stones giving context and meaning to memories of living and working in the landscape over the life-course. As landscape theorists argue, each person is differentially located in relation to the landscape, and therefore draws together a different set of experiences, memories, and knowledge practices in making the world meaningful. A landscape perspective holds together differing, perhaps alternative memories and values in relational tension with one another. Through developing the concept of landscape as a social process for the early modern period, we can reveal the overlapping, intersecting, and at times conflictual memories told and retold among neighboring households and social groups. Memories that were formed through everyday practices and social relationships, which were in turn given tangible form in landscapes. Knowledge might have been shared by others, yet still deponents would offer up the past as their experience, their own life histories were remembered in relation to the landscape as an extension of household space.

An integrated landscape and social perspective offers useful insights into the politics of memory and uses of the past within local societies, as meanings were not simply known, but were continuously created and co-created with others. Considerations of landscape illustrate the diverse, at times contradictory memories and meanings given to the same landscapes and places. Furthermore, consideration of how meanings were generated through incorporated practices, including organized rituals and everyday activities, allows for the possibility of discontinuity and change, but also threads of continuity. From a landscape perspective, there is remarkable evidence for long-term patterns of re-use and re-appropriation, whereby certain sites and places appear to have been afforded special meanings, albeit for different purposes, over extensive periods of time. Memory is not just a function of the mind, but was communicated through the recognition of the physical evidence of the past in the landscape, and the physical presence of being in the landscape, moving through it, and taking note of the location of features that bore witness to the actions of past generations. Landscapes and meanings were not static, each generation chose to incorporate, manipulate, perhaps disregard and destroy the physical evidence of the past. Landscapes were constantly changing, from season to season, and over the life-course of individuals. Given that landscapes were changing whether through human or natural processes, and contemporaries were deeply aware of this, we can begin to understand the authority given to narrating landscape histories and importance of handing on memories through cultural practices and associations. Above all the evidence reveals the possibilities of exploring landscape as central to the work of memory and interconnections between the collections of people living in rural villages in the early modern period.

CHAPTER SEVEN

Rituals of Memory: Commemorations

PETER BURKE

This chapter is concerned with collective practices designed to remind those taking part about past events and deceased individuals. Many of these practices were ritualized, following traditional forms that onlookers as well as participants could easily recognize and interpret. Some of these rituals expressed religious faith: the daily Catholic Mass, for example, commemorated Christ's sacrifice, while masses for the dead or requiems were said in memory of particular individuals. Many rituals were public, but a few were domestic, carried out within the family or household. Some commemorative rituals were everyday events, but many were special occasions, occurring only once a year or even once a century. They may be regarded as collective performances of memory or of history, *Inszenierung von Geschichte* (Müller 2003: 4). When the event commemorated was a controversial one, the performances may be viewed as so many attempts to control its meaning, so many skirmishes in a war of memory.

Early modern commemorations were important expressions of what is often called "social" or "cultural" memory. It may be useful to distinguish the two concepts, linking them with two traditions of scholarship, one of them French and the other German. In what follows the phrase "social memory" will be employed—following the lead of the sociologist Maurice Halbwachs—to refer to what we might call the "cues" given to individuals by their "memory community" (whether family, village, church, nation, or all of these), in suggesting both what to remember and how to remember it (Halbwachs 1925). What is remembered is a tiny selection from what might be remembered, and the community, large or small, encourages individuals to remember some things and not others, a process sometimes described as "canonization." Commemorative rituals support this process. Under the umbrella of social memory, deliberate attempts on the part of the authorities in church and state to shape the memories of their flocks will also be included, as well as the political exploitation of commemorations.

On the other hand, the phrase "cultural memory" will be used to refer—following Aby Warburg and more recently, Jan and Aleida Assmann —to an archive or repertoire of symbols, images, and stereotypes that accumulate over the centuries (J. Assmann 2011; A. Assmann 2011). This repertoire has been described by the psychologist Jerome Bruner as a "store of narratives," that individuals and groups in a given culture are able to draw upon or re-activate whenever they need them, constructing what has been called a "prosthetic memory" that is not natural in origin but all the same, like an artificial limb, becomes part of the body (Bruner 1994; Landsberg 2004).

Early modern commemorations were sometimes limited, confined to a city or monastery, and sometimes much wider. They took a number of forms, some of them rather modest and others extremely ambitious. What has been called the "vocabulary of commemoration" was often lively but sometimes sober. Commemorative acts included writing poems, singing songs, drinking, delivering sermons or speeches, striking and distributing medals, marching in processions and parades, and re-enacting major events in the past by performing plays and even, on occasion, by rebellion.

Some early modern popular revolts appear to have been viewed by participants as continuations or re-enactments of earlier revolts, memories of which had been transmitted by word of mouth from one generation to another, following an unofficial, indeed clandestine, popular tradition (Haemers 2011: 454–6). In the case of England, it has been noted that in 1485, northern rebels named one of their captains "Jack Straw" in memory of one of the leaders of the peasant revolt of 1381. Another captain was called "Master Mendall" (that is, mend-all), referring to the nickname of Jack Cade, the leader of a rising in Kent and Sussex in 1450. A third was known as "Robin of Riddesdale" after the individual who had led another rising, in 1470 (Harvey 1991; Wood 2013a: 63).

In Flanders, the name of Jacob van Artevelde, the leader of the revolt of Ghent in the mid-fourteenth century, still resonated in the fifteenth century, when other rebel leaders either belonged to his family or took his name. One might speak of a tradition of revolt, and even of its ritualization, at least in the early stages of each event (Haemers 2011: 454). The famous revolt of Naples in 1647 may also be viewed as a kind of re-enactment, since the memory of past revolts and the tradition of fighting for political autonomy were very much alive among ordinary people in the city, assisted by places of memory such as the convent of San Luigi, where a popular assembly had been held in 1620, and Piazza Mercato, where Conradin, who claimed to be King of Sicily, had been beheaded by a rival claimant in 1268 (Villari 2012: 300–13).

Many commemorations contributed to the social memory by effectively telling individuals what to remember. One type of early modern commemoration, known in English as "beating the bounds of the parish," did this with particular force, literal as well as metaphorical. In the week of the Ascension, group of parishioners would walk along the boundaries of the parish, and to reinforce the memories of the younger participants, the boys might be beaten with branches or rods of birch or willow. In this way, knowledge of the parish boundaries was transmitted from generation to generation. We might say that the ritual was a performance of memory, maintaining the identity of the parish and its customary boundaries, custom being defined at this time in a legal formula (itself customary) as a practice "whereof the memory of man runneth not to the contrary" (Hutton 1996; Fletcher 2003). In semi-literate societies such as those of early modern Europe, written records needed to be supplemented and were supplemented by oral testimonies of witnesses who remembered not only boundaries but also events such as donations, weddings, or agreements between landlords and tenants.

Like rituals, material "memorials" kept memory alive, notably the statues of important people in public places—the equestrian statue of Grand Duke Cosimo of Tuscany, erected on Piazza della Signoria in Florence in 1594, for example, or that of Henri IV of France on Place Dauphine in Paris, erected in 1614, soon after the king's death and destroyed during the French Revolution in an act of what may be described as "decommemoration" (in similar fashion, during the English Civil War, supporters of Parliament had removed a statue of Charles I from Charing Cross). Much more common were monuments to the dead displayed in churches, ranging from huge tombs decorated with colored marble for royal and noble families to simple brass plaques for merchants and their wives (Llewellyn 2000). The English name for these installations, "funeral monuments," suggests that the monuments were intended to evoke the memory of the splendid funerals of important people, with long processions of mourners, including poor people who were hired for the occasion, so that the dead and their families would be remembered for their generosity and their magnificence.

Funerals were special occasions for the family but everyday events for the clergy who officiated and for their parishioners. Other rituals of remembrance were special occasions for everyone, including anniversaries and centenaries.

ANNIVERSARIES

Anniversaries were a common form of ritual in early modern Europe. At the domestic level, birthdays were not yet taken very seriously by many people (with exceptions such as Matthäus Schwarz, who worked for the firm of Fugger in Augsburg in the early sixteenth century (Schmitt 2007, 2009)). In Catholic families, however, the annual festival of the patron saint of each family member was a special occasion, while the Jews celebrated Passover (*Pesach*), collectively performing their memory of a historical event, the exodus of the people of Israel from Egypt, as told in the Old Testament (the *Tanakh*).

At the public level, Lutherans celebrated November 11, St Martin's day and the day on which Martin Luther was christened, while Irish Protestants celebrated November 4, the birthday of their hero William III. Guilds had their patrons (St. George for armorers, St. Crispin for shoemakers and so on) and might celebrate their saint's day with a feast. Cities too had their patron saints—St. John the Baptist in Florence, St. Mark in Venice, St. Isidore in Madrid—and an annual festival in their memory might be a magnificent, indeed a memorable occasion, with processions through the streets, houses on the main routes decorated with tapestries, fountains in the squares flowing with wine, shows by actors and acrobats, and many other happenings (Peyer 1955).

The stories told about these saints contained a strong element of fiction, to say the least, but like memories, they evoked the past. Other festivals honored people for whose lives there was more evidence. In early modern England, for instance, the colleges of Oxford and Cambridge commemorated their founders and benefactors with an annual religious service followed by a feast. They still do.

Other anniversaries were celebrated all over the Christian world, notably the birth of Christ on December 25, and his passion and resurrection at Easter. The sufferings of Christ were enacted in the streets and squares of a number of European cities at this season. In Rome, for example, the arch-fraternity of the Gonfalon regularly presented a play about the Passion. The whole of Holy Week was in a sense a single great drama played in a theater without walls, in which the many processions gave large numbers of people walk-on parts.

In Catholic Europe, some of these practices were reinforced during the Counter-Reformation. Milan, for instance, has been described as becoming a "ritual city" in the age of San Carlo Borromeo, who was archbishop there from 1564 to 1584, and his cousin Federico, who held the same office from 1595 to 1631. The urban system was reshaped for devotional reasons. For example, stone crosses were erected in different parts of the city in order to allow the faithful to make the "stations of the cross" in the open air, commemorating Christ's journey to the place of his crucifixion by following his route, transposed from Jerusalem to Milan, in fourteen stages, walking in the steps of Christ and meditating on his Passion (Buratti 1982).

Counter-Reformation Rome, the greatest center of pilgrimage in the Catholic world at this time, offers still more dramatic examples of rituals of commemoration. Pilgrimage was a kind of ritual of initiation, requiring purification by means of confession and communion, the following of a traditional route that included the seven major churches, and the collective remembering of the actions of Christ and the saints (Labrot 1987). In the seventeenth century, visits to the newly discovered catacombs commemorated the lives and deaths of early Christian martyrs. A number of new saints were canonized at this time, both reviving past memories and ensuring future ones. The canonizations were marked by festivities, most spectacularly in 1622 on the occasion of the quintuple canonization of Ignatius Loyola, Francis Xavier, Teresa of Avila, Filippo Neri, and Isidore of Madrid.

Past events, including some recent ones, might also be commemorated every year. For example, the relief of the Dutch city of Leiden, besieged by a Spanish army, on October 3, 1574 was commemorated by sermons, parades, and plays (Pollmann 2017: 105–16). The recapture of Breda by the Dutch on March 4, 1590 (by using a peat barge as a kind of Trojan horse to enter the castle), was celebrated annually. For example, a play was performed on the twenty-fifth anniversary of the event in 1616 (Eekhout 2013: 135).

In France, annual commemorative processions go back to the fifteenth century. Orléans celebrated the relief by Jeanne d'Arc of the siege of the city by the English in 1429, while Paris commemorated the liberation of the city from occupation, again by the English, in 1436. The sixteenth-century wars of religion offered more occasions for this kind of festivity. Ten French cities commemorated the failure of Huguenot sieges, among them Toulouse, where the annual procession took place from 1562 until 1791 (Benedict 2008: 390–97). On the other side, the Calvinist citizens of Geneva celebrated the *fête de l'escalade*, remembering the failed attack on the city by the troops of the Duke of Savoy (the festival continues to this day, but has become more carnivalesque than Calvin would have appreciated).

In England, a series of anniversaries began to be celebrated from the late sixteenth century onwards, thus creating a new national and Protestant calendar to replace the feasts of the saints that had been abolished following the Reformation. The date of Queen Elizabeth's accession to the throne, November 17, was already being celebrated ten years later, in 1568. Accession Day became an annual festival "which had no precedent in earlier reigns and no counterpart on the European continent" (Cressy 1990: 35). The day was marked by the organization of jousts between the courtiers (the "Accession Day Tilts") as well as by popular celebrations such as the mock siege of a castle in Northampton in 1589. News of the celebrations was spread by ballads (Yates 1957; Strong 1959).

Celebrations of the memory of "Good Queen Bess" on November 17 continued well into the seventeenth century. The queen's birthday on September 7 was also celebrated, and so were those of her successors James I, Charles I, and Charles II. January 30, the anniversary of the execution of King Charles I in 1649, was commemorated by royalists who regarded the king as a "martyr," assimilating him to a saint. Britain's return to a monarchy in 1660 was celebrated by "Restoration Day," May 29, also known as "Royal Oak Day," when loyalists wore oak apples in memory of Charles II's escape from the parliamentary army by hiding in an oak tree after he was defeated at the battle of Worcester in 1651. These celebrations helped to shape the "national memory" (Cressy 1989, 1990).

However, following the unsuccessful Catholic plot to blow up the Houses of Parliament on November 5, 1605, it was the fifth of November that became the major early modern English ritual of commemoration, marked by the burning of the effigies of the Pope and of a leading conspirator, Guy Fawkes. Participants recited the verses "Please to Remember/ The Fifth of November/Gunpowder, Treason and Plot/I see no reason/Why Gunpowder Treason/Should ever be forgot." By this means, Protestant England celebrated itself and its freedom from "Popery" (Cressy 1989; Sharpe 2005). The anniversary was used by the Whig party in 1679, 1680, and 1681, when the "Green Ribbon Club" organized "Mock-Processions" of individuals dressed as cardinals, Jesuits, and friars, carrying effigies of the Pope to be burned in public (Figure 7.1). This was a festive way of putting pressure on Parliament to exclude James Duke of York, who was an open Catholic, from succeeding his brother Charles II on the throne (Williams 1958; Furley 1959). Following the Revolution of 1688, November 5 gained a new significance, since it was the date of the landing of William of Orange in England, celebrated by his supporters.

On the model of November 5, the Parliament of 1662 required the commemoration in Ireland of the anniversary of October 23, 1641, the day of the foiling of another Catholic plot, to seize Dublin Castle and massacre Protestants, in a kind of re-enactment of the so-called "Massacre of St Bartholomew" in Paris in 1572. After 1690, October 23

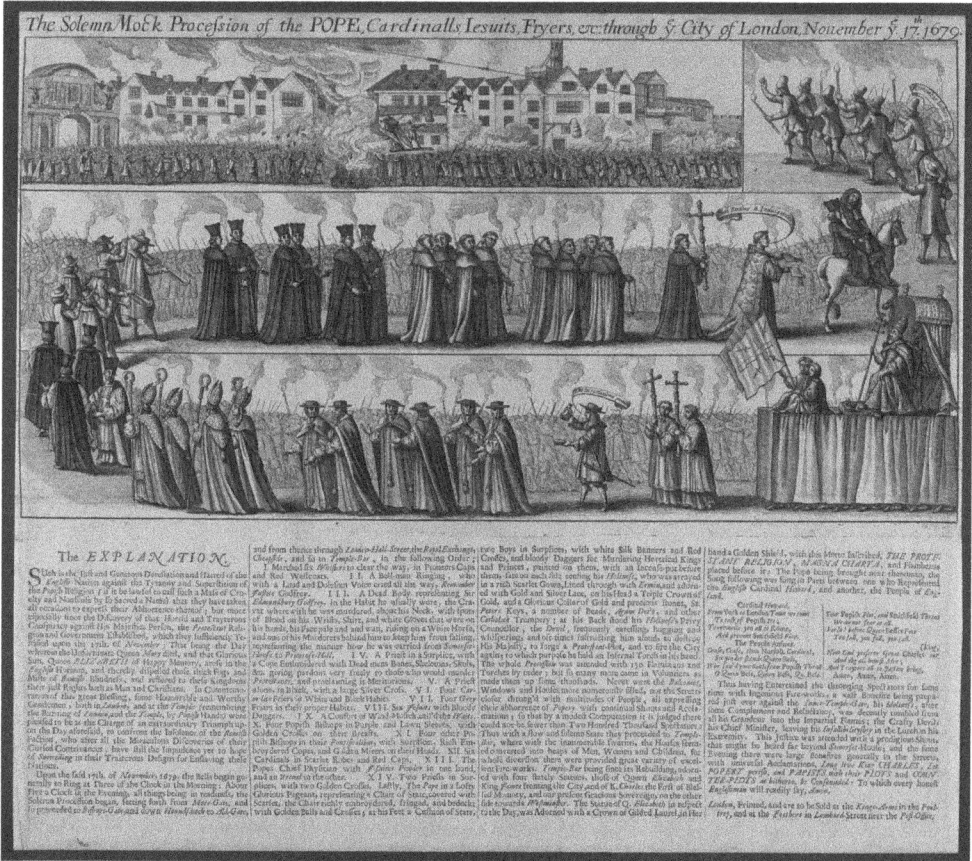

FIGURE 7.1: The Solemn Mock Procession of the Pope, Cardinalls, Jesuits, Fryers &c. through the City of London, November the 17th, 1679. London, printed by G. Croom at the Blew Ball in Thames-Street over against Baynard's Castle, 1684. © The Trustees of the British Museum.

became "one of the principal occasions on the commemorative calendar of Irish Protestants" (Barnard 1991; Kelly 1994: 28–30).

It is often said that memories of the past are stronger in Ireland than they are in England, and the history of Irish commemorations supports this idea. Irish Protestants celebrated the birthday of King William III on August 4 by drinking to his "glorious memory," and they also celebrated the anniversaries of two victories, the Battle of the Boyne on July 1, 1690 (according to the Julian calendar) and the Battle of Aughrim on July 12, in which the armies of William III, the "great deliverer," had rescued Protestants from "Popery" by defeating the forces of his Catholic rival, James II. These dates were marked by processions, parades, banquets, bonfires, fireworks, barrels of wine, and the decoration of houses with orange lilies (since William III was also Prince of Orange). Following the switch to the Gregorian calendar in the eighteenth century, "the Twelfth" came to signify the Boyne, still celebrated by Protestants in Northern Ireland. To understand the importance of these festivities for the Irish Protestant community, we need to remember that although Dublin was a mainly Protestant city in the eighteenth century, it was an island in a sea of Catholics, who were perceived by the Dubliners as a threat. The regular enactment of commemorations of past victories was a means of exorcising this threat and maintaining the solidarity of the Protestant community (Barnard 1991; Kelly 1992, 2000).

In Catholic Europe, there was less emphasis on the commemoration of events, perhaps because of the multitude of annual commemorations of individuals, the saints. However, Pope Gregory XIII did decree the annual commemoration of the Massacre of St. Bartholomew on September 11. The anniversaries of several victories over the Ottoman Empire were also celebrated. Pope Calixtus III made August 6 a feast-day following the defeat of the Turks at Belgrade by the army of János Hunyadi in 1456. Pope Pius V ordered the commemoration of the battle of Lepanto (1571) on the first Sunday of October every year, while in Venice, annual rituals of commemoration took place from 1572 onwards on the feast of the martyr Santa Giustina (Fenlon 2007: 273–92). After the King of Poland, Jan Sobieski, had defeated the Turks and raised the siege of Vienna on September 12, 1683, after asking the Virgin Mary to protect his kingdom, Pope Innocent XI extended the feast of the holy name of Mary to the whole Church. Thus rituals of commemoration encouraged Catholics and Protestants alike to remember certain events in the past and to divide the world into allies and enemies.

CENTENARIES

The centenary is generally treated as an invention of the nineteenth or the late eighteenth century, and the proliferation of this family of festivals is explained by the rise of historicism and nationalism (Quinault 1998). These explanations are extremely plausible, and a third "ism" might be added—secularism, since these commemorative events filled the gap left by the gradual decline of Catholic and Protestant festivals.

All the same, some centenaries (including bicentenaries, tercentenaries, and so on) were celebrated in early modern Europe, and at least a few of them were important, together with other "jubilees," in the sense of fiftieth-year anniversaries, following the Biblical prescription, "ye shall hallow the 50th year" (Leviticus 25:10). The regular papal jubilees, beginning in the year 1300, are the most important of these. During the Jubilee of 1575, for instance, the hospice of Santa Trinità in Rome received more than 170,000 pilgrims, while the number increased to 500,000 for the Jubilee of 1600. Protestant and secular jubilees were also celebrated in the early modern period: Protestants in Pomerania, for instance, celebrated fifty years of the Reformation in that region in 1585.

Irish Protestants, with their traditional predilection for commemorations, celebrated the fiftieth anniversary of the Battle of the Boyne in 1740 in style, with popular parades in Dublin and elsewhere, organized by the Boyne Society and the Protestant Society (Kelly 2000). The state of Pennsylvania celebrated the fiftieth anniversary of its Charter in 1751, buying a "Liberty Bell" for the State House carrying an inscription referring to Leviticus (Fischer 1989: 595).

The panic of the "Year 1000" has often been cited as a sign of concern with centuries in the Middle Ages, but in fact the collective alarm was not focused on that one year at the time, only retrospectively from around the year 1600 (Milo 1991: 64). Interest in a century as a discrete unit of time was increasing in the early modern period, an interest that was both expressed and encouraged by the publication of two ecclesiastical histories. The first was the *Ecclesiastica Historia*, written by a team of Protestant scholars in Magdeburg, edited by Matthias Flacius and published in thirteen volumes from 1559 to 1574. Organized in sections of a hundred years each, the work became known as "the Magdeburg Centuries" and its authors as the "centuriators" (Burckhardt 1971: 8–28). The Catholic response, the *Annales Ecclesiastici* (1588–1607) by Cesare Baronio, devoted twelve volumes to the history of the Church in the twelve centuries from the birth of Christ to the year 1198.

The idea of the century was soon extended from the history of the Church to history in general. In German, the term *Jahrhundert* came into use in the middle of the seventeenth century (Burckhardt 1971; cf. Brendecke 1999). In English, the term "centenary" is first recorded in 1647, and its variant, "centennial," in 1797, while William Cave's history of ecclesiastical writers, published in 1688, was divided into sixteen parts, each corresponding to a century, from the time of the apostles to the time of Luther.

As for the events themselves, which were also described in the early modern period as "jubilees," there was an attempt to revive them (following the ancient Roman precedent of the emperor Antoninus Pius in the second century CE) as early as the year 1421. On that occasion the notary and chronicler Lorenzo de Monacis suggested to the doge that the Venetians celebrate the foundation of their city a thousand years earlier. He was unsuccessful, but he did deliver a speech in honor of the occasion (Poppi 1967: 183–4).

For their part, the Florentines commemorated the 200th anniversary of Dante's birth in 1465 with a fresco by Domenico di Michelino in the cathedral, showing the poet holding an open book and standing between Florence and Heaven. A year later, when the Swiss abbey of Einsiedeln celebrated the 500th anniversary of its foundation, the monks commissioned three engravings of the abbey's famous statue of the Virgin Mary (Landau and Parshall 1994: 49). As the chronological appendix to this chapter shows, this trickle of celebrations gradually became a stream, with five examples (known to me) from the sixteenth century, eight from the seventeenth and seventeen from the eighteenth century (no fewer than fourteen of them in its second half). The rise of what has been called a "culture of jubilees" is clear enough (Müller 1998).

What was found worthy of commemoration? Above all, religious events. In 1515, for instance, the centenary of the burning of Jan Hus as a heretic was commemorated by the striking of a medal inscribed "A hundred years have passed" (*Centum revolutis annis*), presenting Hus as a martyr (Zapalac 1990: 112–13). The most important of all seventeenth-century commemorations was a religious one and took place in 1617.

THE REFORMATION JUBILEE OF 1617

The year 1617 marked one hundred years since Luther posted his famous 95 Theses against indulgences (or at least was supposed to have posted them) on a church door at Wittenberg, thus marking the beginning of what would come to be known as "the Reformation." The event was widely celebrated, beginning with the Faculty of Theology at Wittenberg and spreading more widely. The centenary was marked by an official holiday and by festivals in the German Protestant world, not only in Luther's native Saxony but also in the Calvinist Palatinate (Schönstadt 1978: 10–85; Schönstadt 1982a; Hoyer 1994; Zika [1995] 2003; Flügel 2005; Howard 2016: 11–22). The importance of this particular event helps explain why German scholars have taken the lead in the study of early modern centenaries.

The celebrations were sober ones, quite unlike the feasts of major saints in the Catholic world or indeed the national anniversaries of Protestant England and Ireland, generally celebrated by public drinking as well as bonfires and bells. The main elements of the German jubilee were sermons, hymns, and academic disputations, while the commemorations were themselves commemorated in medals, some of them distributed to children, and also in broadsheets (Figure 7.2). Drinking was forbidden. The closest that these festivals came to entertainment was the music of Heinrich Schütz and the plays written for the occasion, notably the Lutheran clergyman Martin Rinckart's dramatization of the debate on indulgences in *Indulgentiarius confusus*. In 1717, there would be similar commemorations but on a smaller scale, in Hamburg, for instance, in Helmstedt, and in Magdeburg (Schönstadt 1982b; Flügel 2003: 91–5; Cordes 2006; Howard 2016: 22–9).

FIGURE 7.2: Luther medal 1617 (obverse). Latin text on the medal: May it shine forever! Sachsen, Kurfürstentum. Courtesy by Rare Books Collections at the Lutheran School of Theology at Chicago.

Why was this commemorative event so important? The year 1617 was not only the centenary of the posting of the 95 Theses but also the year preceding the outbreak of the Thirty Years' War. Tension between Catholics and Protestants had been increasing for some time and in response, the different groups of German Protestants were moving closer together. The Protestant Union had been formed in 1608, and it was involved in the commemoration in 1617, an event that may be regarded as a collective affirmation of Protestant identity that "helped forge a new sense of history as a communal resource." The celebrations were described at the time as a "jubilee." Rinckart, for instance, called his *Indulgentiarius* a *Jubel-Comoedia*. This was a new term for Protestants, and one that they appropriated from the popes. What is more, Pope Paul V had announced a special jubilee year in 1617. Thus, tension between Catholics and Protestants was expressed and symbolized by the rival jubilees (Schönstadt 1978: 20; Zika [1995] 2003: 211; Loosen 2003: 128–32). In 1717, by contrast, the celebrations were predominantly Lutheran, "the idea of a unified Protestantism being largely a thing of the past" (Flügel 2005: 125–67; Howard 2016: 25).

OTHER RELIGIOUS CENTENARIES

Other commemorations soon followed those of 1617, as if inspired by them. In 1619, the city of Zürich marked the centenary of the calling of Huldrych Zwingli to be pastor of the Grossmünster there. In 1630, Lutherans in Saxony and Hessen commemorated the centenary of the Augsburg Confession (a summary of their beliefs presented to the Diet of Augsburg) with sermons, speeches, songs, processions, and a disputation at the University of Marburg. These actions were once again themselves commemorated in news sheets, pamphlets, and broadsheets, as well as by the striking of medals (Figure 7.3). Martin Rinckart produced another play for the occasion, *Lutherus Augustus*, as well as a better-known hymn, *Nun danket alle Gott*. The Lutherans would celebrate themselves again at the bicentenary of the Confession in 1730 (Galley 1930; Coupe 1966: 75; Marsch 1980; Hänisch 1993; Flügel 2003).

A Catholic response to the Lutheran jubilees was not long in coming, on the initiative of the Jesuits. The Protestants had appropriated and transformed a Catholic practice, but now the direction of appropriation was reversed. The Jesuits were never afraid to steal ideas from the heretics in order to fight them more effectively. They followed the Lutheran model in the year 1640 by celebrating their hundredth birthday or "first century," with celebrations in the church of the Gesù in Rome and the performance of plays in Jesuit colleges in different cities, including Madrid (Shergold 1967: 449), Cologne, Eichstätt, and Graz. One play performed in a catechism school in Cologne included verses claiming that in Europe, India, Brazil, China, and Japan "from today until the end of the world there will be festivals and jubilation" (*Ia heut biss an das endt der welt/man freudenfest und iubel helt*) (Oorschot 1982: 133).

In Antwerp, the Flemish province of the order published a sumptuous commemorative volume, the *Imago Primi Seculi*, with nearly 1,000 pages of poems, prose, and engravings (Oorschot 1982; O'Malley 2015). In response, a number of attacks on the order were published by the opponents of the Jesuits, among them Johann Leonhard Weidner, a schoolmaster from Maastricht, author of *Jubilaeum sive speculum jesuiticum* (Fumaroli 1994). The Jesuits also celebrated in 1722 the centenary of the canonization of Ignatius Loyola and Francis Xavier in 1622, as far away as the Mariana Islands, while in the same

FIGURE 7.3: A broadside commemorating the centenary of the Augsburg Confession, with a colored and partly gilded engraving on vellum by Johann Dürr, showing in the foreground Protestant representatives, presenting the text of the Confession to Emperor Charles V, and in the background various scenes illustrating the main points of the Confession, with engraved lettering and six lines of engraved text. ([Dresden?], 1630). © The Trustees of the British Museum.

year the centenary of the canonization of Filippo Neri was marked in Bologna by the performance of oratorios in praise of the saint.

The Massacre of St. Bartholomew does not seem to have inspired festivities either in 1672 or in 1772. However, in 1762 the city of Toulouse commemorated the bicentenary of the earlier massacre of Protestants there during the French religious wars. In the same year, the Protestant merchant Jean Calas was executed in the same city, accused of murdering his son, who had converted to Catholicism (Bien 1962).

SECULAR COMMEMORATIONS

The Reformation has long been viewed as one of the founding events of the modern world. Two other events of this kind were commemorated in the early modern period, the invention of printing and the discovery of America.

Little notice was taken either of the centenary or of bicentenary of the landfall of Columbus, although it was in 1592 that the enterprising printer Theodore de Bry published an engraving of Columbus reaching Hispaniola. In 1792, on the other hand, there was a cluster of commemorations in the newly independent American Republic, which had begun to celebrate July 4 as Independence Day in 1778. In Boston, for instance, the Reverend Jeremy Belknap delivered "A discourse intended to commemorate the discovery of America by Christopher Columbus." The discourse was followed by a procession and a feast organized by the newly founded Massachusetts Historical Society. In New York, a more popular festival was organized by the Tammany Society, including parades, songs, illuminations, and feasts (Dennis 2002). The occasion was also celebrated in Philadelphia, Baltimore, and Richmond.

In the sixteenth century, it was believed that printing with moveable type had been invented in the year 1440, and so a commemoration took place in 1540, at Wittenberg, thus associating print with the Reformation. Poems were published to mark the occasion (Gehner 1939; Giesecke 1991: 134). In Mainz, where Gutenberg had set up his press, a commemoration took place in 1541. In 1640, five printers celebrated the bicentenary of the invention of printing in Leipzig (the *Jubilaeum typographicum*). One of them, Timotheus Ritzsch, composed verses for the occasion (Flügel and Dornheim 2006: 59–63). Commemorations also took place in Strasbourg, Breslau, Amsterdam, and Prague. Appropriately enough, along with the eulogies (including one by the schoolmaster Christian Gueinz and another, once again, by Martin Rinckart), several histories of printing were published to mark the bicentenary. One of them, by the Dutch scholar Marcus van Boxhorn, claimed that Haarlem, not Mainz, was the birthplace of the invention and that it was Laurens Coster, not Johann Gutenberg, who was the real protagonist (Boxhorn 1640; Mallinckrot 1640; Schrag 1640).

In 1740, the tercentenary was marked by another history of printing, written by the printer Prosper Marchand. Over thirty German towns and a few elsewhere, among them Basel, London and (of course) Haarlem celebrated the event. Three academic theses presented at the University of Altdorf in that year discussed documents concerning Gutenberg (Marchand 1740; Zwahr 1994, 1996; Jensen 2011; Smith 2008–9). The writer Johann Christoph Gottsched delivered a speech "In praise and memory of the invention of printing" at the University of Leipzig, describing the commemoration as appropriate for "a patriotic German" (Gottsched 1976: 116). It may be a little too early to speak of a "national" festival, but in the German-speaking world, the celebration of 1640 as well as 1740 expressed pride in a German invention.

Political events were not forgotten, but they provide relatively few examples of early secular centenaries. The centenary of the German Peasant War of 1525 was not celebrated, though it was certainly remembered, thanks to a play on the subject by that lover of centenaries Martin Rinckart. His *Monetarius Seditiosus Sive Incendia Rusticorum Bellica*, focused on the figure of the radical reformer Thomas Münzer, a leader of the peasants who was executed following the defeat of the rebels. The Peace of Augsburg (1555) was commemorated in both 1655 (Flügel 2005: 87–100) and 1755. The Peace of Westphalia (1648) was commemorated in 1748, another welcome change from the commemoration of battles. In Hamburg, the Senate ordered special church services and the performance of an oratorio by Telemann (Whaley 1985: 194).

In the Dutch Republic in 1772, a *Jubeljaar* commemorated the bicentenary of the taking of the town of Brill by the "Sea Beggars," an event described as liberation from the "Spanish Yoke" and the foundation of the Republic (Barueth 1772). In Vlissingen, which was liberated in the same year as Brill, coins were issued commemorating "two hundred years of freedom." In Vienna in 1783, the centenary of the famous siege of the city by the Turks and its relief by the Poles was commemorated by the performance of a play entitled "The Rewarded Loyalty of the Citizens of Vienna, or 12 September 1683" (Fichtner 2008: 112). It was the turn of the Poles to celebrate in 1883, in the age of nationalism (Dabrowski 2004: 49–74).

In Britain, the "Glorious Revolution" of 1688 was commemorated in 1788 by the revival of the Revolution Society, which now included the radical scientist Joseph Priestley and went on to celebrate the fall of the Bastille in 1789, suggesting that in this case, among others, the commemoration of the past masked a concern with the present and the future (Figure 7.4). In Norwich, a friend of Priestley, the Unitarian minister William Enfield, preached a sermon "On the Centennial Commemoration of the Revolution." In London, church bells rang, the guns of the Tower of London were fired and 400 members of the Revolution Society marched through the streets on their way to dinner at a tavern. In Birmingham, Bristol, York, and other cities, "light-hearted celebrations overlaid with political significance occurred" (Schwoerer 1990: 2–6). However, there was no consensus about the significance of the event commemorated. Indeed, "the celebrations focused and expressed the ideological and political divisions in the nation," in a manner not unlike the French celebrations of the bicentenary of their revolution in 1989 (Kaplan 1995). The centenary "was appropriated by different groups to legitimate very different political positions in the present," whether Whig, Tory, or radical (Wilson 1989: 354, 364).

In Ireland too, a succession of centenaries was celebrated by Protestants between 1788 and 1791 in Belfast, Derry, Drogheda and elsewhere, marking the "Glorious Revolution" of 1688, the siege of Derry and of course the Battle of the Boyne (Kelly 1994: 48).

Celebrations of the centenaries of the foundation of universities, now commonplace, are another early modern tradition. The University of Erfurt marked its centenary in 1492, followed by Basel in 1560. Occasions of this kind gradually became more and more festive. The University of Tübingen marked the centenary of its foundation (in 1477) with celebrations, delayed by an outbreak of plague until 1578, that included banquets, speeches, music, and the performance of a play written by Nicodemus Frischlin, professor of poetry and history, entitled *Priscianus Vapulans*. Not for the last time, one event of this kind seems to have provoked another. Nine years later, in 1587, it was the turn of the University of Heidelberg to mark its bicentenary, which actually fell in 1586 (Müller 1998: 84). There

FIGURE 7.4: Medal commemorating the centenary of the 1688 Revolution, 1788. Obverse: Laureate draped cuirassed bust of William III. Royal Collection Trust, RCIN 443282. © Her Majesty Elizabeth Queen II 2019.

followed Wittenberg's centenary in 1602 and Leipzig's bicentenary in 1609, events that may well have inspired the better-known events of 1617, in which professors at German Protestant universities played a major role. Heidelberg also celebrated its quartercentenary in 1786.

The births and deaths of a few outstanding private individuals, including artists and writers, were also commemorated in public in the early modern period, so many precedents for the romantic cult of heroes. An early example is the commemoration in 1629 of the centenary of the death of the painter Quentin Matsys in Antwerp, the city where he had lived and worked. The bicentenary of the death of the humanist Johann Reuchlin was commemorated in 1722, and the centenary of the death of the poet Martin Opitz in 1739, when Gottsched delivered another memorial oration. In 1743, it was the turn of Nicholas Copernicus, who was claimed by the Germans as a compatriot. His death in 1543 was commemorated in Leipzig. Once again, Gottsched delivered an oration (Gottsched 1976: 88–114, 157–92).

All these commemorations were minor events compared to the Shakespeare Jubilee of 1769.

THE GREAT SHAKESPEARE JUBILEE

A commemoration of the bicentenary of the birth of Shakespeare in 1764 was discussed at the time, but nothing came of it. Five years later, the famous actor David Garrick organized what became known as "the Great Shakespeare Jubilee" in Stratford-upon-Avon and also in London (Stochholm 1964; Deelman 1964; Brewer 1997: 327–9, 411–2). The events of the Jubilee were, appropriately enough, dramatic and spectacular.

In Stratford, the two days of the celebration, September 6–7, 1769, included the performance of an oratorio, *Judith*, and a dedication ode, both set to music by Thomas Arne, best known for his settings for *God Save the King* and *Rule Britannia*. There was also a horse race, the Jubilee Cup. Heavy rain spoiled the fireworks and prevented the planned pageant from taking place, but the indoor masquerade went ahead. Commemorative medals and handkerchiefs were sold, crowds came to see and hear the events, and the price of accommodation and services soared, leading to criticism of the innkeepers and shopkeepers of Stratford for exploiting their guests (Figure 7.5).

In London, too, the celebrations did not go according to Garrick's plan, since he was anticipated by a rival, George Colman, a dramatist who was also the manager of the Theatre Royal in Covent Garden, where he staged a comedy that was set in Stratford, *Man and Wife: or the Shakespeare Jubilee*. The performance devised by Garrick, entitled *The Jubilee*, took place at the Theatre Royal, Drury Lane and included singing, dancing, and the pageant that had been intended for Stratford. In the long term, the Jubilee had three important effects. It was important in the launching of Stratford as a destination for visitors, in spreading the idea of staging jubilees and in the history of Shakespeare's reputation, launching his cult and helping to turn him into the national hero that he still remains. He was presented by Garrick as a "peculiarly English" dramatist (Deelman 1964: 7, 264, 290; Brewer 1997: 412).

A few years later, the English celebrated another culture hero, George Frederic Handel. In 1784, the centenary of his birth as well as the twenty-fifth anniversary of his death, five commemorative performances of his music took place in London, including one of his famous *Messiah* in Westminster Abbey. These events have been described as "almost certainly the first such public celebration of the music of a particular composer, living or dead" (Brewer 1997: 403–5; Burrows 2004: 39; Drummond 2011: 9–11).

FIGURE 7.5: Shakespeare Jubilee, Stratford-upon-Avon, September 6–8, 1769 organized by David Garrick (1717–79), showing wooden pavilion erected by River Avon and celebrations in progress. Aquatint of 1795.

CONCLUSION

The most important change in rituals of commemoration in the early modern period was the rise of a Protestant calendar in competition with the Catholic one. The Protestant calendar was political as well as religious and contributed to the rise of secular festivals, including centenaries. The number of centenaries commemorated in the second half of the eighteenth century has already been noted. This rise of centenaries would become still more obvious in the centuries that followed, thanks to what might be called contagion, or better, conscious imitation, driven by rivalry, imitating in order to surpass, a process that we have already seen at work in the competition between universities or between Catholics and Protestants.

All the same, there are important contrasts between early modern commemorations and later ones. In his introduction to a landmark study of the history of commemorations, published over twenty years ago, John Gillis proposed a simple but plausible division into "three overlapping phases": the "pre-national" phase of local commemorations, before 1789; the national phase; and the relatively recent "post-national" or cosmopolitan phase (Gillis 1994: 5).

The idea of the three phases, with an emphasis on their overlap, is indeed an illuminating one, although the early modern part of the first phase needs to be described in a more complex way. Early modern anniversaries and centenaries generally supported the identities of imagined communities that were either smaller or larger than the nation, cities on one side and Christendom, or the Catholic or Protestant worlds, on the other.

Late modern commemorations, on the other hand, beginning with the American celebrations of 1778 and 1792, supported national identities: the anniversaries of national independence, for instance, together with the centenaries of the birth and death of national heroes, from generals to poets, and of major events in the nation's history, usually victories, such as the Prussian victory over Napoleon at the battle of Leipzig (1813), celebrated a year later by a "National Festival of the Germans" (Düding 1988). These commemorations may be viewed either as spontaneous expressions of nationalism (which the participants would prefer to call it, "patriotism") or as attempts, mainly by governments, to create it. They were probably a mixture of both.

Late modern commemorations also offer examples of the rise of "civil religion" from the French Revolution onwards, since the cult of the nation was often practiced with quasi-religious fervor and included a new liturgy and new "saints," including martyrs (Ozouf 1976). The Italy of Mussolini offers another clear example of the use of commemorations as part of the "sacralization of politics" or the secularization of devotion on the French model (Gentile 1993). Both the nationalization and the secularization of commemorations, together with their commercialization (already visible in the 1760s in the case of the Stratford Jubilee), reveal major fault-lines between the early modern and the late modern periods.

ANNEXE

Chronology of centenaries

1465 Birth of Dante, 200 years
1466 Swiss monastery of Einsiedeln, 500 years
1492 University of Erfurt, 100 years
1515 Burning of Hus, 100 years
1540 Invention of printing, 100 years
1560 University of Basel, 100 years
1572 University of Ingolstadt, 100 years
1578 University of Tübingen, 100 years
1587 University of Heidelberg, 200 years
1602 University of Wittenberg, 100 years
1609 University of Leipzig, 200 years
1617 Luther theses, 100 years
1619 Calling of Zwingli, 100 years
1625 Peasant War, 100 years
1629 Death of Quentin Matsys, 100 years
1630 Augsburg Confession, 100 years
1640 Foundation of Jesuits, 100 years
1640 Invention of printing, 200 years
1655 Peace of Augsburg, 100 years
1682 Foundation of bishopric of Salzburg, 1,100 years
1700 Coronation of Charlemagne, 900 years
1717 Luther theses, 200 years
1722 Canonizations of Loyola, Xavier, and Neri, 100 years
1722 Death of Johann Reuchlin, 200 years
1730 Augsburg Confession, 200 years
1739 Death of Martin Opitz, 100 years
1740 Invention of printing, 300 years

1743 Death of Copernicus, 200 years
1748 Peace of Westphalia, 100 years
1754 Pilgrimage to Telgte, 100 years
1755 Peace of Augsburg, 200 years
1762 Massacre of Protestants in Toulouse, 200 years
1769 Shakespeare Jubilee, 205 years
1772 Capture of Brill, 200 years
1786 Foundation of Heidelberg University, 400 years
1788 Glorious Revolution, 100 years
1788 Siege of Derry, 100 years
1789 Relief of Derry, 100 years
1790 Battle of the Boyne, 100 years
1792 Discovery of America, 300 years

CHAPTER EIGHT

Remembering and Forgetting

PETER SHERLOCK

INTRODUCTION

In 1532, Niccolò Machiavelli included a chapter in his *Discourses on Livy* entitled "How the Changes in Religious Sects and Languages, Along With Such Occurrences as Floods and Plagues, Erase the Memory of Things" (Machiavelli [1531] 1997: 167–9). In this chapter, Machiavelli wished "to reflect upon how things fall into oblivion." He found two principal causes: first, acts of God such as "pestilence, famine, or flood" that wiped out every trace of whole civilizations and second, the attempts of human societies to erase any record of the deeds of earlier peoples or institutions.

In the former case, the erasure of memory could not be explained or justified and was the result of what modern societies would call natural disasters. In the latter case, however, forgetting was no accident. Oblivion was the result of intentional, conscious acts. The key tools, Machiavelli explained, were religion and language. Indeed, the "first inclination" of a new religion or sect was "to extinguish the old religion" by obliteration "of its institutions, all of its religious ceremonies" and by suppression of "the memory of its ancient theology." Machiavelli did not mince his words in describing how this inclination was put into practice: he alleged that St. Gregory and his contemporaries "pursued every record from ancient times, burning the works of poets and historians, destroying images, and ruining everything else that retained any sign of antiquity." This enforced forgetting was necessary to permit the new theology to take root and flourish, to ensure its truth and power were acknowledged. The best way to accomplish this was through a change of language; Machiavelli argued that the one flaw in Christian attempts to suppress pagan religion was the retention of Latin, allowing a partial survival of the memory of earlier beliefs and identities.

As Cornel Zwierlein (2012: 118) has pointed out, Machiavelli's theory is unusual among early modern theories of remembering and forgetting in placing religious change at its center. Writing on the eve of the Reformation, Machiavelli was remarkably prescient. In the early modern age, Protestants attempted to extirpate what they saw as the heretical doctrine and practice of Catholic medieval inheritance. This was achieved through reinterpreting, remembering in new ways, the scriptures and other theological writings of the early church. But it was also achieved through acts of erasure, including the eradication of religious practice and the use of vernacular languages to spread what Protestants believed to be the light of the true gospel.

Between the fifteenth and seventeenth centuries, the meaning, interpretation, and practice of memory was transformed in European societies. At the very moment that mnemonic techniques such as the famous theatres of memory reached their pinnacle in the hands of sixteenth-century hermetic philosophers, humanist scholars began to argue that memory was an unstable agent for the transmission of knowledge (Yates 1966; Russell 2011: xi–xxii). The ancient and medieval notion that all knowledge worth knowing could be captured in the human memory was gradually displaced by the new technology of printing and the increased circulation of knowledge in books. Memory began a transition to modernity, to a new mentality in which remembering was unreliable.

Attitudes toward forgetting were also transformed. The ancient problem of oblivion, of the loss of knowledge or even loss of self, was to be overcome not by elaborate rote learning or intricate rhetorical devices but by the recording and circulation of information in manuscript and print. Just as unreliable remembering became a vice, deliberate forgetting became a virtue. The exercise of imagination and the desire for innovation actually required the erasure of the mind, the forgetting of old presumptions, ideas, and practices.

These changes were nowhere more pronounced than in the challenges of the Protestant reformation and the Catholic counter-reform which ruptured Christian memorial traditions, from the sacraments to the memory of the dead.

Recent scholarship on remembering and forgetting in early modern Europe has challenged the idea of a linear development in how the past was perceived. Where scholars once attributed a crisis of memory or of historical consciousness to the revolutions at the turn of the nineteenth century, attention to early modern culture suggests a different relationship between memory and social change. The most common historical labels for early modern Europe continue to signify what Christopher Ivic and Grant Williams (2004: 14) have labeled "a formidably deliberate act of forgetting." The "Renaissance" collapsed a thousand years' intermission between antiquity and modernity into the "Middle Ages." The "Reformation" constituted a rupture in memory comparable to but well before the French Revolution, with similar consequences for collective thinking about the past: "The changes brought about by the Reformations of the sixteenth century were momentous indeed, not only because they were accompanied by political shifts and religious wars, or because they divided families, but also because they called into question fundamental relationships between the living and the dead, the sacred and the profane, the material and the spiritual" (Deseure and Pollmann 2013: 325–6).

Judith Pollmann (2017) has argued convincingly that the search for a single "crisis of memory" is misplaced, proposing instead that while new practices of memory emerged in the sixteenth and seventeenth centuries, these did not so much overwrite or replace older methods and habits as supplement them. Thus, antiquarian catalogues of landscapes and historical accounts of the past did not replace or exclude customary evidence in legal judgments, a finding supported by Andy Wood's (2013a) research on custom and memory in local English communities.

Key concepts from the field of memory studies have been adapted to explore how remembering and forgetting were transformed in early modern Europe. William Engel (2004) has argued that for early moderns (as for previous ages), the opposite of Memory was Oblivion, the complete erasure of an aspect of the past. Engel proposes that forgetting is not the same as oblivion, defining it instead as a practice that leaves behind traces of the original material. Reworking Pierre Nora's pursuit of *lieux de mémoire* or "sites of memory," Engel (2004: 22) argues that this distinction allows for the investigation of *lieux d'oubli* or "sites of forgetting." Paralleling the work of Maurice Halbwachs on collective memory, Bradford Vivian (2010: 14) has likewise coined the notion of "public forgetting," defined as a pivotal moment in which an agent or a community articulates a rationale for interrupting or ending a paradigm of memory and configures a new relationship of past, present, and future.

This chapter examines how theories and practices of remembering and forgetting changed in early modern Europe, focusing primarily on English Protestant culture. It commences by reviewing the theoretical foundations and cultural expressions of forgetting and remembering. It then proposes that the Reformation is a prime example of "public forgetting," especially in its liturgical performance, before turning to examine one of the major seventeenth-century "sites of forgetting," the enactment of Acts of Oblivion.

THEORIES OF FORGETTING AND REMEMBERING

The tension between memory and oblivion was widely used as a rhetorical technique in early modern literature. Oblivion was an inexorable, inevitable, destructive force linked to decay and the ravages of time. In swearing the truth of her words, William Shakespeare's Cressida conjured up a classic image of oblivion, in which time itself forgets:

> If I be false, or swerve a hair from truth,
> When time is old and hath forgot itself,
> When waterdrops have worn the stones of Troy,
> And blind oblivion swallow'd cities up,
> And mighty states characterless are grated
> To dusty nothing; yet let memory,
> From false to false, among false maids in love,
> Upbraid my falsehood!
>
> —*Troilus and Cressida*, III.2.1835–42

Antiquarian scholars delighted in the irony that the recognition of oblivion constituted a form of remembering. In a paper to the Society of Antiquaries delivered in London in November 1600, Joseph Holland presented a series of exemplary epitaphs to the dead to reveal the development of the genre over time and to argue for its literary merits. He concluded with an example from St. Paul's Cathedral, London,

> wherein there is great sense comprehended in one word, and yet that word is written upon a large marble stone at the foot of the great staires, ascending up unto the quire in St. Paul's, to wit, OBLIVIO. Notwithstanding the brevity of this, the writer's meaning was not that the person there buried should be forgotten, because he hath sett his arms at the four corners of the stone, which are significant enough to declare who he was.
>
> —Hearne 1720: 259–60

This gravestone's verbal proposition was that the deceased subject was forgotten, erased, absent, yet simultaneously it deployed heraldic language to enable commemoration, re-inscription, presence.

Keeping oblivion at bay required constant work. Erasmus wrote that "like books that stick together from neglect if you do not read them, memory evaporates if not refreshed from time to time" (Hiscock 2011: 24). Shakespeare expanded on this trope in *Troilus and Cressida*, showing how oblivion could make a mockery of memory:

Time hath, my lord, a wallet at his back,
Wherein he puts alms for oblivion,
A great-sized monster of ingratitudes:
Those scraps are good deeds past; which are devour'd
As fast as they are made, forgot as soon
As done: perseverance, dear my lord,
Keeps honour bright: to have done is to hang
Quite out of fashion, like a rusty mail
In monumental mockery.

—*Troilus and Cressida*, III.3.2021–29

But how was the past to be remembered? What was to be forgotten? Jonathan Baldo (2012: 8–9) draws attention to the centrality of this theme in Shakespeare's history plays, arguing that the apparent power of a monarch to control memory, history, and national identity stood in contrast with the strength of local custom and popular nostalgia. Early moderns appealed to the classical idea of *damnatio memoriae*, that memory would fall victim not only to uncontrolled forgetting but also to an intentional oblivion. Stephen Mullaney (2015: 109) highlights the power of the deliberate dismemberment of history in Gloucester's reaction in *Henry VI Part 2* to the news of the king's marriage:

O peers of England, shameful is this league!
Fatal this marriage, cancelling your fame,
Blotting your names from books of memory,
Razing the characters of your renown,
Defacing monuments of conquer'd France,
Undoing all, as all had never been!

—*Henry VI Part 2*, 1.1.105–11

Similarly, as Archbishop Scroop explains to Lord Mowbray in *Henry IV Part 2*, the king is frustrated by memory and history; whenever one problem is consigned to oblivion, two more arise in its place:

For he hath found to end one doubt by death
Revives two greater in the heirs of life;
And therefore will he wipe his tables clean,
And keep no tell-tale to his memory
That may repeat and history his los
To new remembrance.

—*Henry IV Part 2*, 4.2.2406–11

The reference to "wiping his tables clean" points to the ancient notion of memory as an archive, repository, or theater, a notion reproduced in early modern literature by the image of memory as an erasable book or tablet. "Tables" or "Books of memory" referenced in English and Spanish dramatic texts were little notebooks that allowed temporary thoughts to be recorded and later erased. Appearing as props on the stage, most famously in Shakespeare's *Hamlet*, these printed volumes contained pages coated in wax that could be inscribed with a metal stylus and later wiped clean when the memories recorded were no longer needed, or had been transcribed to a more permanent medium (Chartier 2007: 13–27). Remembering and forgetting were interwoven in such objects, which allowed the possessor a small stretch of time in which to determine whether something needed to be recorded permanently or temporarily or could be quickly erased.

Early modern printing and publishing, archiving and collecting seemed to alleviate the threat of effacement of memory symbolized by the wax tablet. But this led to new problems. Whereas sixteenth-century humanists saw boundless possibilities in the perfection of memory, seventeenth-century philosophers had to confront the intolerable weight of the proliferation of knowledge. A boundless memory unlimited by forgetting was excessive, indistinct, and indigestible. Forgetting gradually took on positive attributes, as a necessary aspect to preserve the utility of memory and to facilitate processes of discovery and innovation.

The humanist Juan Luis Vives emphasized the need for training in the mnemonic arts. As the 1558 English edition of his work put it, the human person was "framed and facioned by these three things, knowledge, wit, & Memory" (Hiscock 2011: 91). In commenting on Vives' dictum that "the more you entrust to memory, the more faithfully will everything be stored up; the less, the more faithlessly," Harald Weinrich (2004: 39) points out it evidently never occurred to Vives that "forgetting might have any place in the *res publica litterarum*."

This approach to memory training was the subject of satire. In François Rabelais' *Gargantua* (1534), the lead character is taught in the scholastic fashion, learning the same lessons backwards as well as forward, to ensure complete instruction and retention of knowledge. Yet when Ponocrates, a humanist teacher, takes on responsibility for Gargantua's education, he is unable to make any headway for his student's mind is completely full. The solution is to give the student hellebore, a drug that makes the student forget, wiping out scholastic learning. While forgetting here has a positive value—removal of obsolete information—the humanist method still requires the arts of memory, to instill what is simply a different curriculum organized around new categories and a different use of time (Weinrich 2004: 41–2).

The French writer Michel de Montaigne famously quipped in his 1580 *Essais* that "there is nothing that imprints a thing so vividly on the memory as the desire to forget it" (Frame 1958: 365). Montaigne was drawing here on Cicero's oft-cited account of Themistocles' complaint, that he remembered things he did not wish to remember and could not forget the things he wished to forget. Memory was dangerous because it was uncontrollable. For Montaigne, the act of writing could function in the same way memory operated for previous generations. Writing recorded isolated experiences or events that could later be recalled or reassembled into an interpretative analysis. Thus, for those like Montaigne who had not been trained in the mnemonic arts, ink and paper could take the place of memory by enabling the storage of information about personal experiences (Russell 2011: 95–113).

New techniques of note-taking emerged in response to the challenge of a surplus of information, techniques nicknamed "forgetting machines" by Alberto Cevolini (2016b: 13). Beginning with Erasmus' instructions in his *De copia* (1512) on how to take notes systematically, arranged around affinity and opposition, early modern scholars began to create external memory banks through commonplace books. These assisted the student to displace information from memory onto paper—to forget it—in organized ways that facilitated recall (Yeo 2016).

Richard Yeo (2008) has traced the development of these complex note-taking systems, as they evolved from tools for training the memory for use in the rhetorical arts, to external storage facilities for knowledge. Yeo (2008: 123) demonstrates how the choice of "Heads" used in such systems was reflective of a "common repertoire of ideas, quotations and tropes from a stable body of texts." Yet as notebooks became archives, as they went from being "repositories of the material that individuals *sought* to memorize, they came to be seen as ways of retaining information that could *never* be memorized" (Yeo 2008: 130). As the Enlightenment emerged, it became clear that no longer was it merely permissible to forget, to translate knowledge from the mind to the page, it was in fact necessary to make way for discovery and innovation.

Descartes wrote of his exposure to the humanist arts of memory, ridiculing Thomas Lambert Schenckel's 1593 treatise *De memoria*:

> When I read Lambert Schenkel's provoking stupidities, I reflected that I could easily comprehend everything I had discovered within my powers of imagination, if only I always reduced things to their causes. And if they could be reduced to a single cause, then it becomes clear that for knowledge as a whole no memory is needed [. . .]. Therein consists the true art of memory, and it is completely opposed to the one that blockhead practices. It is not that his art is completely pointless, only that he wastes far too much paper on it because he does not adhere to the right order. The latter consists in putting memory images in a relationship of mutual dependency. Schenkel, in contrast, has intentionally or unintentionally failed to see wherein the key to the whole mystery lies.
>
> —Descartes, *Cogitationes privatae*, quoted in Weinrich 2004: 57

Philosophers such as Descartes not only maligned the arts of memory but also questioned the traditional "Heads" or schema used for the categorization of knowledge, challenging the assumption that the concerns of ancient authors were a reliable framework for either the storage of information or the creation of knowledge (Vivian 2010: 27). As Harald Weinrich (2004: 58) puts it, the initial step of Cartesian method was to eliminate all existing information from the mind in "a comprehensive strategy of forgetting" that removes remembered data "to a methodically regulated oblivion." The second step, the reintroduction of the "forgotten" information for a critical assessment, likewise involves an exercise of the will through "methodologically controlled remembering" (Weinrich 2004: 59–60).

In England, Francis Bacon led the charge to subdue memory for rhetoric's sake to critical recollection for the advancement of knowledge (Sherlock 2010). Bacon believed that innovation and discovery—what he termed inauguration—could only occur through creating a disjuncture with the past, in order to overcome what he characterized as the meanderings and self-referential investigations of previous generations: "generally speaking science is to be sought from the light of nature, not from the darkness of antiquity" (Bacon quoted in Hiscock 2011: 220). His empirical method was constituted around the necessity of forgetting in order to purify knowledge and inquiry, a principle supported by reference to the ancient idea of the wax tablet: "on waxen tablets you cannot write anything new until you rub out the old. With the mind it is not so there you cannot rub out the old until you have written in the new" (Bacon quoted in Hiscock 2011: 226). The way ahead for scholarship was peer review. This required the process of rational deduction to be recorded so that it could be critically assessed by others. Knowledge, especially new knowledge, was confirmed by an experiment that could be successfully repeated rather than attribution of ideas to mutually recognized ancient authorities. As Andrew Hiscock (2011: 236) suggests, "Memory, with its grand store of sense impressions and cognitive associations, must thus give place to meticulous written records, enabling the careful processing of all results with the arrangement of data into tables."

After Bacon's death in 1626, his secretary Thomas Meautys erected a monument for him in St. Michael's Church at St. Albans, England, in a composition which used Bacon's insights in an attempt to fashion his memory (Figure 8.1). The sculpture showed Bacon seated in a chair in an unusually relaxed pose associated with melancholy, nostalgia, and contemplation—fitting attributes as they were linked to the study of philosophy. The Latin epitaph gave Bacon's aristocratic titles, before explaining his "more notable titles, the Light of Science, the Law of Eloquence" concluding "he used to sit like this" (*sic sedebat*). Thus, while the effigy invited the learned viewer to make associations drawn from traditional emblematic forms of representative, the epitaph "he used to sit like this" suggested that the visitor might value empirical observation and critical assessment.

FIGURE 8.1: Monument of Francis Bacon (d. 1626), Church of St. Michael, St. Albans, Hertfordshire, England. Photo: Gary Houston, 2004.

THE REFORMATION AS PUBLIC FORGETTING

These literary and philosophical reconfigurations of memory and oblivion reshaped early modern scholarship and helped give life to the Enlightenment. As is now well-established, the Reformation constituted a more immediate and profound change in remembering and forgetting in early modern Europe. In overturning core beliefs and practices of medieval theology, reformers reshaped and rebuilt memory and tradition (Walsham 2011: 567). In England this included an evolving sense of the church year, as national dramas were converted into new festivals, from the anniversary of the accession of Elizabeth I in 1558, through thanksgiving for the deliverance of James VI and I from the Gunpowder Plot in 1605, to the commemoration of Charles I as a martyr of the Church of England (Cressy 1989).

By far the most prominent and most successful attempt to recast the past in England was John Foxe's *Acts and Monuments* (Hiscock 2011: 90–112). First published in English in a massive volume of 1,471 pages in 1563, it went through four editions in Foxe's lifetime alone, including considerable reworking and extension, and was widely circulated in churches and homes (Figure 8.2). Foxe's work created a history for English Protestantism, emphasizing its apostolic inheritance and especially its persecution in the sixteenth century, by dramatically retelling the lives and deaths of Protestant martyrs under Queen Mary. It also rewrote the history of earlier English Christianity, creating a narrative of corruption and falsehood promulgated by papists and monasteries, and continuing the erasure of former heroes such as Thomas Becket, whom Foxe did not consider a martyr. The *Acts and Monuments* also celebrated memory itself, as a duty owed by the reader to the maintenance and propagation of true religion.

FIGURE 8.2: Woodcut, "The burnyng of the Archbishop of Caunterbury Doctor Thomas Cranmer," John Foxe, *Acts and Monuments* (London, 1563), p. 1572.

If Protestants sought to recreate social memory, they did so by intentional erasure of what they saw as false understandings of the past. The Reformation was unquestionably a site of forgetting. As Alexandra Walsham (2012: 907) writes, "In a world in which the art of remembering was primarily an art of mental visualization, the reformers recognized that removing physical reminders of popish error was vital to the task of transforming mentalities." This was at its most obvious in acts of iconoclasm and the revolution in how the dead were remembered, recently described as a "cultural forgetting of faith" (Karremann, Zwierlein, and Groote 2012: 5).

Eamon Duffy (1992: 494) has illustrated both the richness of late medieval English commemorative religious culture and its programmatic destruction in the sixteenth century, describing Edwardian iconoclasm as "an act of oblivion." As the mass was redefined, altars were torn down and their furnishings removed or destroyed. As the intercession of saints was rejected, statues and liturgical calendars were attacked and defaced by order of the state. As Purgatory was decreed to be a fiction, masses and prayers for the dead were abolished. The very act of defacement—of consigning these ideas to oblivion—was itself prized as a cultural habit. As Philip Schwyzer (2018) points out, sixteenth-century English iconoclasts not only destroyed the heads and hands of hundreds and thousands of statues in churches throughout the kingdom but left the defaced remains in situ as a permanent reminder of the will to forget. Oblivion was conceived by some contemporaries as a productive force, producing both a Protestant culture of memory and a nostalgia for a broken, fragmented past (Karremann, Zwierlein, and Groote 2012: 15; Walsham 2011: 273–96).

Fifteenth-century practices for commemoration of the dead at All Saints', Bristol reveal how pre-Reformation communities thought about memory. "Good doers and wellwillers" were to be remembered annually, their names and deeds of charity to be rehearsed in front of the parishioners. This had two purposes, clearly stated in the All Saints' Church Book: "That they shall not be forgotten but had in remembrance and be prayed for of all the parish and all of them that be to come and also for an example to you that be now living that you may likewise do for yourself and for your friends while they be in this world" (Burgess 2000: 55). Remembrance of the dead produced two benefits: prayers for the departed and imitation of their virtues by the living. In the late medieval world, remembering was reciprocal. Just as the dead had provided for posterity through bequests, so the living would provide for the dead by their prayers and charitable intentions.

After the Reformation, Protestants developed a different approach to memory. They rejected the doctrine of Purgatory and insisted there was nothing the living could do to influence or amend the fate of the dead. Yet, as Peter Marshall (2001: 301) argues, "the memory of the dead was also the memory of the Catholic past. To neglect it too completely was a potentially dangerous form of cultural and social amnesia; to celebrate it too exuberantly an equally dangerous temptation to apostasy." Protestants excised the prayers of the living for the dead from their monuments but continued nonetheless to bury and commemorate the dead in churches and churchyards. By 1631, the English antiquary John Weever ([1631] 2016: 206) (Figure 8.3) defined a monument simply as "a thing erected, made, or written, for a memorial of some remarkable action, fit to be transferred to future posterities." Monuments were no longer for the benefit of the dead, but for the living, who in imitating the example of earlier generations might aspire to a godly life and the assured hope of the resurrection after death (Sherlock 2008: 97–128).

The challenge of commemorating the dead for Protestant communities is exemplified in Andrew Spicer's (2007) study of Calvinist churches in early modern Europe. For the

FIGURE 8.3: T. Cecill, frontispiece to John Weever, *Ancient Funerall Monuments* (London, 1631).

Reformed churches, theological and social memory came into conflict about the issue of intramural burial. This practice was inherited from the medieval church but outlawed by some Calvinists as contrary to the sanctity of the church and potentially a form of idolatry. Thus, in Geneva and Scotland Calvinist regimes initially forbade burial inside the church, although by popular demand the practice was reintroduced in the mid-seventeenth century. In the Dutch Republic intramural burial was hugely popular, with the floors of reformed churches quickly covered from wall to wall with ledger stones dedicated to families and individuals. Established habits of commemorating the dead proved hard to shift; where Catholic churches were repurposed, the chancel remained more popular than the nave. In some places the pulpit became a popular place of burial, perpetuating the customary hierarchy of burial but realigning it with the reformed priorities of post-Reformation sacred geography. One reason for this was that Reformed churches themselves remained or became centers for civic memorialization, including images in glass or paint that glorified key historic events, such as the Dutch Revolt (Spicer 2007: 153–5, 231–2).

Yet the Reformation did not dissolve the community of the living and the dead; instead it reconfigured the relationship. In some Protestant communities, aisles formerly dedicated to singing masses and saying prayers for the dead were converted to burial grounds dominated by monuments. In Lutheran German states, early modern tomb patrons appropriated the "epitaph monument," comprising a portrait or carving of the deceased with their family, a religious image and a text. As Maria Deiters (2012) argues, such memorials represented the dead as if they were continuing to participate in worship alongside the living. This is dramatically illustrated in the epitaph monument for Johann Kötteritz and Caritas Distelmeier, erected in their funerary chapel at St. Nikolai's, Berlin around 1615. The couple are shown richly dressed and devoutly kneeling before the Lamb of God, accompanied by Moses and John the Baptist. Behind them is an image of the church itself, full of people participating in rites of baptism, marriage, communion, and preaching, with the monument itself just visible. The living and the dead are in separate realms, but are represented side-by-side, as if the dead and the living are bound in perpetual remembrance of each other (Deiters 2012: 76–81).

The relationship between the living and the dead was a major controversy in the Reformation, signifying divergent understandings of salvation. Even more profound, however, was the division in Reformation thought and polemic about the nature and function of eucharistic memory.

The centrality of human remembering in the late medieval mass is, as Lucy Wooding (2013) has argued, neatly captured in John Lydgate's verse dating from 1435 and printed in London in 1520:

> Of mementoos at masse there be twayne
> The fyrst remembreth of folke than ben alyve
> The seconde is for them that suffre payne
> Whiche by the masse be releved by theyr lyve
> Out of tormentes clerkes can dyscryne
> Syngynge of masses and crystes passyon
> And remembraunce of his woundes fyve
> May moost avayle to theyr remyssyon.
>
> —Lydgate, 1520[1]

This verse links two forms of memory: the people who remember the living and the dead and the priest who remembers Christ's passion and death, making Christ present in the host and providing the pathway to salvation. To participate in the mass was to participate in a unique act of memory, if indeed it was memory at all, as by the miracle of transubstantiation the suffering Christ became physically and immediately present, eclipsing time and space.

In contrast, Protestant theologies of the Eucharist emphasized commemoration in place of actualization. Where the transubstantiated host of the mass presented the believer with the thing signified—Christ's body and blood—the memorial movement of the Lord's Supper imprinted the effects of Christ's body and blood in the believer's heart. As Thomas Fuller (2016: 212) conceived it in 1640, there was a "great chasm" in time and space between early modern England and first-century Palestine, but this was overcome at the communion table for "Christ here teacheth thee the art of memory, what so long was past is now made present at the instant of thy worthy receiving." The object of memory in the Eucharist for Lutherans was the contemplation of Christ's saving death, made once and for all, a contemplation deepened by the corporeal presence of Christ. For Reformed Protestants, eucharistic remembering focused on the Last Supper as well as on the cross, but with a strict separation between these past moments and the present time (Wandel 2006: 260).

In the Church of England, liturgy was regulated throughout the whole realm in the reign of Edward VI in the form of the *Book of Common Prayer*, issued in 1549 and revised in 1552. The prayer book began with an introduction, "Of Ceremonies," which explained how it was necessary to consign to oblivion liturgies that promulgated erroneous beliefs and practices. The prayer book went on to contend that the purpose of liturgy as prescribed by the Bible was "to stirre uppe the dulle mynde of manne, to the remembraunce of his duetie to God, by some notable and speciall significacion, whereby he might bee edified" (Brightman 1915: 1.42). Liturgical memory was an exercise of the human duty to worship God.

From 1552, the crucial moment in the *Book of Common Prayer* communion service was no longer the repetition of Jesus' words at the Last Supper, "this is my body ... do this in remembrance of me," but the administration of the bread and wine to communicants. The words said to each recipient by the minister (as amended in the 1559 edition of the book to incorporate a phrase from 1549) encapsulated the whole point of the liturgy:

> The body of our Lord Jesus Christ, which was given for thee, preserve thy body and soule unto everlasting life: take and eat this in remembrance that Christ dyed for thee, and feed on him in thy heart by faith with thanksgiving.
>
> The blood of our Lord Jesus Christ, which was shed for thee, preserve thy body and soule unto everlasting life: drinke this in remembrance that Christs blood was shed for thee, and be thankfull.
>
> —Brightman 1915: 2.701

In this liturgy the retelling of the Lord's Supper became a mere chronicle of historic events. In contrast, the words of administration emphasized that the act of memory was an act of thanksgiving undertaken in the heart and mind of the individual communicant (Jeanes 2008: 238). Eucharistic memory in the Church of England was intended by Cranmer and his successors to be a physical act of eating and drinking while calling to mind Christ's suffering and death (Turrell 2014). The role of the priest who consecrated the elements was replaced by that of the minister who instructed the people on how to remember correctly. The communion became an act of thanksgiving for God's grace already received rather than a work to solicit that grace (Null 2000: 26).

The new theology of eucharistic memory was clearly understood by at least some laity. In 1563, John Foxe recorded Lady Jane Grey's response, shortly before her execution in 1554, to her inquisitor's questions about whether she believed she received the body and blood of Christ in the sacrament:

> I thynke that at the supper, I neyther receyue flesh or bloude, but onely breade and wyne: Whiche breade when it is broken, and the wyne when it is dronken, putteth me in remembrance how that for my sinnes the body of Christ was broken, and his bloude shedde on the crosse. And with that bread and wine I receiue the benefites that commeth by the breakyng of his body, and sheding of his bloud for our sinnes on the crosse.
>
> —Foxe 2011: 986

This Protestant act of memory was no mere commemoration and it was not to be taken lightly. As reformer Nicholas Ridley argued, the Lord's Supper was a perpetual remembrance that "far passeth all kinds of rememberances that any other man is able to make, either of himself, or of any other thing: for whosoever receiveth this holy sacrament thus ordained in remembrance of Christ, he receiveth therewith either death or life" (Ridley quoted in Turrell 2014: 145–6). According to the theology of the *Book of Common Prayer*, the Eucharist was of no benefit to anyone other than the godly communicant. This had many consequences: the laity should receive as well as the minister; chantries and masses for the dead were ineffectual and irrelevant; and the vernacular should be employed to ensure the communicants partook of the bread and wine with full comprehension of the act (Turrell 2014: 145).

Not everyone embraced the weighty new responsibility of eucharistic remembrance. English reformers soon found that many people were reluctant to receive the bread and the wine, partly due to fear incited by the dramatic exhortations in the *Book of Common Prayer* on the perils of unrighteous reception (MacCulloch 1996: 510). Godly communicants needed to be in charity with their neighbors, which might involve a public reconciliation with neighbors prior to attending the Lord's Supper (Hunt 1998). The Protestant duty to remember extended well beyond the Lord's Supper, however, as preachers exhorted the people to commit scripture to memory, to learn their catechisms by rote. Memory constituted a defense against the doubt and despair which would assail all believers. The recall of scripture could be an aid in extempore prayer to ward off these threats (Ryrie 2013).

An especially intriguing aspect of early modern culture is the way in which the theological burden of human memory was accompanied by the desire for divine forgetting, whereby God would pardon humans and forgive them for their sins. This pairing of sinful remembering and divine forgetting was held in dramatic tension in John Donne's ninth holy sonnet. Donne (1971: 297) presented them as the means by which spiritual rebellion might be resolved into submission to God (Hiscock 2011: 184):

> If poysonous mineralls, and if that tree,
> Whose fruit threw death on else immortall us,
> If lecherous goats, if serpents envious
> Cannot be damn'd; Alas, why should I be?
> Why should intent or reason, borne in me,
> Make sinnes, else equall, in mee more heinous?
> And mercy being easie, and glorious
> To God; in his sterne wrath, why threatens hee?
> But who am I, that dare dispute with thee
> O God? Oh! of thine onely worthy blood,
> And my teares, make a heavenly Lethean flood,
> And drowne in it my sinnes blacke memorie;
> That thou remember them, some claime as debt,
> I thinke it mercy, if thou wilt forget.
>
> —Donne, 1633

Here a corrupt sinner seeks God's mercy, which may be granted through what Frances Cruickshank (2010: 105) calls a "reverse eucharist." Salvation is achieved not by the traditional act of memory as commanded by Jesus at the Last Supper, but by forgetting. This forgetting is the sinner's repentance, represented by "my tears," mixed with the blood of Christ in a "Lethean flood" that washes away "sinnes blacke memorie." The final couplet links remembering with the debt of sin and forgetting with the mercy of God.

This poetic theology of sinful remembering and holy forgetting was a major theme in Protestant culture. The evangelical emphasis on justification by grace alone, rather than by any human agency, raised the problem of whether or not humans had free will, a problem that extended to the memory. As Nicolas Russell (2011) has shown, Marguerite de Navarre addressed this dilemma in her *Heptaméron* (published in 1558). She suggested that, while sinners were culpable for making a choice to do wrong, they were not entirely free. Deep forces beyond human control meant people could temporarily forget themselves and their guiding values. This type of forgetting was an unstable, involuntary behavior of the human mind leading to immoral choices that departed from what a rational person would truly desire (Russell 2011: 47–8).

The Protestant emphasis on repentance stressed the divine initiative, God's act of forgetting and forgiving the sinful deeds of human. The Church of England's "Homilie of Repentance, and of true reconciliation unto God" in the second Book of Homilies (first published in 1571) repeatedly reminded English congregations that, for penitent, true believers, God will "according to his promise, freely pardon, forgive, and forget all our sinnes," that God will "forgive us all our sinnes, and put them out of remembrance, and from his sight" (*Certaine Sermons* 1623).

Early reformers emphasized the apocalyptic dimensions of belief, pointing to how God was making all things new; faith was about the future, not the past. This meant that inherited tradition was to be questioned, shaken down, set aside. Argula von Grumbach, a remarkable German controversialist of the 1520s, highlighted the deceptiveness of tradition when she wrote, "Do not be led astray by old customs and traditional ways. The Lord says; 'I am the way, the truth, and the life.' John 14. He does not say: 'I am what is customary'" (Matheson 1995: 157). Like many reformers, she emphasized the responsibility of the Christian to acquaint herself with the Bible, the word of God, instead of relying on what they had been taught by their parents: "All this is because they are as well informed about the Bible as a cow is about chess. While it certainly isn't my task to deal with their stock retort: 'I believe what my parents believed'—that is not the end of the matter. For all Christians do have a responsibility to know the word of God" (Matheson 1995: 146).

Forgetting was not only an act to be desired of God; it could also be undertaken fruitfully by the godly Christian. This idea was set forth at length by the preacher Thomas Playfere ([1593] 2016: 238–41) in *The Pathway to Perfection*, his 1593 sermon on the text of Philippians 3:14, "I forget that which is behind, and endeavour myself to that which is before." Playfere demonstrated that the wicked were guilty of pride while the godly were characterized by humility, on account of how they remembered virtues and vices: "Both remember virtues, but the godly remember other men's virtues. The wicked remember their own virtues." This was standard Protestant fare, but Playfere went on to praise forgetting as a godly practice, the habit of divines, in contrast to the vain remembering of philosophers:

> For philosophy is an art of memory, but divinity is an art of forgetfulness. Therefore the first lesson that Socrates taught his Scholar was "remember." For he thought that knowledge is nothing else but a calling of those things to remembrance which the mind knew before it knew the body. But the first lesson that Christ teacheth his scholar is "forget." Hearken, O daughter, says he, and see. Forget thine own country and thy father's house.
>
> —Playfere [1593] 2016: 240

Christian forgetting, based on a catalogue of Christ's miracles performed in the gospels, was about turning away from the old to the new, from former things and present sufferings to the future. This, too, was at odds with classical precepts that valorized the memory of good deeds; Playfere ([1593] 2016: 241) wrote that the godly should not only "renounce the devil and all his works and forget all thy wicked works which are behind thee" but "all thy good works also. For if thou forget them, then will God remember them."

These Protestant ideas about remembering and forgetting were not confined to liturgical and literary cultural expressions but were put into practice in diverse forms from commemoration of the dead to personal daily habits such as self-examination. A monumental brass erected in Stockton church, Wiltshire (Figure 8.4), to commemorate the death of Elizabeth Poticary in 1590 spoke of her virtuous life and good death, for she esteemed heavenly hope above worldly values. The epitaph spoke of her prayerful pleas to God not to forget her (using the words of Psalm 13) and assured the reader that her pleas were not in vain:

> How long wilt thou forgett me Lord: This song,
> In greatest panges was her sweete harmony.
> Forget thee: no: he will not thee forget:
> In booke of lyfe for aye thy name is set.

Writing in the first half of the seventeenth century, Elizabeth Isham recorded her memories of a range of domestic and spiritual matters in her unpublished "Booke of Remembrance." Introduced by remarks such as "I will now call to mind," her recollections included regret at the weakness of her memory and her shame at forgetting. A dominant theme in her

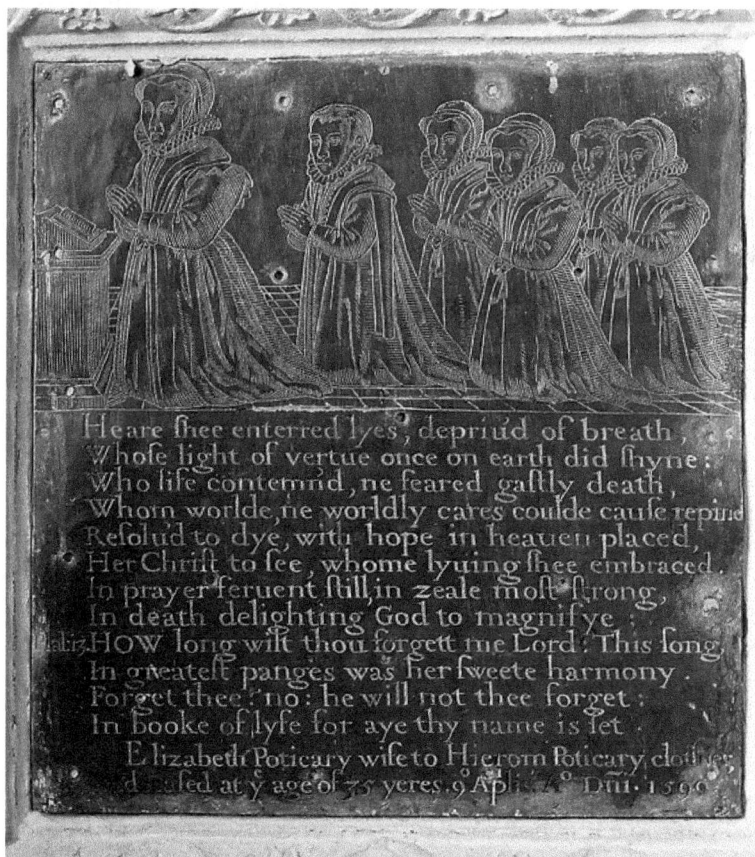

FIGURE 8.4: Monumental brass of Elizabeth Poticary (d. 1590), Church of St. John the Baptist, Stockton, Wiltshire, England. Photo: Mike Searle, 2011.

"Booke" was the theological significance of remembering and forgetting. On the one hand God "hast promised that when the wicked turne from there evill wayes there sinnnes shall noe more be remembered," while on the other Isham herself sinned by "remembering of what I should forget injuries. indignities." For Isham, forgetting—and forgiving—could be a holy act. Remembering, such as bearing a grudge, might be sinful (Ezell 2011).

POLITICAL FORGETTING

The reappraisal of the merits and perils of remembering and forgetting, human and divine, is but one example of the far-reaching consequences of the Reformation. This extraordinary, protracted "public forgetting" divided families and communities and led to a series of confessional wars across early modern Europe. Ending war, justifying victory or creating a lasting peace presented new challenges in the late sixteenth and seventeenth centuries. A common strategy to achieve these ends was deliberate, enforced forgetting, exemplified in one of the most striking sites of forgetting in early modern Europe—the enactment of Acts of Oblivion. Used especially in France and England, these acts sought to offer an amnesty in return for a collective amnesia as a means of responding to the problems of endless civil and religious wars.

In 1598, Henri IV issued the Edict of Nantes in an attempt to conclude the French religious wars and shore up his political and religious authority. The Edict famously dictated that "the memory of everything that has taken place on both sides since the beginning of the month of March 1585 until our accession to the crown, and during the other preceding troubles and on account of them, shall remain extinct and dormant, as of a thing that never happened" (Frisch 2012: 63). This enforced, collective forgetting was the precondition for an enduring peace, reunification of the kingdom, and the security of Henri IV's reign. As Andrea Frisch (2012) has argued, this rhetoric of forgetting subsequently dominated French politics for over a century. The technique was famously repeated in 1685 by Louis XVI in the Edict of Fontainebleau. This time, however, the purpose was to forget the original forgetting: "we judge that we can do nothing better in order to efface entirely the memory of the troubles ... than to entirely revoke the aforementioned Edict of Nantes" (Frisch 2012: 77). Louis insisted that his subjects forget the original forgetting and overlook the reality of continuing religious division in France (Frisch 2012: 78). Paradoxically, the French Edicts drew attention to the very topics they wished to erase: Henri IV's Protestant past; the St. Bartholomew's Day Massacre; the wars of religion (Benedict 2013).

Similar attempts at enforced forgetting were used to try to resolve the civil wars in mid-seventeenth-century Britain and Ireland. The conflicts between the king, the Parliament, and the English, Scottish, and Irish realms were so calamitous that after a decade of war the very institution of monarchy was torn down in 1649 with the execution of Charles I. Yet the whole of English law, politics, and religion was grounded on the concept of monarchy. To resolve this, lawyers, politicians, and philosophers erected a new historical construct that argued for an ancient English constitution which predated the monarchy. In this version of the past, the Norman Conquest of 1066 was reconfigured not as an act of colonization and suppression by a conquering duke, but as a legitimate dynastic succession that left intact the underlying social contract between crown and people which Charles had so profoundly broken. Thus, a fundamental historic event enshrined in tradition, history, and memory was represented as a moment of continuity (Connerton 2008: 60).

From 1642 to 1662, several attempts were made to address the political and historical crisis through Acts of Oblivion (Peters 2017: 46–58). In 1642, Charles I offered his subjects a free and general pardon, an amnesty, in a misguided attempt to reconcile himself with the forces lined up behind the Parliamentarians. This was not only rejected but subsequently contested, when in 1643 the Lords and the Commons indicated their willingness to receive the royal pardon provided that Parliament had the power to determine who would be excepted from it. The prerogative to forget and forgive—or to remember and punish—was hotly contested. In 1651, Oliver Cromwell convinced the Parliament to enact a General Act of Pardon and Oblivion, to prevent the seizure of further estates from the royalists in a bid to alleviate further division, but this was hedged about with so many exceptions that it was destined, it seemed, to bring more bitterness than reconciliation (Worden 1974: 265–70).

Finally, in 1660 following the restoration of monarchy, the Parliament adopted "An act of free and general pardon, indemnity and oblivion." This "pardoned, released, indemnified, discharged and put in utter oblivion" a wide variety of acts, from treason to murder, conducted since 1637, for the purpose of burying "all seeds of future discords and remembrance of the former" (Act of Free and General Pardon, 1660, 12 Car. 2, I). In supporting the Act, the Lord Chancellor Edward Hyde, exhorted the members of Parliament to "teach your neighbors and your friends, how to pay a full obedience to this clause of the Statute, how to learn this excellent Art of Forgetfulness" (Hyde quoted in Shifflett 2003: 108). Not everything could be forgotten, however, and Charles II's mercy had its limits. Several regicides—dead and alive—were to be hanged, drawn, and quartered in punishment for the death of Charles I. In a gruesome public display, the bodies of Cromwell, Ireton, and Bradshaw were disinterred from their graves in Westminster Abbey and given a posthumous execution at Tyburn (Fitzgibbons 2008).

Andrew Shifflett (2003) has highlighted how these Acts of Oblivion were part of a wider cultural interest in clemency, which predated the restoration of monarchy in 1660, paying particular attention to the mid-seventeenth-century English poet Abraham Cowley who advocated in the 1650s for an *ars oblivionalis*, an art of forgetfulness. As Shifflett (2003: 90) puts it, "Cowley's forgetful art was modeled on a history of forgetful acts— *acts* of oblivion that might hold more, not less, political power when converted into *art*." But in the political climate of late seventeenth-century Europe, forgetting in the form of an Act of Oblivion was stubbornly political, more concerned with the demonstration of divine-like power of a ruler or a parliament than with promoting mutual reconciliation, with the virtue of clemency in victory than a reconciliation of divided parties. This sort of forgetting was not an act of forgiveness based on remorse (Van Dijkhuizen 2015).

CONCLUSION

One forgets not by cancellation but by superimposition, not by producing absence but by multiplying presences.

—Eco 1988: 260

This chapter has challenged the assumption that there was an equality to the dialectic of remembering and forgetting in early modern culture. Contemporary dramatists pointed to the subjugation of memory to oblivion, a powerful, ultimately irresistible force. Philosophers and scientists used "forgetting machines," new techniques for organizing, categorizing and circulating information to allow themselves to manage an ever-widening quantity of knowledge. Protestant reformers attacked Catholic attitudes toward memory, especially with regard to the Eucharist. Theologically, Protestants placed a renewed emphasis on the role of divine forgetting of human sin in the drama of salvation. The politics of representing the past were at their most dramatic in attempts to legislate oblivion, moving from the well-worn tropes of amnesty and pardon to turning a blind eye to irreconcilable historic moments. None of these practices replaced or wiped out previous cultures of remembering and forgetting; as Pollmann (2017) and Wood (2013a) argue, they were for the most part additions and superimpositions.

Forgetting was dramatically reworked in early modern Europe. The practice of forgetting could be divided into two broad domains. First was the longstanding view of forgetting as an accident or omission, an error that created absence of knowledge, faith, or understanding. Second, however, was the deliberate erasure of memory. Deliberate forms of forgetting inherited from earlier generations included practices such as *damnatio memoriae*. They also included acts of mercy and pardon by God or by monarchs and parliaments, human regret and repentance. In an age of religious reform and empirical inquiry, in which many communities were driven by a desire for purification, there seemed to be so much that needed to be forgotten: saints, images, liturgies, and prayers; unquestioned authority and old habits of knowledge.

The Renaissance and Reformation were instances of "public forgetting" as they opened the way to new forms of memory by questioning inherited tradition, knowledge, and memory, as they claimed to retrieve purer, older sources of tradition, knowledge, and memory from the ancient world. As forgotten aspects of antiquity were recovered and attempts made to forget or obliterate more recent traditions, the practice of forgetting evolved. On the one hand, forgetting was redeemed as a virtuous, necessary practice, no more so when the human sinner came to seek divine mercy through God's forgetting and forgiving. On the other, forgetting's value remained negative, a way of clearing space for a better future whether on earth or in heaven. As scholars sought to expand knowledge and make new discoveries, and as preachers pointed to godly believing and godly living in the present as the only route to future salvation, the goal of remembering and forgetting was shifted from the past to the future.

NOTES

General Editors' Preface

1   https://www.memorystudiesassociation.org/ (accessed February 3, 2020).
2   Agenda-setting in this respect was Cesari and Rigney (2014). For a review, see Erll 2011: 4–18.

Chapter One

1. Gelders Archief, 0370, inv. 6579.
2. Gelders Archief, 0370, inv. 6579.
3. Gelders Archief, 0370, inv. 6581.
4. "Chronycke der Nederlanden, 1500–1693," Royal Library Brussels, Ms 21769, p. 103.

Chapter Three

1. Isaac Newton, "Questiones quædam Philosophicæ" (Certain Philosophical Questions), Cambridge University Library (hereafter CUL) Add. MS 3996 fols 88^r–135^r, at fol. 108^r. See McGuire and Tamny 1983: 393 for a modernized "Expansion" of the transcription (which I have used) and 392 for the original.
2. [James Duport], "Dr. Duport's Rules," CUL Add. MS 6986, [p. 17].
3. When translating the Latin *reminiscentia*, Hobbes used "Remembrance."
4. *De dignitate et augmentis scientiarum* is the enlarged Latin translation of the *Advancement of Learning* (1605); see Bacon 1963: vol. 4, 273–498 and vol. 5, 3–123.
5. See Yates 1966: 24–5, 28–31 for the doubts of Cicero and Quintilian about memory for words.
6. Burton's *The Anatomy of Melancholy* appeared in 1621.
7. Aubrey 2016: vol. 1, 269. The word "chambers" may refer to rooms in the college rather than niches in the wall of a building, such as the chapel.
8. The artificial language proposed in John Wilkins, *An Essay towards a Real Character, and a Philosophical Language* (1668) was based on a classification and ordering of categories intended to aid memory. See Lewis 2007.
9. MS Osborn b112, Beinecke Rare Book and Manuscript Library, Yale University.
10. CUL Add. MS 3996 fols 88^r–135^r; transcribed in McGuire and Tamny 1983: 328–465; also at http://cudl.lib.cam.ac.uk. See also http://www.newtonproject.sussex.ac.uk.
11. McGuire and Tamny 1983: 6. This estimate is based on a judgment about the similarity of hand, ink and pen. Westfall 1993: 26 estimates "forty-five headings."
12. See British Library (hereafter BL) Add. MS 41846, fols 194–204, at fols 201^v and 198^r. The BL catalogue describes this as "Design for an index cabinet with instructions for use, by a friend of Sam. Hartlib." See Cevolini 2017. The Prussian émigré, Samuel Hartlib (*c*. 1600–62) was an educational reformer and "intelligenzer" in London.
13. This comment occurs in a letter from London of 8/18 October 1641 to his friends in Leszno, Poland.

14. This paperbook is titled "Comentarius solutus sive pandecta, sive ancilla memoriae" (BL Add. MS 27278); in Bacon 1963: vol. 11, 39–95.
15. Boyle, "Introduction to my loose Notes Theological" [1670s–1680s], Boyle Papers (BP), Royal Society of London, vol. 5, fols 16–34, printed in Boyle 1999–2000, vol. 14, 277–83, at 283.
16. Lewis and Short 1966 record that in classical Latin *adversaria* meant "turned toward one," and hence "adversaria in mercantile language, a book at hand."
17. Boyle [1660s–1680s], "Of the several degrees or kinds of natural knowledge," BP vol. 8, fols 184^r–187^r, at fol. 184^r.
18. For more detailed accounts, see Yeo 2014: 175–84; and Locke 2019: 27–56.
19. BL Add. MS 28728, fols 58–59^v. In the "Méthode nouvelle" it is "une Classe" ([Locke] 1686: 323).

Chapter Four

1. Pages in this early modern book, as well as in others quoted hereafter, are identified by "signatures" (markings allowing printers to assemble books in the correct order, since many parts were being printed and hung out to dry all at once). In the early days of printing, page numbering was sporadic, often incorrect, and indicated only on the *recto* (right) page. The "r" of a signature indicates the *recto* side of a page, and "v," the *verso*, or back. Also, throughout, early modern orthography and idiosyncratic printers' spellings have been regularized silently; and, all translations are the author's unless otherwise indicated.
2. *Hamlet*, 2.2.116–19 (Shakespeare 2006). All quotations from Shakespeare follow this edition.
3. So too the larger sweep of the drama—namely "that *Hamlet*, both character and play, is deeply troubled by memory, and that this reflects the intellectual, cultural, and ideological conflicts current at the time at which Shakespeare was writing it" (Lees-Jeffries 2013: 11–35).
4. All quotations from Gratarolo's text (1553) follow the first English translation (1562).
5. On the sources accounting for this maxim, see *Theaetatus,* 152, 166c (Plato 1961), and *Lives of the Eminent Philosophers,* 2.9.51–53 (Diogenes Laertius 1925).
6. Willis refers to a painted shield ("scutcheon") and to tournament devices ("imprese"), which consisted of an image and motto collectively disclosing some secret intention or aspiration of the bearer. The compilers of emblem books mentioned are Theodore de Bèze (1519–1605), the French Protestant theologian who wrote *Icones* (1580); Andrea Alciato (1492–1550), the Italian humanist and author of the trend-setting *Emblematum libellus* (1531); and Henry Peacham (1578–1644), the English poet and miscellany writer, who compiled *Minerva Britanna* (1612).
7. The focal metaphor of venturing beyond—or returning back through—the Pillars of Hercules is a recurring motif on the frontispieces of Bacon's works (Corbett and Lightbown 1979: 186).
8. Andrea Frisch (2016) has examined with admirable clarity the broader cultural and epistemological implications of this claim with respect to early modern memory.

Chapter Five

1. The classic statement is Panofsky 1972: 42–113. See, more recently, inter alia, Rijser 2012.

2. See Clucas 2015, which emphasizes the importance of the Aristotelian tradition during the sixteenth and seventeenth centuries and associates the Platonic and oratorical approaches with the preceding period.
3. Cf. Hans Baldgun Grien's New Year's drawing with cavorting witches (1514, Albertina, Vienna).
4. A carefully considered challenge to the idea that the thistle refers to fidelity in love has been registered by Stumpel and van Kregten (2002), in which case the *Small Fortune* might even more readily suggest instability in love.
5. Machiavelli genders the imagery, but the basic idea can be found earlier in (Rucellai 1960: I, 103–12), where *fortuna* is contrasted with *caso*, *fortuna* being that against which virtue may protect us.
6. Presumably taking the bridle to connote Temperance, and adding the snake to signify Prudence; the etching was copied by Wenceslas Hollar in 1626. See also an etching attributed to Adam Elsheimer, *c*. 1597, British Museum S 2756.
7. She makes an intriguing forerunner to the *Melencolia* of 1514, likewise a middle-aged, winged woman, but one trapped rather than triumphant—it is possible that Dürer himself, like Aldegrever later, started meditating on the bridles and then extrapolated well past the idea of the reined-in Prudence to the thoroughly stalled Melencolia. Aldegrever in 1529 produced a variant inscribed "Respice Finem" (B. VIII 404.134), which combines elements of the *Nemesis* with others from *Melencolia*. The *Melencolia* is often supposed to owe its basic iconographic impulse to Ficino's teachings on the subject. The *Nemesis* is also worth remembering when looking at Caravaggio's triumphant *Amor* (Berlin): both are unusually realistic depictions of figures of dominance, both potentially meant to amuse to some degree.
8. Contrast Botticelli's *Mystic Crucifixion* (Harvard Art Museums, *c*. 1500), where the threat to Florence is palpable.
9. In a letter of 1544 from Niccolò Martelli (Pope-Hennessy 1985: 336); the letter was to Domenico Rugasso (Rabboni 2009: 260). Dürer (Conway 1889: 70), predicts that his Heller altarpiece will keep its freshness for 500 years, "if it is kept clean."
10. Castiglione, who started his book with a preface in which he disavowed the general admiration for Boccaccio, and instead criticized his use of language as outmoded as well as being natural only for Tuscans, might be thought in some degree to have revived the project of the *Decameron*. Castiglione would have recognized that his work, like Boccaccio's, featured young people gathered in competitive conversation, the record of which was meant to charm its readers through pleasant laughter.
11. Buried with Lorenzo is Alessandro de' Medici, the first Duke of Florence and the man whose assassination occasioned the making of Michelangelo's *Brutus*, which we might think of as his counter to Poliziano's history of the Pazzi Conspiracy, in which Giuliano de' Medici, brother of Lorenzo il Magnifico, was assassinated and which was commemorated by two medals by Bertoldo, 1478. These last two are both buried in the New Sacristy, opposite the altar wall, without monument.
12. Vasari 1991: 457 also contrasts envious Fortune with ability, in reference to the incomplete state in which the New Sacristy was left by Michelangelo. Envy was portrayed as an old woman in Mantegna's *Battle of the Sea Gods* engraving, the other half of which was copied in pen and ink by Dürer in 1494.
13. Machiavelli discussed the same instance from Livy in his *Discourses* (published in 1531), noting that Livy approved of Manlius's severity, though to his mind such severity was appropriate to a republic, a more gentle rule for a prince (Machiavelli 1950: 476–82, Book III, ch. xxii). See further Viroli 2012: 62–71.

14. Chantelou 1985: 133: "I replied [to Mattia de' Rossi, Bernini's assistant architect] that Michelangelo had done great things, but it was he who had introduced license into architecture because of his ambition to be original and not to imitate any of his predecessors; it was he who was the inventor of cartouches, of masks, of broken cornices, which he had used to advantage for he had a profound sense of design. Those who had wanted to imitate him had not had the same success for they lacked his basic knowledge."
15. Cf. Donatello's relief in the pediment of Donatello's tabernacle for *St Louis of Toulouse*; see also Pettazzoni 1946.

Chapter Six

1. The National Archives (hereafter TNA), E134/3Jas1/Mich39.
2. TNA, E134/38Eliz/Hil 24; TNA, E178/1538; Norfolk Record Office (hereafter NRO), PD254/171.
3. NRO, PD254/171.
4. TNA, E133/8/1234.
5. TNA, E134/28Eliz/Hil5.
6. TNA, E134/28Eliz/Hil5.
7. TNA, E178/1538.
8. NRO, PD254/171.
9. NRO, PD254/171; TNA, E133/8/1234.
10. TNA, E134/28Eliz/Hil5.
11. TNA, E134/3Jas1/Mich39.
12. TNA, E134/3Jas1/Mich39.
13. TNA, E134/3Jas1/Mich39.

Chapter Eight

1. For a modern edition, see Wooding 2013: 22.

BIBLIOGRAPHY

Ad Herennium: De ratione dicendi (1954), trans. Harry Caplan, Cambridge, MA: Harvard University Press.

Agrippa, Heinrich Cornelius von Nettesheim ([1531] 1569), *The Uncertainty and Vanity of the Arts and Sciences*, London: Henry Wykes.

Aitzema, Lieuwe van (1663), *Historie of Verhael van Saken van state en Oorlogh, in, ende ontrent de Vereenigde Nederlanden, beginnende met 't uytgaen vanden Treves*, The Hague: Johan Veely.

Aitzema, Lieuwe van (1669), *Saken van Staet, In, ende omtrent de Vereenigde Nederlanden, Beginnende met het Jaer 1645, ende eyndigende met het Jaer 1656*, The Hague: Johan Veely.

Allirot, Anne-Hélène (2013), "Longchamp and Lourcine: The Role of Female Abbeys in the Construction of Capetian Memory (Late Thirteenth to Mid-Fourteenth Century)," in Elma Brenner, Meredith Cohen, and Mary Franklin-Brown, eds, *Memory and Commemoration in Medieval Culture*, 243–60, Farnham: Ashgate.

Amelang, James S. (1998), *The Flight of Icarus: Artisan Autobiography in Early Modern Europe*, Stanford, CA: Stanford University Press.

An act of free and general pardon, indemnity and oblivion. Anno 12 Caroli II CAP XI, in Danby Pickering (1763), *The Statutes at Large, from the Thirty-ninth Year of Q. Elizabeth to the Twelfth Year of K. Charles II inclusive*, vol. VII, 419–35, Cambridge: Printed by Joseph Bentham. Available online at British History Online: http://www.british-history.ac.uk/statutes-realm/vol5/pp226-234 (accessed January 18, 2018).

Anderson, F.H. (1948), *The Philosophy of Francis Bacon*, Chicago: University of Chicago Press.

Aristotle (1972), *De memoria et reminiscentia*, in Richard Sorabji, *Aristotle on Memory*, 47–60, London: Duckworth.

Aristotle (2004), *De memoria et reminiscentia*, trans. Richard Sorabji, Chicago: University of Chicago Press.

Assmann, Aleida (2008), "Canon and Archive," in Astrid Erll and Ansgar Nünning, eds, *Cultural Memory Studies: An International and Interdisciplinary Handbook*, 97–107, Berlin: De Gruyter.

Assmann, Aleida (2011), *Cultural Memory and Western Civilization: Functions, Media, Archives*, Cambridge: Cambridge University Press.

Assmann, Jan (1992), *Das kulturelle Gedächtnis: Schrift, Erinnerung und politische Identität in frühen Hochkulturen*, Munich: Beck.

Assmann, Jan (2008), "Communicative and Cultural Memory," in Astrid Erll and Ansgar Nünning, eds, *Cultural Memory Studies: An International and Interdisciplinary Handbook*, 109–18, Berlin: De Gruyter.

Assmann, Jan (2011), *Cultural Memory and Early Civilization: Writing, Remembrance and Early Civilization*, Cambridge: Cambridge University Press.

Aston, Margaret (1973), "English Ruins and English History: The Dissolution and the Sense of the Past," *Journal of the Warburg and Courtauld Institutes* 36: 231–55.

Atia, Nadia and Jeremy Davies (2010), "Editorial," *Memory Studies* 3 (3): 181–6.

Aubery, Louis (1687), *Mémoires pour servir à l'histoire de Hollande et des autres Provinces-Unis*, Paris: Jean Vilette.

Aubrey, John (2016), *John Aubrey: Brief Lives with an Apparatus for the Lives of our English Mathematical Writers*, 2 vols, ed. Kate Bennett, Oxford: Oxford University Press.

Augustine of Hippo (1992), *Confessions*, ed. and trans. Henry Chadwick, Oxford: Oxford University Press.

Bachelard, Gaston (1994), *The Poetics of Space*, trans. Maria Jolas, Boston: Beacon Press.

Backus, Irena (2003), *Historical Method and Confessional Identity in the Era of the Reformation (1378–1615)*, Leiden and Boston: Brill.

Bacon, Francis ([1597] 1826), "De Haeresibus," in *Meditationes Sacrae*, ed. G. Woodfall, *The Works of Francis Bacon*, vol. 10, London: Rivington.

Bacon, Francis ([1597] 1892), "Of Heresies," in James Spedding, Robert Leslie Ellis, and Douglas Denton Heath, eds, *The Works of Francis Bacon*, vol. 7, London: Longmans.

Bacon, Francis (1605), *Of the Advancement and Proficience of Learning*, London: Printed for Henrie Tomes.

Bacon, Francis ([1620] 2004), *The Instauratio magna, Part II: Novum organum and Associated texts*, in Graham Rees, ed., *The Oxford Francis Bacon*, Vol. 11, Oxford: Clarendon Press.

Bacon, Francis (1620), *Novum Organum Scientiarum*, London: John Bill.

Bacon, Francis (1640), *Of the Advancement and Proficience of Learning*, London: Printed by L. Lichfield, for R. Young & E. Forrest.

Bacon, Francis (1963), *The Works of Francis Bacon*, 14 vols, eds J. Spedding, R.L. Ellis, and D.D. Heath, Stuttgart: F. Frommann.

Bacon, Francis (2012), "Letter of Advice to Fulke Greville (*c.* 1589)," in Alan Stewart, ed., *The Oxford Francis Bacon. I. Early Writings 1584–1596*, 207–12, Oxford: Oxford University Press.

Baggerman, Ariane, Rudolf Dekker, and Michael Mascuch, eds (2011), *Controlling Time and Shaping the Self: Developments in Autobiographical Time since the Sixteenth Century*, Leiden and Boston: Brill.

Baldinucci, Filippo (1847), *Notizie dei professori del disegno*, Florence: Batelli.

Baldinucci, Filippo (1966), *The Life of Bernini*, trans. Catherine Enggass, University Park: Pennsylvania State University Press.

Baldo, Jonathan (2012), *Memory in Shakespeare's Histories: Stages of Forgetting in Early Modern England*, New York: Routledge.

Barlow, Edward ([*c.* 1703] 1934), *Barlow's Journal of his Life at Sea in King's Ships, East and West Indiamen & Other Merchantment from 1659 to 1703*. Transcribed from the original manuscript by Basil Lubbock, 2 vols. London: Hurst & Blackett Ltd.

Barnard, T.C. "The Uses of 23 October 1641 and Irish Protestant Celebrations," *English Historical Review* 106 (1991): 889–920.

Bartsch, Adam von ([1805] 1970), *Le peintre graveur*, 22 vols. in 4, B. De Graaf, Nieuwkoop.

Barueth, Johan (1772), *Hollands en Zeelands Jubeljaar. Of tweenhonderdjarige gedagtenis der verlossing van het Spaansche jok en grondlegging van Neerlands republiek*, Dordrecht: Walpot.

[Basse, William] (1630), *A Helpe to Memory and Discourse*, London: Printed by T.B. for Leonard Becket.

Bayly, C.A. (2004), *The Birth of the Modern World, 1780–1914*, Oxford: Blackwell.

Beaumont, Agnes ([*c.* 1675] 1998), "The Narrative of the Persecution of Agnes Beaumont," in John Stachniewski and Anita Pacheco, eds, *Grace Abounding, with Other Spiritual Autobiographies*, 191–224, Oxford: Oxford University Press.

Bedford, Ronald, Lloyd Davis, and Philippa Kelly (2007), *Early Modern English Lives: Autobiography and Self-Representation 1500–1660*, Aldershot: Ashgate.

Beecher, Donald and Grant Williams, eds (2009), *Ars Reminiscendi: Mind and Memory in Renaissance Culture*, Toronto: Centre for Reformation and Renaissance Studies Publications.

Belot, Jean (1654), *Oeuvres*, Lyon: Claude de la Rivière.

Bender, Barbara (1998), *Stonehenge: Making Space*, Oxford: Berg.

Bender, Barbara (1999), "Subverting the Western Gaze: Mapping Alternative Worlds," in Peter J. Ucko and Robert Layton, eds, *The Archaeology and Anthropology of Landscape: Shaping your Landscape*, 31–45, London and New York: Routledge.

Benedict, Philip (2008), "Divided Memories? Historical Calendars, Commemorative Processions and the Recollection of the Wars of Religion during the Ancient Regime," *French History* 22: 381–405.

Benedict, Philip (2013), "Shaping the Memory of the French Wars of Religion. The First Centuries," in Erika Kuijpers, Judith Pollmann, Johannes Müller, and Jasper van der Steen, eds, *Memory Before Modernity: Practices of Memory in Early Modern Europe*, 111–25, Leiden: Brill.

Berger, Stefan, Heiko Feldner, and Kevin Passmore, eds (2020), *Writing History: Theory and Practice,* London: Bloomsbury Publishing.

Berger, Susanna (2017), *The Art of Philosophy: Visual Thinking in Europe from the Late Renaissance to the Early Enlightenment*, Princeton, NJ: Princeton University Press.

Berns, Jörg Jochen and Wolfgang Neuber, eds (1993), *Ars memorativa: zur kulturgeschichtlichen Bedeutung der Gedächtniskunst 1400–1750*, Tübingen: Niemeyer.

Betz, Frederick (2011), *Managing Science*, Heidelberg: Springer.

Bien, David (1962), *The Calas Affair: Persecution, Toleration, and Heresy in Eighteenth-Century Toulouse*, Princeton, NJ: Princeton University Press.

Blair, Ann (2010), *Too Much to Know: Managing Scholarly Information before the Modern Age*, New Haven, CT: Yale University Press.

Blake, Emma (2007), "Space, Spatiality and Archaeology," in Lynn Meskell and Robert W. Preucel, eds, *A Companion to Social Archaeology*, 230–54, Oxford: Blackwell.

Blaugdone, Barbara (1691), *An Account of the Travels, Sufferings and Persecution*, London: T.S.

Bloch, David (2007), *Aristotle on Memory and Recollection: Text, Translation, Interpretation, and Reception in Western Scholasticism*, Leiden: Brill.

Bloemendal, Jan (2007), "De dramatische moord op de Vader des Vaderlands. De verhouding tussen vier typen toneel in de vroegmoderne Nederlanden," *De Zeventiende Eeuw* 23 (1): 99–117.

Bolgar, Robert Ralph (1963), *The Classical Heritage and its Beneficiaries*, Cambridge: Cambridge University Press.

Bollandus, Joannes, Michel Natalis, Adrianus Poirters, Laurentius Uwens, and Abraham van Diepenbeeck (1640), *Af-beeldinghe van d'eerste eevwe der societeyt Iesv*, Antwerp: Plantiinsche drvckeriie.

Bolzoni, Lina (2001), *The Gallery of Memory: Literary and Iconographic Models in the Age of the Printing Press*, trans. Jeremy Parzen, Toronto: University of Toronto Press.

Bolzoni, Lina (2011), "Giulio Camillo's Memory Theatre and the Kabbalah," in Ilana Zinguer, Abraham Melamed, and Zur Shalev, eds, *Hebraic Aspects of the Renaissance: Sources and Encounters*, 14–26, Leiden and Boston: Brill.

Bolzoni, Lina (2012), *Il lettore creativo. Percorsi cinquecenteschi fra memoria, gioco, scrittura*, Naples: Guida.

Bolzoni, Lina (2017), "The Memory Theatre of Giulio Camillo: Alchemy, Rhetoric, and Deification in the Renaissance," in Peter J. Forshaw, ed., *Lux in Tenebris: The Visual and the Symbolic in Western Esotericism*, 66–80, Leiden and Boston: Brill.

Bosman, Lex (2004), *The Power of Tradition: "Spolia" in the Architecture of St. Peter's in the Vatican*, Hilversum: Verloren.

Botero, Giovanni ([1589] 1956), *The Reason of State*, eds and trans. P.J. Waley and D.P. Waley, London: Routledge & Kegan Paul.

Boxhorn, M.Z. van (1640), *De typographica artis inventione et inventoribus dissertatio*, Leiden: H. de Vogel.

Boyle, Robert (1999–2000), *The Works of Robert Boyle*, 14 vols, eds Michael Hunter and Edward B. Davis, London: Pickering & Chatto.

Bradley, Richard (2002), *The Past in Prehistoric Societies*, London: Routledge.

Brendecke, Aendt (1999), *Die Jahrhundertwenden: eine Geschichte ihrer Wahrnehmung und Wirkung*, Frankfurt: Campus.

Brewer, John (1997), *The Pleasures of the Imagination: English Culture in the Eighteenth Century*, London: HarperCollins.

Brightman, Frank Edward (1915), *The English Rite: Being a Synopsis of the Sources and Revisions of the Book of Common Prayer*, 2 vols, London: Rivingtons.

Brinsley, John ([1612] 1968), *Ludus literarius: or, the Grammar Schoole*, Menston: The Scolar Press.

Brinsley, John (1612), *Ludus literarius: or, the Grammar Schoole*, London: Printed [by Humphrey Lownes] for Thomas Man.

Bruner, Jerome (1994), "The 'Remembered' Self," in Ulric Neisser and Robyn Fivush, eds, *The Remembering Self: Construction and Accuracy in the Self-Narrative*, 41–54, Cambridge: Cambridge University Press.

Bryson, Bill (2011), *Seeing Further: The Story of Science, Discovery, and the Genius of the Royal Society*, New York: Harper Perennial.

Bullough, G. (1935), "The Murder of Gonzago," *The Modern Language Review* 30 (4): 433–44.

Bunyan, John ([1666] 1998), *Grace Abounding, with Other Spiritual Autobiographies*, eds John Stachniewski and Anita Pacheco, Oxford: Oxford University Press.

Buratti, Adele (1982), "L'azione pastorale dei Borromeo a Milano e la nuova sistemazione urbanistica della città," in Adele Buratti, ed., *La città rituale*, 9–55, Milan: Angeli.

Burckhardt, Jacob ([1860] 1960), *The Civilization of the Renaissance in Italy*, trans. S.G.C. Middlemore, rev. and ed. Irene Gordon, New York: Mentor.

Burckhardt, Johannes (1971), *Die Entstehung der Jahrhundertrechnung. Ursprung und Ausbildung einer historiographischen Technik von Flacius bis Ranke*, Göppingen: Kümmerle.

Burgess, Clive (2000), "'Longing to be Prayed for': Death and Commemoration in an English Parish in the later Middle Ages," in Bruce Gordon and Peter Marshall, eds, *The Place of the Dead in Late Medieval and Early Modern Europe*, 44–65, Cambridge: Cambridge University Press.

Burke, Peter (1969), *The Renaissance Sense of the Past*, London: E. Arnold.

Burke, Peter ([1978] 1994), *Popular Culture in Early Modern Europe*, 2nd edn, Aldershot: Ashgate.

Burke, Peter (1989), "History as Social Memory," in Thomas Butler, ed., *Memory: History, Culture and the Mind*, 97–113, Oxford: Blackwell.

Burke, Peter (1997), "History as Social Memory," in his *Varieties of Cultural History*, 43–59, Cambridge: Polity.
Burke, Peter (2001), "The Sense of Anachronism from Petrarch to Poussin," in C. Humphrey and W.M. Ormrod, eds, *Time in the Medieval World*, 157–73, Woodbridge: York Medieval Press.
Burrows, Donald (2004), "Handel, George Frederic," in *Oxford Dictionary of National Biography*, Oxford: Oxford University Press, vol. 25.
Burton, Robert ([1621–38] 1927), *The Anatomy of Melancholy*, 3 vols, London: G. Bell & Sons.
Burton, Robert ([1621] 1989), *The Anatomy of Melancholy*, 3 vols, eds Thomas C. Faulkner, Nicholas K. Kiessling, and Rhonda L. Blair, Oxford: Oxford University Press.
Cameron, Euan (2012), "Primitivism, Patristics, and Polemic in Protestant Visions of Early Christianity," in Katherine Van Liere, Simon Ditchfield, and Howard Louthan, eds, *Sacred History: Uses of the Christian Past in the Renaissance World*, 27–51, Oxford: Oxford University Press.
Candau, Joël (2005), *Anthropologie de la mémoire*, Paris: Armand Colin.
Capp, Bernard (2003), *When Gossips Meet: Women, Family and Neighbourhood in Early Modern England*, Oxford: Oxford University Press.
Carpenter, Richard (1642), *Experience, Historie, and Divinitie. Divided into five Books*. London: Printed by R.C. for Andrew Crooke.
Carruthers, Mary (1990), *The Book of Memory: A Study of Memory in Medieval Culture*, Cambridge: Cambridge University Press.
Carruthers, Mary (2008), *The Book of Memory: A Study of Memory in Medieval Culture*, 2nd edn, Cambridge: Cambridge University Press.
Carruthers, Mary and Jan M. Ziolkowski, eds (2002), *The Medieval Craft of Memory: An Anthology of Texts and Pictures*, Philadelphia: University of Pennsylvania Press.
Castiglione, Baldassare (1967), *The Book of the Courtier*, trans. George Bull, London: Penguin.
Castillo Gómez, Antonio (2006), *Entre la pluma y la pared. Una historia social de la escritura en los Siglos de Oro*, Madrid: Akal.
Cellini, Benvenuto (1985), *Vita*, Milan: Rizzoli.
Cellini, Benvenuto (1998), *Autobiography*, trans. George Bull, London: Penguin.
Certaine sermons or Homilies appointed to be read in churches, In the time of the late Queene Elizabeth of famous memory (1623), London: I. Bill. Online edition at: http://www.anglicanlibrary.org/homilies (accessed January 19, 2018).
Cevolini, Alberto (2006), *De arte excerpendi. Imparare a dimenticare nella modernità*, Florence: Leo S. Olschki.
Cevolini, Alberto, ed. (2016a), *Forgetting Machines: Knowledge Management Evolution in Early Modern Europe*, Leiden and Boston: Brill.
Cevolini, Alberto (2016b), "Knowledge Management Evolution in Early Modern Europe: An Introduction," in Alberto Cevolini, ed., *Forgetting Machines: Knowledge Management Evolution in Early Modern Europe*, 1–34, Leiden: Brill.
Cevolini, Alberto, ed. (2017), Thomas Harrison. *The Ark of Studies*, Turnhout: Brepols.
Chantelou, Paul Fréart (1985), *Diary of the Cavaliere Bernini's Visit to France*, trans. M. Corbett, Princeton, NJ: Princeton University Press.
Chappell Lougee, Carolyn (2002), "Emigration and Memory: After 1685 and After 1789," in Rudolf Dekker, ed., *Egodocuments and History: Autobiographical Writing in Its Social Context since the Middle Ages*, 89–106, Hilversum: Verloren.
Chappell, Sophie-Grace (2017a), "Aristotle," in Sven Bernecker and Kourken Michaelian, eds, *The Routledge Handbook of Philosophy of Memory*, 396–407, London: Routledge.

Chappell, Sophie-Grace (2017b), "Plato," in Sven Bernecker and Kourken Michaelian, eds, *The Routledge Handbook of Philosophy of Memory*, 385–95, London: Routledge.

Chartier, Roger (1982), "Intellectual History or Socio-Cultural History?" in Dominick LaCapra and Steven L. Kaplan, eds, *Modern European Intellectual History: Reappraisals and New Perspectives*, 25–45, Ithaca, NY: Cornell University Press.

Chartier, Roger (1998), *Cultural History: Between Practice and Representations*, Cambridge: Cambridge University Press.

Chartier, Roger (2007), *Inscription and Erasure: Literature and Written Culture from the Eleventh to the Eighteenth Century*, trans. Arthur Goldhammer, Philadelphia: University of Pennsylvania Press.

Chedgzoy, Kate (2007), *Women's Writing in the British Atlantic World: Memory, Place and History, 1550–1700*, Cambridge: Cambridge University Press.

Chedgzoy, Kate, Elspeth Graham, Katharine Hodgkin, and Ramona Wray (2018), "Researching Memory in Early Modern Studies," *Memory Studies* 11 (1): 5–20.

Ciappelli, Giovanni (2014), *Memory, Family, and Self: Tuscan Family Books and Other European Egodocuments (14th–18th Century)*, trans. Susan Amanda George, Leiden and Boston: Brill.

Clarke, Danielle (2018), "Memory and Memorialization in the Psalmes of Mary Sidney, Countess of Pembroke," *Memory Studies* 11 (1): 85–99.

Clucas, Stephen (2015), "Memory in the Renaissance and Early Modern Period," in Dmitri Nikulin, ed., *Memory: A History*, 131–75, Oxford: Oxford University Press.

Cohn, Samuel K., Jr. (1992), *The Cult of Remembrance and the Black Death: Six Renaissance Cities in Central Italy*, Baltimore: Johns Hopkins University Press.

Collins, Jeffrey R. (2005), *The Allegiance of Thomas Hobbes*, Oxford: Oxford University Press.

Comenius, Iohannes Amos (1672), *Orbis Sensualium Pictus [. . .] translated into English by Charles Hoole, for the use of young Latine scholars*, London: T.R & N.T. Mearne.

Condivi, Ascanio (1999), *The Life of Michelangelo*, ed. Hellmut Wohl, trans. Alice Sedgwick Wohl, University Park: Pennsylvania State University Press.

Connerton, Paul (1989), *How Societies Remember*, Cambridge: Cambridge University Press.

Connerton, Paul (2008), "Seven Types of Forgetting," *Memory Studies* 1 (1): 59–71.

Conway, W.M., ed. and trans. (1889), *Literary Remains of Albrecht Dürer*, Cambridge: Cambridge University Press.

Corbett, Margery and R.W. Lightbown (1979), *The Comely Frontispiece: The Emblematic Title-Page in England 1550–1660*, London: Routledge and Kegan Paul.

Cordes, Harm (2006), *Hilaria Evangelica Academia: Das Reformationsjubiläum von 1717 an den deutschen lutherischen Universitäten*, Göttingen: Vandenhoeck and Ruprecht.

Coreth, Anna (1982), *Pietas Austriaca. Österreichische Frömmigkeit im Barock*, München: R. Oldenbourg Verlag.

Costello, William T. (1958), *The Scholastic Curriculum at Early Seventeenth-century Cambridge*, Cambridge, MA: Harvard University Press.

Coster, Will and Andrew Spicer, eds (2005), *Sacred Space in Early Modern England*, Cambridge: Cambridge University Press.

Costerus, Franciscus (1595), *Bewiis der ovder catholiicker leeringhe*, Antwerp: Ioachim Trognæsius.

Couliano, Ioan P. (1987), *Eros and Magic in the Renaissance*, trans. Margaret Cook, Chicago and London: University of Chicago Press.

Coupe, William A. (1966), *The German Illustrated Broadsheet in the Seventeenth Century: Historical and Iconographical Studies*, vol. 1, Baden-Baden: Heitz.

Covington, Sarah (2013), "'The Odious Demon from Across the Sea'. Oliver Cromwell, Memory and the Dislocations of Ireland," in Erika Kuijpers, Judith Pollmann, Johannes Müller, and Jasper van der Steen, eds, *Memory before Modernity: Practices of Memory in Early Modern Europe*, 149–64, Leiden and Boston: Brill.

Cressy, David (1989), *Bonfires and Bells: National Memory and the Protestant Calendar in Elizabethan and Stuart England*, London: Weidenfeld and Nicolson.

Cressy, David (1990), "The Protestant Calendar and the Vocabulary of Celebration in Early Modern England," *Journal of British Studies* 29 (1): 31–52.

Crook, John (1706), *A Short History of the Life*, London: T. Sowle.

Crooke, Helekiah (1616), *A Description of the Body of Man*, London: Printed by William Jaggard.

Cruickshank, Frances (2010), *Verse and Poetics in George Herbert and John Donne*, Farnham: Ashgate.

Cummings, Brian (2002), *The Literary Culture of the Reformation: Grammar and Grace*, Oxford: Oxford University Press.

Dabrowski, Patrice M. (2004), *Commemorations and the Shaping of Modern Poland*, Bloomington: Indiana University Press.

Dane, John ([*c.* 1670] 1854), "John Dane's Narrative" ("A Declaration of Remarkabell Prouedenses in the corse of my lyfe"), *New England Historical and Genealogical Register*, April: 147–56.

Darnton, Robert (1984), *The Great Cat Massacre and Other Episodes in French Cultural History*, New York: Basic Books.

Davis, Natalie Zemon (1977), "Ghosts, Kin and Progeny: Some Features of Family Life in Early Modern France," *Daedalus* 106 (2): 87–114.

Davis, Natalie Zemon (1995) *Women on the Margins: Three Seventeenth-Century Lives*, Cambridge, MA: Harvard University Press.

De Moor, Tine (2009), "Avoiding Tragedies: A Flemish Common and its Commoners under the Pressure of Social and Economic Change during the Eighteenth Century," *Economic History Review* 62 (1): 1–22.

Dear, Peter (2009), *Revolutionizing the Sciences*, Princeton: Princeton University Press.

Debus, Allen (1970), "Harvey and Fludd: The Irrational Factor in the Rational Science of the Seventeenth Century," *Journal of the History of Biology* 3 (1): 81–105.

Debus, Allen and Michael T. Walton (1998), "Preface," in Alan G. Debus and Michael T. Walton, eds, *Reading the Book of Nature: The Other Side of the Scientific Revolution*, vii–xvi, Kirksville, MO: Sixteenth Century Journal Publications.

Décultot, Elizabeth, ed. (2003), *Lire, copier, écrire: Les bibliothèques manuscrites et leurs usages au XVIIIe siècle*, Paris: Centre National de la Recherche Scientifique.

Deelman, Christian (1964), *The Great Shakespeare Jubilee*, London: Joseph.

Deiters, Maria (2012), "Epitaphs in Dialogue with Sacred Space: Post-Reformation Furnishings in the Parish Churches of St Nikolai and St Marien in Berlin," in Andrew Spicer, ed., *Lutheran Churches in Early Modern Europe*, 63–96, Farnham: Ashgate.

Dennis, Matthew (2002), "The Eighteenth-Century Discovery of Columbus: The Columbian Tercentenary (1792) and the Creation of American National Identity," in William Pencak and Matthew Dennis, eds., *Riot and Revelry in Early America*, 205–28, University Park: Pennsylvania State University Press.

Deseure, Brecht and Judith Pollmann (2013), "The Experience of Rupture and the History of Memory," in Erika Kuijpers, Judith Pollmann, Johannes Müller, and Jasper van der Steen, eds., *Memory Before Modernity: Practices of Memory in Early Modern Europe*, 315–29, Leiden: Brill.

Diogenes Laertius (1925), *Lives of the Eminent Philosophers*, vol. 2, ed. R.D. Hicks, Loeb Classical Library, Cambridge, MA: Harvard University Press.

Donne, John (1967), *Selected Prose*, selected by Evelyn Simpson, eds Helen Gardner and Timothy Healy, Oxford: Clarendon Press.
Donne, John (1971), *Poetical Works*, ed. Herbert J.C. Grierson, Oxford: Oxford University Press.
Dragstra, Henk, Sheila Ottway, and Helen Wilcox, eds (2000), *Betraying Our Selves: Forms of Self-Representation in Early Modern English Texts*, Basingstoke: Palgrave Macmillan.
Drexel, Jeremias (1638), *Aurifodina artium et scientiarum omnium, excerpendi sollertia*, Antwerp: Apud viduam Ioannis Cnobbari.
Drummond, Pippa (2011), *The Provincial Music Festival in England, 1784–1914*, Farnham: Ashgate.
Düding, Dieter (1988), "Das Deutsche Nationalfest von 1814," in Dieter Düding, Peter Friedemann, and Paul Münch, eds, *Öffentliche Festkultur: Politische Feste in Deutschland von der Aufklärung bis zum Ersten Weltkrieg*, 67–88, Reinbek: Rowohlt.
Duffy, Eamon (1992), *The Stripping of the Altars: Traditional Religion in England 1400–1580*, New Haven: Yale University Press.
Dunton, John (1705), *The Life and Errors*, London: S. Malthus.
Dyer, Christopher and Richard Jones (2010), *Deserted Villages Revisted*, Hertfordshire: University of Hertfordshire Press.
Eco, Umberto (1988), "An *Ars Oblivionalis*? Forget It!" trans. Marilyn Migiel, *PMLA* 103 (3): 254–61.
Eekhout, M.F.D. (2013), "Celebrating a Trojan Horse: Memories of the Dutch Revolt in Breda, 1590–1650," in Erika Kuijpers, Judith Pollmann, Johannes Müller, and Jasper van der Steen, eds, *Memory Before Modernity: Practices of Memory in Early Modern Europe*, 129–47, Leiden: Brill.
Eggert, Katherine (2015), *Disknowledge: Literature, Alchemy, and the End of Humanism in Renaissance England*, Philadelphia: University of Pennsylvania Press.
Eisenstein, Elizabeth L. (2012), *The Printing Revolution in Early Modern Europe*, 2nd edn, Cambridge: Cambridge University Press.
Elyot, Thomas (1531), *The Book named the Governor*, London: Thomas Berthelet.
Emison, Patricia (2004), *Creating the "Divine" Artist from Dante to Michelangelo*, Leiden: Brill.
Emison, Patricia (2012), *The Italian Renaissance and Cultural Memory*, Cambridge: Cambridge University Press.
Engel, William E. (1995), *Mapping Mortality: The Persistence of Memory and Melancholy in Early Modern England*, Amherst, MA: University of Massachusetts Press.
Engel, William E. (2002), *Death and Drama in Renaissance England: Shades of Memory*, Oxford: Oxford University Press.
Engel, William E. (2004), "The Decay of Memory," in Christopher Ivic and Grant Williams, eds, *Forgetting in Early Modern English Literature and Culture: Lethe's Legacies*, 21–40, London: Routledge.
Engel, William E., Rory Loughnane, and Grant Williams, eds (2016), *The Memory Arts in Renaissance England: A Critical Anthology*, Cambridge: Cambridge University Press.
Erasmus, Desiderius ([1512] 1978), *De Ratione Studii*, in Craig R. Thomson, ed., *Literary and Educational Writings 2: De Copia /De Ratione Studii*, trans. Betty I. Knott, Vol. 24 of *Collected Works of Erasmus*, 661–91, Toronto: University of Toronto Press.
Erasmus, Desiderius (1974, 1988), *The Correspondence of Erasmus*, trans. R.A.B. Mynors and D.F.S. Thomson, vols. 1 and 9, Toronto: Toronto University Press.
Erll, Astrid (2011), *Memory in Culture*, trans. Sara B. Young. Basingstoke: Palgrave Macmillan.

Erll, Astrid and Ansgar Nünning, eds (2008), *Cultural Memory Studies: An International and Interdisciplinary Handbook*, Berlin and New York: De Gruyter.

[Eusebius] (1737), *Enchyridion chronologicum Carmelitarum Discalceatorum Congregationis Italiae, sub titulo S.P. Eliae Prophetae digestum A.P. Eusebio ab omnibus sanctis Definitore Provinciali Provinciae Romanae, ac ejusdem Congregationis Historico generali [. . .]*, Rome: Rochi Bernabò.

Evans, Arise (1653), "A Narration of the Life, Calling, and Visions of Arise Evans," in *An Eccho to the Book, called Voyce from Heaven*. Printed for the Authour, and are to be sold at his House in Long-Alley, in Black Friers.

Evans, Katherine and Sarah Cheevers (1663), *A True Account of the Great Tryals and Cruel Sufferings*, London: Robert Wilson.

Ezell, Margaret J.M. (2011), "Elizabeth Isham's Books of Remembrance and Forgetting," *Modern Philology* 109 (1): 71–84.

Fanshawe, Ann ([1676] 1979), *The Memoirs of Anne, Lady Halkett and Ann, Lady Fanshawe*, ed. John Loftis, Oxford: Clarendon Press.

Febvre, Lucien and Henri-Jean Martin ([1958] 2010), *The Coming of the Book: The Impact of Printing, 1450–1800*, trans. David Gerard, eds Geoffrey Nowell-Smith and David Wootton, London: Verso.

Fenlon, Iain (2007), *The Ceremonial City: History, Memory and Myth in Renaissance Venice*, New Haven: Yale University Press.

Fentress, James J. and Chris Wickham, eds (1992), *Social Memory*, Oxford: Blackwell.

Feuchtwang, Stephan (2010), "Ritual and Memory," in Susannah Radstone and Bill Schwarz, eds, *Memory: Histories, Theories and Debates*, 281–98, New York: Fordham University Press.

Fichtner, Paula Sutter (2008), *Terror and Toleration: The Habsburg Empire Confronts Islam, 1526–1850*, London: Reaktion.

Fischer, David Hackett (1989), *Albion's Seed: Four British Folkways in America*, New York: Oxford University Press.

Fitzgibbons, Jonathan (2008), *Cromwell's Head*, Kew: The National Archives.

Fitzherbert, Dionys [c. 1608], MS. e Mus 169, Bodleian Library, Oxford; (2010) ed. and intr. Katharine Hodgkin, *Women, Madness and Sin in Early Modern England: The Autobiographical Writings of Dionys Fitzherbert*, Farnham: Ashgate.

Flather, Amanda (2007), *Gender and Space in Early Modern England*, Woodbridge, Suffolk: Royal Historical Society, Boydell Press.

Fletcher, David (2003), "The Parish Boundary: A Social Phenomenon in Hanoverian England," *Rural History* 14: 177–97.

Flower, Harriet A. (2006), *The Art of Forgetting: Disgrace and Oblivion in Roman Political Culture*, Chapel Hill: University of North Carolina Press.

Flügel, Wolfgang (2003), "Zeitkonstrukte im Reformationsjubiläum," in Winfried Müller, ed., *Das historische Jubiläum*, 77–100, Münster: LIT.

Flügel, Wolfgang (2005), *Konfession und Jubiläum. Zur Institutionalisierung der Lutherischen Gedenkkultur in Sachsen, 1617–1830*, Leipzig: Leipziger Universitätsverlag.

Flügel, Wolfgang with Stefan Dornheim (2006), "Die Universität als Jubiläumsmultiplikator in der Frühen Neuzeit," *Jahrbuch für Universitätsgeschichte* 9: 51–70.

Foucault, Michel (1984), "Of Other Spaces: Utopias and Heterotopias," trans. Jay Miskowiec, *Architecture /Mouvement/ Continuité*, October: 1–9.

Foucault, Michel (2001), *Fearless Speech*, ed. Joseph Pearson, Los Angeles, CA: Semiotext(e).

Fox, Adam (2000), *Oral and Literate Culture in England 1500–1700*, Oxford: Oxford University Press.

Fox, George ([c. 1675] 1997), *The Journal of George Fox*, ed. John Nickalls, Philadelphia: Religious Society of Friends.

Foxe, John (2011), *The Unabridged Acts and Monuments Online or TAMO (1563 edition)*, Sheffield: HRI Online Publications. Available online at: http//www.johnfoxe.org (accessed January 15, 2018).

Frame, Donald M., trans. (1958), *The Complete Essays of Montaigne*, Stanford: Stanford University Press.

Frisch, Andrea (2006), "Montaigne and the Ethics of Memory," *L'Esprit Créateur* 46 (1): 23–31.

Frisch, Andrea (2012), "Caesarean Negotiations: Forgetting Henri IV's Past after the French Wars of Religion," in Isabel Karremann, Cornel Zwierlein, and Inga Mai Groote, eds, *Forgetting Faith? Negotiating Confessional Conflict in Early Modern Europe*, 63–79, Berlin: De Gruyter.

Frisch, Andrea (2016), "Montaigne on Memory," in Philippe Desan, ed., *The Oxford Handbook of Montaigne*, 648–62, Oxford: Oxford University Press.

Fuller, Thomas (2016), "Selected Works," in William Engel, Rory Loughnane, and Grant Williams, eds, *The Memory Arts in Renaissance England: A Critical Anthology*, 211–15, Cambridge: Cambridge University Press.

Fumaroli, Marc (1994), "*L'Imago Primi Saeculi* (1640) et ses adversaires," in *L'école de silence: le sentiment des images au XVIIe siècle*, 325–42, Paris: Flammarion.

Furley, O.W. (1959), "The Pope-burning Processions of the Late Seventeenth Century," *History* 44: 16–23.

Gabriele, Matthew (2011), *An Empire of Memory: The Legend of Charlemagne, the Franks, and Jerusalem before the First Crusade*, Oxford: Oxford University Press.

Galley, Alfred (1930), *Die Jahrhundertfeiern der Augsburgischen Konfession von 1630, 1730 und 1830*, Leipzig: Dörffling and Franke.

Gaposchkin, M. Cecilia (2008), *The Making of Saint Louis: Kingship, Sanctity and Crusade in the Later Middle Ages*, Ithaca and London: Cornell University Press.

Gassendi, Pierre ([1641] 1657), *The Mirrour of True Nobility and Gentility: being the life of the renowned Nicolaus Claudius Fabricus Lord of Peiresk, Englished by W. Rand*, London: J. Streater for Humphrey Moseley.

Geertz, Clifford (1973), *The Interpretation of Cultures*, London: Fontana Press.

Gehner, R.F. (1939), "Printing's Quincentenary," *The Educational Forum* 4: 93–4.

Gentile, Emilio (1993), *Il culto del littorio: la sacralizzazione della politica nell'Italia fascista*, Rome: Laterza.

Gertsman, Elina (2010), *The Dance of Death in the Middle Ages: Image, Text, Performance*, Turnhout: Brepols.

Gestel, Cornelis van (1725), *Historia sacra et profana archiepiscopatus Mechliniensis; Sive descriptio archi-diocesis illius; Item urbium, oppidorum, pagorum, dominiorum, monasteriorum, castellorumque sub eâ, in XI. decanatus divisa. Cum Toparcharum Inscriptionibus Sepulchralibus [. . .] Tomus Secundus*, The Hague: Christiaan van Lom.

Giesecke, Michael (1991), *Der Buchdruck in der frühen Neuzeit*, Frankfurt: Suhrkamp.

Gillis, John R. (1994), "Memory and Identity: The History of a Relationship," in John R. Gillis, ed., *Commemorations: The Politics of National Identity*, 3–24, Princeton, NJ: Princeton University Press.

Gish, Dustin (2013), "Taming the Shrew: Shakespeare, Machiavelli, and Political Philosophy," in Bernard J. Dobski and Dustin Gish, eds, *Shakespeare and the Body Politic*, 197–220, Lanham, MD: Lexington Books.

Glückel of Hameln ([c. 1690–1719] 1962), *The Life of Gluckel of Hameln, 1646–1724, Written by Herself*, ed. and trans. Beth-Zion Abrahams, London: Horovitz Publishing Company.

Goldmann, Lucien (1967), *The Hidden God. A Study of Tragic Vision in the Pensées of Pascal and the Tragedies of Racine*, 17, London: Routledge.

Gotherson, Dorothea (1661), *To all that are Unregenerated, a call to Repentance from dead works*, London: Robert Wilson.

Gottsched, Johann Christoph (1976), *Ausgewählte Werke*, vol. 9, part 1, Berlin and New York: De Gruyter.

Graham, Elspeth, Hilary Hinds, and Elaine Hobby, eds (1989), *Her Own Life: Autobiographical Writings by Seventeenth-Century Englishwomen*, London: Routledge.

Gratarolo, Guglielmo ([1553] 1562), *The Castel of Memorie*, trans. William Fulwood, London: Rouland Hall.

Grazia, Margreta de (2010), "Anachronism," in Brian Cummings and James Simpson, eds, *Cultural Reformations: Medieval and Renaissance in Literary History*, 13–32, Oxford: Oxford University Press.

Green, Ian (2016), *Humanism and Protestantism in Early Modern English Education*, London: Routledge.

Gruzinski, Serge (2017), *La machine à remonter le temps. Quand l'Europe s'est mise à écrire l'histoire*, Paris: Fayard.

Guglielmo Ebreo of Pesaro (1993), *De practica seu arte tripudii / On the Practice or Art of Dancing*, ed. Barbara Sparti, Oxford: Clarendon.

Guntzer, Augustin (2010), *L'histoire de toute ma vie: autobiographie d'un potier d'étain calviniste du XVIIème siècle*, trans. Monique Debus Kehr, Paris: Honoré Champion Editions.

Gusdorf, Georges ([1956] 1980), "Conditions and Limits of Autobiography," in James Olney, ed., *Autobiography: Essays Theoretical and Critical*, 28–48, Princeton, NJ: Princeton University Press.

Gysius, Johannes (1616), *Oorsprong en voortgang der Neder-landtscher beroerten ende ellendicheden*, Leiden: Henrick Lodewijcxsoon Haestens.

Haemers, Jelle (2011), "Social Memory and Rebellion in Fifteenth-Century Ghent," *Social History* 36: 443–63.

Halbwachs, Maurice (1925), *Les cadres sociaux de la mémoire*, Paris: Alcan.

Halbwachs, Maurice ([1952] 1992), *On Collective Memory*, ed. and trans. Lewis A. Coser, Chicago: The University of Chicago Press.

Hänisch, Ulrike Dorothea (1993), *"Confessio Augustana Triumphans": Funktionen der Publizistik zum Confessio Augustana-Jubiläum 1630*, Frankfurt: Lang.

Harris, Tim (1995), "Problematising Popular Culture," in Tim Harris, ed., *Popular Culture in England c.1500–1850*, 1–27, Basingstoke: Macmillan.

Hartlib, Samuel (1642), *A Reformation of Schools*, London: Michael Sparke.

Harvey, E. Ruth (1975), *The Inward Wits: Psychological Theory in the Middle Ages and the Renaissance*, London: Warburg Institute.

Harvey, I.M.W. (1991), *Jack Cade's Rebellion of 1450*, Oxford: Clarendon Press.

Havens, Earle (2001), *Commonplace Books: A History of Manuscripts and Printed Books From Antiquity to the Twentieth Century*, New Haven: University Press of New England.

Hayes, Alice (1723), *A Legacy, or Widow's Mite, left by Alice Hayes to Her Children and others*, London: J. Sowle.

Hearne, Thomas (1720), *A Collection of Curious Discourses Written by Eminent Antiquaries upon Several Heads in our English Antiquities*, Oxford: Printed at the Theatre.

Heidegger, Martin ([1957] 2002), *Identity and Difference*, trans. Joan Stambaugh, Chicago: University of Chicago Press.

Hendon, Julia (2010), *Houses in a Landscape: Memory and Everyday Life in Mesoamerica*, Durham and London: Duke University Press.

Héroard, Jean (1868), *Journal de Jean Héroard sur l'enfance et la jeunesse de Louis XIII (1601–1628), Tome Premier 1601–1610*, eds Eudore Soulié and Edouard de Barthélemy, Paris: Firmin Didot.

Hindle, Steve (2000), "A Sense of Place? Becoming and Belonging in the Rural Parish 1550–1650," in Alex Shepard and Phil Withington, eds, *Communities in Early Modern England: Networks, Place, Rhetoric*, 96–114, Manchester: Manchester University Press.

Hindle, Steve and Beat Kümin (2009), "The Spatial Dynamics of Parish Politics: Topographies of Tension in English Communities c. 1350–1640," in Beat Kümin, ed., *Political Space in Pre-Industrial Europe*, 151–74, Farnham: Ashgate.

Hinds, Hilary (2011), *George Fox and Early Quaker Culture*, Manchester: Manchester University Press.

Hiscock, Andrew (2011), *Reading Memory in Early Modern Literature*, Cambridge: Cambridge University Press.

Hiscock, Andrew (2018), "Debating Early Modern and Modern Memory: Cultural Forms and Effects: A Critical Retrospective," *Memory Studies* 11 (1): 69–84.

Hobbes, Thomas (1629), *Thucydides's History of the Peloponnesian War*, London: Henry Seile.

Hobbes, Thomas ([1640] 1969), *The Elements of Law, Natural and Politic*, 2nd edn, ed. Ferdinand Tönnies, London: Frank Cass.

Hobbes, Thomas ([1651] 2012), *Leviathan*, 3 vols, ed. Noel Malcolm, Oxford: Clarendon Press.

Hobbes, Thomas (1651), *Leviathan; or the Matter, Form, and Power of a Commonwealth*, London: Andrew Crooke.

Hobsbawm, Eric (2000a), "Introduction: Inventing Traditions," in Eric Hobsbawm and Terence Ranger, eds, *The Invention of Tradition*, 1–14, Cambridge: Cambridge University Press.

Hobsbawm, Eric (2000b), "Mass-Producing Traditions: Europe, 1870–1914," in Eric Hobsbawm and Terence Ranger, eds, *The Invention of Tradition*, 263–307, Cambridge: Cambridge University Press.

Hodgkin, Katharine (2008), "Dreaming Meanings: Some Early Modern Dream Thoughts," in Katharine Hodgkin, Michelle O'Callaghan, and S.J. Wiseman, eds, *Reading the Early Modern Dream: The Terrors of the Night*, 109–24, Abingdon: Routledge.

Hodgkin, Katharine (2013), "Women, Memory and Family History in Seventeenth-Century England," in Erika Kuijpers, Judith Pollmann, Johannes Müller, and Jasper van der Steen, eds, *Memory Before Modernity: Practices of Memory in Early Modern Europe*, 297–313, Leiden: Brill.

Holdsworth, Richard (1956–61), "Directions for a Student in the Universitie," in H.F. Fletcher, ed., *The Intellectual Development of John Milton*, 2 vols, vol. 2, 623–55, Urbana: University of Illinois Press.

Hoogstraten, Antoine II de Lalaing, count of ([1568] 1836), "'Nouvelles des Pays-Bas', 5 June 1568," in G. Groen van Prinsterer, ed., *Archives ou correspondance inédite de la maison d'Orange-Nassau (première série). Tome III: 1567–1572*, Leiden: Luchtmans.

Hooke, Robert (1665), *Micrographia, or, some Physiological Descriptions of Minute Bodies made by Magnifying Glasses*, London: Printed by Jo. Martyn and Ja. Allestry.

Hooke, Robert (1667), "A Method for Making a History of the Weather," in Thomas Sprat, *The History of the Royal Society of London, for the Improving of Natural Knowledge*, 173–9, London: The Royal Society.

Hooke, Robert (1705), "A General Scheme, or Idea of the present state of Natural Philosophy," in Richard Waller, ed., *The Posthumous Works of Robert Hooke*, 1–70, London: Printed by S. Smith & B. Walford.

Hooke, Robert (1968), *The Diary of Robert Hooke, 1672–1680: Transcribed from the Original in the Possession of the Corporation of the City of London (Guildhall Library)*, eds Henry W. Robinson and Walter Adams, London: Wykeham Publications.

Houston, Rab (2016), "People, Space, and Law in Late Medieval and Early Modern Britain and Ireland," *Past and Present* 230: 47–89.

Howard, Thomas Albert (2016), *Remembering the Reformation: An Inquiry into the Meanings of Protestantism*, Oxford: Oxford University Press.

Hoyer, Siefried (1994), "Reformationsjubiläen im 17.und 18. Jahrhundert," in Katrin Keller, ed., *Feste und Feier. Zum Wandel städtischer Kultur im Leipzig*, 36–48, Leipzig: Edition Leipzig.

Huarte, Juan ([1575] 1594), *The Examination of Mens Wits. Translated by M. Camillio Camilli, Englished by [Richard Carew]*, London: R. Watkins.

Huizinga, Johan ([1919] 1996), *The Autumn of the Middle Ages*, trans. Rodney J. Paton and Ulrich Marnmitzsch, Chicago: University of Chicago Press.

Hulse, Clark (1990), *The Rule of Art: Literature and Painting in the Renaissance*, Chicago: University of Chicago Press.

Hunt, Arnold (1998), "The Lord's Supper in Early Modern England," *Past and Present* 161: 41–55.

Hunt, Arnold (2010), *The Art of Hearing: English Preachers and Their Audiences, 1590–1640*, Cambridge: Cambridge University Press.

Hunt, Lynn (1989), "Introduction: History, Culture, Text," in Lynn Hunt, ed., *The New Cultural History*, 1–22, Berkeley: University of California Press.

Hunter, Michael (2009), *Boyle: Between God and Science*, New Haven and London: Yale University Press.

Hutchinson, Lucy ([c. 1664–71] 2000), *Memoirs of the Life of Colonel Hutchinson*, ed. N.H. Keeble, London: Phoenix Press.

Hutton, Patrick A. (1993), *History as an Art of Memory*, Hanover, NH: University Press of New England.

Hutton, Ronald (1996), *The Stations of the Sun: A History of the Ritual Year in Britain*, Oxford: Oxford University Press.

Ingold, Tim (1993), "The Temporality of the Landscape," *World Archaeology* 25 (2): 152–74.

Ingold, Tim (2000), *The Perception of the Environment: Essays on Livelihood, Dwelling and Skill*, London: Routledge.

Isham, Elizabeth (c. 1639), "'Booke of Rememberance', MS. RTC01 no. 62, Princeton University. Transcripts at 'Constructing Elizabeth Isham 1609–1654'," eds Elizabeth Clarke and Erica Longfellow (2008). available online at: http://www2.warwick.ac.uk/fac/arts/ren/projects/isham/ (accessed January 10, 2018).

Ivic, Christopher and Grant Williams, eds (2004), *Forgetting in Early Modern English Literature and Culture: Lethe's Legacies*, London: Routledge.

Jacobs, Roel (2006), *Een kleine geschiedenis van Brussel*, Tielt: Lannoo.

Janssen, Geert (2014), *The Dutch Revolt and Catholic Exile in Reformation Europe*, Cambridge: Cambridge University Press.

Jeanes, Gordon P. (2008), *Signs of God's Promise: Thomas Cranmer's Sacramental Theology and the Book of Common Prayer*, London: T & T Clark.

Jenkins, Harold, ed. (1982), *Hamlet* by William Shakespeare, London: Methuen.

Jensen, Kristian (2011), *Revolution and the Antiquarian Book: Reshaping the Past, 1780–1815*, Cambridge: Cambridge University Press.

Johanson, Kristine (2016), "On the Possibility of Early Modern Nostalgia," *Parergon* 33 (2): 1–15.

Jones, Andrew (2007), *Memory and Material Culture*, Cambridge: Cambridge University Press.

Jones, Ann Rosalind and Peter Stallybrass (2000), *Renaissance Clothing and the Materials of Memory*, Cambridge: Cambridge University Press.

Judovitz, Dalia (1988), *Subjectivity and Representation in Descartes: The Origins of Modernity*, Cambridge: Cambridge University Press.

Junius, Franciscus (1595), *Vita nobilis & eruditi viri Francisci Ivnii*, ed. Paullus Merula, Leiden: ex off. Plantiniana apud F. Raphelengium.

Juste, Théodore (1855), *Les Pays-Bas sous Philippe II. Histoire de la Revolution du XVIe siècle. Tome second (1565–1572)*, Brussels: Méline, Cans et Compagnie.

Kaplan, Steven L. (1995), *Farewell Revolution*, Ithaca, NY: Cornell University Press.

Karremann, Isabel, Cornel Zwierlein, and Inga Mai Groote, eds (2012), *Forgetting Faith? Negotiating Confessional Conflict in Early Modern Europe*, Berlin: De Gruyter.

Kelly, James (1994), "'The Glorious and Immortal Memory': Commemoration and Protestant Identity in Ireland, 1660–1800," *Proceedings of the Royal Irish Academy* 94c: 25–52.

Kelly, James (2000), "The Emergence of Political Parading, 1660–1800," in T.G. Fraser, ed., *The Irish Parading Tradition*, 9–26, Basingstoke: Macmillan.

Kempe, William (1588), *The Education of Children*, London: Thomas Orwin.

Kilburn-Toppin, Jasmine (2013), "Material Memories of the Guildsmen. Crafting Identities in Early Modern London," in Erika Kuijpers, Judith Pollmann, Johannes Müller, and Jasper van der Steen, eds, *Memory before Modernity: Practices of Memory in Early Modern Europe*, 165–81, Leiden and Boston: Brill.

Koslofsky, Craig M. (2000), *The Reformation of the Dead: Death and Ritual in Early Modern Germany, 1450–1700*, London: Macmillan.

Kossmann, E.H. and A.F. Mellink, eds (1974), *Texts Concerning the Revolt of the Netherlands*, Cambridge: Cambridge University Press.

Kristeller, Paul Oskar (1948), "Introduction to *Oration on the Dignity of Man*," in Ernst Cassirer, Paul Oskar Kristeller, and John Herman Randall, Jr., eds, *The Renaissance Philosophy of Man*, 215–22, Chicago: University of Chicago Press.

Kristeva, Julia (1986), "Women's Time," in Toril Moi, ed., *The Kristeva Reader*, 187–213, Oxford: Blackwell.

Kuijpers, Erika, Judith Pollmann, Johannes Müller, and Jasper van der Steen, eds (2013), *Memory Before Modernity: Practices of Memory in Early Modern Europe*, Leiden: Brill.

Kuwakino, Koji (2016), "From *domus sapientiae* to *artes excerpendi*: Lambert Schenkel's *De memoria* (1593) and the Transformation of the Art of Memory," in Alberto Cevolini, ed., *Forgetting Machines: Knowledge Management Evolution in Early Modern Europe*, 58–78, Leiden and Boston: Brill.

Labrot, Gérard (1987), *L'image de Rome: une arme pour la Contre-Réforme, 1534–1677*, Seyssel: Champvallon.

Landau, David and Peter Parshall (1994), *The Renaissance Print: 1470–1550*, New Haven: Yale University Press.

Landsberg, Alison (2004), *Prosthetic Memory*, New York: Columbia University Press.

Lawson, A.J., E.A. Martin, and D. Priddy, eds (1981), "The Barrows of East Anglia," *East Anglian Archaeology* 12, Report for Norfolk Museums Service, Suffolk County Council and Essex County Council.

Le Goff, Jacques (1992), *History and Memory*, trans. Steven Rendall and Elizabeth Claman, New York: Columbia University Press.
Lechner, Joan Marie (1962), *Renaissance Concepts of the Commonplaces*, New York: Pageant Press.
Lees-Jeffries, Hester (2013), *Shakespeare and Memory*, Oxford: Oxford University Press.
Lemnius, Levinus (1576), *The Touchstone of Complexions*, London: Thomas Marsh.
Lewis, Charlton T. and Charles Short ([1879] 1966), *A Latin Dictionary*, Oxford: Clarendon Press.
Lewis, Rhodri (2007), *Language, Mind and Nature: Artificial Languages in England from Bacon to Locke*, Cambridge: Cambridge University Press.
Libby, Alexandra (2015), "The Solomonic Ambitions of Isabel Clara Eugenia in Rubens' *The Triumph of the Eucharist* Tapestry Series," *Journal of Historians of Netherlandish Art* 7 (2): 1–24.
Llewellyn, Nigel (2000), *Funeral Monuments in Post-Reformation England*, Cambridge: Cambridge University Press.
[Locke, John] (1686), "Methode Nouvelle de dresser des Recueuils," *Bibliothèque Universelle et Historique* 2: 315–40.
Locke, John ([1690] 1975), *An Essay Concerning Human Understanding*, ed. Peter H. Nidditch, Oxford: Clarendon Press.
Locke, John ([1693] 1989), *Some Thoughts Concerning Education*, eds John W. Yolton and Jean S. Yolton, Oxford: Clarendon Press.
Locke, John ([1697] 1823), *Mr Locke's Reply to the Right Reverend the Lord Bishop of Worcester's Answer to his Second Letter*, in *The Works of John Locke*, 10 vols, a new edn, corrected, vol. 4, 191–498, London: Thomas Tegg.
Locke, John (2019), *Literary and Historical Writings*, ed. J.R. Milton in collaboration with Brandon Chua, Geoff Kemp, David McInnis, John Spurr, and Richard Yeo, Oxford: Oxford University Press.
Loon, Gerard van (1723), *Beschryving der Nederlandsche historipenningen: of beknopt verhaal van 't gene sedert de overdracht der heerschappye van keyzer Karel den Vyfden op koning Philips zynen zoon, tot het sluyten van den Uytrechtschen vreede, in de zeventien Nederlandsche gewesten is voorgevallen*, vol. 1, The Hague: Christiaan van Lom, Isaac Vaillant, Pieter Gosse, Rutgert Alberts, and Pieter de Hondt.
Loosen, Iris (2003), "Die 'universalen Jubiläen' unter Papst Paul V," in Winfried Müller, ed., *Das historische Jubiläum: Genese, Ordnungsleistung und Inszenierungsgeschichte eines institutionellen Mechanismus*, 117–38, Münster: LIT.
Louthan, Howard (2009), *Converting Bohemia: Force and Persuasion in the Catholic Reformation*, Cambridge: Cambridge University Press.
Lundin, Matthew, (2012), *Paper Memory: A Sixteenth-Century Townsman Writes His World*, Cambridge, MA: Harvard University Press.
Lundin, Matthew, Hans Medick, Mitchell Merback, Judith Pollmann, and Susanne Rau (2015), "Forum: Memory before Modernity: Cultures and Practices in Early Modern Germany," *German History* 33 (1): 100–22.
Mac Carthy, Ita (2020), *The Grace of the Italian Renaissance*, Princeton: Princeton University Press.
MacCulloch, Diarmaid (1996), *Thomas Cranmer: A Life*, New Haven: Yale University Press.
Machiavelli, Niccolò ([1531] 1997), *Discourses on Livy*, trans. Julia Conaway Bondanella and Peter Bondanella, Oxford: Oxford University Press.
Machiavelli, Niccolò ([1532] 1950), *The Prince and The Discourses*, trans. Luigi Ricci and Christian Detmold, New York: Random House.
Magnússon, S.G. (2003), "The Singularization of History: Social History and Microhistory within the Postmodern State of Knowledge," *Journal of Social History* 36: 701–35.

Magnússon, S.G. (2016), "Views Into the Fragments: An Approach From a Microhistorical Perspective," *International Journal of Historical Archaeology* 20: 182–206.

Malcolm, Noel (2004), "Thomas Harrison and his 'Ark of Studies': An Episode in the History of the Organization of Knowledge," *The Seventeenth Century* 19: 196–232.

Mallinckrot, Bernard (1640), *De ortu ac progressu artis typographiae*, Cologne: Kinchius.

Marchand, Prosper (1740), *Histoire des origines et des premiers progres de l'imprimerie*, The Hague: Le Viet and Paupie.

Marsch, Angelika (1980), *Bilder zur Augsburgischen Konfession und ihren Jubiläen*, Weissenhorn: Konrad.

Marshall, Peter (2001), *Beliefs and the Dead in Reformation England*, Oxford: Oxford University Press.

Marshall, Peter (2017), *1517. Martin Luther and the Invention of the Reformation*, Oxford: Oxford University Press.

Martin, Craig (2014), *Subverting Aristotle: Religion, History, and Philosophy in Early Modern Science*, Baltimore: Johns Hopkins University Press.

Martines, Lauro, ed. (1994), "The Fat Woodcarver" by Antonio Manetti, trans. Murtha Baca, in *An Italian Renaissance Sextet: Six Tales in Historical Context*, New York: Marsilio.

Mascuch, Michael (1997), *Origins of the Individualist Self: Autobiography and Self-Identity in England, 1591–1791*, Cambridge: Polity Press.

Massey, Doreen (1995), "Places and their Pasts," *History Workshop Journal* 39: 182–92.

Matheson, Peter, ed. (1995), *Argula Von Grumbach: A Woman's Voice in the Reformation*, Edinburgh: T & T Clark.

Matussek, Peter (1999), "The Computer as Theater of Memory," Vortrag gehalten am 27. 11. 1999 im Max-Planck-Institut für Wissenschaftsgeschichte, Berlin. available online at: http://www.peter-matussek.de/Pub/V_26.pdf (accessed September 20, 2017).

Matussek, Peter (2001), "The Renaissance of the Theatre of Memory," *Janus* 8: 4–8.

McAreavey, Naomi (2018), "Building Bridges? Remembering the 1641 Rebellion in Northern Ireland," *Memory Studies* 11 (1): 100–14.

McGuire, J.E. and Martin Tamny (1983), *Certain Philosophical Questions: Newton's Trinity Notebook*, Cambridge: Cambridge University Press.

McLuhan, Marshall (1969), *The Gutenberg Galaxy: The Making of Typographic Man*, Toronto: Signet.

Merrill, Michael (1976), "Interview with E.P. Thompson," in H. Abelove, et al. eds, *Visions of History*, 5–25, Manchester: Manchester University Press.

Milo, Daniel S. (1991), *Trahir le temps (histoire)*, Paris: Les Belles Lettres.

Misztal, Barbara (2003), *Theories of Social Remembering*, Berkshire: Open University Press.

Moine, Claudine ([c. 1645] 1989), *You Looked at Me: The Spiritual Testimony of Claudine Moine*, ed. and trans. Gerard Carroll, Cambridge: James Clarke & Co.

Montaigne, Michel de (1958), *The Complete Essays of Montaigne*, trans. Donald Frame, Stanford: Stanford University Press.

Montaigne, Michel de (1991), *The Essays*, trans. M.A. Screech, London: Penguin.

Mörke, Olaf (2010), *Willem van Oranje (1533–1584). Vorst en "vader" van de Republiek*, Amsterdam: Atlas.

Mormiche, Pascale (2009), *Devenir prince. L'école du pouvoir en France, XVIIe-XVIIIe siècles*, Paris: CNRS Éditions.

Moryson, Fynes ([after 1609] 1918), "Morysons reis en zijn karakteristiek van de Nederlanden," ed. J.N. Jacobsen Jensen, *Bijdragen en Mededeelingen van het Historisch Genootschap* 39: 214–305.

Moss, Ann (1996), *Printed Commonplace-Books and the Structuring of Renaissance Thought*, Oxford: Clarendon Press.
Muir, Edward (1997), *Ritual in Early Modern Europe*, Cambridge: Cambridge University Press.
Mulcaster, Richard (1581), *Positions Concerning the Training up of Children*, London: Thomas Vautrollier.
Mulcaster, Richard (1582), *The First Part of the Elementary*, London: Thomas Vautrollier.
Mullaney, Steven (2015), *The Reformation of Emotions in the Age of Shakespeare*, Chicago: University of Chicago Press.
Müller, Winfried (1998), "Erinnen an die Gründung. Universitätsjubiläen, Universitätsgeschichte und die Entstehung der Jubiläumskultur in der frühen Neuzeit," *Berichte zur Wissenschaftsgeschichte* 21: 79–102.
Müller, Winfried, ed. (2003), *Das Historische Jubiläum: Genese, Ordnungsleistung und Inszenierungsgeschichte eines institutionellen Mechanismus*, Münster: LIT.
Nadav-Manes, Yael (2006), "The Nature of *Historia* in Leon Battista Alberti's *De Pictura* (1435)," *Forum Italicum* 40: 8–21.
Neuber, Wolfgang (2009), "Mnemonic Imagery in the Early Modern Period: Visibility and Collective Memory," in Donald Beecher and Grant Williams, eds, *Ars Reminiscendi: Mind and Memory in Renaissance Culture*, 69–81, Toronto: Center for Reformation and Renaissance Studies.
Nicolson, Marjorie Hope (1960), *The Breaking of the Circle: Studies in the Effect of the New Science on Seventeenth Century Poetry*, rev edn, New York: Columbia University Press.
Nora, Pierre (1989), "Between Memory and History: *Les Lieux de Mémoire*," *Representations* 26 (Special Issue): 7–24.
North, Roger (1984), *General Preface and Life of Dr John North*, ed. Peter Millard, Toronto: University of Toronto Press.
Norwood, Richard ([1639] 1945), *The Journal of Richard Norwood, Surveryor of Bermuda*, ed. and intr. Wesley Frank Cravan and Walter B. Hayward, New York: Scholars' Facsimiles and Reprints, for the Bermuda Historical Monuments Trust.
Null, Ashley (2000), *Thomas Cranmer's Doctrine of Repentance: Renewing the Power to Love*, Oxford: Oxford University Press.
O'Malley, John W. (1993), *The First Jesuits*, Cambridge, MA: Harvard University Press.
O'Malley, John W., ed. (2015), *Art, Controversy and the Jesuits: The Imago Primi Saeculi (1640)*, Philadelphia: St Joseph's Press.
Olick, Jeffrey K., Vered Vinitzky-Seroussi, and Daniel Levy, eds. (2011), *The Collective Memory Reader*, Oxford: Oxford University Press.
Ong, Walter (1991), *Orality and Literacy: The Technologizing of the Word*, London and New York: Routledge.
Ong, Walter (2012), *Rhetoric, Romance, and Technology: Studies in the Interaction of Expression and Culture*, Ithaca: Cornell University Press.
Oorschot, T.G.M. van (1982), "Die erste Jahrhundertfeier der Gesellschaft Jesu (1640) in Kölner Katechismusspielen," in Richard Brinkman et al., eds, *Theatrum Europeum: Festschrift für Elida Maria Szarota*, 127–52, Munich: Fink.
Ozouf, Mona (1976), *La fête révolutionnaire, 1789–1799*, Paris: Gallimard.
Panofsky, Erwin (1972), *Renaissance and Renascences in Western Art*, New York: Harper and Row.
Parkinson, John (1640), *Theatrum Botanicum*, London: Thomas Cotes.
Parshall, Peter (2013), "Graphic Knowledge: Albrecht Dürer and the Imagination," *Art Bulletin* 95 (3): 393–410.

Peter of Ravenna ([1491] 1548), *The Art of Memory, that Otherwyse is Called the Phenix*, trans. Robert Copland, London: Wyllyam Myddylton.

Peters, Erin (2017), *Commemoration and Oblivion in Royalist Print Culture 1658–1667*, London: Palgrave Macmillan.

Pettazzoni, R. (1946), "The Pagan Origins of the Three-headed Representation of the Christian Trinity," *Journal of the Warburg and Courtauld Institutes* 9: 135–51.

Peyer, Hans Conrad (1955), *Stadt und Stadtpatron im mittelalterliche Italien*, Zurich: Europa.

Placcius, Vincent (1689), *De arte excerpendi, vom Gelährten Buchhalten liber singularis quo genera et praecepta excerpendi*, Hamburg: G. Liebezeit.

Plat, Hugh (1594), *The Jewell House of Art and Nature*, London: Bernard Alsop.

Plato (1961), *Collected Dialogues of Plato Including the Letters*, eds Edith Hamilton and Huntington Cairns, New York: Pantheon.

Platter, Thomas ([c. 1573] 1839), *The Autobiography of Thomas Platter*, trans. Elizabeth McCaul, London: n.p.

Playfere, Thomas ([1593] 2016), "The Pathway to Perfection (1593)", in William Engel, Rory Loughnane, and Grant Williams, eds, *The Memory Arts in Renaissance England: A Critical Anthology*, 238–41, Cambridge: Cambridge University Press.

Pliny the Elder (1938–63), *Naturalis Historia*, 10 vols, trans. H. Rackham, London: W. Heinemann.

Pollmann, Judith (2008), *Het oorlogsverleden van de Gouden Eeuw*, Leiden: s.n.

Pollmann, Judith (2011), *Catholic Identity and the Revolt of the Netherlands, 1520–1635*, Oxford: Oxford University Press.

Pollmann, Judith (2017), *Memory in Early Modern Europe, 1500–1800*, Oxford: Oxford University Press.

Pollmann, Judith and Erika Kuijpers (2013), "Introduction: On the Early Modernity of Modern Memory," in Erika Kuijpers, Judith Pollmann, Johannes Müller, and Jasper van der Steen, eds, *Memory Before Modernity: Practices of Memory in Early Modern Europe*, 1–23, Leiden: Brill.

Pope-Hennessy, John (1985), *Italian High Renaissance and Baroque Sculpture*, New York: Vintage Books.

Popkin, R.H. (2003), *The History of Scepticism from Savanarola to Bayle*, Oxford: Oxford University Press.

Poppi, M. (1967), "Ricerche sul notaio e cronista veneziano Lorenzo de Monacis," *Studi Veneziani* 9: 153–86.

Purver, Margery (2013), *The Royal Society: Concept and Creation*, repr. edn, London: Routledge.

Quinault, Roland (1998), "The Cult of the Centenary, c. 1784–1914," *Historical Research* 71: 314–23.

Quintilian (1961), *The Institutio Oratoria*, trans. H.E. Butler, Loeb Classical Library, Cambridge, MA: Harvard University Press.

Rabboni, Renzo (2009), "Fra Aretino e Varchi: le lettere (e le rime) sull'arte di Nicolò Martelli," *Italianistica: Rivista di letteratura italiana* 38 (2): 251–69.

Raleigh, Walter (1614), *History of the World*, London: Walter Burre.

Raylor, Timothy (2008), "Review of Thomas Festa, *The End of Learning: Milton and Education*," *Milton Quarterly* 42 (3): 218–22.

Recorde, Robert (1556), *Castle of Knowledge*, London: Reginalde Wolfe.

Rhodes, Neil and Jonathan Sawday (2000), "Paperworlds: Imagining the Renaissance Computer," in Neil Rhodes and Jonathan Sawday, eds, *The Renaissance Computer: Knowledge Technology in the First Age of Print*, 1–17, London and New York: Routledge.

Ricoeur, Paul (2000), *La mémoire, l'histoire, l'oubli*, Paris: Seuil.
Ricoeur, Paul (2004), *Memory, History, Forgetting*, trans. Kathleen Blamey and David Pellauer, Chicago and London: University of Chicago Press.
Ridley, R.T. (1986), "To be Taken with a Pinch of Salt: The Destruction of Carthage," *Classical Philology* 81 (2): 140–6.
Rijser, David (2012), *Raphael's Poetics: Art and Poetry in High Renaissance Rome*, Amsterdam: Amstrdam University Press.
Rio Barredo, María José del (2010), "Rituals of the Viaticum: Dynasty and Community in Habsburg Madrid," in Melissa Calaresu, F. de Vivo, and J.P. Rubies, eds, *Exploring Cultural History: Essays in Honour of Peter Burke*, 55–76, Farnham: Ashgate.
Rivet, André (1642), *Instruction du prince chrestien. Par dialogues, entre un jeune Prince, & son directeur*, Leiden: Ian Maire.
Robey, Tracy E. (2013), "*Damnatio memoriae*: The Rebirth of Condemnation of Memory in Renaissance Florence," *Renaissance and Reformation / Renaissance et Réforme* 36 (3): 5–32.
Rodgers, Christopher, Eleanor Straughton, Angus Winchester, and Margherita Pieraccini (2011), *Contested Common Land: Environmental Governance Past and Present*, London and Washington DC: Earthscan.
Rogers, John (1653), *Ohel or Beth-Shemesh: A Tabernacle for the Sun*, London: R.I., and G. & H. Eversden.
Roller, Matthew B. (2010), "Demolished Houses, Monumentality, and Memory in Roman Culture," *Classical Antiquity* 29 (1): 117–80.
Romberch, Johannes Host von (1520), *Congestorium Artificiose Memorie*, Venice: Giorgio Rusconi.
Rossellius, Cosmas (1579), *Thesaurus Artificiosae Memoriae*, Venice: Antonio Padovani.
Rossi, Paolo ([1960] 2000), *Logic and the Art of Memory: The Quest for a Universal Language*, trans. Stephen Clucas, Chicago: University of Chicago Press.
Rossi, Paolo (1968), *Francis Bacon from Magic to Science*, trans. Sacha Rabinovitch, London: Routledge & Kegan Paul.
Rowlandson, Mary White ([1682] 1977), *A True History of the Captivity and Restoration of Mrs Mary Rowlandson*, New York: Garland Publishers.
Rucellai, Giovanni (1960), *Il suo zibaldone*, ed. Alessandro Perosa, London: The Warburg Institute.
Russell, Nicolas (2011), *Transformations of Memory and Forgetting in Sixteenth-Century France: Marguerite de Navarre, Pierre de Ronsard, Michel de Montaigne*, Newark: University of Delaware Press.
Ryrie, Alec (2013), *Being Protestant in Reformation Britain*, Oxford: Oxford University Press.
Sabean, David Warren and Simon Teuscher (2007), "Kinship in Europe: A New Approach to Long-Term Development," in David Warren Sabean, Simon Teuscher, and Jon Mathieu, eds, *Kinship in Europe: Approaches to Long-Term Development (1300–1900)*, 1–16, New York and Oxford: Berghahn.
Sacchini, Francesco ([1614] 1615), *De ratione libros cum profectu legendi libellus . . .*, Sammieli: F. du Bois.
Safley, Thomas Max (2000), *Matheus Miller's Memoir: A Merchant's Life in the Seventeenth Century*, Basingstoke, Hampshire: Macmillan.
Sanderus, Antonius (1629), *Le grand theatre sacré du duché de Brabant [. . .] Tome Premier. Seconde Partie VI*, The Hague: Chrétien van Lom, 1629.
Saunders, J.B. de C.M. and Charles D. O'Malley (1973), *The Illustrations from the Works of Andreas Vesalius of Brussels*, New York: Dover.

Saunders, Richard (1671), *Physiognomy and Chiromancy [. . .] whereunto is added the Art of Memory*, 2nd edn, London: H. Brugis, for Nathanial Brook.
Savage, Kirk (2009), *Monument Wars: Washington, D.C., the National Mall, and the Transformation of the Memorial Landscape*, Berkeley: University of California Press.
Sawday, Jonathan (2007), *Engines of the Imagination: Renaissance Culture and the Rise of the Machine*, London: Routledge.
Schama, Simon (1995), *Landscape and Memory*, New York: Random House.
Schiffman, Zachary S. (1984), "Montaigne and the Rise of Skepticism in Early Modern Europe: A Reappraisal," *Journal of the History of Ideas* 45 (4): 499–516.
Schiffman, Zachary S. (2011), *The Birth of the Past*, Baltimore: Johns Hopkins University Press.
Schmitt, Jean-Claude (2007), "La naissance de l'anniversaire," *Annales H.S.S.* 62: 793–835.
Schmitt, Jean-Claude (2009), *La naissance de l'anniversaire*, Paris: Arkhè.
Scholten, Fritz (2003), *Sumptuous Memories: Studies in Seventeenth-Century Dutch Tomb Sculpture*, Zwolle: Waanders.
Schönstadt, Hans-Jürgen (1978), *Antichrist, Weltheilsgeschehen und Gottes Werkzeug: Römische Kirche, Reformation und Luther im Spiegel des Reformationsjubiläum 1617*, Wiesbaden: Steiner.
Schönstadt, Hans-Jürgen (1982a), "Das Reformationsjubiläum 1617," *Zeitschrift für Kirchengeschichte* 93: 5–57.
Schönstadt, Hans-Jürgen (1982b), "Das Reformationsjubiläum 1717," *Zeitschrift für Kirchengeschichte* 93, 58–118.
Schrag, J.A. (1640), *Bericht von Erfindung der Buchdruckerey in Strassburg*, Strasbourg: Carle.
Schuermans, H. (1870), "La colonne de Culembourg à Bruxelles," *Bulletin des commissions royales d'art et d'archéologie*, 17–107.
Schwoerer, L.G. (1990), "Celebrating the Glorious Revolution, 1689–1989," *Albion* 22: 1–20.
Schwyzer, Philip (2018), "Fallen Idols, Broken Noses: Defacement and Memory After the Reformation," *Memory Studies* 11 (1): 21–35.
Scribner, R.W. (1989), "Is a History of Popular Culture Possible?" *History of European Ideas* 10: 175–91.
Shakespeare, William (2006), *The Oxford Shakespeare: The Complete Works*, 2nd edn, gen. eds Stanley Wells and Gary Taylor, Oxford: Clarendon Press.
Sharpe, James (2005), *Remember, Remember the Fifth of November: Guy Fawkes and the Gunpowder Plot*, London: Profile.
Sharpe, Kevin (2009), *Selling the Tudor Monarchy: Authority and Image in Sixteenth-Century England*, New Haven, CT: Yale University Press.
Shepard, Alexandra (2003), *Meanings of Manhood*, Oxford: Oxford University Press.
Shepard, Thomas ([c. 1646] 1972), "Autobiography," in Michael McGiffert, ed., *God's Plot: The Paradoxes of Puritan Piety*, Amherst: University of Massachusetts Press.
Shergold, N.D. (1967), *A History of the Spanish Stage from Medieval Times until the End of the Seventeenth Century*, Oxford: Clarendon Press.
Sherlock, Peter (2008), *Monuments and Memory in Early Modern England*, Aldershot: Ashgate.
Sherlock, Peter (2010), "The Reformation of Memory in Early Modern Europe," in Susannah Radstone and Bill Schwarz, eds, *Memory: Histories, Theories, Debates*, 30–40, New York: Fordham University Press.
Shifflett, Andrew (2003), "Kings, Poets, and the Power of Forgiveness, 1642–1660," *English Literary Renaissance* 33 (1): 88–109.
Sidney, Philip (1595), *The Defence of Poesy*, London: William Ponsonby.

Small, Jocelyn P. (1995), "Artificial Memory and the Writing Habits of the Literate," *Helios* 22: 159–77.

Smith, Anthony D. (2000), *The Nation in History: Historiographical Debates about Ethnicity and Nationalism*, Cambridge: Polity Press.

Smith, David L. (2008/2009), "Gottsched, Gutenberg's Printing Press and Humankind's Third Creation," *Lessing Yearbook* 38: 137–57.

Smyth, Adam (2010), *Autobiography in Early Modern England*, Cambridge: Cambridge University Press.

Spence, Jonathan D. (1984), *The Memory Palace of Matteo Ricci*, New York: Viking Penguin.

Spicer, Andrew (2007), *Calvinist Churches in Early Modern Europe*, Manchester: Manchester University Press.

Sprat, Thomas (1667), *The History of the Royal-Society of London, for the Improving of Natural Knowledge*, London: The Royal Society.

Starobinski, Jean (1966), "The Idea of Nostalgia," *Diogenes* 54: 81–103.

Stedman Jones, Gareth (1983), *Languages of Class: Studies in English Working-Class History 1832–1986*, Cambridge: Cambridge University Press.

Steen, Jasper van der (2015), *Memory Wars in the Low Countries, 1566–1700*, Leiden and Boston: Brill.

Stirredge, Elizabeth (1711), *Strength in Weakness Manifest: In the Life, Various Trials, and Christian Testimony of that Faithful Servant and Handmaid of the Lord*, London: T. Sowle.

Stochholm, Johanne M. (1964), *Garrick's Folly: The Shakespeare Jubilee of 1769 at Stratford and Drury Lane*, New York: Barnes & Noble.

Stock, Paul, ed. (2015), *The Uses of Space in Early Modern History*, Basingstoke: Palgrave Macmillan.

Strong, Roy C. (1959), "The Popular Celebration of the Accession Day of Queen Elizabeth I," *Journal of the Warburg and Courtauld Institutes* 21 (1/2): 88–91.

Stumpel, Jeroen and Jolein van Kregten (2002), "In the Name of the Thistle: Albrecht Dürer's Self-Portrait of 1493," *Burlington Magazine* 144 (1186): 14–18.

"Suite du rapport rédigé par un secrétaire du Conseil des Troubles, de l'activité de ce dernier organisme pendant la période du 13 janvier 1568 au 6 avril 1568" ([1568] 1961), in A.L.E. Verheyden, ed., *Le Conseil des Troubles. Liste des condamnés (1567–1573)*, Brussels: Paleis der Academiën.

Sutton, John, Celia B. Harriss, and Amanda J. Barnier (2010), "Memory and Cognition," in Susannah Radstone and Bill Schwarz, eds, *Memory; Histories, Theories and Debates*, 209–26, New York: Fordham University Press.

Tarlow, Sarah (2007), *The Archaeology of Improvement in Britain 1750–1850*, Cambridge: Cambridge University Press.

Taurinus, Jacobus (1617), *Na-Sporingh / hoe ende in vvat manieren, De door-luchtighe, ende hoogh-ghebooren vorst, de prince van Orangien, hooghloffelijcker memorie, de beschermenisse deser landen heeft aenghenomen, om de Nederlantsche Belijdenisse / als in allen deelen met Godts woordt accorderende / te mainteneren: en t'gevoelen der Contra-Remonstranten, int stuck vande predestinatie met den aencleven vandien, als Schrifmatich over al in te voeren*, s.l.: s.n.

Taylor, Craig (2006), "The Salic Law, French Queenship, and the Defense of Women in the Late Middle Ages," *French Historical Studies* 29 (4): 543–64.

Tenenti, Alberto (1952), *La vie et la mort à travers l'art du XVe siècle*, Paris: Armand Colin.

Teresa of Avila ([1561–5] 1962), *The Life of St Teresa of Avila, written by herself*, trans. David Lewis, London: Burns and Oates.

The life and death of Queene Elizabeth, from the wombe to the tombe, from her birth to her buriall, (1639), London: John Okes.

Thompson, Ann and Neil Taylor, eds (2016), *Hamlet: Revised Edition*, London: Bloomsbury Publishing.

Thompson, E.P. (1991), *Customs in Common*, London: Merlin Press.

Thurgood, Rose ([c. 1636] 2005), "A Lecture of Repentance," in Naomi Baker, ed., *Scripture Women*, Nottingham: Trent Editions.

Toews, John E. (1987), "Intellectual History after the Linguistic Turn: The Autonomy of Meaning and the Irreducibility of Experience," *American Historical Review* 92(4): 879–907.

Trapnel, Anna (1654), *Anna Trapnel's Report and Plea. Or, a Narrative of Her Journey from London into Cornwal, etc.*, London: Thomas Brewster.

Tribble, Evelyn and Nicholas Keene (2011), *Cognitive Ecologies and the History of Remembering: Religion, Education and Memory in Early Modern England*, Basingstoke: Palgrave Macmillan.

Trigland, Jacobus (1650), *Kerckelycke geschiedenissen begrypende de swaere en bekommerlijcke geschillen, in de Vereenigde Nederlanden voor-gevallen, met derselver beslissinge, ende aenmerckingen op de kerckelycke historie van Johannes Wtenbogaert*, Leiden: Adriaen Wyngaerden.

Tryon, Thomas (1705), *Some Memoirs of the Life of Mr Tho. Tryon*, London: T. Sowle.

Turrell, James F. (2014), "Anglican Theologies of the Eucharist," in Lee Palmer Wendel, ed., *A Companion to the Eucharist in the Reformation*, 139–58, Leiden: Brill.

Uytenbogaert, Johannes (1617), *Copye van seker vertooch onlanghs bij eenighe predicanten der ghereformeerde kercke ghedaen [. . ..] roerende de oudtheyt vande gereformeerde leere*, Delft: Bruyn Harmansz Schinckel.

Van Dijkhuizen, Jan Frans (2015), "Narratives of Reconciliation in Early Modern England: Between Oblivion, Clemency and Forgiveness," in Karl A.E. Enenkel and Anita Traninger, eds, *Discourses of Anger in the Early Modern Period*, 403–35, Leiden: Brill.

Van Mander, Karel (1936), *Dutch and Flemish Painters*, trans. Constant van de Wall, New York: McFarlane, Wane, McFarlane.

Vasari, Giorgio (1991), *The Lives of the Artists*, trans. J.C. and P. Bondanella, Oxford: Oxford University Press.

Vesalius, Andreas (1543), *De humani corporis fabrica*, Basel: Johannes Oporinus.

Villari, Rosario (2012), *Un sogno di libertà: Napoli nel declinio di un imperio, 1585–1648*, Milan: Mondadori.

Vine, Angus (2011), "Commercial Commonplacing: Francis Bacon, the Waste-Book, and the Ledger," in Richard Beadle and Colin Burrow, eds, *Manuscripts Miscellanies c. 1450–1700*, 197–218, Chicago: The University of Chicago Press.

Viroli, Maurizio (2012), *As If God Existed: Religion and Liberty in the History of Italy*, Princeton, NJ: Princeton University Press.

Vittinghoff, Friedrich (1936), *Der Staatsfeind in der römischen Kaiserzeit: Untersuchungen zur "damnatio memoriae,"* Berlin: Junker und Dünnhaupt.

Vives, Juan Luis (1563), *Introduction to Wisdom*, trans. Richard Morison, London: T. Powell.

Vivian, Bradford (2010), *Public Forgetting: The Rhetoric and Politics of Beginning Again*, University Park: Pennsylvania State University Press.

Voet van Oudheusden, A.W.K. (1753), *Historische beschryvinge van Culemborg. Behelzende een naemlyst der heeren van Bosichem, benevens der heeren en graeven van Culemborg . . . der-*

zelver huwelyken, nakooomelingen [. . .] Mitsgaders een beschryvinge van de stad Culemborg, derzelver regeeringwyze, gebouwen [. . .] handvesten, privilegien en voorrechten, enz., Utrecht: J.H. Vonk van Lynden.

Walker, Obadiah (1673), *Of Education Especially of Young Gentlemen. The second impression with additions*, Oxford: Printed at the Theatre.

Walsham, Alexandra (2002), "Reformed Folklore? Cautionary Tales and Oral Traditions in Early Modern England," in Adam Fox and Daniel Woolf, eds, *The Spoken Word: Oral Culture in Britain, 1500–1850*, 178–95, Manchester: Manchester University Press.

Walsham, Alexandra (2011), *The Reformation of the Landscape: Religion, Identity, and Memory in Early Modern Britain and Ireland*, Oxford: Oxford University Press.

Walsham, Alexandra (2012), "History, Memory, and the English Reformation," *The Historical Journal* 55 (4): 899–938.

Walter, John (2006), "Crown and Crowd: Popular Protest and Popular Culture in Early Modern England," in his *Crowds and Popular Politics in Early Modern England*, 14–26, Manchester: Manchester University Press.

Wandel, Lee Palmer (2006), *The Eucharist in the Reformation: Incarnation and Liturgy*, Cambridge: Cambridge University Press.

Wear, Andrew (2000), *Knowledge and Practice in English Medicine, 1550–1680*, Cambridge: Cambridge University Press.

Weever, John ([1631] 2016), "Ancient Funeral Monuments (1631)," in William Engel, Rory Loughnane, and Grant Williams, eds, *The Memory Arts in Renaissance England: A Critical Anthology*, 205–8, Cambridge: Cambridge University Press.

Weinrich, Harald (2004), *Lethe: The Art and Critique of Forgetting*, trans. Steven Rendall, Ithaca: Cornell University Press.

Westfall, Richard S. (1993), *The Life of Isaac Newton*, Cambridge: Cambridge University Press.

Whaley, Joachim (1985), *Religious Toleration and Social Change in Hamburg 1529–1819*, Cambridge: Cambridge University Press.

Whitfield, Peter (2015), *Mapping Shakespeare's World*, Oxford: Bodleian Library.

Whyte, Nicola (2007), "Landscape, Memory and Custom: Parish Identities c. 1550–1700," *Social History* 32 (2): 166–86.

Whyte, Nicola (2009), *Inhabiting the Landscape: Place, Custom and Memory c. 1500–1800*, Oxford: Windgather Press.

Whyte, Nicola (2011), "Custodians of Memory: Women and Custom in Rural England c. 1550–1650," *Cultural and Social History* 8 (2): 153–73.

Whyte, Nicola (2013), "An Archaeology of Natural Places: Trees in the Early Modern Landscape," *Huntingdon Library Quarterly* 76 (4): 499–517.

Whyte, Nicola (2015), "Senses of Place, Senses of Time: Landscape History from a British Perspective," *Landscape Research* 40 (8): 925–38.

Whyte, Nicola (2018), "Spatial History," in Sasha Handley, Rohan McWilliam, and Lucy Noakes, eds, *New Directions in Cultural and Social History*, 233–51, London: Bloomsbury Publishing.

Whythorne, Thomas ([c. 1576] 1962), *The Autobiography of Tomas Whythorne*, ed. James M. Osborn, Oxford: Clarendon Press.

Wilcox, Helen (2006), "Selves in Strange Lands: Autobiography and Exile in the Mid-Seventeenth Century," in Ronald Bedford, Lloyd Davis, and Philippa Kelly, eds, *Early Modern Autobiography: Theories, Practices, Genres*, 131–59, Ann Arbor: University of Michigan Press.

Williams, Sheila (1958), "The Pope-burning Processions of 1679, 1680 and 1681," *Journal of the Warburg and Courtauld Institutes* 21 (1/2): 104–18.

Williamson, Tom (1995), *Polite Landscapes: Gardens and Society in Eighteenth-Century England*, Stroud: Alan Sutton.

Willis, John (1621), *The Art of Memory*, London: W. Jones.

Wilson, Kathleen (1989), "Inventing Revolution: 1688 and Eighteenth-Century Popular Politics," *Journal of British Studies* 28 (4): 349–86.

Wilson, Stephen (2000), *The Magical Universe. Everyday Ritual and Magic in Premodern Europe*, London and New York: Hambledon and London.

Witt, John de (1654), *Deductie, ofte declaratie van de Staten van Hollandt ende West-Vrieslandt [. . .] tot justificatie van't verleenen van seeckere acte van seclusie, raeckende 't employ vanden heere prince van Oraigne [. . .] op den vierden mey 1654 ghepasseert*, The Hague: Hillebrandt Jacobsz van Wouw.

Wood, Andy (1997), "The Place of Custom in Plebeian Political Culture: England, 1550–1800," *Social History* 22: 46–60.

Wood, Andy (1999), "Custom and the Social Organisation of Writing in Early Modern England," *Transactions of the Royal Historical Society* 6 (9): 257–69.

Wood, Andy (2002), *Riot, Rebellion and Popular Politics in Early Modern England*, Basingstoke: Palgrave.

Wood, Andy (2013a), *The Memory of the People: Custom and Popular Senses of the Past in Early Modern England*, Cambridge: Cambridge University Press.

Wood, Andy (2013b), "Deference, Paternalism and Popular Memory in Early Modern England," in Steve Hindle, Alexandra Shepard, and John Walter, eds, *Remaking English Society: Social Relations and Social Change in Early Modern England*, 233–55, Woodbridge: Boydell.

Wood, P.B. (1980), "Methodology and Apologetics: Thomas Sprat's *History of the Royal Society*," *The British Journal for the History of Science* 13 (1): 1–26.

Wooding, Lucy (2013), "Remembrance in the Eucharist," in Andrew Gordon and Thomas Rist, eds, *The Arts of Remembrance in Early Modern England: Memorial Cultures of the Post Reformation*, 19–36, Farnham: Ashgate.

Woolf, Daniel (1991), "Memory and Historical Culture in Early Modern England," *Journal of the Canadian Historical Association* 2 (1): 283–308.

Woolf, Daniel (2002), "Speaking of History: Conversations about the Past in Restoration and Eighteenth-Century England," in Adam Fox and Daniel Woolf, eds, *The Spoken Word: Oral Culture in Britain, 1500–1850*, 119–37, Manchester: Manchester University Press.

Woolf, Daniel (2003), *The Social Circulation of the Past: English Historical Culture 1500–1730*, Oxford: Oxford University Press.

Woolf, Daniel R. (2005), "From Hystories to the Historical: Five Transitions in Thinking about the Past, 1500–1700," *Huntington Library Quarterly* 68 (1–2): 33–70.

Worden, Blair (1974), *The Rump Parliament, 1648–1653*, Cambridge: Cambridge University Press.

Wrightson, Keith (1996), "The Politics of the Parish in Early Modern England," in Paul Griffiths, Adam Fox and Steve Hindle, eds, *The Experience of Authority in Early Modern England*, 10–46, Basingstoke: Palgrave Macmillan.

Wrightson, Keith (2005), "Mutualities and Obligations: Changing Social Relationships in Early Modern England," *Proceedings of the British Academy* 139: 157–94.

Yates, Frances A. (1957), "Elizabethan Chivalry: The Romance of the Accession Day Tilts," *Journal of the Warburg and Courtauld Institutes* 20: 4–25.

Yates, Frances A. (1964), *Giordano Bruno and the Hermetic Tradition*, Chicago: University of Chicago Press.
Yates, Frances A. ([1966] 1999), *The Art of Memory*, repr. edn, London and New York: Routledge.
Yates, Frances A. (1969), *Theatre of the World*, Chicago: University of Chicago Press.
Yates, Frances A. (1978), *The Art of Memory*, repr. edn, London: Penguin.
Yeo, Richard (2007), "Between Memory and Paperbooks: Baconianism and Natural History in Seventeenth-Century England," *History of Science* 45: 1–46.
Yeo, Richard (2008), "Notebooks as Memory Aids: Precepts and Practices in Early Modern England," *Memory Studies* 1: 115–36.
Yeo, Richard (2010), "Loose Notes and Capacious Memory: Robert Boyle's Note-taking and its Rationale," *Intellectual History Review* 20: 335–54.
Yeo, Richard (2014), *Notebooks, English Virtuosi, and Early Modern Science*, Chicago: The University of Chicago Press.
Yeo, Richard (2016), "Notebooks, Recollection, and External Memory: Some Early Modern English Ideas and Practices," in Alberto Cevolini, ed., *Forgetting Machines. Knowledge Management Evolution in Early Modern Europe*, 128–54, Leiden and Boston: Brill.
Young, Robert F. (1932), *Comenius in England*, Oxford: Oxford University Press.
Zapalac, Kristin Eldyss Sorensen (1990), *In His Image and Likeness: Political Iconography and Religious Change in Regensburg, 1500–1600*, Ithaca: Cornell University Press.
Zerubavel, Eviatar (1997), *Social Mindscapes: An Invitation to Cognitive Sociology*, Cambridge, MA: Harvard University Press.
Zika, Charles ([1995] 2003), "The Reformation Jubilee of 1617," reprinted in his *Exorcising Our Demons: Magic, Witchcraft and Visual Culture in Early Modern Europe*, 197–236, Leiden: Brill.
Zwahr, Hartmut (1994), "Zur Entstehung eines nationalen Gedächtnisses. Die Leipziger Jahrhundertfeiern zum Gedenken an die Erfindung des Buchdrucks mit beweglichen Lettern," in Katrin Keller, ed., *Feste und Feiern: zum Wandel städtische Festkultur in Leipzig*, 117–35, Leipzig: Edition Leipzig.
Zwahr, Hartmut (1996), "Inszenierte Lebenswelt: Jahrhundertfeiern zum Gedenken an die Erfindung der Buchdruckerkunst," *Geschichte und Gesellschaft* 22: 5–18.
Zwierlein, Cornel (2012), "Forgotten Religions, Religions that Cause Forgetting," in Isabel Karremann, Cornel Zwierlein, and Inga Mai Groote, eds, *Forgetting Faith? Negotiating Confessional Conflict in Early Modern Europe*, 117–27, Berlin: De Gruyter.

CONTRIBUTORS

Alessandro Arcangeli is Associate Professor of Early Modern History at the University of Verona, Italy. He is a cultural historian with research interests in leisure and dance (in Europe and in cultural encounters), as well as the body, passions, and medical thought. He is the author and editor of various academic publications in these fields. He has also worked on cultural history methodologically and historiographically, both with reference to Italy and in a wider perspective (see his *Cultural History: A Concise Introduction*, Routledge, 2012). From 2013 to 2017 he served as Chair of the International Society for Cultural History.

Peter Burke is Professor Emeritus of Cultural History and Life Fellow of Emmanuel College, University of Cambridge. He is also a fellow of the British Academy and member of the Academia Europea. He is a specialist in the social and cultural history of early modern Europe as well as in theoretical and methodological questions of historical research. His most recent books include *What is the History of Knowledge?* (Polity, 2015), *Secret History and Historical Consciousness from Renaissance to Romanticism* (Edward Everett Root, 2016), and *Exiles and Expatriates in the History of Knowledge, 1500–2000* (Brandeis University Press, 2017).

Patricia Emison, Professor at the University of New Hampshire, is the author of several books on the Italian Renaissance, including *The Italian Renaissance and Cultural Memory* (Cambridge University Press, 2012). *Moving Pictures and Renaissance Art History* is forthcoming from Amsterdam University Press. She contributed "The forest around the fir tree: looking for Marcantonio's art," to an exhibition curated by Edward Wouk, *Marcantonio Raimondi, Raphael, and the Image Multiplied* (Whitworth Art Gallery, 2016), and wrote *The Shaping of Art History: Meditations on a Discipline* (Pennsylvania State University Press, 2008).

William E. Engel (PhD, University of California, Berkeley) was a dissertation research scholar at the Warburg Institute and postdoctoral fellow at the Huntington Library. Currently the Nick B. Williams Professor of Literature at Sewanee, The University of the South, he is the author of five books on literary history and applied mnemonics, including *Mapping Mortality: The Persistence of Memory and Melancholy in Early Modern England* (University of Massachusetts Press, 1995); and co-author (with Rory Loughnane and Grant Williams) of *The Memory Arts in Renaissance England* (Cambridge University Press, 2016). He has a monograph forthcoming from Routledge on *The Printer as Author in Early Modern English Book History*.

Katharine Hodgkin is Professor of Cultural History at the University of East London. She has published extensively on memory, autobiographical writing and early modern cultural history, focusing in particular on spiritual autobiography. Publications in these areas include two books on contemporary memory cultures co-edited with Susannah Radstone (*Regimes of Memory* and *Contested Pasts*, Routledge, 2003, 2005), a monograph on madness and autobiographical writing (*Madness in Seventeenth-Century Autobiography*, Palgrave, 2007), and a co-edited special issue of *Memory Studies*, "Memory and the Early Modern" (2018). She is currently working on a monograph, *The Self in Time: Memory, Subjectivity and Life Writing in Early Modern England*.

Peter Sherlock is Vice-Chancellor of the University of Divinity, Melbourne, Australia. His research examines cultures of death and memory in early modern Europe, especially monumental commemoration, and the intersection of gender and religion. He is author of *Monuments and Memory in Early Modern England* (Ashgate, 2008) and *Practices of Gender in Late Medieval and Early Modern Europe* (Brepols, 2008) edited with Megan Cassidy-Welch. He is currently completing a history of the Tudor and Stuart monuments of Westminster Abbey.

Marek Tamm is Professor of Cultural History at the School of Humanities in Tallinn University and also Head of Tallinn University Centre of Excellence in Intercultural Studies. His primary research fields are cultural history of medieval Europe, theory and history of historiography, and cultural memory studies. He has recently published *Rethinking Historical Time: New Approaches to Presentism* (ed. with Laurent Olivier, Bloomsbury, 2019), *Debating New Approaches to History* (ed. with Peter Burke, Bloomsbury, 2018), an edited volume, *Afterlife of Events: Perspectives on Mnemohistory* (Palgrave, 2015), and a companion to the *Chronicle* of Henry of Livonia, *Crusading and Chronicle Writing on the Medieval Baltic Frontier* (co-edited with Linda Kaljundi and Carsten Selch Jensen, Ashgate, 2011).

Jasper van der Steen is a postdoctoral researcher and lecturer at Leiden University's Institute for History. Against widespread assumptions about the supposed modernity of cultural memory, his first monograph *Memory Wars in the Low Countries, 1566–1700* (Brill, 2015) argues that early modern public memory did not require the presence of state actors, nationalism, and modern mass media in order to play a role of political importance in the Low Countries. He is currently doing research for his second monograph, *The Nassaus and the Family Business of Power in Early Modern Europe*.

Nicola Whyte is an Associate Professor in History at the University of Exeter. She is particularly interested in developing interdisciplinary approaches to the meanings of landscape, place, and memory in Britain since the sixteenth century. She has published on early modern landscapes, agriculture, custom, memory, gender, everyday practices, environmental change, and local conflict. Her first book *Inhabiting the Landscape: Place, Custom and Memory 1500–1800* was published in 2009, and its themes were further developed in, "Senses of Place, Senses of Time: Landscape History from a British Perspective" (*Landscape Research*, 2015). She is currently working on a monograph exploring the concepts of landscape, dwelling, and place for the early modern period.

Richard Yeo is an historian of science, a Fellow of the Australian Academy of the Humanities, and Emeritus Professor at Griffith University, Brisbane. His books include *Defining Science: William Whewell, Natural Knowledge and Public Debate in Early Victorian Britain* (Cambridge University Press, 1993); *Encyclopaedic Visions: Scientific Dictionaries and Enlightenment Culture* (Cambridge University Press, 2001); and *Notebooks, English Virtuosi, and Early Modern Science* (The University of Chicago Press, 2014). He has co-edited special issues of *Parergon* 26 (2009), with Vanessa Smith, and of *Intellectual History Review* 20 (2010) with Ann Blair.

INDEX

Agrippa von Nettesheim, Heinrich Cornelius 62, 85,
Albert of Austria 23–4, 26
Albert the Great 82
Alberti, Leon Battista 83, 93
Alexander the Great 101
amnesia, *see* forgetting
Amsterdam 10, 31, 33, 145
anachronism 4, 5, 19, 20
ancestors 4, 28–9, 35, 37, 45–6
anniversary 10, 32, 137–8, 140, 142, 148
Antoine II de Lalaing, Count 22
Antoninus Pius 141
Antwerp 23, 143, 147
Arcangeli, Alessandro 1
Argula von Grumbach 164
Aristotle 1, 2, 61, 65, 78–80, 82, 98, 102
Arminius, Jacobus 26
Arne, Thomas 147
ars memorativa 14–15
ars memoriae, *see ars memorativa*
ars oblivionalis, *see* arts of oblivion
artificial memory 15, 18, 61–2, 78, 82–3, 92
arts of memory, *see ars memorativa*
arts of oblivion 17
Assmann, Aleida 20, 135
Assmann, Jan 9, 135
Aubery, Louis 30
Aubrey, John 62
Augustine 2, 39–40, 61
autobiography 7, 37–9, 40, 44–5, 47, 54

Baccio Bigio, Nanni di 109
Bachelard, Gaston 52
Bacon, Francis 18, 61–3, 65, 67, 69–71, 73, 80, 84–6, 90–2, 156–7
Baggerman, Ariane 55
Balbín, Bohuslav 25
Baldinucci, Filippo 103
Baldo, Jonathan 154
Baltimore 145
Barlow, Edward 47–8, 50
Barocci, Federico 106

Baronio, Cesare 141
Basel 145–6
Basse, William 58
Beaumont, Agnes 52
Becket, Thomas 6, 158
Bedford 37, 41, 52
Belfast 146
Belknap, Jeremy 144
Bellini, Giovanni 103
Belot, Jean 79, 93
Bembo, Pietro 112
Berlin 161
Bernini, Gian Lorenzo 101, 103, 107–8, 113
Bible 10, 19, 27, 33, 39, 84, 162, 164
Birkenhead, John 62
Birmingham 146
Black Death 8, 10
Blake, Emma 123
Blaugdone, Barbara 53
body 1, 7, 9, 11, 30, 45–6, 49, 52, 58, 77–8, 80–3, 87, 93, 105, 110, 135, 164
Bohemia 25, 35
Bologna 115, 144
Bolzoni, Lina 14–15, 17
Boniface VIII, Pope 25–6
Borghese, Scipione 103
Borgia, Cesare 111–112
Boston 144
Botero, Giovanni 28
Botticelli, Sandro 103, 171 n.8
Boyle, Robert 65, 70–1, 73
Bracciolini, Poggio 83
Brahe, Tycho 86
Breslau 145
Brinsley, John 60, 90
Bristol 146, 159
Brunelleschi, Filippo 99–100, 109
Bruno, Giordano 87, 93
Brussels 21, 23–5, 80
Bry, Theodore de 144
Bunyan, John 45–6, 51–2
Burckhardt, Jacob 5, 7
burial 8, 49, 124–5, 160

Burke, Peter 9, 10, 26, 117, 126, 135
Burton, Robert 50, 62

Cade, Jack 136
Calas, Jean 144
Calixtus III, Pope 140
Calvin, John 27, 138
Cambridge 58, 60, 65–6, 86, 137
Camillo, Giulio 15–16, 87, 93
Canada 54
Canterbury 6
Caravaggio 103
Carpenter, Richard 50
Carruthers, Mary 14
Castiglione, Baldassare 102, 108–12
Cave, William 141
Cellini, Benvenuto 103
centenary 2, 26, 137, 140–3, 145–6, 148–9
Cervantes, Miguel de 102
Cevolini, Alberto 155
Chantelou, Paul Fréart de 101
Charlemagne 149
Charles I 32, 136, 138, 158, 166–7
Charles II 33, 138–9, 167
Charles V 144
Charleton, Walter 65
Cheevers, Sarah 54
Cicero, Marcus Tullius 61, 63, 83–4, 88, 94, 112, 155
Clucas, Stephen 115, 170 n.2
collective memory 13, 47, 78, 98, 122, 153
Colman, George 147
Cologne 82, 143
Columbus, Christopher 144
Comenius, Johann Amos 42, 59, 63, 67, 90, 95
commemoration 2, 8–11, 13, 25–9, 32, 35, 135–6, 138–49, 153, 158–9, 161–2, 165
communicative memory 9
Condivi, Ascanio 113
Connerton, Paul 123
Conradin 136
Coote, Edmund 90
Copernicus, Nicolaus 77, 81, 147, 150
Cort, Cornelis 106
Cosimo de' Medici 100
Coster, Laurens 145
Costerus, Franciscus 25
Counter-Reformation 2, 21, 23, 25–6, 28, 35, 137–8
Cowley, Abraham 167
Cressy, David 10, 32
Cromwell, Oliver 33, 167

Crooke, Helkiah 82
Cruickshank, Frances 163
Cullyer, Peter 125
cultural memory 9, 21, 24, 28, 54, 81, 97, 101–2, 106–7, 112–15, 135
Cummings, Brian 10
custom 6, 9, 122–3, 127, 129, 132, 136, 152, 154
customary law 123, 127

D'Ewes, Simonds 64
damnatio memoriae 5, 6, 23, 154, 168
Dane, John 44, 47–8
Dante Alighieri 94, 149
Davis, Natalie Zemon 40
De Witt, John 32–4
death 8, 11, 15, 19, 30–1, 35, 45, 49, 67, 105, 111, 136, 147, 149, 154, 159, 161–3, 165, 167
Dekker, Rudolf 55
Denmark 86
Derry 146, 150
Descartes, René 65, 80, 85, 88, 99–101, 110, 156
Diogenes of Sinope 88
Dioscorides, Pedanius 81
Distelmeier, Caritas 161
Donatello 102
Donne, John 39, 41, 52, 163
Drexel, Jeremias 64, 66
Drogheda 146
Dublin 141
Duffy, Eamon 159
Dunton, John 44
Duport, James 60
Dürer, Albrecht 97, 102–7, 110
Dürr, Johann 144

Education, *see* pedagogy
Edward III of England 27
Edwards, Elisabeth 127
Eichstätt 143
Elizabeth I 10, 32, 35, 41, 138, 158
Elyot, Thomas 88
Emison, Patricia 97
Enfield, William 146
Engel, William 10, 14, 77, 152
England 6–7, 10–11, 13, 27, 32–3, 38, 41, 47, 50–1, 53, 86, 118, 121, 124–5, 128, 130, 136–40, 142, 154, 156–8, 161
Erasmus of Rotterdam 18, 63, 65, 80, 85, 92, 98, 102, 105, 112–13, 153, 155

Erfurt 146
Estonia 11
Eucharist 8, 19, 28, 161–3, 168
Evans, Arise 45, 52
Evans, Katherine 54
Evelyn, John 70

Fanshawe, Ann 46, 49–50
Fawkes, Guy 139
Fenlon, Iain 13
Ficino, Marsilio 100
Fitzherbert, Dionys 51–2
Flacius, Matthias 141
Florence 5, 7, 17, 100, 105–6, 109, 113, 136–7, 141
Floris I of Culemborg, Count 21, 23
Fludd, Robert 87
Fontana, Giovanni 15, 17
forgetting 1–2, 5, 17, 20, 39, 58, 87, 97–8, 112, 122, 151–6, 158, 159, 163–8
Foucault, Michel 37, 86
Fox, George 53
Foxe, John 158, 162
France 50, 138, 154, 166
Francesco Maria I della Rovere, Duke 111
Francis I 103
Frederick V 26
Freud, Sigmund 40
Frisch, Andrea 166
Frischlin, Nicodemus 146
Fuller, Thomas 57, 161
Fulwood, William 14
funerals 8, 11, 137

Galen of Pergamon 60, 81–2, 110
Galileo Galilei 38, 81, 86–7, 115
Garrick, David 147–8
Gassendi, Pierre 64
Gataker, Thomas 10, 32
Geertz, Clifford 119
Geffrey, Thomas 122–3, 127
gender 46, 98, 119
Geneva 138, 160
Germany 8, 35, 161
Ghent 23–4, 26, 136
Gillis, John 148
Giuliano de' Medici 111, 171 n.11
Gluckel of Hameln 44, 46
Goltzius, Hendrik 105, 107–8
Gomarus, Franciscus 26
Gotherson, Dorothea 40, 46

Gottsched, Johann Christoph 145, 147
Graz 143
Gratarolo, Guglielmo 14, 55, 78, 79
Gregory XIII, Pope 140
Grey, Jane 162
Grotius, Hugo 80
Gruff, Agnus 131
Gueinz, Christian 145
Guilds 11
Guntzer, Augustin 41, 44, 48
Gusdorf, Georges 37, 39
Gutenberg, Johannes 145
Gysius, Johannes 23

Haarlem 145
Halbwachs, Maurice 135, 153
Hamburg 142, 145
Handel, George Frederic 147
Harris, Tim 117
Harrison, Thomas 67
Hartlib, Samuel 95
Heidegger, Martin 82
Heidelberg 147
Helmstedt 142
Hendon, Julia 126
Henri III of France 13
Henri IV 166
Henri IV of France 28, 136, 166
Henry VIII 5, 88, 122
Héroard, Jean 28
Hessen 143
Hippocrates 60
Hiscock, Andrew 156
historical culture 4
historiography 5, 10–11, 118
history writing, see historiography
Hoare, Richard 70
Hobbes, Thomas 58, 60–1, 80
Hobsbawm, Eric 19
Hodgkin, Katharine 37
Hofer, Johannes 55
Holdsworth, Richard 60, 64, 66
Homer 102
Hooke, Robert 57, 73, 86
Hoole, Charles 42
Horace 63, 113
Howell, Hugh 132
Huarte, Juan 60
humanism 1, 2, 4, 18
Hunford, Cicely 127
Hunyadi, János 140
Hus, Jan 35, 141, 149

Hutchinson, Lucy 41, 45
Hyde, Edward 167

identity 2, 7, 9–10, 18, 32, 37, 45, 47, 86, 99, 117, 119, 122–3, 127, 129–30, 132, 136, 143, 148, 151, 154
Ignatius Loyola 138, 143
images 1, 4–5, 8, 11, 15, 17–18, 27, 38, 61, 75, 77, 82, 84, 87, 90, 92–4, 100, 105, 114–15, 135, 151, 156, 160, 168
Ingold, Tim 13, 119–20
Innocent XI, Pope 140
Ireland 6, 32, 139–40, 142, 146, 166
Isham, Elizabeth 39, 165
Isidore of Madrid 138
Italy 5, 7, 10, 86, 111, 149
Ivic, Christopher 152

James I 138
James II 140
James IV 3
James VI 32, 158
James, Duke of York 139
Jeanne d'Arc 138
Jerusalem 137
Jesuits 25, 84, 139, 143, 149
Johanson, Kristine 55
Jones, Andrew 11
Julius II, Pope 110–11

Kempe, William 90
Keyser, Hendrick de 31
knowledge 1, 6, 14–15, 18, 39, 48, 60, 65, 70, 75, 77–8, 80–1, 83–5, 87–90, 92–6, 100, 110, 115, 119–20, 123–4, 127, 129, 132, 136, 152, 155–6, 164, 168
Kristeva, Julia 46
Kuijpers, Erika 13, 20, 86, 118
Kötteritz, Johann 161

landscape 13–14, 25, 52–4, 78, 104, 118–21, 123–5, 127–33, 152
Lechner, Joan Marie 65
Leiden 138
Leipzig 147, 149
Lemnius, Levinus 82
Leo X, Pope 109
Leonardo da Vinci 83
Leroi-Gourhan, André 78
Libby, Alexandra 19
lieux de mémoire, see places of memory
lineage 30, 45, 46

literacy 8–9, 90, 117
Locke, John 58–61, 70–2
London 52, 57, 86, 90, 93, 139, 145–7, 153, 161
Lorenzo de Monacis 141
Lorenzo il Magnifico 100
Lougee, Chappell 50
Louis IX 27–9, 35
Louis XIII 28
Louis XIV 101
Louis XVI 166
Low Countries, *see* the Netherlands
Lull, Ramón 93
Lummenaeus à Marca, Jacobus 26
Lundin, Matthew 8
Luther, Martin 2, 10, 110, 113, 137, 141–2, 149
Lydgate, John 161

Machiavelli, Niccolò 65, 80, 105, 111–12, 151
Madrid 19, 29, 49, 137, 143
Maertensz, Clement 27
Magdeburg 141–2
Magnússon, Sigurður, 118
Mainz 145
Mantua 111
Marafioto, Girolamo 15
Marburg 143
Marchand, Prosper 145
Marguerite de Navarre 163
Marie de l'Incarnation 54
Marshall, Peter 159
Masaccio 105, 110
Massey, Doreen 47
material memory 7
Matsys, Quentin 103
Meautys, Thomas 157
Melanchthon, Philip 18, 65
memorials 11, 124, 136, 161
memory books 37
memory palace 38, 55, 94
memory studies 1, 13, 19, 24, 38, 152
memory theatre, *see* memory palace
Michelangelo 98, 100–3, 105–11, 113
Michelet, Jules 108
Michelino, Domenico di 141
Milan 137
Miller, Matheus 43–4
Milton, John 62
modernity 6, 55, 98, 101–2, 107, 110, 112, 118, 130, 152

INDEX

Moine, Claudine 53
Molière 102
Montaigne, Michel de 80, 88, 92, 98–9, 101, 110, 112, 155
Montefeltro, Federico da 112
monument 11, 20, 120, 124, 129, 131–2, 136–7, 154, 159–60
monumental time 46
More, Henry 65
More, Thomas 102
Moryson, Fynes 31
Mulcaster, Richard 90
Mullaney, Stephen, 154
Mussolini, Benito 149
Mörke, Olaf 31
Münzer, Thomas 145

Napoleon 149
narrative 6, 28–9, 33, 35, 37, 39, 44–8, 51–2, 54, 87, 97, 158
nationalism 19, 21, 24, 35, 140, 145, 149
Neave, Thomas 125, 128
Neri, Filippo 138, 144
Netherlands 6, 15, 21, 23–7, 30, 33, 103
New England 44, 48
New York 145
Newton, Isaac 58, 65–6, 68, 87
Nixon, Anthony 32
Nora, Pierre 152
Norfolk 121, 124
North, John 66
North, Roger 66
Norwich 146
Norwood, Richard 40–1, 45, 48, 51
nostalgia 13, 35, 38, 45, 55, 154, 157, 159
notebooks 58, 60, 63–5, 67–3, 75, 154, 156

objects, *see* things
oblivion, *see* forgetting
Opitz, Martin 147, 149
oral memory 9, 10, 122
orality 9
Orléans 138
Ovid 63, 65
Oxford 52, 60, 86, 88, 93, 137

painting 12, 14–15, 29, 93, 98, 100, 103, 113, 115
Palestine 161
Paris 53, 136, 138–9
parish 6, 124, 128–9, 136, 159

Parkinson, John 81
Paul II, Pope 26
Paul III, Pope 25
Paul IV, Pope 26
Paul V, Pope 107, 143
pedagogy 14, 87, 90, 96
Peiresc, Nicolas Fabri de 64
Peter of Ravenna 84
Petrarch 4, 111, 113
Philadelphia 145
Philip II of Spain 19, 21, 23, 29, 34
Philip III 29
Philip IV 29
Philip VI of France 27
Pia, Emilia, 112
Pico della Mirandola 83
Pirckheimer, Willibald 97, 102, 113
Pius V, Pope 140
Placcius, Vincent 64, 66
places of memory 13, 52, 53, 90, 136
Plat, Hugh 84
Plato 1, 65, 90, 100, 111
Platter, Thomas 41, 45
Playfere, Thomas 164
Pliny 65
Pliny the Elder 57
Pollmann, Judith 11, 13, 20, 86, 118, 127, 152, 168
popular culture 117
Poticary, Elizabeth 165
power 1, 11, 19, 21, 24–5, 28, 33, 52–4, 64, 80, 100, 102, 110–11, 119, 122, 151, 154, 167
Prague 145
Priestley, Joseph 146
printing 1, 2, 9–10, 14, 18, 38, 78, 83, 144–5, 149, 152, 155
Protestantism 5, 9, 25, 143, 158
Ptolemy 110
Purgatory 11, 159

Quintilian 83–4, 88

Rabelais, François 102, 155
Raleigh, Walter 82
Ramus, Peter 78, 90, 92–3
Raphael 98, 107–10, 115
recollection 1–2, 6, 8, 49, 52, 59, 61–2, 64–5, 70–1, 73, 75, 87, 156
Recorde, Robert 77, 89
Reformation 2, 8–11, 21, 23, 25–8, 32, 35, 47, 98, 104, 138, 141–2, 144–5

205

Renaissance 1, 4–5, 7, 13–14, 18, 38, 58, 62, 65, 78, 80, 83, 87–8, 93, 99, 108, 112, 152, 168
Reuchlin, Johann 147, 149
rhetoric 2, 6, 15, 26, 80, 83–4, 88, 92, 97, 156, 166
Ricci, Matteo 62
Richmond 145
Ricoeur, Paul 13, 37, 40, 46
ricordanze 7
Ridley, Nicholas 162
Rinckart, Martin 142–3, 145
Ritzsch, Timotheus 145
ritual 2, 6, 8–10, 13
Rivet, André 31
Roberts, John 129
Romano, Giulio 109
Romberch, Johannes 94–5
Rome 25, 83, 100, 105, 113, 137–8, 140, 143
Rosselli, Cosma 17
Rossellius, Cosmas 94, 96
Rowlandson, Mary 48–9
Rubens, Peter Paul 19–20, 29
Rudolf I of Habsburg, Count 28–9
Russell, Nicolas 163
Rutland, Thomas 128–9

Sacchini, Francesco 64, 66
Sarto, Andrea del 109
Saunders, Richard 93
Savonarola, Girolamo 99, 113, 115
Saxony 26, 142–3
Schenckel, Thomas Lambert 17, 156
Schenkel, Lambert 156
Schwarz, Matthäus 137
Schwyzer, Philip 159
Schütz, Heinrich 142
science 15, 18, 73, 77, 80–1, 84, 86–7, 90, 95, 156
Scotland 32, 160
Scribner, Bob 119
Scultori, Diana 98–9
Selden, John 62
self-narrative, *see* autobiography
self-writing, *see* autobiography
Seneca the Elder 57
Seneca the Younger 63
Shakespeare, William 77, 93, 102, 111, 147–8, 150, 153–4
Sharpe, Kevin 28
Sharping, John 125
Shepard, Thomas 41

Sherlock, Peter 5, 11, 151
Shifflett, Andrew 167
Sidney, Philip 92
Simonides 57
site of memory, *see* place of memory
Sixtus IV, Pope 26
Sobieski, Jan 140
social memory 6, 127, 135–6, 159–60
Soderini, Piero 100
Southwell, Robert 65–6
Spain 19, 23, 29, 31–2
Spicer, Andrew 159
Sprat, Thomas 74, 87
Stillingfleet, Edward 60
Stirredge, Elizabeth 46
Strasbourg 145
Suarez, Francisco 61

Tacitus 65
Tallinn 11–12
Tamm, Marek 1
Taurinus, Jacob 27
Telemann, Georg Philipp 145
Terence 98, 102
Teresa of Avila 41, 138
things 4, 8, 11, 20, 55, 58, 62, 82, 93–4
Thirty Years' War 21, 143
Thomas Aquinas 82, 84
Thucydides 80
Thurgood, Rose 42
Toulouse 138, 144
transmission 2, 6, 8–11, 13–14, 87, 152
Trapnel, Anna 54
trauma 6, 8, 58
Tryon, Thomas 41, 45
Tübingen 146

Underwood, Peter 125
Uytenbogaert, Johannes 27

Valla, Lorenzo 108
van Artevelde, Jacob 136
van Boxhorn, Marcus 145
van Ceulen, Cornelis Janssen 50
van der Steen, Jasper 19
van Heemskerck, Jacob 31
van Leyden, Lucas 106
van Loon, Gerard 23
van Mander, Karel 105
Vasari, Giorgio 100, 105, 109–10, 112
Velázquez, Diego 100

Venice 13, 17, 97, 137, 140
Vermeer, Johannes 100
Veronese, Paolo 4, 113
Vesalius, Andreas 79, 80, 82, 87
Vienna 140, 145
Virgil 63, 102
Vitruvius Pollio 83
Vives, Juan Luis 91–2, 155
Vivian, Bradford 153

Wales 6, 52, 118, 120
Walker, Obadiah 60–1, 67, 88, 93
Walsham, Alexandra 13, 25, 47, 159
Warburg, Aby 135
Weever, John 159–60
Weidner, Johann Leonhard 143
Weinrich, Harald 156
Weinsberg, Hermann 7
Whyte, Nicola 13, 117
Whythorne, Thomas 43, 45
Wildens, Jan 29
Wilkins, John 169 n.8
William II 31

William II of Nassau 33
William III 33, 137, 140, 146
William of Orange 27, 30–1, 33, 139
Williams, Grant 152
Willis, John 84
Witt, John de 33
Wittenberg 145, 147
Wood, Andy 9, 13, 152, 168
Wooding, Lucy 161
Woolf, Daniel R. 21
Wren, Christopher 86

Xavier, Francis 138, 143

Yeo, Mary Louise 75
Yeo, Richard 57, 155
York 146
Ysbrantsz, Jan 27

Zepper, Wilhelm 9
Zerubavel, Eviatar 127
Zwierlein, Cornel 151
Zwingli, Huldrych 98, 143, 149